Sermons, Addresses and Reminiscences and Important Correspondence

Sermons, Addresses and Reminiscences and Important Correspondence, With a Picture Gallery of Eminent Ministers and Scholars

By
E. C. Morris

Edited
By
J. Mitchell

E. C. Morris, D. D.

Sermons, Addresses and Reminiscences

and

Important Correspondence,

With a Picture Gallery of Eminent Ministers and Scholars.

By

E. C. Morris, D. D.

Introduction
By R. H. Boyd, D. D.

NASHVILLE, TENN.:
NATIONAL BAPTIST PUBLISHING BOARD.
1901.

ENTERED ACCORDING TO ACT OF CONGRESS, 1901,
BY E. C. MORRIS.

**Prepared for publication and edited by
Press Publication.**

Sermons, Addresses and Reminiscences and Important Correspondence, With a Picture Gallery of Eminent Ministers and Scholars.

By

E. C. Morris, D. D.

Introduction By R. H. Boyd, D. D.

Edited By J. Mitchell

NASHVILLE, TENN.:
NATIONAL BAPTIST PUBLISHING BOARD.
1901.

**ENTERED ACCORDING TO ACT OF CONGRESS, 1901,
by E. C. MORRIS.**

Sermons, Addresses and Reminiscences

PREFACE.

The only apology made for giving this book to the public, is the earnest desire which the author has to inspire young men of the race, and especially those of the Baptist faith, who were born and reared under much more favorable circumstances than he, to greater deeds of usefulness, and to leave to the denomination a written testimony of what was accomplished by the Negro Baptists of the United States in the first years of their separate effort at Christian work. The speeches and sermons contained in this volume are not given out as an exhibition of literary talent, nor is any claim made of perfection in their construction. But they are the promptings of a heart and mind full of love for the cause of the Master and for a race that has long been oppressed and is now struggling to improve its condition in every honorable way. The writer firmly believes in the possibilities of the race and has firmly advocated that the nearly two millions of colored Christians which God has added to the Baptist churches as a mass, are an heritage, and that it is the imperative duty of Negro Baptist leaders to develop this mighty force for the glory of God and the further redemption of the race. The facts presented will be more appreciated, when it is remembered that the wonderful development and unparalleled success of the denomination form the work of only a few years. But this is the most potent argument in favor of what can be done when a united effort is made at self-help. The author has great admiration for those friends of the race who have contributed so much for the educational and religious training of the same; but he believes that people who have been helped become very unworthy when they fail to make an effort to help themselves.

Sermons, Addresses and Reminiscences and Important Correspondence

Sermons, Addresses and Reminiscences and Important Correspondence

CONTENTS.

- Preface
- Introduction
- Educational Sermon
- Infallible Proofs of the Perpetuity of Baptist Principles
- Sanctification
- The Brotherhood of Man
- Sermon (to a class of ministers)
- Sermon (delivered to Holy Trinity Baptist Church, Philadelphia, Pa.)
- Origin of the Baptists
- The Demand for a Negro Baptist Publishing House
- Address delivered before the Baptist Foreign Mission Convention, September, 1895
- Negro Baptists--Retrospective and Prospective
- Annual Address to the National Baptist Convention, 1898
- Address to Colored Baptists
- Annual Address to the National Baptist Convention, 1899
- Annual Address to the National Baptist Convention, 1900
- Nineteenth Annual Address before the Arkansas Baptist State Convention, 1900
- Annual Address of the Closing of the Arkansas Baptist College, 1901
- Annual Address to the National Baptist Convention, 1901
- Reminiscences
- "President E. C. Morris of the National Baptist Convention Arraigns his Critics" . . . . .
- National Baptist Catechism
- Important Correspondence
- "Dr. E. C. Morris favors the Negro Publishing House Project"
- Biographical Sketch (from Preachers' Magazine)
- Biographical and Otherwise . . . . .
- DIRECTORY OF ORDAINED MINISTERS.
    - Alabama . . . . .
    - Arkansas . . . . .
    - District of Columbia . . . . .
    - Florida . . . . .
    - Georgia . . . . .
    - Indian Territory . . . . .
    - Kansas . . . . .

Sermons, Addresses and Reminiscences and Important Correspondence

- o Kentucky . . . . .
- o Louisiana . . . . .
- o Maryland . . . . .
- o Mississippi . . . . .
- o Missouri . . . . .
- o North Carolina . . . . .
- o South Carolina . . . . .
- o Tennessee . . . . .
- o Texas . . . . .
- o Virginia . . . . .
- o West Virginia . . . . .

Sermons, Addresses and Reminiscences and Important Correspondence

PICTURE GALLERY.

- Rev. G. L. P. Taliaferro, D. D
- Rev. A. N. McEwen
- Rev. L. L. Campbell, D. D. . . . . .
- Rev. A. R. Griggs, D. D. . . . . .
- Rev. Caesar Johnson . . . . .
- Mr. P. Kneeland . . . . .
- Rev. H. C. Pettis . . . . .
- Rev. G. B. Howard, D. D. . . . . .
- Rev. J. R. Bennett . . . . .
- Rev. William Jarrett . . . . .
- Hon. G. W. Lowe . . . . .
- Rev. J. P. Barton . . . . .
- Rev. G. W. Longwood . . . . .
- Rev. Geo. W. Dudley . . . . .
- Prof. R. E. Bryant . . . . .
- Rev. J. H. A. Cyrus . . . . .
- Rev. E. H. McDonald . . . . .
- Rev. C. S. Dinkins, D. D. . . . . .
- Rev. H. C. Cotton, ...
- Rev. C. H. Parrish, D. D. . . . . .
- Hon. J. W. Lyons . . . . .
- Rev. A. H. Miller . . . . .
- Rev. W. F. Graham . . . . .
- Rev. Willis Anthony Holmes . . . . .
- Rev. I. G. Bailey . . . . .
- Rev. E. Arlington Wilson . . . . .
- Rev. E. Green . . . . .
- Rev. Benj. W. Farris . . . . .
- Rev. J. J. Blackshear . . . . .
- Rev. Robt. Mitchell, D. D. . . . . .
- Rev. William Beckham . . . . .
- Rev. R. H. Boyd, D. D. . . . . .
- Rev. C. S. Brown, D. D. . . . . .
- Rev. Wm. H. Phillips, D. D. . . . . .
- Rev. J. D. Humphrey . . . . .
- Rev. J. F. Thomas . . . . .
- Dr. J. A. Dennis . . . . .

Sermons, Addresses and Reminiscences and Important Correspondence

- Rev. P. S. L. Hutchins . . . . .
- Rev. J. C. Battle . . . . .
- Rev. W. G. Parks . . . . .
- Dr. C. L. Fisher . . . . .
- Dr. Harvey Johnson . . . . .
- Rev. H. C. Howell . . . . .
- Prof. Jas. H. Garnett, A. M., D. D. . . . . .
- Rev. H. W. Bowen, D. D. . . . . .
- Rev. J. W. McCrary . . . . .
- Rev. S. A. Mosely, D. D. . . . . .
- Dr. S. E. Smith, ...
- Rev. A. A. Cosey . . . . .
- Rev. W. H. Jernagan . . . . .
- Rev. H. R. McMillan . . . . .
- Rev. W. H. Anderson, D. D. . . . . .
- Rev. C. B. Brown . . . . .
- Rev. W. H. McRidley, A. M., D. D. . . . . .
- Dr. W. H Suggs . . . . .
- Prof. A. W. Pegues, Ph. D. . . . . .
- Rev. E. B. Topp . . . . .
- Mr. John S. Trower . . . . .
- Prof. Joseph A. Booker, A. M., D. D. . . . . .
- Mrs. M. C. Booker . . . . .
- Rev. S. L. Cannon . . . . .
- Rev. D. H. Harris . . . . .
- Rev. J. Anderson Taylor, D. D. . . . . .
- The Morris Family . . . . .
- Rev. C. T. Stamps, B. D. . . . . .
- Rev. G. W. Raiford . . . . .
- Rev. J. H. Eason, D. D. . . . . .
- Mrs. W. F. Graham . . . . .
- Rev. L. G. Jordan, D. D. . . . . .
- Mr. I. E. Alsup . . . . .
- Hon. Taylor G. Ewing . . . . .
- Rev. E. W. D. Isaac, D. D. . . . . .
- Rev. S. E. Griggs, B. D. . . . . .
- The Boyd Family . . . . .

Sermons, Addresses and Reminiscences and Important Correspondence

Sermons, Addresses and Reminiscences

INTRODUCTION.

Whenever a man sees fit, by tongue or pen, to address his fellowmen, the minds of the parties addressed instinctively pass back of the thought given to the man giving it. Thus the man and his word are made to go hand in hand, each aiding in determining the value of the other. Many would seek to disassociate what they *say* from what they *are,* but the people will not have it so.

"Is not this the carpenter, the son of Mary," is a question that will be asked of all who seek to enlighten the multitude. It is in response to this well known demand of the public that this introduction is written. As you shall ponder over the ripened thought of the distinguished author, we trust that the picture, which we herein seek to draw of his personality, shall reinforce his words, since the character of the tree is known to determine the character of the fruit it bears.

Rev. E. C. Morris, D. D., occupies one of the most important posts in the world. We are aware of the tremendous nature of the assertion, which we have just made, and yet we adhere to it.

It is quite evident to the observant mind that the Twentieth Century is to witness a rejuvenation of the great African race. The Negro is slowly but surely awakening from his long slumber and will soon step forward to take a man's part in the great world problems. He who has made a study of the condition of the Negro in all countries is aware of the fact that the Negroes of the United States are far in advance of all others. We, therefore, are in the van of the coming army. We are to blaze the way to be the first to plant and defend the flag of our new hopes. The dominating influence of this advance guard is to be religion. In religious affairs, the Negro Baptists being numerically stronger than any other Negro denomination in the United States, must play the leading role. Of this host of Baptists, Rev. E. C. Morris, D. D., President of the National Baptist Convention, is the acknowledged leader. When we consider that he is to largely influence the Baptists; that the Baptists are to largely influence the race life in America; that the race in America is to largely determine the destiny of the entire Negro race; that the Negro race is ere long to largely determine the current of human history: when we consider these incontrovertable facts it must be admitted that we state a plain truth when we say that Rev. E. C. Morris, D. D., occupies one of the most important posts in the world.

While the holding of an exalted position creates a presumption in a man's favor, it is not conclusive evidence that he is a great man.. There must also be considered how he obtained his eminence and what achievements while there can be placed to his credit.

We shall now view Dr. Morris in the light of these suggestions.

Let it be said in the outset that Dr. Morris' exalted station is due to no accident. Beginning at the very bottom round of the ladder of life, he has climbed his way step by step to the dizzy heights of fame. Pure in life, sound in judgment, eager for all that tends toward human progress, industrious, persevering, with a hopeful, cheerful mien, he has journeyed onward, winning and holding friends, until his name is the symbol of goodness and greatness in thousands upon thousands of homes.

Since the coming of freedom, the great, inchaotic mass of Negro Baptists has been wrestling with the problem of combining their strength for aggressive work in the Master's Kingdom. When, after years of experimenting, the Negro Baptists of the United States in convention assembled, decided to coalesce and form one great body, they began to cast around for a leader for the united hosts. They had before them an abundance of material from which to make a choice.

Each State represented could boast of a favorite son, to whose credit could be placed many notable achievements in the religious world. But the eyes of the Convention passed by all the rest of these and fell upon the pride of Arkansas, the Rev. E. C. Morris, D. D. His life lay spread before them. It was a record so full of worldly work as to inspire full confidence in all. His ability and his character were guarantees that the honor of the Convention would not suffer in his hands. Around him the thoughts of his brethren congealed, and he was escorted to his exalted position, the first leader of the consolidated hosts of Negro Baptists.

It was the sheer force of merit and conspicuous adaptability to the work that procured for Dr. Morris this mark of distinction. Having set forth the influences that brought about his election, we now advance a word as to his work as President.

Whoever has attended Negro assemblages knows the thorns in the way of the presiding officer. To be impartial in the midst of such conflicting interests and diversities of opinion; to remain calm while the surroundings are anything but calm; to pilot a body through floods of discussion to definite, creditable action, is a work not easy of accomplishment.

And yet Dr. Morris has been perfect master of the situation. So skillful have been his labors that not a reef has been struck by the ship while his hand has guided the helm. Since his incumbency, project after project has been proposed and carried to success. Among the notable achievements wrought during his administration, we may mention the publication of a series of Sunday school helps, the founding of the National Baptist Young People's Union, the establishment of co-operation with the American Baptist Missionary Union and with the Southern Baptist Convention (white).

Those familiar with the work of the departments named, can see the immense character of the work inaugurated under the administration of Dr. Morris. We may also add that the work of giving the Gospel to foreign lands has been prosecuted with more vigor and success during his administration than in all the previous history of the denomination. It is pre-eminently fitting that so great and so worthy a man should give to the world a book. He can thus become a daily companion of the great army of his admirers who find delight in his wisdom of speech.

By publishing a book he will treasure up for future generations the thoughts that have been of such great value to this generation. More and more will he become the inspiration of the youth of the race, who shall seek to walk in his footsteps.

The estimate of Rev. E. C. Morris, D. D., and his labors, which I have given in these few pages, is not based upon hearsay. My acquaintance with him has extended over a period of twenty-two years, the last six of which have been spent in intimate association with him in denominational work. So close has been our relationship that the suggestion has often been made that the two of us were one. Having known Dr. Morris so long and intimately, being fully aware of his great worth and work, it has been a source of genuine pleasure to me to pen these few lines by way of introducing to you a volume that will bring uplifting power to all who are blessed with the privilege of perusing its pages.

Yours very truly,

R. H. BOYD.

SERMONS.

EDUCATIONAL SERMON.

[Preached before the Baptist Educational Convention at Montgomery, Ala., September, 1894.]

Text:--"The light of the body is the eye: if therefore thine eye be single, thy whole body shall be full of light. But if thine eye be evil, thy whole body shall be full of darkness. If therefore the light that is in thee be darkness, how great is that darkness!"

Brethren of the Convention: I recognize in the appointment which I am about to fill, a very responsible duty. Those of you who have consulted the program for this service have seen that the Annual Sermon of the Educational Convention would be preached at this hour. It is expected, of course, that what will be said in this discourse will enable the people to see what good is to come from the Educational Convention, which has been recently organized. Just as a man whose sight has grown dim from age would adjust his glasses to behold tiny objects with accuracy, so will you doubtless draw my remarks before you to see what good there is in the Educational Convention. This organization is the youngest of our national bodies, and does not come before the people with the hope or desire of supplanting either of the older organizations among us; but it comes to do a specific work, which is not assumed by either of the others. And it comes using the same words, which our Heavenly Father used when darkness was brooding upon the face of the great deep. In order to remove the confusion and establish order, He said, "Let there be light." And the fact that many of the people are yet in darkness and ignorance as to the educational status of our denomination, is one of the great reasons why the leaders have launched this organization. We are anxious that the truth may be known about us as a denomination of Christians. For years, the Negro Baptists of the world have been held up to the ridicule of the other denominations. Their ministers have been classed as the most ignorant of the race and their manner of worship has been called a modified form of heathenism. This grave charge has stood before the world for a generation. But I tell you to-night that the charge was never true of us as a whole, for from the days of slavery until now, the leading Baptist preachers and the intelligent and progressive element in our churches have composed the vanguard of God's great army among the Negro Christians of the world. And the only reason I assign for the ignorance of those who thus falsely charge us, is that their eyes are evil.

It is not my purpose in this discourse to give you any figures setting forth the educational status of the Negro branch of the Baptist denomination in the United States, as that matter has been looked after by our statistician, and is now a matter of history. But we do hope to at least impress you with the fact that the organization of this Convention was a pressing necessity in order to give stimulus to the educational work among us. As a body cannot be perfect without eyes, so neither is a people what they should be without a medium through which they can see and be seen. Hence, we present in our first proposition, "The Educational Convention as a Means to Show the Progress and Possibilities of the Negro Baptist Denomination."

The Lord Jesus, who is and ever will be the Great Head of the Church, in that wonderful sermon on the Mount, gave the world many rules which will ever be the governing power of his Church. By noticing carefully the preceding chapter you will observe that he there introduces the law of abrogation, by first calling attention to what was said by them of old time. Then he gives to them what is to be the law in the kingdom of grace and the penalty of violating that law.

But under the paragraph from which we take our text, the blessed Master rises to what we call the loftiest pinnacle of eloquence and plunges into the very essence of his Gospel by saying, "Lay not up for yourselves treasures upon earth, where moth and rust doth corrupt, and where thieves break through and steal: But lay up for yourselves treasures in heaven, where neither moth nor rust doth corrupt, and where thieves do not break through nor steal: For where your treasure is, there will your heart be also." This beautiful context fully sets forth what is to follow. Here it is that we form the opinion from the illustration given that the Christian religion is the light of the world, that its beneficent influence is to the world what the eye is to the body. If this view of his sermon be correct, then we have within our reach the means by which every man is to enter into the kingdom of God, and should be impressed with the responsibility, which devolves upon us as *"the light of the world."* The text brings to mind this parable: If you were passing through the crowded streets of this capital city and should see standing at some conspicuous corner a poor blind beggar with his hand extended for help, you would doubtless be moved with compassion. Perhaps the first thought would be of Bartimeus, who, when he heard the tramp of the multitude, after enquiring the cause, began to cry, "Jesus, thou Son of David, have mercy on me." They (the disciples) charged him to hold his peace, but he cried the more, "Thou Son of David, have mercy on me."

When Jesus had commanded him brought to him, he asked him, "What wilt thou that I should do unto thee?" The blind man answered, "Lord that I might receive my sight?"--the very thing which the penitent are asking to-day.

Brethren, the great task resting upon the Church to-day is to convert the world to Christ and give spiritual sight to those who are blind. Indeed, you are to aid in opening the eyes of the world and help to establish that singleness of purpose and doctrine which is so beautifully portrayed in the words of Jesus when he prayed, "That they may be one, even as we are one." (John 17:22.) That these glorious results will at someday be realized, I have not the slightest doubt, but they can be sooner accomplished by organization than without it. There should be a recognized head to all of our great Baptist concerns and there should be something on which we can safely rely for truthful data concerning ourselves as a denomination and to which others may look for reliable statistics. This Educational Convention seeks to be the means by which the world may see us as a body of Christian believers, and know the truth concerning the doctrines, which we preach, and that we may know our own strength and the advance, which we are making against the kingdom of darkness.

It necessarily follows, that to assume this responsible position in the denomination, the purposes of the Convention should be well defined. "If therefore thine eye be single, thy whole body shall be full of light." It has been said that the eye of the soul, in a moral sense, is the intention. When we speak of a person having an evil eye, we mean that that person is jealous, envious, grudging, unstable, etc.; hence, to have a single eye is to have the object of our intention single, pure and good. It is said that if there be a devided aim, if there is a cataract or skin between any of the humors, that the rays of light will never make any distinct impression on the internal seat of sight. If this be true in a natural sense, it is true also in a moral sense. If the moral eye--the intention of the soul--be single to serve God and secure heavenly treasures, it directs the whole person's actions; but if we are biased or prejudiced in our intentions, we are sure to be led aside to follow after the traditions of men rather than the commandments of God. There must be a singleness of purpose in Christian work, if we are to succeed along the lines laid out by the Savior. Every cataract should be cut off and the soul's intentions clearly set forth by these great conventions, which meet annually to devise ways and means to do the work of our Master. In doing this, we will prove ourselves to be a sword rather than peace to the terrified millions about us. Such a position is necessary in order to fill the world with the true light.

You will let your minds for a moment go to the rugged slope upon the mountainside where Jesus has retired for rest, followed by his chosen disciples. And as he seats himself in a convenient place, you will observe the disciples crouching at his feet, waiting to learn of his great wisdom. You will further observe from the words of Jesus that their intentions are not single. Perhaps the various forms of religion, the desire for place or position, have clouded their minds. The upturned faces of the great multitude in the valley below has doubtless made an impression upon them, for in that multitude there must be Pharisees, Sadducees, Jews and Gentiles, and people representing all forms of religion; hence the necessity now of indoctrinating them that their minds and hearts may be set upon the truth as is embodied in the Gospel which they are to preach and teach. It seems appropriate for me to say, if indeed they have left all to follow Christ and there is no desire in them to turn back to the world, their eye is single, and, therefore, they are full of light. But if they are yet undecided and are thinking of what to-morrow will bring forth or how they will be cared for by the people, or if they are thinking upon whether it be possible to follow him and at the same time serve the world, they are full of darkness. And if they are in this latter condition, how dense is the cloud that hangs over their minds! "Ye cannot serve God and mammon." When Israel forsook God under the leadership of Ahab, and the prophet of the Lord had been driven into exile, one of the first things, which the prophet of the Lord said after assembling the people, was, "How long halt ye between two opinions. If God be God serve him, and if Baal be God serve him." Elijah here indicates that that singleness of purpose which had been so characteristic of Israel to serve God had departed and that the people were divided as to who was the true God, etc.

It is perhaps not out of place to make the admission that those who know the least about the Negro Baptists as a denomination, are the members of our own churches. Very many people are Baptists without being able to give an intelligent reason why they are Baptists. The Educational Convention seeks to enlighten them and put in the minds and hearts of the great army of our followers that same knowledge, zeal and courage that is possessed by many of the leaders who have done such a marvelous work in the last twenty years. The great work of training and religiously educating the people has just begun. All of the years of the past have been spent in preparation for the campaign now before us. But the time has come to push the battle for an educated ministry as well as for an educated pew to the very last ditch. We must not rest until we have informed the people and put upon the tongue of every Baptist the names of such schools as Shaw University, Spellman Seminary, Roger Williams University, Richmond Theological Seminary, State University, Ky., Leland University, Benedict College, Bishop College, Selma University, Arkansas Baptist College, Jackson College, Guadalupe College, Hearne Academy, Howe Institute, Arkadelphia Academy, Natchez College and many others which I do not call to mind just now. These are among the many strong citadels of the denomination and their power and influence should be known by and read of by men. Our own constituency should be taught to know them and should learn to love, honor and serve them. Nor should we be content with teaching the people the names of these institutions and the great work they are doing for the cause of the race and Christianity; but they should be brought to know and put in touch with the thousands of pious Christian gentlemen who have come forth from the schools as polished shafts from the quiver, and we should seek to make place for them to work among our people. I repeat that "If thine eye be single, thy whole body shall be of light."

By way of digression, permit me to call your attention to a remark made by our blessed Savior to his disciples, when he sent them forth to preach and teach. It is this: "Behold, I send you forth as sheep in the midst of wolves: be ye therefore wise as serpents, and harmless as doves." (Matt. 10:16.) This same advice comes down to all of God's minister's to-day. The great work of convicting the world of error and converting it to truth is no less important now than it was when Christ spoke these words, and it will require much wisdom and discretion on the part of our ministry to overcome the many false religions, which have gotten such a firm, hold upon the people. Peter, the fisherman from Galilee, led the services on the day of Pentecost, and by the aid of the Holy Ghost was instrumental in the converting of thousands in a day. But when the church had to contend with spiritual wickedness in high places; when Governors were to be made to tremble and Kings to confess; when angry mobs were to be dispersed by simple Gospel truth clothed with superhuman eloquence. Christianity needed a Paul who was not only a classical scholar but who sat at the feet of Gamaliel in Jerusalem until he became thoroughly furnished in Biblical knowledge. This Convention aims to inspire a greater desire among the young men to prepare themselves for the high calling of the ministry.

THE SAD RESULT OF DIVIDED LEADERSHIP.

One great lesson is yet to be learned by us. It is on the proper regard for our leaders. Every preacher in our ranks has learned that every Baptist church is an independent organization and from that they have concluded, many of them, that every preacher is independent and equal in importance to every other one. Few have learned that there is an interdependence, which makes us all workers together, and that some are to lead and direct while others are to follow. The example of carrying matters to Jerusalem to receive the counsel and advice of the older and well-informed disciples has been set aside, and in many cases the courts are resorted to to settle matters of the church. "If the blind lead the blind, both shall fall into the ditch." (Matt. 15:14.) There are many religions in the world and all are seeking the confidence of the people, and all claim to be the Church of Christ This, of course, cannot be true. But so zealous are the representatives of these different organizations, in pressing their views upon the minds of the people, that really intelligent professors of religion claim to be puzzled over the question of who is right and who is wrong.

We must learn to be firm, for if our doctrines are right, they should be pressed with all the power and vigor of our soul. We should convince the world that we are not reeds to be shaken by the wind. The Lord Jesus loves and honors a man who is firm and true to a principle. When the disciples of John the Baptist had delivered the message of John to Christ and departed, Jesus began to say to the multitude, "What went ye out into the wilderness to see? A reed shaken with the wind? But what went ye out for to see? A man clothed in soft raiment? Behold, they that wear soft clothing are in king's houses. But what went ye out for to see? A prophet? Yea, I say unto you, and more than a prophet. For this is he, of whom it is written, Behold, I send my messenger before thy face, which shall prepare thy way before thee." And then he proceeds to pronounce the greatest eulogium ever spoken of man. "Among them that are born of women there hath not risen a greater than John the Baptist." Above all things, be a man-- one that cannot be shaken by heresies like a reed by the "wind," "Having done all to stand, stand therefore."

Brethren, the work of educating and evangelizing the world is before us and much of it devolves upon us. Jesus, that hero of Calvary who led the monster, Death, in chains, is our leader and he stands now upon the lofty summit of Gospel truth and says, "All power in heaven and in earth is given into my hands," "Go ye therefore, and teach all nations, baptizing them in the name of the Father, and of the Son, and of the Holy Ghost: teaching them to observe all things whatsoever I have commanded you: and, lo, I am with you always, even unto the end of the world. Amen." And so long as these inspiring words can be heard, and the victorious Banner of the Cross can be seen in front of us, we should take courage and go forward, not fearing our foes, and leaving the results with God. And when the advancing hosts of hell come in view, say in the words of the poet:

>"My soul, be on thy guard;
>Ten thousand foes arise;
>The hosts of sin are pressing hard
>To draw thee from the skies.

>"O, watch and fight and pray;
>The battle ne'er give o'er;
>Renew it boldly every day,
>And help divine implore.

>"Ne'er think the victory won,
>Nor lay thine armor down;
>Thy arduous work will not be done
>Till thou obtain thy crown.

>"Fight on, my soul, till death
>Shall bring thee to thy God;
>He'll take thee, at thy parting breath,
>To his divine abode."

INFALLIBLE PROOFS OF THE PERPETUITY OF BAPTIST PRINCIPLES.

[Denominational Sermon delivered before the National Baptist Convention at Kansas City, Mo., 1898.]

Text:--"These are they which came out of great tribulation." (Rev. 7:14.)

The world has never known the whole truth about the Baptists, and will, perhaps, never know it until there is a complete triumph of those principles, which distinguished them as a denomination of Christian believers. Baptists are as much a phenomenon to the other religious sects and Christian professors' today as they were in the early centuries when cruel persecutions, hunger and death haunted them day and night; when they deemed it an honor to suffer and to die for the cause of their blessed Master.

I do not fear the criticism that may follow after I tell you that the history of the Baptists covers all the time from the days of John the Baptist until now, with the possible exception of that "time and half a time" spoken of in the prophecy of this book, where the Church appears to be in obscurity, but by no means is it extinct. It is, so to speak, in the period of its infancy, like the smoldering spark beneath the heap of ashes. The Church rested upon the arm of God, gathering strength from his warm bosom, while the angry waves of the adversary rushed about her. But in the fullness of time, she came forth as bright as the morning, fair as the moon, clear as the sun, and as terrible as an army with banners, irresistible, invincible, destined to cover the whole earth.

THE AUTHENTICITY OF THE CHURCH.

The regal authority by which the church exists is not questioned by any who believe the Bible to be the Book of God, for it is clearly set forth in that book that God is the founder of his church, Proofs of this may be found as far back as the days of Abraham or Moses, who looked forward to "a city which hath foundations, whose maker and builder is God," or to the time when the scepter should depart from Judah, and be given into the hand of him who would gather the people together.

But I shall not go so far back as Moses to get these infallible proofs of the authenticity of the church. I will call your attention to a more recent prophecy found in the book of Daniel (2:44), which reads: "In the days of these kings shall the God of Heaven set up a kingdom, which shall never be destroyed: and the kingdom shall not be left to other people, but it shall break in pieces and consume all these kingdoms, and it shall stand forever." The first question that arises after reading this prediction is, "Has this prophecy been fulfilled? Have the days of the kings spoken of come? And have their kingdoms been destroyed?"

By consulting Luke 3:1, 2, you will find these words, which immediately precede the preaching and baptism of John, the son of Zacharias: "Now in the fifteenth year of the reign of Tiberius Cæsar, Pontius Pilate being governor of Judea, and Herod being tetrarch of Galilee, and his brother Philip tetrarch of Ituraea and of the region of Trachonitis, and Lysanias the tetrarch of Abilene, Annas and Caiaphas being high priests, the word of God came unto John the son of Zacharias in the wilderness." This I take to be a clear enunciation of the conditions of those who, under Roman authority, held the scepter of power over both church and state. This, too, is at a time when the Roman Empire is at its zenith and challenges the admiration of the world, and at a time when those who had been entrusted with the sacred oracles of God were in absolute subjugation to Roman authority, notwithstanding the fact that the scepter (religious authority) was still held by the trembling hand of Judah. At such a time and under such conditions, John the Baptist, the greatest of Baptist preachers, appears in the wilderness of Jordan. Without any formal introduction, without a flourish of trumpets and banners, the Baptist comes forth with a voice, which attracted the attention of the people of Jerusalem and of Judea and of all the region round about Jordan. He notifies them that "the kingdom of heaven is at hand." I would not have you think for a single moment that it is my purpose to impress you that John the Baptist was the founder of the church, for he was not, and that there may be no mistake, the record says, "He was not that light, but was sent to bear witness of that light" (John 1:8). And again when John gracefully tells those who ask him, "Who art thou," that "I am the voice of one crying in the wilderness*** I indeed baptize you with water unto repentance: but he that cometh after me is mightier than I, whose shoes I am not worthy to bear: he shall baptize you with the Holy Ghost and with fire." (Matt. 3:11.)

We must not pass by this inspiring scene, which rushes like a sunbeam before our eyes as we approach this place. It is the most inspiring scene that heaven ever looked upon, or that ever engaged the attention of the world. May heaven listen and the world stand in breathless silence, as the record of Christ's baptism is told by the inspired writer. "Then cometh Jesus from Galilee to Jordan unto John to be baptized of him. But John forbade him, saying, I have need to be baptized of thee, and comest thou to me? And Jesus answering said unto him, Suffer it to be so now: for thus it becometh us to fulfill all righteousness. Then he suffered him. And Jesus, when he was baptized, went up straightway out of the water: and, lo, the heavens were opened unto him, and he saw the Spirit of God descending like a dove, and lighting upon him: And lo a voice from heaven, saying, This is my beloved Son, in whom I am well pleased." (Matt. 3:13-17.) So plain, unmistakable, is the evidence here given that no kind of comment is necessary.

But Jesus having waited the full time under the Levitical law before entering upon his ministry, now proceeds to call about him those whom he had chosen to be his companions and apostles, that they might be witnesses of all that he said and did, and be prepared to carry forward the work after his ascension. And when he had gone about sufficiently to cause the people to form an opinion of him, he said to his disciples, "Whom do men say that I, the Son of man am? And they said, Some say that thou art John the Baptist; some, Elias; and others, Jeremias, or one of the prophets. He saith unto them, But whom say ye that I am? And Simon Peter answered and said, Thou art the Christ, the Son of the living God. And Jesus answered and said unto him, Blessed art thou, Simon Barjona: for flesh and blood hath not revealed it unto thee, but my Father, which is in heaven. And I say also unto thee, That thou art Peter, and upon this rock (the immovable faith that you have that I am the Christ) I will build my church; and the gates of hell shall not prevail against it." (Matthew 16:13-18.) The first words to engage our attention in this remarkable answer are "I will build," which expression implies that the work was to be done, and that it was done in its completeness is manifest in these words, which, like thunder, fell from the lips of that blessed Christ as he hung upon the cross--"It is finished." And after being in the grave for three days, he comes forth and says to an astonished world, "All power is given unto me in heaven and in earth. Go ye therefore, and teach all nations," etc. Hence, the church derives its authority from God, for God and Christ are one.

THE GLORIOUS HISTORY OF THE CHURCH.

This grand old church has a most glorious history. The first baptism of blood came upon the Great Head of the Church. Having led the way through trials, persecutions, ignominious sufferings and death, the Son of God leaves this warning to those who are to follow him: "For if they do these things in a green tree, what shall be done in a dry?" And with a complete victory over death, hell and the grave, he commissions his disciples to "Go into all the world and preach the gospel to every creature," giving to them at the same time the promise, "I will be with you."

The work of the church began at Jerusalem under the immediate direction of the Holy Spirit on the day of Pentecost, and from the great outpouring of the Spirit on that day, has, as I have said, continued unto this day, and will continue to roll on until the "Gospel of the kingdom shall be preached in all the world for a witness unto all nations; and then shall the end come." None of the Protestant churches (in these, of course, I do not include Baptists) can lay claim to having had their beginning there, for it is said of the Baptists, "It may be seen that the Baptists who were formerly called Ana-Baptists, and in later times Mennonites, were the original Waldenses and have long in the history of the church received that origin and as such may be justly termed the only Christian community which has stood since the days of the apostles." (History of Religious Denominations, p. 42.) But as we run through the musty pages of history and look at the blood and fire through which the church has come, we are inclined to think that the road has been a dark and dreary one. But a second look will bring out the brilliancy of those glorious pages, filled with immortal deeds of those whose very names are stars on the horizon of that invincible kingdom and serve as beacon lights to cheer and encourage the weary pilgrims who are yet in the way to that unclouded glory.

The world without Christ cannot see any greater men than those who have led great armies and sat as rulers of great nations. It points with pride to such men as Napoleon, Cromwell, Hannibal, Washington and Grant; and the Christian cannot help admiring the courage, pluck and brilliancy of these great warriors and leaders. But these great men had great armies to follow them to encourage and cheer them as they went from conquest to victory. But when we come to a John, a Peter, a Paul, a Silas, who, oftentimes alone, sometimes with shackles on their limbs, with a cross before their eyes and a guillotine over the head, would profess willlingness to die, if need be, for the cause of the Master; and, as we look into the face of the trembling governor and hear the testimony of the trial-king, that he is almost persuaded to be a Christian by the irresistible argument of a Christian in chains, we conclude that no just comparison can be made between these great characters as the former were great with men; the latter, great with God and man. But as we look upon the causes, which they respectively represent, we ask:

> "Where are the kings and empires now
> That of old, went and came?
> Thy church, O God, is praying yet,
> A thousand years the same."

But one of the most glorious features of this grand old church is that her history is one unbroken chain of events and progress. It is that amazing sight which appeared to Moses in Midian, the burning bush, but not consumed. The fires of tribulation and persecution have followed the Church of God in all these years of its existence, and perhaps will follow it to the end of time. It is by reason of the principles held by the Baptists to-day and the fact that these are the same principles which characterized the earlier Christians and brought on them suffering and death, that justifies us in the claim that ours is the only Christian denomination that can lay claim to apostolic succession. In this claim, we are not without evidence. It is said in the Encyclopedia of Religious Knowledge: "Their principles have subjected them to persecution from age to age and to such principles they have counted it a glory to be martyrs. Though their own blood has flown freely, they have never shed the blood of others." What was true of the early apostles is true of those who are their successor's to-day.

BAPTISTS ARE THE PIONEERS OF RELIGIOUS FREEDOM.

In 1636, according to Judge Story, a law was enacted in Rhode Island through and by them (Baptists) that conscience should be free and that men should not be punished for worshipping God in the way they are persuaded. The doctrine which is repugnant to all free people (the union of church and state) and which has, wherever it has been maintained, made the minister the vehicle of the political demagogue, has been wiped from the statute books of our country, and largely, if not altogether, this has been done through Baptist influence. And it was not accomplished without blood and tears. I have only to call up the names of Henry, Arnold, Lollard, Wycliffe, Tyndall, Milton, Bunyan, Gale, Hill, Booth, Butterworth, Carey, Ward, Fuller, Hall, Foster, Gregory, Roger Williams, and a host of others whom I need not mention, to awaken your thoughts to the cruel persecution to which Baptists were subjected even in the last three or four centuries. While some of these were not Baptists by their church connection, they believed as Baptists now believe, viz.: in baptism and liberty of conscience. The influence planted in the State of Rhode Island by the first Christian Baptist churches has permeated every State in this great Union and practically shaped the laws and policies of every local government between the two great oceans.

It is the firm unmovable stand that they (Baptists) have taken for religious freedom that has made it possible for other denominations of Christians to stand. While others may hold their episcopal orders from some great dignitary or potentate, it is nevertheless true that it is by the grace of God and the grace of the Baptists that they have been permitted to keep house outside of the Old Roman Home (the Catholic Church). It has been a war to the hilt. The old red dragon who had sought to destroy the child as soon as it was born has been continuously after the church and even now is contending against her. But the promise of Jesus inspires courage." "Lo, I am with you always, even unto the end of the world." My brethren, the transcendent beauty of our Church lies in the fact that every page of its history is ornamented with blood and cruel persecution, and so common has it become for Baptists to be the rejected and despised of all others, that they look for those very conditions and often ask, in song:

> "Must I be carried to the skies
> On flowery beds of ease,
> While others fought to win the prize,
> And sailed through bloody seas?"

Notwithstanding the beginning was small, the mustard seed has become a great tree, and the stone cut out without hands has become a great mountain and will fill the whole earth.

You have, perhaps, expected me to speak to you more particularly of the denominational work as carried on by Negro Baptists, and I shall now address myself to that feature of the work. For many years, owing to certain social conditions which have existed in this and other countries, the work of white and colored Baptists, has been carried on in separate societies and churches. This ought not to be and will not always be the case, for, as a rule, white and colored Baptists believe alike. But since they are separate, we may look at the work carried on by our own people, and in doing so we will not go beyond that period which recognizes the Negro as a man in a national sense. Immediately following the emancipation of the Negro of this country came the church and schoolhouse, and, contrary to the predictions of many, the Negro panted after these "as a hart panteth for the water brook," and in a very brief period, he was prepared for the work of preaching the Gospel and teaching others of the race. From the first, it was not known just what the Baptists were doing, for it was several years before we commenced to keep books. Those who traveled most formed the opinion that Negro Baptists were pretty well up. In view of the glorious history that our church had made, the fact that she bore the honor of being a friend to education and was the pioneer in agitating religious liberty and the first to send the Gospel to a foreign land, we came together in 1886, to count up and see what the denomination had been doing, and, to our own surprise, we had as many people in our churches as all the other denominations among our people combined; had more high schools and colleges and more children in these schools and almost two preachers to their one. The figures were astounding. We could hardly believe them, and the other folks said it was not so. And as our figures were not official, we waited quietly until after the census report of 1890 had been compiled. We found our figures not only verified, but that we had 182, 758 more than all others combined. Here is the Government report:

African Methodist Episcopal	452,725
African Union Methodist Protestant	3,415
African Methodist Episcopal Zion	349,788

Congregational Methodist	319

Colored Methodist Episcopal	129,383
Colored Cumberland Presbyterian	13,439
Colored members in M. E. Church	100,000
Colored members in Prot. Episcopal Church	20,000
Colored members in Presbyterian Church	20,000
Colored members in Congregational Church	12,000
Colored members in Christian Church	25,000
Colored members in Roman Catholic Church	100,000
Total outside Baptist Church	1,226,069
Total number of Colored Baptists	1,408,827
Leaving a majority over all for the Baptists,	182,758

Since that time, we have been making a net increase at the rate of forty thousand a year. This is the work of colored Baptists in our own country and to these figures may be added the number in our churches in Liberia and the various mission stations in Africa and the work of the Baptists in Jamaica and other islands. In the work of Christian education, we lead all the others; and not counting the magnificent colleges and seminaries built by the American Baptist Home Mission Society, we have fifty-four colleges and high schools of our own. Many of these schools will compare favorably with the best colleges in the land.

A most significant fact, which tells of the indomitable energy of Negro Baptists, is that while our race is only one-eighth of the entire population of the whole country, they represent three-eighths of all the Baptists and fully one-half of all the Negro Christians. So when Dr. MacArthur pays a tribute to Baptists for their rapid increase from 1870 to the present, he might have said that that increase was largely due to the ability of Negro Baptist preachers in making disciples of men.

The Baptist denomination stands for the best thought and highest ideal of a democratic form of government, and because of their unrelenting war for the absolute separation of church and state, many of them have suffered martyrdom at the hands of monarchs, kings and potentates. Our own country owes a debt of gratitude to the Baptists for the absolute liberty of conscience which it never will finish paying. We need only to refer you to the life and times of Baxter, and to Cromwell, the Speaker of whose Parliament, it is said, was a Baptist preacher, and many of the men and generals who followed him, to show the active part taken by the Baptists in the great reforms of a few centuries ago and their active participation in the American Revolutionary War, which was, indeed, fought upon these very principles for which the name Baptist stands to-day.

HONORED FOR THE SUFFERING ENDURED.

The Son of God, as he sat upon the Mount of Olives and told of the destruction of the temple, said, "This gospel of the kingdom shall be preached in all the world for a witness unto all nations; and then shall the end come." (Matt. 24:14.)

It can be said without fear of successful contradiction that Baptists have suffered more, have sacrificed more lives on account of their loyalty to the doctrines of Jesus Christ, than any other denomination of Christians; and we are glad to be counted worthy of suffering for the cause, and, in the name of that crowned Prince who sacrificed his own life that he might save the lives of those who had fallen into the pits of eternal night. The eloquent words spoken by Paul as he stood, as it were, in sight of the guillotine, "I am now ready to be offered, and the time of my departure is at hand. I have fought a good fight, I have finished my course, I have kept the faith: henceforth there is laid up for me a crown of righteousness, which the Lord, the righteous Judge, shall give me at that day," etc., have been a source of inspiration to Christian ministers in all the time since they were uttered, and will continue to be until the consummation of all things or when the Church of God shall be called out, as it were, upon the musty hills of Zion and wave their palms, emblems of victory, before the throne and before the Lamb; and as the question is asked, "Who are these arrayed in white robes and whence came they?" the answer shall be proclaimed throughout the heavens, "These are they which came out of great tribulation, and have washed their robes, and made them white in the blood of the Lamb."

SANCTIFICATION.

[Sermon before the Arkansas Baptist State Convention, in 1899.]

Text:--"Sanctify them through thy truth: thy word is truth." (John 17:17.)

That there is such a doctrine as Sanctification taught in the Scriptures must be admitted. And that this doctrine has been wantonly perverted and misunderstood must also be admitted. But I am charitable enough to say that many who have misunderstood and misinterpreted this doctrine have done so from honest convictions which had formed in their hearts on account of incompetent teachers. But it is not my purpose to attempt to set up an argument in answer to that class of persons who are preaching the doctrine of sinless perfection, or bodily holiness. Such an attempt would be only a waste of time in an unsuccessful effort to turn Ephraim from his idols. Indeed, if argument were needed to prove the fallacy of that contention, I would need only to refer to the statement of the Apostle Paul, found in 2 Cor. 12:9, and the reply which he claims to have received from the Lord, viz.: "My grace is sufficient." Hence, I shall present to you the doctrine of Sanctification as I find it in God's Word, and as illustrated by those who were first entrusted with the responsibility of preaching it.

The word "sanctify" means to set apart, or appoint to service. "Sanctify ye a fast, call a solemn assembly, gather the elders and all the inhabitants of the land into the house of the Lord your God, and cry unto the Lord." (Joel 1:14.) Again, the same prophet says, "Blow the trumpet in Zion, sanctify a fast, call a solemn assembly." (Joel 2:15.)

Here is a call to service, a getting ready for a meeting in which to worship God; a laying aside of secular matters, that for the time, the whole being may be devoted to the service of God, and thereby turn back the calamity which was about to come upon the nation. This call to sanctification, or forming a solemn assembly, does not imply that the individuals are entirely purged from sin. But it does mean that they are to turn to God with their whole hearts, and to put themselves in absolute obedience to his commands. The wonderful prayer of the Son of God from which our text is taken was uttered perhaps on the night before his crucifixion. Those for whom this prayer was directly made had been with him for three years, and were fully decided as to their religious course; yet, they had so many imperfections that it was necessary that this remarkable prayer be made. The very wording of it implies that they were not perfect and that perfection had to be brought about by an implanting and growth of the Word. The group of disciples who are with the Son of God when these words are spoken are the same men who were gathered at his feet when he went up into the mountain away from the multitude and said to them, "If thine eye be single, thy whole body shall be full of light;" *i. e.,* if you have gotten your whole being drawn in from the cares of the world; if you are able now to have no thought for food or raiment or even for your life, then you are full of light. But was this the case with these men who had seen not only the miracles which the Son of God had wrought, but had seen the spirit of God on him and heard the word of God proclaiming him as his only begotten Son. Nay, they were still at times filled with doubts, such as fill every believer when the clouds of the adversary rise over his head. Notwithstanding all that, Christ had said and done, and this wonderful prayer in their presence, on that very night, Peter denied that he ever knew him. And after the awful tragedy on Calvary, Thomas declared that he would not believe him risen except he could put his finger in the nail prints and thrust his hand into the wounded side of the Redeemer. Even after this, one of those discouragements which so often rush upon believers caused Peter to lead the little band back to their former occupation--that of fishing. But the Son of God was on the bank early in the morning and with a voice so tender as to awaken every thought of the past, he calls to them, "Children, have ye any meat?" They answered him, "No." And he said unto them, "Cast your net on the right side of the ship, and ye shall find." The fact of their imperfection is made manifest by the divine direction, which led to the great draught of fishes. Continuing, Jesus says, "Simon, son of Jonas, lovest thou me more than these?" None will doubt that Peter loved Jesus, but the desires of the flesh had not been overcome. The leaven, however, was at work and would finally leaven the whole lump. Before leaving this remarkable prayer, let us read the nineteenth verse of the same chapter. "And for their sakes I sanctify myself, that they also might be sanctified through the truth." Please note these words, "might be," which suggest that Sanctification is a progressive work. It begins in regeneration, which is itself a work of the Holy Spirit, and when accomplished, affects the individual in a manner above his comprehension and justifies the statement of Paul when he says, "He which hath begun a good work in you will perform it until the day of Jesus Christ. He will carry on the work begun," etc. Sanctification, while having its root (beginning) in regeneration, implies justification and the final perseverance of the believer. For one cannot consistently be set apart to a work that is not approved of (by) him for whom he works; nor can we hope to reach the stage of perfection without persevering to the end. Hence, the ground of one's justification will determine the extent of his sanctification. "Therefore, being justified by faith we have peace with God." This justification does not rest upon our own righteousness, but upon the righteousness of the Son of God. Hence, the faith is in the fact that God was in Christ reconciling the world unto himself, "not imputing their trespasses unto them," as shown in 2 Cor. 5:19. If there were not a mighty war going on in us, why should the question be asked, "Who shall separate us from the love of Christ?" If there is a place for the evil desires to bring on a war, sin has not been entirely eradicated. The Son of God illustrates the work of the Holy Spirit in the believer in this parable, "The kingdom of heaven is like unto leaven, which a woman took, and hid in three measures of meal, until the whole was leavened." Just as the particles of leaven (yeast) worked their way until they had touched every atom of the meal, so will the Spirit, in its work of sanctification, continue to work in the believer until every superfluity of life has been touched and the whole being has been brought under its influence.

The early apostles did not understand or teach that men were perfect in the beginning of Christian life. We read in Ephesians, the fourth chapter, eleventh and fourteenth verses inclusive, "And he gave some, apostles; and some, prophets; and some, evangelists; and some, pastors and teachers; For the perfecting of the saints, for the work of the ministry, for the edifying of the body of Christ: Till we all come in the unity of the faith, and of the knowledge of the Son of God, unto a perfect man, unto the measure of the stature of the fullness of Christ." Here it is plainly taught that God has employed all the means here outlined to bring us unto that state of perfection to make us like unto Christ. Great and wonderful, indeed, is the work of sanctification! In the second epistle of Peter 1:5, 6, we are shown that regeneration only begins our Christian life.

He says, "Add to your faith virtue; and to virtue, knowland to patience, godliness; and to godliness, brotherly kindness; and to brotherly kindness, charity." All these graces, according to the Apostle Peter, are to be acquired after one enters the Christian life. Again, in the second epistle, 3:18, he says, "Grow in grace and in the knowledge of our Lord and Savior Jesus Christ." We understand by this growth that perfection is not reached in regeneration, but that we are kept by the power of God through faith unto salvation. But since there is such a doctrine as Sanctification, to what extent does it possess our being? God having begun a good work in us, will carry it on unto the day of Jesus Christ. This, which is the experience of one Christian, is the experience of all. "I find, then, a law that when I would do good, evil is present. For I delight in the law of God after the inward man." May that inward man control in all our lives, and the sanctifying influence of the Spirit abide in our hearts. So very often we find ourselves with Paul, saying, "O wretched man that I am; who shall deliver me from the body of this death?" It is the sinful nature that imprisons our soul, etc. Having received the sanctifying influence of the Holy Spirit in our hearts, we set about a cultivation of it with an anxious desire that we may become more and more like Christ each day. The deformity which sin has brought on us will only be lost in the regeneration of the world. Like the doctrine of baptism, sanctification implies a resurrection of the body. "It is sown a natural body, it is raised a spiritual body." (1 Cor. 15:44.) If the bodies in which we live and die are to be changed by the power of God from mortal to immortal, then they cannot be holy until that change has taken place. "But we shall all be changed." (1 Cor. 15:51.) In conclusion I would say, my brethren, that it is safe to follow that grand old doctrine set forth in the "Declaration of Principles," namely, "Sanctification is the work of the Holy Spirit, begun in regeneration and carried on in the life of the believer unto the end, or unto the perfect day."

THE BROTHERHOOD OF MAN.

"I am Joseph your brother, whom ye sold." (Genesis 45:4.)

The text and theme which we here present comes down to us from the patriarchs of old. They present to us a rule and sentiment which should find place in the hearts of every Christian, and should direct our conduct towards our fellow-man, and especially to those who are of the household of faith wherever dispersed around the globe. The ties of blood relation are prominent in the beautiful truths presented by the Scriptures, from which my text is taken. They enable the speaker (Joseph) to rise above all privations and difficulties of the past and to forgive all the injuries inflicted, even the jealous, murderous rage of angry brothers who sought his utter destruction, and enables him to come forward and acknowledge them as his equals, notwithstanding their impoverished condition. And to remove any embarrassment which these guilty brothers might feel at a remembrance of their past conduct towards him, Joseph hastily tells them that it was God's purpose that he should be thus sent ahead of them, that he might preserve life. We cannot always understand the purposes or plans of the All wise God in his dealings with his people, nor are we at all times prepared to accept willingly the orders of his Providence or the wisdom of his counsel. But he surely knows what is best for us, for he can see the end from the beginning, and knows of every obstacle which lies in our path, from the cradle to the grave. One of the hymn-writers has rightfully said:

> "Judge not the Lord by feeble sense,
> But trust him for his grace;
> Behind a frowning providence
> He hides a smiling face."

Joseph, who is the central figure in my text, was at an early age the fondest hope of an aged but indulgent parent, and was the brightest gem in a pious home, which fact was the cause of his brothers' hatred. But the fact that his mind was susceptible of Divine revelations which you perhaps would call dreams, added to the hatred which they had for him, and so fierce became their rage that they plotted among themselves to kill him. But the counsel of Reuben prevailed and they cast him into a pit, and as they were eating they lifted up their eyes and saw a company of Ishmaelites. They took Joseph out of the pit and sold him to these traders who were on their way to Egypt, etc. Perhaps the darkest part of the picture which I shall attempt to draw, is where an effort is made to deceive the aged father and lead him to believe that Joseph had been destroyed by some wild beast, etc. Those who traffic in human flesh lose their respect for pious, consecrated humanity and will resort to any kind of diabolism to cover up their crimes.

Slavery has existed in some form or other in nearly all ages of the past. But in some instances it proved to be a blessing in disguise, while in others it formed some of the most blood-curdling, revolting scenes in the history of the world. It has separated husband and wife, parents and children, brother and sister, and broken the cords of affection which nature and nature's God have entwined around the hearts of a happy family. But these cruel separations do not, in all cases, last forever. Sometimes they are of short duration and work for the persecuted party "a far more exceeding and eternal weight of glory." When the God-appointed time came around that the brothers of Joseph should meet with him whom they had sold, and there be humiliated by their own conduct toward him, he brings forward all the true manhood in his great soul and says, "Now therefore be not grieved, nor angry with yourselves, that ye sold me hither; for God did send me before you to preserve life."

The theme of our discourse carries us beyond blood relationship and introduces us to an unexplored field of humanity which recognizes one common Father--God, and one common brother--man.

THE BROTHERHOOD OF MAN NOT A NEW DOCTRINE.

The doctrine of the brotherhood of man is sustained both by law and by grace. But the Church has apparently gone to sleep upon this great doctrine and allowed political, economical and social questions to relegate it to the background, thereby silencing one of the most effective weapons of the Christian religion. The opponents of this heaven-appointed doctrine have endeavored to create a prejudice against it by claiming that it teaches the social equality of the races and classes, and we are forced to admit that they have, in a measure, been successful. For many so-called Christians are so very reserved in their manner of worship that they refuse to come in contact with the common people, for fear that they will have to otherwise associate with them. But, my friends, this doctrine does not teach the social equality of the races nor the classes, beyond that rule given to the world by the Son of God, which says, "Therefore, all things whatsoever ye would that men should do to you, do ye even so to them." Hence, your sociality is based upon your own choice. If you do not desire the association of men of a different race or class, you are not required to associate with them. But is there not a difference between our social and religious life? Is not every man our brother who has accepted Christ Jesus as his Saviour? The Syro-Phenician woman had no legal, social or racial rights which would warrant her in approaching the Son of God, but she had a religious right, and she contended for that right. Christ is not the Saviour of any particular race or class, but "whosoever will may take the water of life freely."

Class and race antipathy has been carried so far in this great Christian country of ours, that it has almost destroyed the feeling of that common brotherhood, which should permeate the soul of every Christian believer, and has shorn the Christian Church of that power and influence which it would otherwise have, if it had not repudiated this doctrine. The Apostle Peter is a notable example of those who believed that racial lines should direct in the conduct of the preaching of the Gospel of Jesus Christ. But when God had convinced him by suspending a great vessel from Heaven which enclosed all manner of four-footed beasts, creeping things and fowls of the air, he at once confessed his ignorance and went with the men who sought him. And when they had come to the house of Cornelius, Peter said, "Ye know how that it is an unlawful thing for a man that is a Jew to keep company, or come unto one of another nation; but God hath shewed me that I should not call any man common or unclean," etc., etc. Cornelius tells Peter for what purpose he calls him, etc. Peter answers and says, "Of a truth I perceive that God is no respecter of persons." While Paul waited at Athens' for Silas and Timotheus, whom he had sent for, and, seeing the idolatry of the city, it caused his very soul to yearn for an opportunity to declare unto the people the Gospel of Jesus Christ. His earnest and fearless presentation of the truths of the Gospel brought out certain philosophers of the Epicureans and of the Stoics, who said to Paul what such persons will say to-day when the truth is given without compromise or apology, "May we know what this new doctrine, whereof thou speaketh, is?" After Paul's mild rebuke of their ignorant or misguided worship of the unknown God, he proceeds to tell them that God "hath made of one blood all nations of men for to dwell on all the face of the earth." The whole world is to-day indebted to Paul for the prominence he gave to this all-important doctrine at Mars Hill. We know that the doctrine is not a popular one and that none can accept and practice it, except such as are truly regenerated. But the man who has been brought into the new and living way by the birth which is from above, by contrasting his own depraved and sinful nature with the pure, immaculate character of the Son of God after meditating what that matchless Prince underwent for him, can get inspiration and courage to acknowledge every man his brother who has enlisted under the banner of the Cross, and accepted the same Christ as his Saviour.

For nearly nineteen hundred years the church has been upon the field, and has been opposed by all the powers that the adversary could marshal. No opportunity has been or is overlooked, or passed, by those who are opposed to the principles of Christianity, but all are brought into play to weaken it, even to the equality of the races and the classes. But, sad to say, many church members have too often sided with the world, and especially so when this doctrine of the fatherhood of God and the brotherhood of man is presented. In the beginning only two classes were considered, Jews and Gentiles.

But with the multiplicity of religions has come a multiplicity of races and classes, and so prominent have the lines of cast been, that many Christians of the same faith cannot worship at the same altar; that God, who is no respecter of persons, is not pleased with the service which his chosen embassadors are rendering, and he will not always chide. The commission which he gives is without regard to race, color or condition, but is that the Gospel be preached to every creature, not over the telephone or through the medium of the phonograph, but by the human voice, coming in direct contact with the people, all the people. If they are low, take their hands and lift them up. If too high, call them down. "Christ Jesus came into the world to save sinners," not white sinners, nor black sinners, nor red sinners, but sinners. The wise man Solomon who doubtless had an eye single to the division and opinions of men, where class is arrayed against class, and race against race, looked beyond the active scenes of life back to Mother Earth from whence we all were taken, and back to which we all must go, and says, "The rich and the poor meet together; the Lord is the maker of them all."

But let us not despair: the church will make to righteousness and put on her beautiful garments and her ministers will, ere long, declare that there be no North, no South, no East and no West; no black and no white, but we shall be one in Christ Jesus. And the complete fulfillment of that prophecy concerning Israel will be made manifest in his redeemed, which says. "After those days, saith the Lord, I will put my law in their inward parts, and write it in their hearts; and will be their God, and they shall be my people. And they shall teach no more every man his neighbour, and every man his brother, saying, Know the Lord: for they shall all know me, from the least of them unto the greatest of them.

When the Christians at Galatia were divided over this perplexing question, Paul said to them, "For as many of you as have been baptized into Christ have put on Christ,' and, again, "There is neither Jew nor Greek, there is neither bond nor free, there is neither male nor female: for ye all are one in Christ Jesus."

WHAT THE CHURCH WILL DO IN THE TWENTIETH CENTURY.

Already the great evangelical churches are lining up for more effectual work in the coming century. And this means to me that the white man, the black man, the red man, the yellow man, all who enlist under the banner of the Cross, will form one mighty army to go mightily against the power of darkness and with the great battering ram of the Gospel pitched, as it were, upon the universal brotherhood of man, break down the strong towers of Satan until this government, as well as all the other kingdoms of the world, shall become the kingdoms of our God and his Christ, and he shall reign forever.

SERMON.

[Delivered to a class of ministers.]

Text:--"The good shepherd giveth his life for his sheep." (John 10:11.)

My friends, I have no greater pleasure than to speak of the position of honor and trust which the Lord Jesus has tendered those heralds--shepherds, whom we call preachers. No class of men are more deserving of honor than the ministers of our Lord and Saviour, and there is no class who should be held in more tender regard. Their very calling and the authority by which they enter their work should make a place for them in the affections of the people. Their appointment is by the Holy Ghost, and their duty is to watch for souls. No angel ever performed a tenderer and more worthy function than that performed by the minister of the Gospel in visiting the sick, or performing the last solemn rite when death has claimed the mortality. The minister is sought when marriage is to be solemnized. His counsel is sought on all serious and difficult questions which affect the peace and well being of the home and community, and it always brings good results when followed, because filled with the Divine unction from above. But while the minister is deserving of honor, he can hardly expect it from those who are of the world. He may have a good report of those who are without, but they will not go further, for his work comes in direct conflict with their work. Hence, if not supported by the church, he necessarily will have to yield to the inevitable and flee into another city.

Permit me to say before entering upon a discussion of my text that there is a great deal of doctrine (which is the very essence of the Gospel) found in this chapter. The opening verse goes to show that Christ is the way, the only way to God the Father and into heaven, and implies that those who seek entrance to the kingdom of God in any other way than that laid out by him, will be shut out. It also shows the filial relation which exists between Christ and his people and how impossible it is for one who is born from above to be deceived by those who are the emissaries of the devil; for the sheep know the shepherd's voice. I may say also that the context goes to show that all religions which antedate the coming of Christ to the world and claim to be the Christian religion are false, and all which have their origin since his ascension into heaven are equally false. For Christ Jesus, the Great Shepherd of the sheep, is the only true and living way. All that came before him were thieves and robbers. He is the Great Head of the Church, its only law-giver, or legislator, and personally superintends the work carried on in his kingdom. Those who act as under shepherds get their authority from him and are to execute and not make laws. This was fully understood by the first disciples, and no variation from that rule is anywhere recorded. Paul gave the elders of Ephesus to understand that their appointment was from the Holy Ghost. He said to them, "Take heed therefore unto yourselves, and to all the flock, over the which the Holy Ghost hath made you overseers," etc. The shepherd must know his sheep; the pastor must know his members.

The wonderful power which the shepherd has over the sheep comes from his constant association and contact with them. They learn to love him by reason of his tender care for them, in leading them from pasture to pasture, from one cooling stream to another; in gathering them into the fold and making them secure from the prowling wolves which seek them as prey when the shades of night come on. So must the pastor seek to draw himself into the affections of his people by showing to them that he is careful about their spiritual food. He must know them, for there are the tender lambs (the converts who would be an easy prey for the adversary). Hear what the Good Shepherd has to say about the lambs and the sheep: "Simon, son of Jonas, lovest thou me more than these? He saith unto him, Yea, Lord, thou knowest that I love thee. He saith unto him, Feed my lambs. He saith to him again the second time, Simon, son of Jonas, lovest thou me? He saith unto him, Yea, Lord; thou knowest that I love thee. He saith unto him, Feed my sheep. He saith unto him the third time, Simon, son of Jonas, lovest thou me? Peter was grieved because he said unto him the third time, Lovest thou me? And he said unto him, Lord, thou knowest all things; thou knowest that I love thee. Jesus said unto him, Feed my sheep." (John 21:15,16,17.) No language could be employed that would in a greater degree magnify the care which Christ has for his followers, and how he expects for his ministers to act toward them. Indeed, the pastor, the undershepherd, is to exercise the same care and concern for the well being of the church that Christ would exercise himself.

I. The pastor should know each member by name as well as by sight. Now, there are the aged and worn-out members which must not be overlooked. Jesus loves them now just as he did when they were able to fill their places in church at every service, and the pastor must do the same thing. He may become discouraged sometimes. His salary may not be promptly paid all the time; but he must labor on, for besides the hundredfold which he receives as reward in this life, there is a greater inheritance laid up above. He should know when death has claimed one of his members and should be able at once to recognize just which one it is, for if he should in any way appear as a stranger to the deceased, he will have wounded the hearts of the entire family or intimate friends. In this matter of being acquainted with the members of the church, the deacons can greatly aid the pastor by providing him with the necessary aid, such as a horse and buggy and a man to drive him, so that much time may be saved especially in case of a large membership. Then, the deacons should see to it that the pastor is free from all anxiety, so far as his temporal support is concerned. For his life is to be given for the sheep, and no time is left to the true pastor after he has looked after the welfare of five hundred or a thousand members, to labor for the temporal support of himself and family.

II. He must lead his people. The whole life of the pastor is to be given for his people, the people over whom the Holy Ghost hath made him overseer. Many people are of the opinion that the pastor should give his entire time to the preaching of the Gospel. But let me say just here, preaching is only one of the many duties of the pastor. A hymn writer has said:

> " 'Tis not a cause of small import
> The pastor's care demands;
> But what might fill an angel's heart,
> And filled a Saviour's hands."

Indeed, the least of his duties is to preach the Gospel, to feed the Church of God. The greater responsibility comes when he is to prepare the food so as to suit the various conditions of those to whom he is to minister. Some of them are to have the "sincere milk of the word;" others need stronger food. He is to lead by example as well as by precept. He should not only agitate, but live a temperate life. He must be a model of neatness and precision; always on time at the church service. His outer life must be a living testimony to the world that he "has been with God and learned of him." He must "study to show himself approved of God." He must study every great question of the day. He must know when the political demagogue seeks to enslave the people by unjust legislation and otherwise. He must sound the trumpet when he sees the sword coming and let the people know the proper course to take to prevent their enslavement. For these things, he will be hated and perhaps persecuted, but he should not be moved from the path of duty for fear of persecution. He should bear in mind that it is an honor to be hated for righteousness' sake. "Blessed are ye, when men shall revile you, and persecute you, and say all manner of evil against you falsely."

III. He must give his life for the people. That is, he must spend all the best energies of his life in an effort to lift up the fallen. He may undergo much criticism for going into the hovels and slums to save his people; but he must go. For Christ made himself of no reputation, and it is imperative that we follow his example. The woman who washed the Saviour's feet with tears was a woman out of whom he had cast seven devils. Indeed, it is written: "I came not to call the righteous, but sinners to repentance." The Son of God who is the only true type and the one after whom we must fashion our lives, not only suffered to be persecuted and given a bad name, but willingly laid down his life for his people. The adversary of our souls goes about as a roving lion seeking whom he may devour. He has many ways to lead the young into his alluring traps; but, like David, the pastor must slay the lion, and save the lamb. The lion may assume the form of the saloon or the gambling house. No matter how unpopular it may make the preacher appear, he must oppose them. The lion and the bear which would destroy our Father's flock must be slain. The pastor must not desert because of opposition. His life, all of his life, must be given to his calling. "There is no discharge in this war."

Then, our Great Shepherd will not desert us in death, for he has promised to call before him all nations, and he will separate them one from another, as a shepherd divides his sheep from the goats. When all the best energies of the shepherd's life have been spent and he can no longer lead, feed and protect the flock given to his care, and he shall be brought to the margin of the river, and, notwithstanding some have not heeded his call, the words of God will give cheer--the words to the effect that if they fail to take warning their blood shall be upon their own heads--and as he looks over the surging billows and the thought shall come over his soul, "How can I get through?" then he can say with David,

"The Lord is my shepherd; I shall not want. Yea, though I walk through the valley of the shadow of death, I shall fear no evil: for thou art art with me; thy rod and thy staff they comfort me."

SERMON.

[Delivered to the Holy Trinity Baptist Church, Philadelphia, Pa., April, 1900.]

Text:--"He hath sent me *** to proclaim liberty to the captives." (Isaiah 61:1.)

If this discourse should be confined to an elucidation of the one word *liberty,* it would bring us into an inexhaustible region of thought, and let us out upon a fathomless ocean of felicity. It is one of the sweetest words in all the English vocabulary. Every letter is a diamond stud making the whole the most sparkling gem of the language. Its meaning is self-conveying and extends to every living creature, whether the creature be possessed with the power of reason or merely led by blind, unreasoning instinct. Each creature realizes the true meaning of liberty, whether intelligent or ignorant, rational or irrational. The beneficent influence of this word reaches to every people and every clime. The heathen and savage tribes of earth, such as the roaming red man, the savage bushman, the stupid Chinaman--all enjoy liberty of body. Even the beasts of the forests and the cattle of the field realize what it is to have liberty. The winged fowls of the heavens and the finny tribes of the sea are miserable and discontented when confined to prison walls, or shut in from the liberty given them by their Creator. But it is man, the masterpiece of divine architecture, with which my subject deals. He was born amid the freedom of a heavenly paradise prepared by divine wisdom, and suited to every condition of his holy state, in which he was unrestrained in all things which were necessary to his perfect happiness. But having violated the command of the Maker, man was driven from the Garden of Eden under a heavy penalty--one which he could not pay. Having voluntarily imprisoned his own soul and finding himself totally unable to release it from the thraldom of sin, he showed his disgust or abhorrence of soul bondage by his opposition to physical bondage--a thing which has been characteristic of man in all the ages of the past. Perhaps the most notable instances cited in Bible history are those in the accounts of the bondage of the Israelites to the Egyptians, and the Jews to the Babylonians, evidenced by such passages as, "I have surely seen the affliction of my people which are in Egypt, and have heard their cry by reason of their task-masters," (Ex. 3:7) etc. "For there they that carried us away captive required of us a song; and they that wasted us required of us mirth" (Ps. 137:3), etc.

Perhaps no more emphatic declaration was ever issued, touching upon the liberty of human beings than the Preamble to the Declaration of Independence by the American people, and there is not a gem of literature outside of the sacred writings more brilliant. The man who wrote it, and those who signed it spoke more wisely than they knew, and have sent rolling down the rugged hills of time, a sentiment which is destined to cover the whole earth. It is this: "We hold these truths to be self-evident; that all men are created free and equal; that they are endowed by their Creator with certain inalienable rights; that among these are life, liberty, and the pursuit of happiness." It was in an old Virginia town that Patrick Henry, facing an anxious assembly of his country-men, gave utterance to these words, "Give me liberty or give me death." Many poor slaves in years gone by, who were inspired by such words as these, sacrificed their lives in the attempt to liberate themselves from a cruel physical bondage. Nor was there any peace until the shackles had been broken from the limbs of every slave. It was a desire for absolute freedom that caused the fathers of our country to rise up as one man, throw off the British yoke and declare their independence.

THE GREAT LIBERATOR.

But no comparison can be made of the physical bondage, which has held so many of the human family in its heartless grasp, with the bondage of the soul to sin. But in the fulness of time we beheld one coming down to us from the eternal hills, who is in every way fully capable of sympathizing with fallen man in his imprisoned state, and to release him from Satan's grasp.

> "Down from the shining courts above,
> With joyful haste He fled;
> Entered the grave in mortal flesh
> And dwelt among the dead"

The awful depths into which sin had plunged man can better be imagined than described in words. The fact that man had lost favor with his Creator, was shut out of Paradise and held under the dreadful penalty that "the soul that sinneth must die," rendered him a most miserable creature. Think of one who has been tried under the laws of his country by a jury of his countrymen, and, having been convicted, still cherishes hope in executive clemency, his longing eyes filled with tears of hope as he looks to see coming to him a pardon, which will free him from the awful guillotine or gallows. Who can contemplate or portray the joy of one doomed to death when he has been assured, just before the time appointed for execution, that a full pardon has been granted him? And yet it is the great privilege of every man to receive such a pardon. Indeed, every man is in need of a pardon, for all have sinned and all are doomed to eternal death, except such as receive the pardon which is found only in the Gospel of Jesus Christ and borne to a guilty world by the heralds of the cross.

THE AUTHORITY OF CHRIST TO LIBERATE.

The perfect liberty of that soul freed from the awful consequence of sin, death--"for the wages of sin is death"--and its hope of an ultimate triumph over the power of darkness, lies in the ability of the Liberator to sustain his proclamation. A proclamation to free may also carry with it a promise of indemnity for all who are included in said proclamation. The Son of God was vested with all the regal authority of heaven, to proclaim liberty to the captives of sin and hell, and paid the price for their ransom, notwithstanding the fact that that life was a continuous life of suffering and finally an ignominious death upon the cross. But his power to save from sin and to bring from the prison house (the grave) those who believe in him is made manifest in his triumphant resurrection from the grave, the evidence of which is superabundant both by the testimony of his enemies as well as that of his friends (Matt. 28:13; Luke 24; Mark 16; John 19). Having proclaimed the liberty to those who were bound, he engages to keep them against the evil day through the fostering care of the Holy Spirit. "Being confident of this very thing, that he which hath begun a good work in you will perform it until the day of Jesus Christ" (Phil. 1:6). The proclamation of liberty to the soul must be borne by the ministers of the Gospel of Jesus Christ, and since the bondage of sin is so grievous and its consequence so terrible, each minister should exclaim with Paul, "Woe is unto me, if I preach not the Gospel."

The liberty which the Gospel gives is not confined alone to the freedom of the soul, but it gives also physical liberty and recognizes the "Fatherhood of God and the brotherhood of man." Indeed, the full and complete liberty of the world, when all caste, racial and national lines shall be obliterated, will come only when "this Gospel of the kingdom shall be preached into all the world for a witness unto all men." Even now where the Gospel is preached and believed as it should be, there is one common brotherhood. How important, then, that the plain, simple Gospel be preached, that heaven's greatest proclamation may fall upon the ears of a lost world!

One cannot think of that matchless name, "Jesus," the name of the one who came to

> "Rescue the perishing,
> Care for the dying,"

without recognizing in him an all-sufficient Saviour.

> "How sweet the name of Jesus sounds
> In a believer's ear!
> It soothes his sorrows, heals his wounds
> And drives away his fear."

But, alas! that name is only sweet in the ears of the believer. The man who will not believe that the message of salvation was for him will remain a slave to sin and hell and will turn even the messenger from his door, choosing to remain a bondman and reap the awful result, eternal death. He who enjoys that perfect liberty of the soul by reason of his acceptance of the Lord and Saviour Jesus Christ, is indeed a happy man. His hope is not limited to the present existence, but it goes beyond the grave, "for if in this life only we have hope, we are of all men most miserable." He who brought this proclamation to fallen man has passed through death and the grave and leaves the blessed assurance, "Be of good cheer, I have overcome the world." If he has overcome the world, all who believe in him will also overcome and stand with him after the consummation of all transitory things. "For we know in part," but then we shall be brought into that perfect liberty which will be free from all anxiety and care, because we shall be forever with the Lord.

ORIGIN OF THE BAPTISTS.

(Denominational Sermon preached before the National Baptist Convention at Richmond, Va., September, 1900.)

Text:--"The same was in the beginning with God." (John 1:2.)

The origin of a thing cannot be considered aside from the source from which it came. The text given in connection with the subject on which I am to speak sets up the claim that Baptists have their origin in Christ, who himself antedates the formation of the world, and that the beginning of their work in the world was made manifest with the advent of Christ and the choosing of the first disciples. This, on the face of it, is indeed a startling claim, considering, too, that there are so many other great denominations in the world, all claiming to be representatives of the Church of Christ. Hence, to define the claim which I here make, it will be necessary to prove the continued succession of those principles held by the Baptists from the days of Christ until now; that these principles are inseparable from the Church of Christ. But before coming to this, in order that you may know that the origin of the Baptists (that is, if Baptists represent the Church of Christ) was in Christ even before he came into the world, it will not be out of place to consult that prophecy which refers directly to the coming of his kingdom. In the forty-fourth verse of the second chapter of the book of Daniel we have this prophecy: "In the days of these kings shall the God of heaven set up a kingdom, which shall never be destroyed: and the kingdom shall not be left to other people, but it shall break in pieces and consume all these kingdoms, and it shall stand forever."

The commission or authority under which the churches of Christ are to operate must have its beginning (or authority) in Christ. The "Go ye into all the world, and preach the gospel to every creature," is an order of Divine appointment and has been in effect ever since it fell from the Divine lips. It did not have its origin with the establishment of the Greek Catholic Church, in the fourth century, to say nothing of those of a more recent date of organization, but had been proclaimed and pushed with vigor and determination during all the time between the ascent of the Son of God and the establishment of these later systems, and must continue to be the only authority under which the Gospel is to be preached.

You will pardon me for this quotation from one of the greatest preachers of the nineteenth century: "The covenant of grace was made before the covenant of works, for Christ Jesus, before the foundation of the world, did stand as its head and representative. And we are said to be elected according to the foreknowledge of God the Father." Perhaps the most important feature of this prophecy is that which says, "It shall not be left to other people," or, in other words, the kingdom, or the Church of God, will be of Divine and not human origin and that Christ will forever remain the Great Head of the Church or Churches; thus stamping all creeds, which claim a founder other than Christ, as human and not divine.

It is also worthy of note that the kingdom is to stand forever. Now if there has been any time since the days of Christ when this kingdom has ceased to exist, then our argument falls to the ground. Kingdoms, monarchies, and so-called churches have arisen and crumbled to the earth. Ancient Babylon, whose magnificence and glory had reached to the heavens and whose ruler defied the God of Heaven, as she reveled in her iniquity, was at last astounded by the mysterious appearance of a Divine hand writing on the wall (while Belshazzar conducted his impious feast), etc., etc., and is now the home of bats, scorpions and every kind of hateful bird and reptile. Rome, the once proud mistress of the world, whose wicked Emperor looked complacently on while the blazing fagots were pushed around the charred remains of martyred saints and mocked at the shrieks of agony as their souls went upward through the flames of persecution, has lost her glory. Jerusalem, that magnificent city in which stood the temple of God and in which Jehovah delighted to meet his saints, because she threw down the altars of God, crumbled and fell in less than half a century after the prediction made by the Son of God, that "There shall not one stone be left upon another that shall not be thrown down." But the church of God is yet standing and will continue to successfully resist all attacks that may be made in the future.

The first visible or audible token we have of the approach of the kingdom of Christ is when John the Baptist appeared in the wilderness of the Jordan. (Matt. 3:1-3.) In connection with this announcement let us examine Luke 3:1-2, and see if it accords with "the days of these kings" referred to by Daniel. "Now in the fifteenth year of the reign of Tiberius Cæsar, Pontius Pilate being the governor of Judea, and Herod being tetrarch of Galilee, and his brother Philip, tetrarch of Iturea and of the region of Trachonitis, and Lysanias the tetrarch of Abilene, Annas and Caiaphas being high priests, the word of God came unto John, the son of Zacharias, in the wilderness," etc. If these days correspond to the prophecy of Daniel--and we believe they do--it may be seen that both John and Christ were born at the time of these kings; and if this fulfillment of that prophecy is genuine, we may trace the genealogy of the Son of God from his birth to his baptism, and from his baptism to the time when he stood upon Olivet, as if reviewing the work and making a forecast of the future, and ascended to Heaven upon a cloud, leaving the promise that "I will send you another Comforter." But without any statement concerning his life from his birth to his baptism, except to say that he was subject to his parents till he was thirty years old, or the time when he was baptized by John in the river Jordan. After leaving the waters of the Jordan and circulating sufficiently among the people to give them an opportunity to form an opinion as to who he was, he asked his disciples, "Whom do men say that I, the Son of man, am? And they said, Some say that thou art John the Baptist; some, Elias; and others, Jeremias, or one of the prophets. He saith unto them, But whom say ye that I am? And Simon Peter answered and said, Thou art the Christ, the Son of the living God, And Jesus answered and said unto him, Blessed art thou, Simon Barjona: for flesh and blood hath not revealed it unto thee, but my Father which is in heaven. And I say also unto thee, that thou art Peter, and upon this rock I will build my church; and the gates of hell shall not prevail against it." (Matt. 16:13-18.)

You will please notice the statement, "I will build my church," which accords with the statement of the prophet that it should not be left to other people, and also repudiates the idea that the church existed in any recognizable form before his advent and thereby destroys the claim of Judahism. The characteristic points which set forth the Church of Christ are the doctrines which he gave the church to be observed by it. Now, it remains for us to prove that we have sacredly maintained those doctrines in all the days of the past. What are the doctrines established by Christ? There are a few of the fundamental doctrines of Christ which we desire to make prominent and which are sustained by Baptists (with all the others), such as "Salvation by Grace," "Justification by Faith," "Baptism of Believers Only," "Final Perseverance of the Saints," etc. Following these special doctrines come the ordinances of the kingdom, viz.: Baptism and the Lord's Supper, and how they are to be observed. That Christ commanded these ordinances may be seen from the following: Matt. 28:19; Mark 16:15-16; 1 Cor. 11:24-26.

For an elucidation of the doctrines we are dependent upon the Apostles who were intimately associated with the Son of God for three years. The Council of Apostles and elders held for the specific purpose of allaying the dissension which arose over the question of "Salvation," arrived at this conclusion: "But we believe that through the grace of the Lord Jesus Christ, we shall be saved," etc. (Acts 15:11, etc.) Paul in his letter to the Romans (3rd chapter, 24th verse) says,

"Being justified freely by his grace through the redemption that is in Christ Jesus." Thus, it is shown that our salvation rests wholly upon the grace of God as made manifest in his Son, Jesus Christ. Peter also says, "Of which salvation the prophets have inquired and searched diligently, who prophesied of the grace that should come unto you. (1 Peter 1: 10.) Perhaps the most significant and far-reaching of these references is the one found in Ephesians 2:8: "For by grace are ye saved through faith; and that not of yourselves: it is the gift of God."

Were the early Apostles and writers who held forth these doctrines Baptists? The primary definition given to the word "Baptist," is *one who believes in immersion for baptism.* And if this definition is applied to Christ and his Apostles, it is clear, then, that they are all Baptists, for they were baptized of John in Jordan and did themselves baptize in the same river, those who professed faith in the Saviour. (John 3:22). To sustain the contention, I quote from history the following:

"Mosheim, with all his violent prejudices against the Baptists, in relating the history of the primitive church, has given a description which will not apply to his own church, the Lutheran, nor to any sect in Christendom, except the Baptists. The churches in those early times were entirely independent, none of them subject to any foreign jurisdiction, but each one governed by its own rulers and laws. For, though churches founded by the Apostles had this peculiar difference shown them, that they were consulted in doubtful and difficult cases, yet they had no judicial authority, no sort of supremacy over the others, nor the least right to enact laws for them."

A bishop during the first and second century was the person who had the care of one Christian assembly."

"Baptism was administered in the first century without the public assemblies, in places appointed for that purpose, and was performed by the immersion of the whole body in water."

In this account, Mosheim is sustained by the Scriptures, for the Apostles, after receiving the command from the lips of the Messiah, to disciple all men and baptize them, understood that they were to immerse them, for Philip, who was of the earliest disciples, baptized the eunuch, going down into the water, and coming up out of the water after having baptized him. And Paul, who was a later disciple still, not only recognized immersion as the only mode of baptism which would set forth our death to sin, but also recognized it as being the strongest proof setting forth the resurrection of the dead. (Romans 6: 4; 1 Corinthians 15: 29-42.)

The practice of these early Apostles was kept up for many years without undergoing a change. But it had been plainly predicted that the church would go into obscurity; not that it would be extinct, but that it would be in the wilderness. Here was cited the bitter persecution by the Roman Catholics. (Rev. 12.) But it is not a question whether the individuals representing the Church of Christ lived or died, but whether the principles lived, and whether there has been a people in the world that has held to these principles during all the Christian era.

One of the best historians has said: "It may now be seen that the Baptists, who were formerly called Ana-Baptists, but in later times Mennonites, were the original Waldenses, and may, therefore, be justly termed the only Christian community which has stood since the days of Christ and the Apostles. That is to say, that the principles which the Baptists hold were held also by the Ana-Baptists and by the Mennonites." (History of Religious Denominations of the World, p. 42.)

Martin Luther, who is given credit of being the greatest Christian reformer, in his works expressed great surprise at finding a sect of people who held practically the very same views and principles as those which he advocated, with slight variations, at the beginning of the Reformation. These people were ready to join Luther and did co-operate with him until he attempted to introduce infant baptism. This being contrary to their principles, and not in accord with the early teachings of the disciples, they dissented, holding as Baptists now believe, that none are proper subjects for baptism except believers. These little characteristics, so to speak, are the things which caused the people to speak of Baptists as a "peculiar sect."

Now, to the foundation of this subject, Christ Jesus is the origin of the Baptists. If Christ was in the beginning with God, then the Baptists were also in the beginning, for if their origin is not in Christ, they have none; and if they have no origin, then they are like Melchisedec, without beginning of days or ending of life. If our origin is in Christ and he is the head and body of the church, he then is, indeed, the church. "Ye are indeed many members but one body." For the Baptists claim to be the only people who claim him to be the only founder or head of their churches. Others can trace their origin to some good or great man, while Baptists have no founder other than Christ; and if he is not their foundation they are without one--simple air castles to be blown about by the wind, for, indeed, they recognize no bishop or potentate on earth. Nor do they believe that any human being can be the founder of such a system of faith and practice as the one to which they subscribe their lives and fortunes. Their doctrines are all in the Bible and are, therefore, as old as the Bible. Baptists believe that John the Baptist was a man sent from God, but that Heaven only gave him the honor of introducing the Son of God, who is the embodiment of the Church--the Alpha and Omega. The figures and shadows of the Church set forth in prophecy all go to show that the Baptists represent the true intent and purpose which God had in mind before the incarnation of his Son. References made by Paul to the baptism of the children of Israel, as they were baptized in the cloud and in the sea, and which is sometimes diverted into a proof that sprinkling is baptism, can be understood by bringing that same people down to the Red Sea; and as the waters of the sea stand up as a wall on either side and the mystical cloud which has led them passes over them and stands between them and their enemy--the passing over of this cloud and the mighty walls of the sea together would effect a complete burial and justify the statement of Paul when he says, "Therefore, we are buried with him by baptism." The ordinance of baptism is inseparable from the Baptists for indeed there can be no Baptists without baptism. And if baptism was introduced before the coming of Christ into the world and Christian baptism came with his advent, the origin of the Baptists may be traced back to my text, "The same was in the beginning with God."

Christ is not only the foundation of the Church and the beginning of Christian history, but he is the object to which all the ancient and sacred history pointed before his incarnation. Was Christ a Baptist? is a question which can be answered by asking, *Was he baptized?* If he was baptized, he was a Baptist or else baptism will not make one a Baptist. If he was a Baptist, then the Baptists originated in him, for he is the first and the last, the beginning and the ending of all things.

We conclude by saying that nothing is more clearly set forth than the eternity of the Son of God, and the eternity of his church. In speaking of this, Solomon says, "The Lord possessed me in the beginning of his way, before his works of old. I was set up from everlasting, from the beginning, or ever the earth was. When there were no depths, I was brought forth; when there were no fountains abounding with water. Before the mountains were settled, before the hills was I brought forth; while as yet he had not made the earth, nor the fields, nor the highest part of the dust of the world. When he prepared the heavens, I was there: when he set a compass upon the face of the depth * * * Then I was by him, as one brought up with him: and I was daily his delight, rejoicing always before him; rejoicing in the habitable part of his earth; and my delights were with the sons of men." (Prov. 8:22-31.)

Paul, the great Apostle to the Gentiles, recognizes this eternal existence when he says, "According as he has chosen us in him before the foundation of the world." The origin of the Baptists was in Christ, Christ was in the beginning with God. Far beyond the granite hills of time, nestling in the varied colors reflected in the foundation walls of jasper, sapphire, chalcedony, emerald, sardonyx, crysolyte, and the topaz, were the everlasting principles which characterize the Church of Christ, the mysterious analysis of the Word made flesh "and dwelt among us, and we beheld his glory." Notwithstanding the exalted place I have endeavored to give the churches of Christ in this discourse, John says, "It doth not yet appear what we shall be." But we shall be like unto his own glorious body, for we shall be with him, and shall see him as he is. Amen.

THE DEMAND FOR A NEGRO BAPTIST PUBLISHING HOUSE.

[Address delivered before the National Baptist Convention at Washington, D. C., in 1893.]

Brother President, Members of the Convention, Ladies and Gentlemen:

The Executive Board of your Convention has done me the honor to request that I speak to you upon the demand for a Negro Baptist Publishing House. I confess that I feel a degree of pride in coming before you, especially to speak upon a matter which lies very near my heart. Much of what I shall say is in support of the report of the committee which has just been read to you by Rev. J. H. Frank, and I would have you know in the beginning that we are in perfect accord on the matter of a publishing house. In presenting this matter we would have you know also that it is not the purpose of the friends of this movement to antagonize any person or organization in our effort to establish a Negro Baptist Publishing Company, but to discharge a duty which we feel that God has put upon us--to leave a legacy to our posterity. The first reason I advance for such an enterprise is:

1. IT IS NEEDED FOR RACE EMPLOYMENT.

The colored Baptists represent about five-eighths of the entire colored population of the United States, and about the same proportion of the wealth. In education they are on a parity with all the other denominations among the colored people. This fact will hardly be questioned by any who have acquainted themselves with the Negro literati of America. But although we note with pleasure that the Negro without regard to denomination or religion has made wonderful progress in the higher branches of education, it is a lamentable fact that some of the ablest scholars of the race have been forced to occupy very menial positions, because there is such little organization among our people that they are not willing to place their genius and learning at our command. When education tends indirectly to force our men and women out of the service for the race, it is not having the desired nor the intended effect. And if we stop educating, we go backward toward slavery and eternal obscurity. We must encourage education or the few years of freedom which we have enjoyed become but a recurrent middle age in the life of obscurity, which history may take time to record for us. We must encourage education by creating establishments for the employment of scholarship. it is no doubt true that we can trust the simplicity of our polity and the correctness of our doctrine as a sufficient cohesive to forever hold our large numbers; but it is our duty to set a premium on our church connection, and to show that while it costs something materially to become a Baptist, it is worth something materially to be a Baptist. If the large army of Baptist young people who are increasing at such a rapid rate are not encouraged to bookmaking, clerkships, superintendencies, and management by us, whither shall they go as they come forth from the colleges and universities, with religion and learning suited for this very demand? Is it true that some have said that we cannot afford to organize any feature of religious work merely for the sake of giving employment, and yet employment is inseparable from organization. It is a resultant element of force that bides its time, but comes in, nevertheless.

I am not one of those who takes a pride in feeding the leopard of race prejudice, by drawing and making prominent the color-line, and yet at times I feel like saying with Paul, "That I have great heaviness and continual sorrow in my heart. For I could wish that myself were accursed from Christ for my brethren, my kinsmen according to the flesh." I am led to believe that we can more successfully bestir our people by persuading them to properly cultivate race pride by inaugurating enterprises of their own than in any other way. Again,

2. IT IS NEEDED FOR RACE DEVELOPMENT.

Nothing teaches a man or a set of men so well as duty. If the scholars and workers of our race find that they are the sponsors of a great concern like the one we have in contemplation, nothing else will so inspire them to make master strokes for the race. If we never have books to write and criticise, we shall never be able to write and criticise written productions. If we never have to conduct the business side of our religion, we shall never know how. The lives that were lost for our freedom, the sacrifices that have been made for our social elevation, the heroism in common life that has been put forth for our intellectual development are all legacies left to us with the understanding that we would not always sit at the gate called beautiful and beg for privileges, power, and prominence * * * since our faith in freedom has been lost in sight and our freedom has become a blessed reality, if we do not proceed to do some work which history will rejoice to record, our unworthiness of the good deeds done us will stand out as the most prominent feature in our racial life. The solution of the so-called race problem will depend in a large measure upon what we prove able to do for ourselves. In political and denominational relations, we must not fail to remember that the country has not forgotten our past condition and present status, and through every avenue possible, whether civil or religious, political or denominational, we are in duty bound to use every means within our reach in bringing forth a better day, and present to the country a more strongly developed race. And again,

3. IT IS NEEDED AS A REQUEST TO OUR POSTERITY.

The one idea which stands paramount in the bosom of every proud Anglo-Saxon and throbs in his every vein, is to leave a legacy to his posterity. This is the ring that they gave to the organic law of our country when they wrote, "We, the people of the United States, * * * And to secure the blessings of liberty to ourselves and posterity." * * * It is a great pity at leastt in religious matters, that our children were not here included, but they were not. And the exclusion is no fault of ours, but is due to the mistakes of the fathers of this country and the prejudice which like a smoking flax their children will not quench. But we are in duty bound by virtue of what has been done for us, by the providence of God, to provide better things for our children, than our fathers were allowed to prepare for us. He who lives not in the future might as well not live at all.

4. IT IS NEEDED AS A BUSINESS ENTERPRISE.

The great apostle to the Gentiles, in writing to the Thessalonians (4:11), said: "Study to be quiet, and do your own business."

If there is any one thing in which the colored Baptists are behind their brethren of other denominations, it is in business enterprises of this kind, and the fact is a serious one when we consider how many Baptist young people there are who are looking to us to lift up a standard for the people, and while we have such numerical strength, and hence are able to foster one of the very kind of enterprises which the race and the denomination need, our scholarship is going largely unexercised and unremunerated, and the young people who are preparing for the higher art connected with such work are proceeding with but little hope. Are these young people who are preparing themselves for the printing press, the counting house, and other places of usefulness, to be told that there will be no demand for them so long as our books, tracts, and periodicals can be published in the great establishments already in operation? And shall we not be able to rise above the humiliating position of telling them that these great societies cannot afford to give you such employment as will be commensurate with your learning, nor can they give you that recognition which our large patronage justly deserves, for such action would be an insult to many of our white brethren? We should venture, if we fail. But we cannot fail. Success will follow our earnest and righteous effort; our history will be written to our pride and God's glory; the genius of our men shall be recorded, their names shall live forevermore. We will not perish by our own posterity, but our children in all time to come will view with gratitude and pride the record of their father's deeds. The demand for a Negro Baptist Publishing House is imperative.

The report of the Committee on Publishing House was read by its Chairman, Rev. J. H. Frank:

Washington, D. C.

To the American National Baptist Convention:

DEAR BRETHREN--Your Committee on Publication House submits the following report with recommendations for your approval. At the last meeting of the Convention, the following preamble and resolutions were adopted:

WHEREAS, Inasmuch as there is great necessity for the organization of the long contemplated Publication Society and Book Concern; and inasmuch as it is an unquestionable fact that we have both the intellectual and financial ability to successfully operate such an establishment, *if we will do so;* and inasmuch as it is plainly evident that as a denomination we shall never attain to the broad influence and elevated dignity worthy of so vast a body of Baptists, so long as our literary productions remain unpublished, our work unsystematized, and its success remains dependent upon the option of our friends for prosecution. And further, inasmuch as there are now extant hundreds of literary and theological productions from the pens of colored Baptists, eminently worthy of publication and issuance, and which should be published for the good of the people, but because our friends care not to publish them, they remain unpublished, hence are lost to the denomination and the world. Therefore be it

Resolved, By the A. N. B. C. in annual session assembled, that a special committee, one from each State and Territory here represented, to be selected by the respective delegations and appointed by the president, with five from the country at large, be and are hereby authorized to effect plans for and proceed to the organization of the A. N. B. C. Publication Company and Book Establishment, to be operated under the direction of this Convention; and that said company shall have full power to secure buildings, machinery, and all necessary apparatus, or to make ample arrangements otherwise for the publication of Baptist and other literature.

The following is the committee: Rev. C. L. Purce, Ala.; Rev. John H. Frank, Ky.; Rev. G. W. Lee, Washington, D. C.; Rev. G. B. Howard, W. Va.; Rev. E. C. Morris, Ark.; Rev. M. W. Gilbert, Fla.; Rev. E. J. Fisher, Ga.; Rev. H. C. Green, La.; Rev. H. W. Bowen, Miss.; Rev. C. Johnson, N. C.; Rev. H. E. Clemmens, Tenn.; Rev. J. L. Dart, S. C.; Rev. P. F. Morris, Va.; Rev. W. M. Alexander, Md.; H. Watts, Texas; Revs. A. N. McEwen, C. H. Parrish, W. B. Johnson, A. Binga, E. K. Love, at large.

For reasons considered good, but little has been done during the year.

The resolutions were not approved unanimously. Quite a number of our most able brethren voted in the negative, and hundreds of prominent Baptists of America did not vote at all, because they were absent. We want and need the support of these strong forces, and must not rush off without them. Doubtless the brethren who voted their disapproval are honest, and their convictions must be respected. Time, we think, will place them with us.

A concern of such magnitude cannot be developed in a year--no, not in five years, perhaps. Much of the enthusiasm that appears when new measures are agreed upon is enthusiasm only, and that not of the genuine kind, and often the importance of a proposition *can not be realized in a day.* Hence, we thought it wise to allow the matter to "lie in state," if so to speak, for these months, that all distorting media might be removed and the stupendous affair might loom up before us in its true character. Then all would realize the responsibility it involves.

Before business begins we should know what support can be relied upon. The majority of our schools and churches now patronize the American Baptist Publication Society, and some of them deal with the Southern Baptist Convention. We must ascertain what proportion of the denomination will purchase Sunday school periodicals and other publications of their own brethren.

It is much easier to pass resolutions than it is to maintain a publication house, and we, when we do begin, must begin an institution that will live a hundred years.

The time is riper for our establishment than ever before, the reason therefor the Rev. E. C. Morris, D. D., will give, hence, with that feature our report does not deal. Suffice it to say that no careful observer can fail to see that contemporary races do not accord us our rights.

With scarcely an effort to receive subscriptions, certainly no appeals have been sent out, we can report as the result of one letter, a copy of which was sent to each, about fifteen brethren have given their names for one hundred dollars each, and we believe that a thousand such can be found in America. After prayerful consideration of this stupendous affair, we conclude that it is of God and will succeed, if not in our day, in that of our children.

RECOMMENDATIONS.

- 1. That the preamble and resolutions adopted at the last annual session in Savannah, Ga., looking toward the establishment of a publication society and book concern, be reaffirmed.
- 2. That there be constituted a Board of Management, to be composed of life members and life directors, into which the general officers and the directors from the States represented in the Convention shall have full power and authority to operate.
- 3. That the payment of twenty-five (25) dollars shall constitute any regular Baptist a life member of the Convention; the payment of one hundred (100) dollars shall constitute one such person a life director, and any State contributing one hundred (100) dollars shall be entitled to a director, to be elected by the Convention, at its annual session.
- 4. That any Baptist church or Baptist organization contributing annually to the publication work of the Convention shall be entitled to representation in its annual meetings.
- 5. That the constitution of the Convention be so revised by the committee on publication as to conform with the foregoing rule, and that it report to the Convention next Monday.
- 6. Further, that the present Committee be continued to perfect the plans, and be authorized to appoint such members of the Convention to assist them as they may desire in filling such vacancies as may occur.

J. H. FRANK, *Chairman.*

Rev. E. C. Morris, D.D., of Arkansas, then addressed the Convention upon "The reasons for establishing a Publishing House."

The report of the committee was then adopted after an animated discussion.

On motion of Rev. J. H. Frank, the address of Rev. E. C. Morris, D.D., on "Reasons for Baptist Publishing House," was indorsed and ordered for publication for general distribution.

ADDRESS.

[Delivered before the Baptist Foreign Mission Convention at Atlanta, Ga., September, 1895.]

Brethren of the Convention, Ladies and Gentlemen:

By the aid of a kind Providence we have been brought together in another annual session for the purpose of devising plans and means for the furtherance of the Gospel of God's dear Son in heathen lands. And in commencing this address, I wish to assure you that I fully appreciate the distinguished honor which this service does me and I share fully in the hope which has been echoed by the Negro Baptist press of the country, that this meeting will be an improvement upon all preceding ones.

I fear no criticism when I say that you represent the intelligence and loyalty of the greatest religious society among Negro Christians in the world--greatest, because it represents one-half of the Negro population in the United States, and greatest because of the work it seeks to do and is doing in the land of our ancestors.

We are now passing the fifteenth milestone in the history of this organization, and are now undergoing the most severe criticisms which have come upon us since our birth; but I do not wish to be understood as objecting to any criticisms which may be brought against the management of our affairs, but, to the reverse, I invite it. For our blessed Master hath said: "By their works ye shall know them." But I wish further to assure you that we have made a history which, when compared with the history of like societies among other people, is not one to be ashamed of.

It may appear to you to be somewhat out of place for me to reach beyond the present administration, to gather matter for this report, but to me it seems that the exigencies of our work demands that the public should know what we have been doing, if we are to have any claim upon their charitable offerings in the future. The unbiased and charitable minds will grant that for a people who were themselves just seventeen years from bondage, to attempt to enter Africa, that long-neglected land, and plant there the banner of the cross among her millions of superstitious and idolatrous worshippers, was a great undertaking. But God's time is always opportune. Hence when he put it upon the hearts of the Baptists in Virginia to send out Rev. W. W. Colley to sound the trumpet and call together the great Baptist family in this country, with a view of organizing them into a Convention to send the gospel into heathen lands, the Holy Spirit went with him as was manifested when the roll of states was called in that historic old city, Montgomery, Ala., in 1880. For it was there ascertained that the missionary chord in every Southern state had been touched, and that our leaders were in full sympathy with the movement.

In the organization of the Convention it pleased the brethren to place in the lead that grand old man, a prince in Israel, W. H. McAlpine, who wore the robes of his office with credit and honor. It was not expected that we would accomplish a great deal neither the first nor the second year, but beyond our expectations, much was done. Our dear Brother Cosby, who was there, was reënforced by the Convention's sending out Brother and Sister Presley and Brother McKenney, and later Brothers Coles, Topp and Diggs. Brother Colley also returned and entered the field. I would not attempt to portray in words the sacrifices which these good brethren made in order to impress you with the work which has been accomplished through this organization, but it is nevertheless due them to say that they left all to follow Jesus. And while we are here to-day enjoying the blessings of life, the bodies of some of them are buried beneath the burning sands of Africa. One returned home to die; and still others have lost their health and wrecked a stalwart frame in their efforts to obey the Divine injunction, "Go." "Greater love hath no man than this, that a man lay down his life for his friends." The unsettled and hasty minds are not prepared for the reverses that are sure to come in such a work. There was a time in the life of Job before his affliction that his name was the synonym of wealth and honor. God tried him by taking from him all that he had. Yet Job did not despair, but said: "Though he slay me, yet will I trust him." But remember well, that after his affliction, he was restored to double the amount of his former possessions and his latter state was happier than his former. We have had some like experiences in this work. Reverses have come and the clouds have lowered. A war that broke out among the Vey tribe, among which we were laboring, and utterly destroyed all that we had there, and like the servants of Job, Brother and Sister Coles were only left to tell us. But, thank God, of the seed that had been planted there, some fell in good ground, and by the aid of the Holy Spirit and the courage and zeal of Brother Hayes, we still hold the field in Liberia and will not surrender it until every enemy of the Cross has been conquered; yea, until this gospel of the kingdom shall have been preached "in all the world for a witness."

That we have made mistakes we do not deny, for the work of foreign missions was entirely new to us; much of our first efforts were experiments and some of the plans adopted have not been entirely satisfactory to the Board. But in a great society like this, plans and methods cannot be changed in a day without serious effect upon the work. But I wish to say to you that if errors have been committed by the management of your affairs, it was because of the intense desire of the leaders to push forward the work of missions in heathen lands. Over confidence in you has caused the Board, no doubt, to be a little hasty in some matters, believing that you would be as zealous at your homes as you seem to be at the meetings. But I am glad to say that we have always been able to afford relief to our missionaries before any real suffering came upon them.

The Board has been diligent and faithful in all matters pertaining to the work of this Convention. They have spent much time and means in trying to gather information that would more fully prepare them to understand the condition of our fields in Africa. Books and pamphlets have been published by Brothers Coles, Colley, and Topp, setting before the world the vast resources of that great Continent and the anxiety of the people to hear the Gospel of Jesus Christ. And in addition to these, the Board sent Rev. Dr. Vassar to Africa that he might make a personal examination of the field and surroundings. His report is a matter of record, and needs no comment from me. Brethren, I feel called upon to mention these things because it is thought by many that our work has not progressed as reported. But permit me to remind you of one significant fact. Unless our great and powerful churches throughout the Union give to this work their hearty support, we cannot succeed as we desire; nor should their leaders complain because of the little that is done.

There are times that try men's souls, and the year which has just passed over us is one of them. Our whole nation has stood almost paralyzed for two years past over the financial agitation which has overshadowed all other questions before the American people. The panic which we brought on by this agitation has been felt in every avenue of life; hence the Church did not escape, and it has been very difficult to get money for any purpose. But we have not failed to use voice and pen in behalf of this cause and I am glad to say that our efforts have not been entirely vain.

Rev. R. A. Jackson and his devoted wife, who are in charge of our work in Cape Town, South Africa, have put new inspiration in the work by the cheering reports which they send from that faraway land. They have been there a little over a year and have built up a converted membership which numbered forty-five on the 24th of July, last. Brother Jackson is the only Negro Baptist preacher in all South Africa and the church which he established is the only Negro Baptist church known to South Africans. Surely his going to that land was directed by the Holy Spirit. His way there has by no means been smooth and pleasant, for he has encountered many difficulties. At one time he was threatened with death if he attempted to obey his Master by burying his converts in baptism. But he writes that "none of these things moved me," that God had stood by him in his work, and that he is now being received and recognized by the powers that be as well as by Christians of other denominations. Time will not permit me to quote as extensively from his letter as I should like. But there are some things which the Negro Baptists of this country should know, for surely if there is any one thing that will stir the denomination to do more for the redemption of Africa, it is the fact that other nations are preying upon the poor ignorant African and that some of their missionaries are the willing allies to carry out their infamous designs.

"The native policy of the colony and imperial government is more destructive than slavery. The laws are made to demoralize, degrade, degenerate, expel, and annihilate the natives. England destroyed the aborigines, and that is the proud boast of her citizens to-day. One of her majesty's servants told me that it would be the result of England's work in South Africa. I quote from history the following: 'The tribe of Sandili decreased from 31,000 to 3,700; that of Mahala from 23,000 to 6,500. The entire population of British Kaffrasia decreased from 105,000 to 38,000.' There are said to be many methods for 'grinding the native low.' One is liquor poison. There is a kind of drink here that cannot be found anywhere else on earth called 'the young wine,' made expressly for the natives. All who drink it burst open like a roasted potato. It should be named Death. There is another drink prepared for the native called Dop, and it should be named Devil, for it is one of his means of destroying men's souls.

"A man told me the other day that he saw it published in the Cape Town paper that no private citizen would be permitted to wear a uniform, and expressed great joy at the same. As the old uniforms are sold in lots of thousands of pieces and at auction, I thought it a blessing to the poor natives who are only the purchasers of such clothing. But the man said it is a blessing from God that the sale of these uniforms to natives be stopped, and then, looking at me, he said: 'You do not see the point?' I confessed I did not, and he said, 'I will show you. The old clothes cannot be sold until condemned and when the inspection is over, they are disinfected.' But that is good, said I, for then those who wear them do not take any skin diseases. 'Ah!' said the black man, 'that is just where the trouble comes in. The disinfectant is a deadly poison, and whoever puts on those clothes is forever doomed. Their whole body breaks out in great incurable sores or boils, and thousands die.' This same man told me of a strong, healthy tribe that was destroyed by the government forcing the entire tribe to be vaccinated.

"The English are the most subtle of all the nations here. They send out missionaries among the people. These educated hypocrites have ever been the forerunners of the English army. And then, there is that vagabond of earth, the trader who is sent into adjoining tribes to plunder them and when he gets his plunder, he is usually run out by the natives and takes refuge among the so-called missionaries. This cunning fraud, who has the government at his back, from which he gets clergymen's instructions, goes to the chief for protection, and thereby gets permission to build a fort and castle for the reception of thousands of English soldiers who come as friends of the preacher's tribe. Then it is that a commissioner is appointed, and he in turn appoints magistrates. The missionary is invariably made commissioner over the very tribe to which he was sent to preach the gospel of peace. And he then, in the name of the government, declares war.

"There are some white missionaries who, when they leave home to go to Africa, are full of the Holy Ghost; but when they reach the Dark Continent (which is daily being made darker by so-called Christian people) they are told that they are not wanted here to teach these people, and unless the minister yields to them he is told that he had better go back to England or America. A minister of the Wesleyan Church came here, built a church, and could not open it because Negroes who had helped build it were admitted in it.

"If the Negroes in Africa are to be brought out of darkness into the light and liberty of the gospel, it must be done by Negroes. White missionaries, who wish to do right and practice what they preach to the black man, are told that they are not wanted here. I repeat that English freedom here is worse than slavery in other countries. If you, brethren of the National Convention, could hear the native

South African praying in his own tongue, that God may open your hearts to help them, I am sure you would do more for them."

Brother Jackson concludes his letter by saying: "I fully understand now what Bishop Turner and Hon. John P. Green meant when they said that the Englishman considers no one a Negro except the real black man. But this is England's dodge to divide us, and while I have breath I shall ever be proud of being a Negro. God knows my heart is for my race; I love the sight of the blackest face."

Much of Brother Jackson's letter is omitted, but enough has been quoted from it to show you that we have in him a missionary worthy of his steel, and that he is entitled to the hearty support of this Convention.

But, my brethren, there is another motive which should more forcibly drive us into a support of this great work. It is that Jesus has commanded it. He has said to us to go into all the world, and as we look out into the world we see millions of people who are perishing for the want of the gospel of peace; and in that great number we behold our own ancestors with uplifted hands and anxious hearts, saying, "Bring us the bread of life; come and help us;" and while we cannot and must not be selfish in heeding the Macedonian cry which comes from other parts of the world, it does seem to me that God intends to redeem Africa through the instrumentality of her own sable sons. And if this is his purpose, it is not in anywise at variance with his plans in dealing with his people in olden times. I digress a little here to say that the time to parade and boast of the good and great men among us and of our superior numbers is past, and the time now is when we must get down to business in every department of our Church work. We must show to the world that our powers are not limited to getting men into the Church, but that we know how to utilize these superior forces to the glory of God and the cause of humanity. We must not only cultivate the fields already open, but must open new fields at home and abroad, to give strength and encouragement to those already in operation. Every day new and unexplored fields are opening up before us, and the colleges and seminaries are turning out scores of educated young men and women who are ready to sacrifice all for Christ and the race. And it devolves upon the leaders in the denomination to open up the avenues and give means and moral support to these young men and women, that they may go forth sowing the precious seeds. Brethren, I may be criticised for appealing so strongly in behalf of my own race, but how can I do otherwise when I see that it (the race) is everywhere spoken against?

UNIFICATION OF THE NATIONAL BODIES.

This Society being the senior member of our national organizations, I deem it proper that I should say a few words upon the matter of unification which has been agitated by the leaders in the three great societies for the last year, and which has been given prominence in some of our papers. In advocating the union of these organizations I do not wish to be understood as underestimating the importance of either of the others, for while I have the honor to represent the Foreign Missionary Convention, I nevertheless feel an equal interest in each of the others. They are indeed equal in importance, for while this one seeks to give the gospel to the heathen, the others seek to educate and prepare men and women for the very work which this one is endeavoring to do. But the question first to be determined is: Will the unification of these organizations impair the usefulness of any one of them as they now exist? I think not, and am rather inclined to the belief that it will add to the strength and usefulness of all; because, first, the work which is now being imperfectly done by the Conventions, on account of the brief time alloted to each, can be well done by boards which will have charge of the work from the beginning to the end of the year, and these can make their reports annually to the Convention, each bearing the same or equal relation as the other to the Convention. The adoption of a plan which will give us one great National Convention, will be a step far in advance of anything yet accomplished by Baptists in this country.

In conclusion I would say that during the one year that I have had the honor to be styled the President of the Foreign Mission Convention, every opportunity has been used to create a greater interest in the work and to bring forward that old-time enthusiasm which was characteristic of our meetings a few years ago. With an abiding faith in the justice and righteousness of the cause we represent, and with great hope for the future, I am your obedient servant.

NEGRO BAPTISTS--RETROSPECTIVE AND PROSPECTIVE.

[Delivered in Boston, September 15, 1897.]

Brethren of the Convention, Ladies and Gentlemen:

Again, by the providence of an all-wise God, we have been brought together in another annual meeting of our Convention, at a most opportune time and place; a time when the race is being tried in the balance of public opinion, as to its progress as citizens, and as Christian followers of the meek and lowly Nazarene, and at the place which can boast above all others, that her citizens were the first to strike the blow which felled the monster, slavery, and broke the shackles from four and a half millions of bondmen. I cannot too strongly urge upon you the importance of this meeting, for the simple reason that it represents nearly five-eighths of the Afro-American Christians on this Continent, and is, therefore, the most representative body that has or may hereafter meet to devise plans for the extension of Christs's kingdom, and the uplifting of a race of people who are only thirty-four years from a cruel bondage.

I congratulate myself upon having the honor to address the representatives of such an organization. I assure you that it is a source of supreme pleasure to me to be here, and I want to thank you, one and all, for the uniform courtesy and loyal support you have given me during the three years I have had the honor to preside over your deliberations. There may have appeared on the surface, at times, differences of opinion as to the best methods of doing the work of the Convention; but how could it have been otherwise, with such an army of leaders as we have, all endeavoring to put forth the best plans for the advancement of the race and denomination? But no matter how much we have differed in the past, we come here a grand, united army, a million six hundred thousand strong of the G. A. R. (Grand Army of the Redeemer), with our colors flying, bearing the significant declaration, "One Lord, One Faith, and One Baptism." And having firmly planted this banner in the homes of a majority of our people in the South, we are now moving on the East. And permit me to say in this connection, that when these chosen men of God, carved in ebony, shall be permitted to publish the gospel of God's dear Son to every creature, and not forced to preach it to creatures of their own race, there will be a wonderful change of belief among the white Christians of this country.

But this narrow, selfish condition is by no means the fault of the colored ministry, nor are they in any respect responsible for the fact that the Christian Churches of to-day are silent upon the wrongs heaped upon the race daily, all over the land. But rest assured that God has a remedy for all the wrongs in his Church, and in his own time and way will apply it. But, my brethren, you will bear in mind that there are notable exceptions to what I refer to here as "religious proscription;" for it is a matter of fact that there are here in Boston and other great cities of our country, those who believe in and practice the doctrine delivered at Mars Hill by the eminent Apostle to the Gentiles, that "of one blood God created all nations of men." And it is due this city to say, that when every door in the land was closed to the advocacy of universal liberty, an effectual door was opened here and the great and much-revered William Lloyd Garrison, though encountering many dangers and hardships, was finally permitted to use pen and tongue in favor of the abolition of the slave trade and of slavery. It would not perhaps be too great a speculation for me to say that that noble life which passed to its reward eighteen years ago is not dead, but he having lived to see the complete triumph of the principles for which he contended, his spirit is now associated with such noble spirits as Wendell Phillips, Charles Sumner, and our own Frederick Douglass, who are looking upon these inspiring scenes as a result of their labors and bidding us God speed.

Only one generation has passed since those of us who walk in peace here were held as chattels, and the ground upon which we walk was once made crimson with the blood of those who, like Patrick Henry, thought death preferable to bondage.

Perhaps it was the hand of an all-wise Providence that ordered this meeting to this place, for it was here that the first blood for American independence was shed, and it was here that the old "Liberator," which set fire to the hearts of the loyal people of the nation to battle for the freedom of the slaves, was born. And most of you who come to this Convention are the direct beneficiaries of those contentions. You are the living testimony that the many lives sacrificed for our freedom, and the volumes of money spent for the elevation of the freedmen were not spent in vain. But I am reminded just here of a most touching statement made by a prominent gentleman representing one of the great Baptist societies of the North and East. After reviewing the relations of the two races in the South, and reminding his audience that nearly all the old abolitionists who had sacrificed, many of them, their fortunes and social pleasures, that they might enlist in the cause of freedom's cry, had been gathered home, he said: "Another king had come upon the throne which knew not Joseph." This statement for a long time lingered in my mind, and has produced the thought that if they had gone to their reward, the sons and daughters of these good and great men are here, and that the examples of the fathers are not yet erased from their memories. So we come to them, we come to the people of this nation, and say to-day: "Draw near unto us, and be not afraid; for we are (I am) the descendants of Joseph, your brother, whom ye sold. It was not you, but it was God who sent us hither."

We are representing what thirty-four years of freedom have done for a nation of people--showing to the world, what we as a wing of the great Christian army have accomplished, and our plans for future work. This Convention was organized and has been steadily at work as a separate and distinct body of Christians for seventeen years; made separate in a country for which we have done more, to the man, to build up than any other people in it, and by a people whom we have served for two hundred and fifty years. It is perhaps well for us, if not for the other race, that we have been compelled to have these separate organizations; for it is clear to my mind that had it been otherwise, the possibilities of the race, and especially that part represented by the colored Baptist, would not have been drawn out and made manifest as they have. There would not have been such a host of intelligent, self-reliant, practical leaders among us, nor would we have been able to show to the world our devotion to God's cause by pointing to the thousands of magnificent and costly church edifices and the scores of high schools and colleges built, supported, and managed by the Negro Baptists in this country.

My brethren, the forcing of these separate institutions was a blessing in disguise. Persons who have been helped and who have received alms at the beautiful gate, are too liable to remain there, if not bidden to rise up and walk. And it is by reason of the fact that we have been made to support institutions of our own that the powers of the race have been developed. The men among us who know best how to build and operate educational institutions, and to superintend missions and other Christian work, are the men who have done it.

PROGRESS AND WORK OF COLORED BAPTISTS.

The progress of colored Baptists has been phenomenal, so far as the increase in numbers is concerned. They have a majority over all the other colored denominations combined. Indeed I take it that much of the time used by others in seeking prominence in the world has been by Baptists devoted to winning souls to Christ, believing that "greatness in the sight of the Lord" is far better than worldly honor and distinction. Like their white brethren of the same faith, they have shown themselves the true friends of education, and have planted schools in every Southern State, and these are rapidly multiplying until in some States they have as many as a half dozen of these Christian schools. The value of their church property, which is rated at ten million dollars, is evidence conclusive that progress has been made in the line of church building. But the greatest and most difficult task is yet to be performed. The millions of our people who are yet to be developed morally, socially, and intellectually, present a problem to the thoughtful men and women of our race which is not easy of solution. And much more of the responsibility of this great task rests upon Baptists than upon any other denomination for the simple reason that most of the colored Christians are in our churches.

Then again, the colleges and seminaries are turning out thousands of educated men and women, who are fitted by education and training to perform any of the practical duties of life; but these find, when they have finished their school days and come out to enter the public arena, that every avenue is closed against them, and, if given employment at all, it is of the most menial kind. Such a condition not only discourages those who have spent years in preparing themselves for usefulness in life, but those who may have children whom they desire to educate, are caused to inquire: "What kind of employment can they get?" To my mind there is only one alternative, and that is for the Negroes to concentrate their means, both in secular and religious matters, and operate such enterprises as will give remunerative employment to the young men and women of the race. Such a concentration of means will open the avenues in other spheres.

Our progress in literature compares favorably with that of other denominations; but perhaps the greatest progress made in this line is by the Negro Baptist press. No class of men in the denomination is more deserving of special mention and of the endorsement and support of the Convention than the editors and proprietors of the thirty-two Negro Baptist papers. They have stood up fearlessly in defense of the race and denomination, and have, at the same time, without money and without price, earnestly contended for the faith once delivered to the saints.

SPECIAL OBJECTS.

One of the special objects of the Convention is to do mission work in foreign lands. This work was undertaken by colored Baptists in 1880, and has been earnestly and faithfully prosecuted ever since. It was, indeed, a great undertaking, especially in the face of the history our white brethren had made in this work. Many precious lives had been sacrificed, and many thousands of dollars had been spent by them in earnest efforts to give the Gospel to our ancestors in Africa, and yet such little results had followed. But with faith in God, and believing that he has reserved this field to be successfully entered by the colored Christians in this land (their emancipation and the removal of the fear of the African fever being almost simultaneous) the effort to give the Gospel to the heathen in Africa was made. For a while the success of our labors appeared to be great, but the Foreign Mission Board soon found that many discouragements awaited them, and for a while it looked as if all the powers of the adversary had combined against us, and that we would be compelled to abandon the work in Africa and commence operations elsewhere. But at the most critical period in this work it seemed that the finger of God pointed Rev. R. A. Jackson to go to Cape Town, South Africa, and there attempt an entrance into the Dark Continent. As soon as this fact was made known to our Board, it at once grasped the opportunity, and accepted the work as its own, and have vigorously prosecuted it from that day to the present.

You are all familiar with the perplexing conditions which confronted our Board at the time of Dr. Luke's death. But I am glad to say that nearly all those embarrassments have been removed, and through the earnest, faithful efforts of Rev. L. G. Jordan, our most efficient Corresponding Secretary, coupled with the wise and prudent management of our Foreign Mission Board, the work is in a most healthy condition. The number of missionaries has been increased from two to five during the year, and the work extended a thousand miles in the interior. A much greater interest has been created among our people in this country toward this work, and they appear to be in hearty sympathy with the Board.

The Foreign Mission Board is endeavoring to raise six thousand dollars with which to build a chapel at Cape Town, which is the principal station now held by us. The effort should meet with immediate success, for delay in the matter of building the chapel will greatly retard the work so auspiciously begun there.

It will hardly be denied that the work of giving the Gospel to the heathen in Africa lies nearer the heart of our people than any of the special objects of our Convention, and if the twelve thousand pastors can be induced to lay the matter before their churches, sufficient means will be at once given to put the work where it rightfully belongs.

I regret that I am not able to report any foreign work in any other country. Indeed, it looks a little selfish that Afro-American Christians should confine their missionary labors to Africa. But the Board hopes soon to be able to make a beginning elsewhere.

HOME MISSION BOARD.

The Home Mission Board, created by the consolidation of the three Conventions, has, by the direction of the Convention at its last session, devoted its efforts during the year to the publication of Sunday school literature.

The success of the venture has been most wonderful, and has by far surpassed the expectations of its most sanguine friends. As a matter of course, there was some opposition, and I think, in the most, it was from honest, pure motives, for the simple reason that there were already Baptist societies in this very class of work, and one of these, at least, had for thirty-five years been a direct benefactor of our people, and was at the time, and is now, supporting missionaries and colporters among our people; and in addition to this beneficient work, it is distributing Bibles, tracts, and other helps to the needy.

But when the people were brought face to face with the fact that people live in the deeds they do, and that their deeds were immortal and that to be something they must do something, and the only way by which they could leave their "footprints on the sands of time" was to put those prints there, all opposition faded like mists before the sun. I cannot refrain from saying in this connection that if there ever were an enterprise put on foot by the colored Baptists, which is deserving of and should have the indorsement of Baptist Christians, white and black, the world over, it is the publishing department of our Convention. It should be encouraged by the white Christians, because it will clearly demonstrate to them that the millions of dollars spent for the education of the Negro, and the social pleasure sacrificed, and the ostracism endured by those who came among us and lived the last thirty years, were not in vain; but as the rainbow reflects the colors of the sun, just so in the success of this enterprise they can see the fulfilment of that promise: "He that goeth forth and weepeth, bearing precious seeds, shall doubtless come again with rejoicing, bringing his sheaves with him."

But it should be encouraged and supported by every Negro in the land for a thousand reasons, for not since "the morning stars sang together, and all the sons of God shouted for joy," has there been such an opportunity presented to the sons of Ham--an opportunity to show to the world that they are endowed by their Creator with the same genius and capacity with which other men are endowed, and that God, in making choice of men to write expositions of his Word, is no respecter of persons, and that they leave as a heritage for their children the writing and doings of their fathers. To me the duty is imperative. We must either foster this enterprise of the denomination, else permit ourselves and the rest of our race who are in Baptist churches to be forever lost to future generations so far as our religious work is concerned. But without further discussing the matter of carrying on these publications, I wish to remind you that the predictions one year ago have been more than realized; and instead of the Board coming to this meeting with a debt to be cancelled, it is prepared to report more than 700,000 copies of periodicals handled since January 1, 1897; and that instead of issuing nothing but "backs" which cover the brain of white men, as charged, the Convention Teacher and Advanced Quarterly are the absolute products of Negro brain, and these will compare favorably with any of the kind issued by any society of this country; and that twenty-six Negro men and women have been employed in the preparation and handling of this work. These have been paid, and all other bills have been promptly met as they came due, and I think I can safely say that the Home Mission Board does not owe a dollar that it cannot pay at a moment's warning--and all out of receipts arising from the sales, and not from gifts or bequests.

EDUCATIONAL BOARD.

Up to the present time nothing has been done by the Educational Board, except to publish a magazine, and it was deemed expedient by the managers of that enterprise to form a joint stock association for the purpose of more successfully operating a plant that would assure the perpetuity of the magazine. It would, in my judgment, be a wise thing to consolidate the work of the Home Mission and Educational Boards, and let them begin to plan at once for what I believe is inevitable--*i. e.,* that colored Baptists enter into coöperation with, and assume a part of, all the educational work carried on by the societies of the North and East among colored people in the South.

Experience in the matter of educational institutions dictates that a change of policy is necessary, and already the American Baptist Home Mission Society has adopted this change of policy in some sections of the country.

I need not remind you that the terrible race proscription throughout the whole country has caused most of the colored people to look upon all white men with suspicion, and it is sometimes difficult for one of the representatives of the great and beneficent societies of the North to get a respectful hearing among our people. And I do not attach any blame to these people for this suspicion, for they are continually reminded that they are Negroes, and as such, are unfit for the company of white men. They are shown that they must have separate churches, separate schools, separate church societies, separate cars, separate hotels, separate barber shops, separate burying grounds, and if God could be influenced by such tomfoolery there would be a separate heaven prepared. And this sentiment is not local, but national; for while the Negro in the South is deprived of the civil privileges he is entitled to under the Constitution, in the North he is deprived of admission into the trades where he might get such remunerative employment as will in the future give him financial standing in the country. These things ought not to be; hence, in order to open the way for the truly good and philanthropic people who, above everything else, desire to help uplift the race and establish universal brotherhood, a coöperative plan should be agreed upon that would place a part of the burden, officially and otherwise, upon the colored people themselves.

SIMMON'S MEMORIAL FUND.

It was agreed by this Convention to create a fund not to exceed five thousand dollars, the interest of which was to be devoted to the education of the children of Dr. William J. Simmons, the first President of this Convention. So far the effort has been futile as far as the permanent fund is concerned. And I would advise a reconsideration of that proposition, and that a yearly pension be given Mrs. Simmons, the same as that given Mrs. Lucy A. Coles. These widows should not be neglected, for their husbands laid down their lives in the cause we represent.

On the 27th of last month the sad news of the death of Rev. M. Vann, of Chattanooga, Tenn., ex-President of this Convention, was borne over the wires, and it came like a clap of thunder from the clear sky. Having been with him the previous week, and talked to him of this meeting and of the future plans of our respective Boards, made the matter doubly serious to me. But his was to go from labor to reward, while ours is to toil on until we shall finish our course. He was truly a good and great man, whose influence for good in this Convention was unbounded. In his death we sustain an irreparable loss. But his exit from the militant army makes a notable accession to the army triumphant. In conclusion, permit me to say that I cannot too strongly urge upon you the necessity of wise and prudent deliberation. We must go down from this place after having convinced the people of this nation, and the people of the world, of our ability to faithfully and honestly discharge the duties incumbent upon our Boards, and to honestly account as stewards of God's Church for all the means intrusted to our care. And let me remind you also that there is no compromising grounds between Baptists and other Christian societies, but that the fight for a baptized New Testament Church is to be kept up until every Christian is brought under one polity, and there is one Shepherd and one fold. If there is any credit to be attached to the doctrine of a millenium period, those who believe in it may rest assured of one thing, and that is, it will never come so long as the professed followers of the Lord Jesus Christ are divided as they are.

IF CHRIST SHOULD COME TO BOSTON.

This city has long borne the reputation of being one of the greatest religious centers in the world. Her citizens are honored and revered for their broad, humanitarian views and their loyal support of Christian institutions. But if Christ should come to Boston and did not stop at the grand old Methodist Church, that fact would create such a stir among the friends of Wesley that an indignation meeting would be held upon the Common in Boston to denounce him. And should he not go among our Episcopal brethren of the Church of England, the elders of that faith would doubtless meet, pass resolutions, and fill every daily paper with the statement: "An impostor in the city; beware!" While our brethren of the Presbyterian faith would try to prove by the oracles of old that he is not the predestined Son of God, or else he would have come to them; and if not with the Catholics, they would repudiate him, because he failed to bring St. Peter along. And if he failed to come to this meeting and declare the Baptists to be the only people who have kept sacred the commandments and ordinances of the Church from the time he went away until now, we could be ready to unite with all the congregational societies, and send up a cry that would rend the heavens: "Crucify him!"

The thing most needed in the world to-day is a Congress of the religions of the world, with a view of getting at a oneness of the following of Jesus Christ. This can be done, and it should be done, and if not done, the banner of the Christian Church will not be successfully carried among the heathen world.

PRESIDENT'S ANNUAL ADDRESS.

[Delivered at Kansas City, Mo., September, 1898.]

Brethren of the Convention, Ladies and Gentlemen:

It is by the grace of God that we are again permitted to meet in another annual Convention. Our purpose in gathering here as the representatives of a great Church organization are manifold, and are of vital interest to the struggling race of people as well as to our own denomination. We are here to review the past with the hope of a better planning for effectual work in the future. Words are inadequate to express the very high appreciation which I have for the privilege of addressing the most prominent representatives of my people, persons upon whose shoulders rests, in a great degree, the weal or woe of ten millions of Negroes.

In the outset I want to thank you sincerely for the repeated honors which you have thrust upon me in choosing me for your President. I have endeavored to serve honestly and faithfully the trust reposed in me, and have at no time been unmindful of the fact that no greater honor lies within the gift of a people than the leadership of their denominational interests. This organization represents the largest and most invincible army of Negro Christians in the world, as well as a sisterhood of churches which has done more toward lifting up the masses of an emancipated race than any other denomination among our people.

Our presence in this great Western city is to serve notice upon the world that we are yet in the field, eighteen hundred thousand strong, to renew the conflict and press the battle for right principle and an uncompromising Gospel into all the world for a witness unto all people.

The difficulties of the past year have been many, and the obstacles very great. The clouds have at times been so very thick that nearly every great leader was hidden from view; but when those clouds would break away and the smoke of battle would rise from the field, we could look out and see them, as Jackson, "standing like a stone wall." The most serious difficulties which we have encountered the past year have been from within. In a great organization like ours, we have "many men of many minds," and in a denomination which grants to every man the right to think, act, and interpret for himself, since he does not transcend the authority of the Bible, it is expected that some disagreements will arise; but we count such as light afflictions and console ourselves with the thought that "they will endure for only a season."

A very grave misunderstanding--and, I may add, misrepresentation--grew out of our meetings held in Boston one year ago. I do not charge that any one with willful intent has tried to disrupt our National Convention, but it is known to every man who attended that meeting that it has been held before the world in a false light by some of our brethren who ought to have known better. I am charitable enough, however, to say that the brethren doubtless were honest in the publications made and believed they were right.

The people of our country have been told that the Boston meeting was a "mob," that "the right of free speech was suppressed," and that "visiting white brethren were treated with the utmost discourtesy." These statements have had some effect upon the work, but have not prevented its success, for

"Truth, crushed to earth, shall rise again."

The truth of the matter is that the greatest, grandest, most enjoyable, and most orderly meeting ever held by our National Convention was the one held at Boston. The people of that grand city, without regard to race, color, or condition, united in helping to make the meeting a complete success, opening to us the most historic hall and grandest churches, and turning out in large numbers and mingling freely with the members of the Convention; and they were a unit in their praise of the meeting. As to there being the slightest discourtesy toward any class of our visitors, it can be said that such a statement is entirely without foundation. So far as the charge that the color line was drawn is concerned, I would say that it, too, is without the semblance of truth. The fact is generally known that the National Baptist Convention is an organization composed of messengers from regular Baptist churches, associations, conventions, etc.; and while our constitution does not mention the fact, it is understood that all these are organizations among the Negro Baptists. Our white brethren recognize it thus, and, therefore, none of their churches or conventions send any messengers to our meetings. However, I venture to say, that should they do so, such messengers would be received on perfect equality with our own. At most of our meetings we have had fraternal messengers from the great societies among our white brethren, and it is useless for me to say that in every case they have been cordially received and given a most hearty welcome; and I hope the day will never come when we will not have the fraternal visits of these brethren. Moreover, I wish to assure you that there is no desire on the part of the management of the Convention to widen the breach or to encourage further separation between the "white" and "colored" Christians in this country; but the management is not blind to the fact that the white and colored people in this country are as separate in nearly every profession and calling of life as if they lived in different worlds. We verily believe that the time will come when there will be no separate Christian institutions, and would gladly welcome such a day; but as the day has not yet come, and the "strong," who should bear the infirmities of the "weak," are not yet ready to obliterate those lines, the thing for us to do is to go forward, do something, get something, so that when the day shall come around to unite the Baptist forces of America in one great society we will have something to offer as a separate and distinct race of people.

Another thing which has, perhaps, somewhat hindered our progress, is the fact that our country has been engaged in war with another nation. While some of the wisest and greatest men of our country deprecate war, and did all in their power to prevent it, nevertheless there was no way out of having an armed conflict with Spain and maintain our honor as a Christian nation. When our Chief Magistrate had done all in his power to prevent active hostility, and at the same time bring about a peaceable settlement of the inhuman, uncivilized, Cuban war; and when he saw that his own and other Christian charities that were being extended to the starving women and children, whose husbands and fathers were fighting for freedom, had been challenged and resisted by Spanish arms, his great heart, which met with quick vibration from seventy million other hearts, rose up and said that Spanish barbarity and misrule must cease. You know the result up to this time.

But the war is not yet ended, notwithstanding the fact that peace negotiations are now pending and actual hostilities have ceased. Through the mists that rise over the battlefield and in the ragged ranks of the poor and oppressed slaves of Spanish tyranny, the Church of God sees an opportunity to plant the banner of the Cross in places made more accessible by the triumphant victory of the American flag. Wherever the flag of our country has been borne in triumph the principles of religious liberty have also been carried.

THE AMERICAN FLAG A SYMBOL.

That grand old flag is a significant symbol to every patriotic American. Its colors and peculiar arrangement are object lessons, and inspire love for home and native land. To me it is an emblem of resplendent beauty. Not only do the stars represent the sisterhood of the States, but they recall the beautiful sentiment spoken by Job when he says, "Canst thou bind the sweet influences of Pleiades, or loose the bands of Orion?" while the beautiful colors recall the bow of promise which God has placed in the clouds, and inspire confidence that the principles which our flag represent shall be extended to every nation.

Our race in this country, for many years held as slaves, and not now enjoying the full and complete protection of that flag, challenges the whole country to find a class of people more loyal. Wherever and whenever it has been placed in the hands of the ebony-hued sons of America its folds have not been allowed to trail in the dust. The American Negro can look through the "region of terror" to which he has been subjected and from which he now suffers, and see the ultimate triumph of those principles which lie at the very foundation of our government--that "all men are created free and equal," etc. He believed that the success of this flag in the Revolutionary War would bring a better day, and followed it then; he followed it under Jackson without the hope of reward, and he saved it from dishonor in the Civil War; he also bravely led the charge under those colors at Santiago, and will ever remain loyal to it until this is in deed and in truth

"The land of the free and the home of the brave."

MOB VIOLENCE.

One of the most serious menaces of our country to-day is the unbridled spirit of mob violence, which, I am sorry to say, seems to be on the increase. There seems to be an unholy alliance between some of the officers of the law and the mob to overturn the very foundation on which our government rests. This condition of affairs cannot long exist without seriously affecting the whole country. The causes which have in many instances led to the taking of human life without judge or jury are held up as an excuse for the mob's shameful work. While I insist that our ministers should speak out in no unmistakable terms against every class of crime, and especially the most heinous of all crimes--rape-- at the same time I insist that the men who gather for no other purpose than to empty their revolvers into the body of helpless criminals, are themselves guilty of a crime which shall cry out from the ground, and God will, if the people do not repent and turn away from this sin, overthrow the government; and I call to the Church to-day in the words of another, "To your knees! to your knees! O Church!" and let us move this blight from our land! Bear in mind that God has said: "Vengeance is mine."

OUR FOREIGN WORK.

The Foreign Mission Board has labored against great odds during the past year, greater odds than any which have confronted it in any year of its existence, and yet with perhaps greater success. It was thought that the apparent differences which existed between the Board and the ex-members of the Richmond Board had been satisfactorily settled when the chairman of the Louisville Board agreed at Boston to yield every point and accept whatever plan the brethren at Richmond might suggest; and it was not known that a portion of the brethren were bent on splitting the Convention until after the adjournment of the meeting. When the question of dividing the country into districts for more effectually doing foreign mission work was raised by the Virginia delegation at Boston, the attention of the Convention was called to the fact that such an order had been made one year previous, and the Secretary informed the Convention that the work of districting the country was then in progress. It was thought that this fact would give general satisfaction, and the Board was advised to proceed at once to form said districts. This the Board proceeded to do; but it developed that this was not satisfactory to some of the brethren, and that nothing short of an independent organization would be acceptable. Just what success the District Convention has had I am unable to say, but I am sure that no cause has ever existed in this body which would in any way justify the action of the brethren in an attempt to divide our forces in this great work.

THE WORK OF THE TWO BOARDS COMPARED.

From the organization of the Foreign Mission Convention, in 1880, to the consolidation of the three conventions, in 1895, the Foreign Mission Board was located at Richmond, Va. Since that time the Board has been located at Louisville, Ky. It has been my pleasure to be an ardent supporter of the foreign mission work under both of these Boards, and I have an unbiased knowledge of the work accomplished by both of them. For years the Board at Richmond labored through its missionaries to maintain mission stations on the West Coast of Africa among the Vey tribes. I need not tell you the sad story of how we were driven out of that country, and that Brother Coles, who was the last to preach there, and Sister Coles, barely escaped with their lives. I do not attach any blame to the Board at Richmond for the misfortunes which befell the work under its charge. They did the best they could, and all that they did has been destroyed; and when the Board at Louisville took charge of the work, they had but little more than the name with which to commence. Brother Jackson, who had gone out to Africa of his own account, was subsequently taken up; and an effort was made through him to establish a mission station at Cape Town, South Africa. The present Board has been on the field for only three years, and has fourteen missionaries actively engaged. While it has had some reverses, it is too magnanimous to charge any Christians in this country with it.

That you may know of some of the things with which Baptists have to contend, I give you here an exact quotation from a letter received from Brother John Tule, who went to Africa since the adjournment of our meeting at Boston:

"I reached here in May last, and from that time I have preached, and have baptized twenty-one precious souls, and went to the Petty Chief for a mission site. After his consent, we went to work and made three thousand bricks with our own hands; and, in spite of that, the Wesleyan (Methodist) missionaries went to the chief and offered him money to drive us out of his locality, and there and then came he and his tribe, armed, and broke all our bricks; and we went to the magistrate of that district, who demanded the contract of our Board as their authorized agent, but were unable to produce one, and then and there were warned not to preach in that district."

The fact that these missionaries were forced to leave the country has caused some of our brethren to accuse the Board of not giving them the proper support. "Consistency, thou art a jewel!"

The Foreign Mission Board has not been as aggressive as I think it might have been; but when I consider the unwarranted attacks made by our own brethren and the effort of some to lead the people away from the Convention, I wonder how it has done so well.

HOME MISSION BOARD.

This is the Board whose work has caused so much comment and which has caused many of our good brethren to criticise severely the action of the National Baptist Convention in authorizing the Board to begin the publication of Sunday school periodicals; but the wisdom of that act will be seen in the success which has crowned the efforts of the Home Mission Board in this special line of work. It is needless now that I say a single word in defense of this great undertaking on the part of the Negro Baptists, but it is necessary that something be said concerning the charges which have been brought against the project and against its friends. It has been said that those of us who have fostered this enterprise and have contended that it was a necessity in order to show to the world that we are worthy of the sacrifices made for our race, and also for the purpose of training ourselves in the management of great concerns, are ungrateful creatures, and are drawing the color line by endeavoring to have a business of our own and then attending to it. The charge is a grave one, and should be given more than a passing notice; for if it be true that we have suffered more on account of that thing called the "color line" than any other people in the country, and if it be true that in less than forty years we have forgotten the wonderful sacrifices of men and means for the elevation of our race, which had been driven to the lowest depths of degradation by slavery, then such miserable wretches as we are unfit for the association of good people; but I wish to say that the charge is without foundation, and we challenge the whole country to find a set of men who have done more to obliterate the "color line" in our religious societies or who have shown by their acts more of the true spirit of gratitude than those who are the friends to the enterprise. Before this enterprise had a beginning those who are now fostering it endeavored in every honorable way to secure a proper recognition of our leading men in the publication house which had for thirty years been our benefactor and was at the time receiving ninety per cent of our patronage. No undue haste was taken in the matter, but for years the question was discussed in our meetings and brought to the attention of the Board of the Publication Society; and when "patience ceased to be a virtue," we then set about laying a foundation for ourselves.

I sincerely believe, my brethren, that God, who is now carrying the race through a period of transition without a parallel in its history, has permitted this to come upon us for our own good. There can be no comparison between our Publication Board's work and that of other societies in like work. It required many years for some of these to even reach the place to publish a paper to accompany a few tracts which they issued; others began with borrowed capital; but we commenced with nothing but faith in God and the justice of our cause.

I am glad to say to you that, notwithstanding we were accused of issuing "backs which covered white men's brains," in less than two years from the date of our first issue we are turning out more than 200,000 periodicals each quarter, and that the entire work, from the janitor in the printing office to the editor at his desk, is done by our own people, and that the machinery on which the work is done and the building in which it is done are the property of this Convention; and I may add that this Board has in its employ thirty men and women of our race, all of whom are paid regularly from the Secretary's office once every quarter. The Board's report will show the financial standing of the Publication Department, and I need not enlarge upon that; but shall I not ask you to share with us the joy we have in the fact that we can no longer be regarded as mere consumers in the literary world, but that we may be justly termed producers, and that five thousand of the best Negro Sunday schools in this land buy that literature from the counter made by this Convention and from the hands of the very men you appointed to stand behind it?

"Praise God from whom all blessings flow;
Praise him, all creatures here below."

EDUCATIONAL WORK.

You will recall the fact that I recommended the consolidation of the Home Mission Board and the Educational Board in my report at Boston one year ago. Since no action was taken upon the recommendation, I will say that, aside from the publication of the magazine, nothing has been done. Dr. Johnson has endeavored to get his Board together to plan for assisting in the educational work of the denomination, but to no avail. There is a broader and greater opportunity before this Board than before either of the other Boards. However, I am still of the opinion that the work of the two Boards should be consolidated. The magazine has been allowed to fall upon the hands of a few, and yet it has been a success--not as great a success as it deserves, for it must be made to represent in the highest degree the best thought and best literary talent in the denomination; and this can be done by the Convention's giving to it the support it deserves.

COÖPERATION.

Much has been said during the year on the matter of cooperation between the white and colored Baptists along educational lines in the South. I have been free, as an individual, to express myself in favor of coöperation; but I am for that cooperation which indeed coöperates. The work of the National Baptist Convention has been held up as an obstacle to the cooperation of the Baptist societies in the work of missions and education among the Negroes in the South. Neither the Convention nor its officers, at any time, in any way, desired or attempted to discourage the plan, nor has the Board nor the Convention ever been asked to consider or in any way advise in the matter; and until the other Baptist societies recognize that there is in existence such a thing as a National Baptist Convention, no official notice will be taken of the coöperative plan. Personally, I would welcome the day when a plan could be entered into that would not only obliterate the color line, but at the same time wipe out all sectional lines; but the burden of this great undertaking will fall first and heaviest upon the shoulders of our white brethren, who must open the way for co-operation in all the branches of work carried on by the Baptists in this country.

A PLEA FOR UNITY.

Many well-disposed, devout, Christian brethren, who desire no doubt to see the very best things done for the race and the denomination, have deemed it expedient, in order to secure the aid and coöperation of our stronger brethren, to play neutral upon the work of this Convention and some have said we should surrender all and let other societies do the work we are endeavoring to do. Such an action would be without precedent, and, if followed, would destroy every atom of manhood there is in the members of our churches. Brethren, what we need, and what we must have if we are ever to command the respect of our white brother, is *unity*. "Behold, how good and how pleasant it is for brethren to dwell together in unity!" is as applicable to-day as it was in the days of the Psalmist. We have 1,600,000 people who are as loyal to their Churches as any that ever lived; and if we can succeed in getting the 14,000 Baptist ministers united in the great work before us, no power on earth can prevent our carrying to success every object of this Convention. If you will indulge the speculation, I will say that I believe that an all-wise Providence has the matter in hand, and that he is effectually using the other race to drive ours together; for those who yesterday were the most bitter opponents of Negro enterprises--Negro Conventions, Negro Churches, Negro Associations, Negro papers, Negro magazines, Negro song books etc.--are to-day loudest in their claim for such organizations. I need not give the reasons, for every daily paper in the land furnishes the reason why we should be united; but let us hope that the day will come, and that by our unanimity of action we will help to bring it on, when there will be "neither Jew nor Greek."

As I come to consider the discussion in our own ranks, I am constrained to say, in the words of Hosea: "My people are destroyed for lack of knowledge: because thou hast rejected knowledge, I will also reject thee, that thou shalt be no priest to me: seeing thou hast forgotten the law of thy God, I will also forget thy children." My brethren will you hear me for my people's sake, for the generations that are to follow us? Is there no way by which we can prevent the systematic methods used to keep our people divided and to make them war against each other in everything, from a small grocery store to the greatest religious society among us? Wherever and whenever an honest effort is made to do anything for the race, persons can be found who, like Catiline, sit in counsel with us, and on going out immediately seek to overthrow every plan laid. When I look at these things, I am in full sympathy with Paul when he says: "I have great heaviness and continual sorrow in my heart. For I could wish that myself were accursed from Christ for my brethren, my kinsmen according to the flesh."

> "Help us to build each other up,
> Our little stock improve;
> Increase our faith, confirm our hope,
> And perfect us in love."

Do not think me pessimistic. I have faith in God and in the ultimate unity and triumph of our Churches in this work, for I think I can see through the dim vista of time, as we go forward and grasp the problems of life and keep pace in the steady march of civilization, one Grand Army of Christian Believers; and I can hear the tramp of an unnumbered throng, like the voice of many waters, and, listening still, I can hear the voice of that multitude as they raise the old battle cry of "One Lord, one faith, and one baptism;" and in that grand procession, as they march against the powers of darkness, I can see the Galilean Jew sitting in the chariot with the Ethiopian eunuch, and their song is: "The kingdoms of this world are become the kingdoms of our Lord, and of his Christ; and he shall reign forever and ever."

Sermons, Addresses and Reminiscences and Important Correspondence

ADDRESS TO COLORED BAPTISTS.

Helena, Ark., February, 1898.

Dear Brethren: As President of the National Baptist Convention, I have for some time felt it a duty to speak to you upon those matters which have been discussed so liberally by the colored Baptist press for the last four months, and which are of vital interest to us as an organized body of Christian workers.

In sending forth this address, I am not unmindful of the fact that as President of your Convention, all of my official acts are subject to open criticism, nor do I wish to be understood as objecting to any criticism that may be made against me as a public servant. But I had rather a thousand times be severely censured by the press of our Church than have the denomination suffer a single loss. And it is this fact which impels me to speak to you through this medium.

Since the adjournment of the meeting held in Boston (and which would have gone down in history as the greatest ever held by colored Christians had it been permitted to stand in its true light before the world, and which has made that impression upon all who are not biased or prejudiced) many things have been said which openly reflected upon the officers of the Convention. If the charges made are true, the present officers of the Convention are unfit for membership in a Christian organization, to say nothing of their official connection. And as this matter appears so very grave to me, you will readily see why I take so much time and pains in laying these things before you.

The National Baptist Convention (if we include the Foreign Mission Convention) was organized eighteen years ago. The primary object was to give the gospel of Jesus Christ to the heathen in Africa and elsewhere, as Providence might direct. The organization of the Foreign Mission Convention, and the subsequent organization of the American National Baptist Convention, developed the fact that the colored Baptists were capable of doing far more work, both home and foreign, than they were doing; hence came the agitation to "enlarge the place of thy tent," which resulted in the creation of the Home Mission Board.

As strange as it may seem, it is nevertheless true that no opposition has ever developed against the colored Baptists doing work on foreign fields, and not until the Convention undertook to do work on the home field has there been any discontent anywhere. We have had the honor to be a member of the Convention from its organization to the present, and for fourteen of the eighteen years of its existence we had the honor to be a follower under the leadership of some of the best men in the denomination, and it is a happy reflection that in all those years we were satisfied to have the leaders lead, and are the better prepared to follow now, that we have had four years' experience of leadership. But coming to the thing which called forth this address, we would say that the charge has gone to the world that "no persons were recognized in the Boston meetings, except those who were favorable to certain movements," meaning the publication of Sunday school literature by the Home Mission Board. If the above charge is true, the President of the Convention is a very bad man, unless it be that none were present who opposed "the certain movements." But we are glad to say that the President does not feel hurt at such an unwarranted charge, and is willing to bear the stigma for Jesus' sake and the good of the denomination.

But what is the truth about the whole matter? When the time came to arrange a programme for the Boston meeting, a call was issued for a meeting of the Board at Nashville in June, 1897. In response to said call seven members of the Board met, four of whom were persons known to be opposed to the publication of Sunday school literature by the Home Mission Board of the National Baptist Convention, and two of the four were then and are now in the employment of the A. B. P. S. But neither of these expressed any opposition on that occasion, for, as sensible men, they knew that they had a plain duty to perform, and went forward and did it. Every person suggested by either of the four gentlemen referred to for a place on the programme was accepted without challenge. When the programme had been completed, it was left with the Secretary (who is also a missionary under the A. B. P. S.) to print and bring to the meeting at Boston, and when presented there it was adopted without opposition. It may be seen from this that the programme was regular, and that it was not a "cut and dried affair," as charged. But there is a matter of very grave import which the critics have omitted to mention--*i. e.,* after the adjournment of the St. Louis meeting, several of the persons who were opposed to the publication of Sunday school literature by the Home Mission Board, prophesied that that Board would come to the Boston meeting with a great debt to be canceled by the Convention out of funds sent up for foreign mission purposes. Some of these prophets were on the ground ready to oppose any such diversion of the people's money. Be it said to the credit of these prophets, they were very orderly and gave no trouble to the Convention until after the report of the Home Board had been read, which showed that the Board had handled over 700,000 periodicals, and had received in nine months $5,000 in cash, had given away three hundred dollars' worth of literature to needy schools, and had a net balance of $89 to the credit of the Convention. It was then that they began to cut themselves with lances, and to cry aloud. In the midst of this great disappointment, these same men looked around and saw in the Convention some of our most distinguished "white" brethren, and apparently it occurred to them that the whole thing should be turned over to the "white" brethren, for they had never witnessed such wonderful management by the black men before. But as the officers of the Convention did not do this, those disappointed brethren made the charge that visiting "white" brethren were not treated with due courtesy. It is the misfortune of some people not to know what courtesy is, and this may be true of the President; but he has learned from following up the anniversaries of other Baptist societies, that only those persons are given a place on the platform who have been invited to speak at those anniversaries.

But the circumstances which have surrounded our people for all the years of our freedom have been such as to make matters entirely different with us; hence instead of following the precedent set by other societies we suspended the rule and had as many as four of our "white" brethren speak to the Convention. And I wish to say just at this point that there is no complaint on the part of the officers of the Convention towards the "white" visiting brethren. Their presence in our meetings is always desired and appreciated. For we know that their work is largely among our people, and therefore they have the same rights and privileges in our meetings that others have, and would not choose to have it otherwise. We are glad to say also that the impression sought to be made on the minds of the people to the effect that strained relations exist between the officers of the National Baptist Convention and the "white" Baptists of the country is false *in toto*. All intelligent Baptists, North and South, approve of the "colored" Baptists doing whatever they can for themselves.

There is still another objection urged to the National Baptist Convention, and which in my judgment is the most unreasonable of all, that is, "the Convention is too large and unwieldy." It has been the battle cry of the denomination for many years to try and win the world over to the Baptist way of doing things, and to their faith in the teachings of Jesus Christ. And now that God has given success to our efforts, complaint is made that the Convention is too large. The remedy suggested is the organization of District Conventions. The constitution which regulates the membership of our Convention was prepared and adopted by many of the men who are now complaining. And these brethren know that it provides for life and annual membership. If the fee for these is too small, the remedy would be to amend the constitution. So long as the present constitution is in force, if ten thousand Baptists who are in regular standing with their respective churches choose to attend the Convention and otherwise meet the requirements, they must be received on perfect equality.

But the President is not of those who think the representation should be reduced. Indeed, he would rather see the number increased. Not for the purpose of raising money, for this should not be an object of our annual meetings. Money should be given to the respective Boards during the year in sufficient quantities to do the work of the denomination, and our annual meetings should be for the purpose of receiving the reports of these Boards and planning and adopting methods for future work. Then, again, these gatherings give fresh inspiration to the messengers, who, after coming in personal contact with each other and with the work, go to their homes filled with the zeal and spirit inspired by the success of their Boards.

As to the matter of districting the country for foreign mission purposes, the President and other officers of the Convention are in hearty accord. But, since the matter of forming these districts was referred to the Foreign Mission Board, and that Board set to work at its first meeting to carry out the instructions of the Convention, it does not seem proper that brethren from any section should assume to take the matter in hand to organize the district and profess, at the same time, that it is not their purpose to antagonize the National Baptist Convention. As a matter of course, as free men, they have the right to make as many organizations as they may choose. But it is not in harmony with common sense to say that the exercise of that right, in the face of the action of the Convention, is not antagonistic to the National Convention. If the authority of the National Baptist Convention is recognized as these brethren profess that it is, then there will be two agencies at work in the same field, for the territory embraced in the District Convention has been included in the plans adopted by the Foreign Mission Board. And if the brethren in the district recently organized refuse to receive and acknowledge the right of the Foreign Mission Board or its agent to work in its territory, then the profession of loyalty to the Convention falls to the ground. But if the brethren in the "first district" are sincere in a desire expressed to advance the cause of foreign missions, why not have the Secretary appointed by them report to the National Foreign Mission Board and save the people the expense of holding a District Convention?

I trust that I shall not give offense to any one when I say that I fear that the whole matter of complaint has grown out of a desire for prominence (office), and, in saying this, I do not include many persons who have honestly and faithfully contended for the organization of District Conventions. But it would not be just to the hundreds of thousands of Baptists who are giving no attention to the complainers, if I did not say a few words commendatory of their faithfulness.

We confess that the work of foreign missions has not progressed as was the desire of the leaders. When we were called from the ranks in 1894, to the presidency, we found but little to rally around; indeed, the work had gone down. But we knew the fault was not with the Board--then located at Richmond--but was due to two causes: the first and greatest being the fact that our mission station on the West Coast of Africa among the Vey tribe had been broken up by a war between the natives. Hence we devoted our efforts to rallying the people so as to get a representative gathering the following year at Atlanta, Ga. As to the success of the efforts we will leave others to tell. But we say, with some degree of modesty, that the work began from that meeting to take on some of the old-time energy that was characteristic of the Convention in its early years.

From the adjournment of the Convention in 1895 to the meeting at St. Louis the work was entirely under a new management, with headquarters at Louisville, Ky. The Board did fairly well during the year. But it was not until after the meeting at St. Louis that there seemed to be any discontent. You will bear in mind that it was at this meeting that the publication of the Sunday school literature was ordered by the Convention. The first objection urged was that it would retard the work of foreign missions, but when it was found that the Foreign Mission Board at Boston reported greater success than in any previous year, the "bottom dropped out of that theory." Hence it appears that there is a certain class among us who are trying to find fault with everybody and everything, and don't think that any progress should be made unless it be under the leadership of some of this class.

The President is pleased to say that notwithstanding the reports sent out to the contrary, the National Baptist Convention is in a healthy condition, and, from present indications, all of the Boards will more than double their work the present year; and that instead of there being any strained relations between our Convention and other Baptist societies, the best of feeling exists on our part. It is not the purpose of our society to antagonize the work of any other, but to do as we have been doing--prosecute to the extent of our ability the work committed to us by the Convention.

E. C. MORRIS, *President.*

PRESIDENT'S ANNUAL ADDRESS.

[Delivered before the National Baptist Convention at Nashville, Tenn., September, 1899.]

Brethren of the Convention, Ladies, and Gentlemen:

Again, by permission of a kind Providence, I have the honor of coming before you to deliver my annual address as President of your great Convention. I congratulate you upon the wonderful record and unparalleled progress made by the Baptists since the organization of this Convention. It came into existence at the right time and for the very purposes it has so ably served--viz., to save this wing of our great and invincible denomination from disgrace; to show that in the onward movement of the great army of God in the world Negro Baptists are a potent factor. Until thrown into separate organization, such as this, it was not known what part those of our race in Baptist churches were bearing in the mighty conquest against the kingdom of darkness and in the upbuilding of the Master's kingdom on earth.

The wisdom which dictated such an organization was, in my opinion, divine. Had it not been divine, the strong and well-organized forces which have conspired to overthrow every enterprise put on foot by this Convention would have succeeded. But I am glad to say that instead of being overthrown, the Convention and its enterprises are stronger to-day than at any time before, and it has, by its peerless record, drawn to it many who once stood in open rebellion against its objects. It has been my opinion for some time that the leaders in this Convention have been for many years misunderstood, and, therefore, misrepresented, and that when the real objects and policy of the leaders are fully known all opposition will cease, and we will have the encouragement and coöperation of all the great Baptist societies in the country.

I wish to repeat what I have said on several occasions: that this Society entertains no ill will toward any other Christian organization in the world. It seeks to be on friendly terms with all, and the charge that this organization means to draw the color line, and thereby create prejudice in "Negro" Christians against "white" Christians, is without foundation. We admit, however, that practically, and not constitutionally, the color line has been drawn by the establishment of churches and schools for the "colored people" and the employment of missionaries, colporters, etc., to the colored people, which has resulted in the organization of associations and conventions by the Negroes in more than half of the States in the Union. And since these organizations exist, it is the duty of all to do everything in their power to build up the cause of Christ in and through these agencies.

But if these separate organizations did not exist, there is a reason for the existence of a National Baptist Convention, because, owing to the agitation of the slavery question, the white Baptists of the North and South had divided into two societies, represented respectively by Northern Baptists and Southern Baptists and when the cause of the division had been removed, the Northern Baptists went immediately to work to educate and evangelize the emancipated. The Southern white people soon fell in line and began by a system of taxation to aid the emancipated in acquiring a common school education, and many of the Southern white ministers lent their aid in church work. But their organizations remained separate and are separate to-day. Hence, it was one of the prime objects of the promoters of this Convention to obliterate all sectional lines among Baptists and have one grand national society, which would know no North, no South, no East, no West; and in this we have been successful. From Maine to California we are one, notwithstanding the efforts of designing men to disrupt the Convention by making false publications concerning it. If you will pardon the particular reference, I will say that one of our number who for three years held official position in this Convention had published in a little paper out in North Carolina the startling statement that the "Convention has departed from the New Testament standard and has turned into an ecclesiastical body; and that it exists for political purposes, the President exercising his powers the year round, attempting to dictate the policy for one million seven hundred thousand Baptists." Others of our ranks have styled us ingrates--all because we

> "Dare to be a Daniel,
> Dare to stand alone!
> Dare to have a purpose firm!
> Dare to make it known!"

But against all we have marched steadily on, and disproved all that has been said, until we have enlisted the coöperation of the most thoughtful Negro Baptists throughout the civilized world. We have endeavored to avoid any entangling alliances with other Baptist organizations, but have prayed for and sought to maintain friendly relations with all. I cannot account for the apparent disposition of some of our Baptist societies to ignore utterly the existence of the

National Baptist Convention. Since the Negro Baptists in all the States of this great Union are in harmony with the work of this Convention and are contributors to its objects, there can be no good reason why any organization should attempt to form alliances with the respective States to do the very work which the Convention is endeavoring to do. In the matter of Cuban missions, notwithstanding the fact that this Convention has declared its purpose to do mission work in Cuba, other Baptist societies which had a similar purpose in view, consulted and even had correspondence with persons not officially connected with the National Convention upon the matter of coöperation. This breach of fraternal courtesy is not understood, except it be that others think that they can more easily handle our people by having them divided than by recognizing an organization with an official Board or Boards empowered by the constitution to act for the whole body. That the time will come when all the Baptist societies in America will recognize the existence of this Society, I have not the slightest doubt; but for reasons known only to themselves they have not done so yet.

A prominent minister of our denomination told me a few weeks ago at Greenville, Miss., that he had opposed the work of the National Baptist Convention because he did not think it possible to get the Negro Baptists of this country organized, and that their notions of church independence and church sovereignty were such as to preclude any such thing as a national organization. "But," says he, "I see you are about to get them together." I was a bit modest in giving a reply at that time, but I will assure you, my brethren, that the time is not far away when our organization will be so systematic that at the pressing of a button the Baptists from Maine to California and from the Canadian border to the Gulf of Mexico will spring to action as one man, and there will be a oneness of faith, a oneness of purpose in holding forth the truths of that Book which teaches that there is but one God.

I stated that the Convention had declared its purpose to do mission work in Cuba. And it did, at the meeting held in Kansas City one year ago, appoint a commission to visit the island with a view of ascertaining the moral, religious, and educational status of the Cuban people. An appeal was made to the churches to send up money to pay the expenses of the commissioners, and I am glad to say that many churches responded to the appeal and sent money to the Treasurer of our Convention. The commission, owing to the unsettled state of affairs, thought it would be a useless expenditure of money to go there at the time designated by the Convention; hence, the money sent is now in the treasury subject to the orders of the Convention. The principal points in Cuba had been entered through the agency of our Foreign Mission Board and other Baptist societies before the time had come for the committee to go out, so that we may say, Baptist missions are already under way in Cuba. Providence seems to have favored us in that Rev. Campbell and wife were secured by our Board, and that Dr. C. T. Walker and Rev. Richard Carroll were given chaplaincies in the army. Dr. Walker succeeded in gaining one hundred conversions while there, and you may surmise the rest. We are in duty bound to aid in carrying the Gospel to the Cuban people. Like the black troopers who went up El Caney and saved the lives of their white comrades from destruction, so must the Negro Baptists of this country join their white brethren in carrying the Gospel of the Son of God to that people.

THE PHILIPPINE AFFAIR.

Before the Cuban question had been settled and Spain had been forced to take her barbarous hand off those people, a war broke out in the Philippine Islands, and our country is one of the principals in that conflict. The United States, having given Spain $20,000,000 for the Spanish possessions in the Archipelago, attempted to secure those rights and was met by all the force the Filipinos could command. While the scene of operation is a great way off, the situation is far more serious than is generally thought. More than 40,000 Americans are there exposed to the malarial conditions of the country and the determined spirit of a relentless foe.

The policy of our government in the prosecution of the Philippine war has been severely criticised, and even now, many are openly opposing the further prosecution of the war. Necessarily, Christians are opposed to armed conflicts and bloodshed. And we contend that all international questions can and should be settled by arbitration. The war which is now upon us has divided our country into two strong factions--viz., Expansionists and Anti-Expansionists, and the contention growing out of the points of this division makes the horizon dark with commotion, and calls to Christians everywhere to appeal to that God who holds the reins of governments, that he might intervene and establish peace among the nations.

LAW AND ORDER VERSUS A RACE PROBLEM.

In our domestic relations to this country, many of our people feel that they have a just cause to complain of the treatment they receive at the hands of the people among whom they live. And the man is indeed blind who cannot see that the race feeling in this country has grown continually for the last two decades. But since the organic law of the land stands unimpeached, there is room left to inquire, Is it only race hatred, or is it not the out-growth of a lawless spirit which has taken possession of many of the people in this country? Perhaps it appeared when this spirit of anarchy first took hold in this country that it was directed to a particular class or race of people. But that can no longer be said. For, indeed, it is evident that those who will forget themselves so far as to take the laws into their own hands and hang, shoot down, and burn helpless Negroes, will ere long turn and slaughter one another. Indeed, such is the case now. Mob violence is not confined to any particular section of our country. The same disregard for law and order which exists in the South when a Negro is involved, exists in the North when the miners or other laborers are involved. The people have become crazed and have lost their respect for the law and the administrators of the law, and unless there is a change no man will be secure in life or property. The apologies which are being given for the mob's shameful work, by no means remove the fact that there is a growing disregard for the laws of our country. I would counsel my people everywhere to be law-abiding, no matter how much they may suffer thereby. It does not stand to reason that the whole race is a set of cowards because the inhuman treatment administered to members of our race is not resented. But one thing is true: the men who will take the laws into their own hands and thereby prevent the piercing rays of the letter and spirit of the law from shining through the courts upon the crimes committed, are themselves a set of cowards. Ministers of the Gospel and good people everywhere should lift their voices against all classes of crime which is blackening the record of our country. The man who will not lift his voice in defense of the sacredness of the home and the chastity of the women in this country, is unworthy to be called a man. It is but right that the man who breaks over the sacred precincts of the home and perpetrates a dastardly deed--it is but right that he be made to pay the penalty of the inhuman act. But let all such be done by and through the law. The wisest and most prudent men of our country foresee the evils which threaten the perpetuity of our republican institutions if the present disregard for law and order be kept up. The agitations which are going on will soon bring a reaction. Reason will again be enthroned; the laws of the country, like the laws of God will be supreme; and from the least to the greatest, the people will "submit to every ordinance of man, for the Lord's sake." Those who are inclined to the opinion that there is a great "Race Problem" confronting us, are asked to look beyond racial lines for a moment and behold the civil strife in many of the States in the Union where the State militia, United States marshals and sheriffs with strong guard, are called upon to protect life and property, to stand and guarantee the moving of the wheels of commerce, while the cries of hungry women and children force husbands, fathers, and brothers to wage open conflict with the administrators of the law, and then they will modify their opinion as to a race problem and agree that a serious law and order problem confronts the people of this country.

LOCAL DISSENSION.

The work of the National Baptist Convention has been somewhat hindered by local dissensions, most notably in Georgia and Virginia. The National Convention officers have endeavored to steer clear of local disturbances which have divided our brethren in several of the states, notwithstanding the fact that in one State (Virginia), the contention was made that the National Convention was responsible for the opposition to the cooperative plan as carried on by the Home Mission Society. The charge was made without reason. No men regret more than the officers of this Convention that our people should divide into factions in their state and national work; nor have the officers of the Convention at any time interfered with the coöperative plans adopted in any of the states. We have frequently expressed ourselves in favor of coöperation in all lines of Christian work, and have not changed our opinion in the matter. But when I say this, I mean to be understood as favoring that the plans to be drawn and the conditions to be met and followed should be mutually agreed upon by all the parties concerned in the work; that the plans should be such as not to lift up one and humiliate the other; but to place all upon absolute equality in Christian work, making fitness the only essential in promotion of one above the other. But recent developments go to show that this country is not yet ready for the kind of coöperation I have in mind. I insist, however, that coöperation in any of the states which will force a division of the Baptists in their organizations of long standing, should be discontinued and the plans so changed as to meet the reunited body. The National Baptist Convention does not hope to gain anything by reason of these divisions, but pleads for unity in every state, even though, for the time being, the Convention should lose all its support in those states.

DISTRICT CONVENTION.

Much has been said concerning the utility of a District Convention. At first it was said that the organization was to antagonize the National Baptist Convention in Foreign Mission work. But the leaders of the movement insisted that they had no such purpose, and made the representation at the Kansas City meeting that they proposed to work in harmony with the National Baptist

Convention; but recent developments go to show that the leaders of the District Convention have endeavored to induce some of our missionaries to resign work under the Foreign Mission Board and accept work under the District Convention Board. If this be true, and the issues are thus drawn, without any words of abuse or ill-feeling toward the promoters of the District Convention, the National Baptist Convention will proceed to occupy the entire field in so far as our representatives are received by the churches. There can be no doubt of the people being in favor of one grand national society among the colored Baptists, and any effort or scheme to defeat that object will be repudiated.

FOREIGN MISSIONS.

The all-important question of the hour is that of Foreign Missions. The Foreign Mission Society is the oldest of our national organizations and has a greater claim upon our people than any other, for it indeed represents the spirit and mission of the Master, as well as his Church. No man can be true to Christ and refuse to support the cause of missions. And, yet, I am sorry to say, that many of our churches have turned a deaf ear to the urgent appeals of the Board for means to support our missionaries, and have really joined in with our enemies to deride the Board when it failed to pay the salaries promptly.

While there has not been as much adverse criticism during the present year as the past, there has been some. Our Baptist papers have been more considerate of the Board's responsibilities, and have not permitted so many things which are intended to impede the progress of the Foreign Mission work, to find circulation through them.

It has been difficult for the Board to keep in harmony with some of the workers in South Africa. The Board deemed it wise and expedient that Rev. R. A. Jackson be dropped from the list of missionaries, and I am informed that he was paid up in full. I am of the opinion that the Board should place a ticket at the disposal of Brother Jackson in case he desires to return to this country. Brother and Sister Tule have resigned, and I am told that their salaries were paid in full. This leaves only eleven workers on the field at this time. I am of the opinion that much of the dissatisfaction arose on account of the fact that our tireless and earnest Corresponding Secretary does not give enough personal attention to the duties of his office. No man can give satisfaction in that office who attempts to traverse the country from one end to the other. If the churches of this country are to be reached and stirred up to their duty in the work of Missions, it must be done by a system different from the one followed for the last five or six years. I have not the slightest doubt that the Foreign Mission Board has done the best it could, under the circumstances. But with a little more aggressiveness on the part of the officers of that Board, many of the circumstances which hinder the work very materially will be removed. A new impetus must be given to this department of our work. We can no longer hope to retain the confidence and respect of other peoples of the world, unless we do more for the redemption of the heathen, and especially those of our fatherland. If it should appear that we are a little selfish in our missionary operations, we can offer the just apology that the heathen of Africa are by far the most neglected of any on the globe--less money is being given for their evangelization than for any others. This Convention will not rise to the full dignity of a great missionary organization until it has at least fifty active workers on the field. This can and should be done. As the Foreign Mission Board will give a full report of its work for the year, I shall not say more on this theme just now, but will ask you to consider some recommendations respecting the work of the Board which I will mention later.

HOME MISSION BOARD.

The Home Mission Board was constitutionally established in September, 1895. But in 1896 it brought into existence one of the most notable heritages the Negro Baptist ever did, or ever will have, in that our Publishing House was then established. This enterprise was started with nothing save faith in God and the justice of the cause, backed by Negro brain and ambition. And to-day ten thousand dollars' worth of real property, sixteen thousand dollars' worth of printing material and machinery, an average monthly distribution of nearly two thousand dollars' worth of periodicals, sixty-eight ardent workers and writers of our own race, causing a pay-roll amounting to one hundred dollars per day, speak out in one tremendous voice and tell whether or not we have made progress. The sun has forever gone down on any race of people who will not encourage and employ their literary talent. How could the Negro Baptists ever hope to be or do anything while thy were committing literary suicide? From year to year scores of our young men and women were graduating from school without the slightest hope or encouragement, in a land where the color of their skin debars them from a liberal or equal chance with others. Were we to stand still and do nothing? No. Our Home Mission Board put forth an effort to remedy this condition to some extent, and it has been successful so far.

The Baptists have read a little history, and are endeavoring to profit by the mistakes and useful deeds of others. They find that the literary standing of the Greeks and Romans keeps them before the world as a vivid example of ancient progress, and they are quoted with pride the world over by many of the ripest scholars of the day. Furthermore, we will find by reflection that although the former were the slaves of the latter, by the excellent reputation of Grecian philosophers, teachers, etc., the Romans at the same time were only too glad to bow at the Grecians' feet to learn from them the secret of that higher power which intellect wields over mere brute force. The Greeks were able to give this knowledge, and never would have become slaves had they only watched carefully their true literary standing, and not gone off into skepticism, and the variegated porch of the poets would, no doubt, have still been in use had it not been that "cooks were in as great demand as philosophers." It has been well said that "no man who persists in thinking can be kept in bondage."

If we mean to improve, why should we not make an attempt at the preparation of our Sunday school literature as well as a few books and papers to which we can lay claim? In religion, the key to which comes from the Bible, we must not, as a great Christian society, be found wanting. Then, we must not agree for others to take all the advantage of studying and then writing the Bible lessons as presented to our Sunday schools. If the Negro had no chance to study and interpret the Holy Scriptures, he could only be expected to stand off and talk about what has been prepared by somebody else, and never be able to give authority for what he holds. If we are to preach and teach, we must have some personal, unbridled knowledge of our subjects, and the interest which is at the bottom of this knowledge is caused by the taking on of responsibility. If we have to go through the same test of others (and we do), why not have the same advantages?

The progressive Negro Baptists deliberated on all these things for four or five years, and have consequently given some of their business managers a chance to manage business, their bookkeepers opportunity to keep books, their printers and binders a chance to print and bind, their Bible students and writers impetus to study and write, and their thousands of anxious Sunday school students, both young and old, opportunity to get their lessons from books made by their own brothers in color.

Although the publication of Sunday school periodicals has proved to be an expedient work of Home Missions, this has not been the only work of our Home Board. It is doing no small amount of missionary work in supplying needy stations and in the support of missionary workers. In this latter work the Board hopes to enlarge its operations in the near future.

EDUCATIONAL BOARD.

The progress made by this Board has been very slow, but the plans which have been laid are well laid. It has continued the publication of the magazine under very stringent circumstances. Through the efforts of the Corresponding Secretary, arrangements have been made which will insure the regular and permanent issuance of the magazine from the Publishing House at Nashville. I regret very much that the Board has not yet undertaken the formation of a federation of the schools owned by our people, with a view to aiding them through means solicited by the Board. It is quite evident to me that these institutions cannot become the beneficiaries of philanthropic people until a proper channel is created through which their gifts may be conveyed.

OUR B. Y. P. U.

Too much cannot be said in commendation of the movement of our Baptist young people. We have a vast army in our churches who are yet to be developed into practical, useful Christians, and the effort to form a national organization should meet with the encouragement of all lovers of our grand old Church. Thousands of the best and most highly cultivated young men and women of the race are in our churches, and are capable of performing any and all the duties necessary to lead our young people to success. There is no reason why all the literature used by our B. Y. P. U.'s should not be produced by our own folks. For the first time in the history of our Convention one session will be devoted to the young people's work.

A LOOK AHEAD.

Thirty-six years have passed since the shackles of slavery were broken from the limbs of our people in this country. And these have been years of trial and conflict of which the Negro Baptists have borne no little part. In this brief period they have succeeded in building more schools and colleges than any other denomination of Negro Christians, and have enrolled as members of their churches more than all the rest combined. For this glorious heritage we sincerely thank God, and have a heart full of love for all who have aided in any way to bring about such a condition. But the fact that such a vast army has volunteered to follow the lead of those who contend for the principles enunciated at Olivet and for which the Apostles suffered and died; for which Bunyan, Hall, Roger Williams, Spurgeon, and an innumerable host of others battled to uphold, it is but meet that we pause to ask: What of the future? A very large number of the one million seven hundred thousand Negro Baptists are crude and undeveloped. They know but little of the practical side of Christianity. The work of developing these that they may become the safe guardians of the undying principles which have distinguished our Church in all ages of the Christian era, is no small task. But I assure you, my brethren, that we have the men and means to keep our organization abreast of the times. And we will keep it so if we will only be united and submit to proper leadership, I have no doubt that the census of 1900 will show nearly two million Negro Baptists in census of 1900 will show nearly two million Negro Baptists in this country. Can you as leaders trust that host to support the present and future enterprises as you trusted them in the past to build and support churches all over this land? The charge of mutiny seldom ever comes against a Baptist; and as they have been loyal and true to their local organizations, so will they be to this Convention and every enterprise put in motion by it.

We are nearing the close of the present century, the most remarkable in many respects of all the centuries since the dawn of creation. And, without reference to the wonderful achievements in steam, printing, and electricity, and many more unparalleled discoveries and inventions, I come to say that when the light from the eternal hills announced the birth of the nineteenth century, our race--our fathers and mothers--groaned in the grasp of slavery, and held the place of goods and chattels. But by the direction of an unerring providence, when a little past the meridian of the century, a decree was handed down that the "slaves are and henceforth shall be free." Hence, I conclude that one of the marvels of the century will be that although it opened and looked for sixty-three years on a race of slaves, it closes with that same race a happy, free people, having built more churches and school houses, in proportion to their numbers, than any people dwelling beneath the sun. While the flickering light and agonizing groans of the nineteenth century are being lost in the misty and retreating past, let us look ahead. A little less than sixteen months from now that tireless steed, Time, will come forth and announce the birth of the twentieth century. Already in the distance can be heard the thunder of his neck and the fury of his nostrils, and the inhabitants of the world are preparing to greet his coming. Many of the great Christian societies are planning to make the opening year the most important and aggressive in Christian missions since the beginning of the New Dispensation. Some are asking for a million dollars, some for half a million, and some for still less. And as I see these great societies line up as if on dress parade and call for more men and means to go more strongly against the power of darkness, I am forced to ask: What is the duty of the Negro Baptists? The answer comes back that as the nineteenth century opened upon us as slaves and closed upon us as freemen, so may the Gospel, borne on the tongues of the liberated, set at liberty during the twentieth century, the millions bound in heathen darkness.

In conclusion permit me to set forth the organization and progress of our Convention in words of broken rhyme:

>In eighteen hundred seventy-nine
>The Baptist hosts were thrown in line;
>Then, next year at Montgomery met,
>And for the future plans were set.

>The work of Foreign Missions first:
>In Colley's mind it had its birth;
>He told the truth, both far and near,
>That the heathen must the Gospel hear.

>Like angel voice from heav'n it came,
>And every Baptist said, "Amen!
>We'll come to every call that's made,
>And send the Gospel to their aid."

>The first to take the reins in hand
>Was noble-hearted McAlpin,
>With Foster next to guide the ship
>That made many a perilous trip.

>Virginia, State of great heroes,
>Led forth our force against our foes;
>While Jones, Williams, Vassar and Troy
>Named the men of our employ.

While planning here for greater work,
The Afric' fever 'gan to lurk
On Colley, Pressley, Cosby, Cole,
And Sister Pressley, weak but bold.

McKenney, too, was true and tried,
And, like the three last named, he died.
He held his post though weak and lone
While Topp and Diggs returned home.

A war broke out among the tribes;
It shook confidence on all sides.
The work ran down, until at last,
Our Simmons sounded trumpet blast.

Many have tried to make us fail;
Against them all we have prevailed,
And stand to-day the greatest band
Of any Church in this great land.

If I should call the roll by States
Of all the men whose names are great,
Before the last one had been reached,
My voice would fail me of my speech.

But here are some as true as steel:
Love, Carter, White, McNeal
And Fisher, too, a Georgia man,
With Brawley, Durham in the van.

There's Dr. Graham, Hayes and Fox,
Stood the storm of the equinox,

With Mitchell, Bolden in the van,
And Cyrus, a Convention man.

There are Drs. Gilbert, Raiford, Jones,
And none of whom are thought as drones;
McDaniels, Dart and Robinson
Shine in work like glowing sun.

We've men like Wilhite, Stokes and Booth
Who never fail to speak the truth;
McEwen, Barton, Eason, Grimes
Will keep their State up with the times.

Kentucky, in the foremost rank,
With Parrish, Smith, Stewart and Frank,
There's Gaddie, Kennedy and Ward,
Then, Jordan, Purce in full accord.

Now, Payne, who lives in mountain chains
Of West Virginia, spares no pains,
But always tries to do his part;
He has in him a loyal heart.

Columbia District: there you'll see
Johnson, Champ, Brooks and George Lee,
With Toliver, Miller and Taylor,
They've brought the District into favor.

Anderson, Carr and Davenport,
With more great men, they held the fort
Till Indiana fell in line
With Baptist progress of the time.

The Keystone State we don't despise;
We have there men who're strong and wise:
Howard, Taliaferro and John Trower,
Gordon and others--a mighty power.

Ohio's not too far away,
For Phillips, Christmas and Bailey,
And many more who're very sure
To introduce our literature.

DeBaptiste, Thomas--many more--
Are men who're solid to the core.
They're with us when we are going right.
But wrong oppose with all their might.

Then, Johnson, Waller, 'f Maryland,
With Alexander in the stand,
Are strong in council and debate
As men from any other State.

New England, on our eastern shore,
Led by Phillips and many more:
Like Dixon, Wisher, Benny Farris,
With Adams, Jeter 'nd Rev. Harris.

Coming South again we'll see
Clark and Boyd, of Tennessee;
Dennis, Haynes and J. M. Mason
Who met us at the Union Station.

And Cansler, who's a quiet man,
With Parks, who succeeded M. Vann;

And Hall, Jackson, Ross and Petty,
Who helped to make all things ready.

Let's farther go in sunny clime--
In Mississippi, where we find
Such men as Gayles, Topp and Ford,
With Hamilton, Bowen and Ward.

In Louisiana they've suffered much
From fever, and prevented such
As Jackson, Clanton, Hamilton
From doing as they would have done.

But never mind, they'll be on hand
With Bryan and Davidson, great men,
To see that our old flag shall go
All the way to th' Gulf of Mexico.

And crossing o'er to Texas line
We find a host who all the time
Contend for every inch of ground:
But treat them right and they'll be found,

In closed up ranks of those who think
That Negro Baptists ought to drink
From wells dug out by their own hand,
And make themselves 'mongst others grand.

There's Griggs and Isaac, two great men--
They've pulled the "Old Convention" train;
Abner, Collier, Campbell and Beckham
Have challenged them at every station.

Sermons, Addresses and Reminiscences and Important Correspondence

But when they gathered at their place,
To save the Baptists from disgrace,
They left their diff'rences at home
And entered in the work as one.

But Kansas men are not afraid
To catch Missourians hands and aid
In lifting up our enterprise,
Which gives employment to the wise.

These Western heroes whom I name,
Have worked for God and not for fame:
Bacote and Cohron, Coles and Grant,
And Countee, Wilson, Moore and Bank.

Way out on Pacific slope
Eugene Harris has stretched our rope;
California, too, is in our band,
With Brinkley, who's a Memphis man.

Arkansas, she has stood the test,
And gives her plans to all the rest:
"Be men, and help yourselves to rise,
But do not any friend despise."

The closing words of this long rhyme
Will be to you, who, for a time
Informed the world that we were quacks
And issued nothing else but "backs."

But since you've found that we were not
Engaged in putting up a plot,

Will you not tell both far and near
What you have seen and what you hear?

Then in three years from that great day
When at St. Louis we all did say:
"We'll start a plant; we can but fail
No matter how that some may rail--"

And now you see in this short time,
The faithful ones who fell in line
Have built up such an enterprise
That makes you look on with surprise.

At the conclusion of the address the following offered by Rev. W. B. Johnson, D. D., was unanimously adopted.

WHEREAS, We have heard with inexpressible delight, the able address of our beloved President, E. C. Morris, D. D.--an address, orthodox in bone, Christlike in spirit, and courageous as well as safe in policy;

Resolved: That we suspend the rule for the commiting of the address to a special committee and adopt the same as the sentiment of the Convention.

Resolved, further, That as a mark of our unwavering confidence in the character and the splendid administrative ability of our President, we do hereby elect him as President by acclamation for another term.

Rev. C. T. Walker, D. D., presented the President with a handsome gavel made of wood selected by him during his stay in Cuba.

PRESIDENT'S ANNUAL ADDRESS.

[Delivered before the National Baptist Convention at Richmond, Va., September, 1900.]

Brethren of the Convention, Ladies and Gentlemen:

In the name of Jesus our Redeemer, and by the guidance of his kind providence, we meet in this historic city in another annual session of our Convention, to hand in our reports as servants in the Master's vineyard and to gather inspiration and means to push forward his cause into all the world. I confess that I feel a special joy at meeting so many of you at this time and place-- in this grand old State which bears the honor of being the "Mother of Presidents," and which has the distinction of being one of the foremost in the Union in point of loyalty to Baptist principles. We are also reminded of our nearness to the place where the first of our race, so far as history gives account, were landed upon these shores two hundred and eighty years ago, not as men, but as goods and chattels. It is quite appropriate that we, the descendants of that few who were landed at Jamestown, should meet here as men, having been lifted up by our contact with other peoples of this nation, and look back upon the scenes of the past to behold "what wonders God hath wrought."

Permit me to congratulate you, in the first place, upon the extraordinary prosperity enjoyed by the people in every part of this great country, and especially the success which has been achieved by the heralds of the Cross who are enlisted under that banner of which you are the representatives. As a great church organization, we can share in the unprecedented prosperity that, like a tidal wave, has swept over our country, and the successful conquests which our nation has waged against error abroad, setting before us an open door which no man can shut. Notwithstanding our nation has been engaged in bloody conflicts with foreign foes, there has been no period in the history of our organization that has been more prosperous than that of the present year. We have maintained our record of making steady increase both in numbers and property throughout the country. Perhaps the most notable evidence of this is found among the colored Baptists of the North and East, where there has been considerable emigration from the South, and where there is a large number of honest, earnest, devoted, consecrated ministers endeavoring to bring the people of their respective fields to a proper acceptance of the Word of God; and we may say also, that our organizations are not sectional, but in the language of the poet,

"Jesus shall reign where'er the sun
Doth his successive journeys run."

This exalted sentiment impels the leaders of the National Baptist Convention. In our effort to carry forward the work of the Convention, we have endeavored to keep in friendly touch with all the Baptist societies in the world. We recognize that while we have separate organizations, our cause is one -- that we have one great aim in view, viz.: the giving of the Gospel of the Son of God to the world, without apology. In this we are glad to say that our relation has been fraternal and pleasant so far, and I think it is growing warmer each year. It is only when irresponsible bigots attempt to espouse the cause of the older societies that misunderstandings gain circulation and prominence. It is, indeed, unfortunate both for the societies and for us that these apparent differences gain circulation. Quite a lengthy article was given to the public in the *Biblical Recorder,* published at Raleigh, N. C., on August 1st, and given further circulation by the *Florida Evangelist,* under the caption, "Questionable Methods of Colored Baptists." The article was a severe arraignment of the Secretary of our Publishing Board. If the friends of the National Baptist Convention had not possessed a personal knowledge of the method and work of that department, they, perhaps, would have been influenced by it. We like criticism when it comes from friends having a veiw to correcting errors for the good of our race and denomination. But so far as this one is concerned, we are in a serious quandary as to whether the editor wrote it from a spirit prompted to benefit the colored Baptists, or whether he was influenced by some one who is an inveterate enemy of our publishing concern. We venture to say that, when the truth is known, some man of our own race, who ought to be rejoicing at its progress, will be found at the bottom of the whole affair. But be the matter as it may, I am glad to say that the reports of the respective Boards to the National Convention have met the hearty approval of the Convention, and convinced all the world not too biased to believe it, that the Negro Baptists are doing work now which gives opportunities and successes to the race which did not come to them when all their contributions went to, and all their work was being done by, the societies operated by the white brethren.

This has been a very busy year with the officers of the Convention. We have spared neither time nor money in a protracted effort to get every part of our denominational forces actively engaged in the support of our respective Boards in their great campaign against sin and error. We have put behind us the mutterings and contentions of those who would seek to stir up strife, and have endeavored to have harmony and unanimity in the work of the Convention. We have endeavored to exercise great patience and charity toward those who seemed to think a National Convention of Negro Baptists unnecessary, as we are sure that time and environment will be sufficient to convince them of the necessity of such an organization. To me, as the "heavens declare the glory of God," so do the signs of the times in church and in State point to the fact that for the Negro to ever be received and given the place of a man in religion, in politics, in business, etc., he must accumulate, he must own, control, or manage enterprises for the development of the race and the blessing of mankind. And this condition of affairs will not give offense to any except those who would prefer to be agents, rather than owners, of such concerns.

You will permit me here to repeat what I have said on former occasions: that the conditions in this country have forced the Negroes to be separate in their churches, associations, and conventions, from their white brethren, and these smaller organizations have, by reason of the same conditions, been forced to form this national society. And since we have this National Baptist Convention, it is imperative that it have a high and noble object; and as this object has been clearly defined, it is unnecessary that I should again attempt to bring it before you.

The man or men who can not see the wisdom displayed in effecting this organization is indeed blind. Before the organization of the National Baptist Convention at St. Louis, Mo., in 1886, our denominational strength as to men and means was a thing unknown. But in the few years we have maintained the principles of our society, there has sprung into activity a spirit to do mission work, educational work, publication work, and the like, which is without a parallel in the history of our race, and which at the same time has developed an army of practical business men as well as inspired others to become great and useful as writers, bookkeepers, typographers, managers, theologians, etc. Since these things are true -- and no one will doubt them -- we would not entertain, by any means, even a suggestion to cease this onward march.

We can not afford to sit idly by for fear of criticism and permit other organizations among Negroes in this country to show the possibilities of the race by undertaking to do something in a way separate from their white brethren, and not do something ourselves in that way. When we can point to the fact that a Board representing the Negro Baptists in this country is successfully operating and supporting mission stations and missionaries in far-off Africa, in Cuba, and in South America, and that our Home Mission Board is supporting missionaries far out in the West, and at the same time operating a publishing plant which is now doing a business of $50,000 a year, supplying fully nine thousand of our Sunday schools with a literature which is acceptable to the very best; and then that we have as a result of separate effort, supplemented by the aid of friends at the North, such institutions as Selma University, Selma, Ala.; State University, Louisville, Ky.; Natchez College, Natchez, Miss.; Guadalupe College, Seguin, Texas; Central City College, Macon, Ga.; Howe Institute, Memphis, Tenn.; Arkansas Baptist College, Little Rock, Ark.; Virginia Seminary, Lynchburg, Va.; and many others of equal importance to our people, we can say, "The Lord hath done great things for us; whereof we are glad." Already we lead all the other denominations among our people in the matter of progressive enterprise; only one thing remains to be done to place the Convention where it properly belongs before the world, and that is to establish and successfully maintain a great National University such as will command the support and respect of all peoples and races -- a University which will be to the Negro Baptists what Brown University is to the white Baptists of the North, the Southern Baptist Seminary is to Southern white Baptists, or Wilberforce is to the African Methodists.

A STEP IN THE RIGHT DIRECTION.

For the first time in the history of our Convention, a step has been taken by the Foreign Mission Board toward coöperation with one of our great Baptist societies of the North. You will recall the fact that when we met one year ago at Nashville, Tenn., great enthusiasm was created by the reception of a letter from Rev. C. S. Morris, who was at that time in South Africa. He had been sent out by an organization of white Baptists in the North in coöperation with our Foreign Mission Board, for the purpose of considering the advisability of establishing industrial missions in South Africa, and also, if possible, to settle the differences that existed between our Board and some of our missionaries in South Africa. On Brother Morris' return to this country, he at once set out to create a sentiment in favor of the mission work which he had planned to do before he left. I shall not speak of the work of that peerless ambassador, as he will come before you in person. But it was upon his suggestion that a conference was held in New York last April between the representatives of the Missionary Union and our Foreign Mission Board, which conference resulted in an agreement to coöperate in the support of Brother Morris while he traveled in this country with a view to creating a wider sentiment and a greater desire to help in foreign missions. This is the beginning of systematic coöperation between the Northern societies and our Convention, and I think it will prove to be a wise project. As to this agreement, the Foreign Mission Board will report in detail, but enough is in evidence to show that our Convention is not hostile to Christian coöperation with other societies.

RETROSPECT.

A brief review of the past as relates to our race and denomination would not be out of place at this time. To look back to the days when our people had just been delivered from a cruel bondage, clothed with ignorance and superstition, having crude, unpolished ideas of religion, no schools or churches, no leaders -- nothing but a helpless mass of humanity -- it is revolting in the extreme. In those days of misery and extreme necessity, among the many agencies which God sent to redeem and lift up these people, was the American Baptist Home Mission Society. I speak of it particularly because of the fact that in this city, the old Lumpkin Jail, which held so many of the slaves for sale, became the seat of the first school for the training of our people under the auspices of that magnificent society. From that feeble beginning has come to us the beautiful Union University, which is, doubtless, the pride of every loyal Baptist in the land. Notwithstanding that it has been but a few years since the emancipation of our race, the distance which we have traveled is very great. We could not have made the journey or the marvelous progress which we have made, had we not been given the aid of such friends as those who foster the work of the Home Mission Society. I can not refrain from referring in this connection to the much revered and greatly lamented Dr. Corey, who spent many years of his noble life in this city, as President of the Richmond Theological Seminary. He was a prince of good men, and perhaps looks from his spiritual abode to-day, with glorious satisfaction, upon this gathering, and into the faces of many whom he trained or gave their first lessons in theology; and his noble spirit, like that of John Brown, is still "marching on." The work of these grand and noble men is immortal, and if there were a disposition or effort on the part of any to destroy it, it would prove futile. But I can say without fear of successful contradiction that there is not the slightest enmity in the leaders of the National Baptist Convention against any of these good and great men or the work which they have done for the elevation of this race. But our method of showing our deep and abiding appreciation for what has been done for us has been misunderstood and misrepresented. The manly, cultivated, God-like ministers and laymen among us believe that the best method of showing their gratitude to those who have helped them is to do something to help themselves and others who are in need. We believe that every effort made for our people during the thirty-five years of the past by the friends of our race is an unanswerable argument that for every school, university, or other enterprise planted and supported by others for the benefit of the Negro Baptists, there should be one, as a supplement, planted and operated by ourselves. How else can we show our appreciation for the help we have received? Words alone will not do it. Deeds are immortal. As we look over the long list of the noble-hearted philanthropists, the hundreds of consecrated teachers and preachers who arose above social caste and associated themselves with our fathers in the days of their early trials in order that such a scene as I have before me be made possible, our hearts go out to them in loving remembrance, notwithstanding most of them have been gathered to their final reward. And so deep is my confidence in the Word of God, I am reminded to repeat the words of Paul, when he said, "Wherefore seeing we also are encompassed about with so great a cloud of witnesses, let us lay aside every weight, and the sin which doth so easily beset us, and let us run with patience the race that is set before us."

But allow me to say that the supplementary institutions planted by the colored Baptists do not seek to supplant those formed by our friends, but rather to augment and enlarge the opportunities of and for our race. It is as necessary that there be mission boards, publication boards, educational boards, colleges, seminaries, academies, etc., owned and operated by the Negroes, as it is for them to own the houses they live in or to have newspapers, dry goods stores, grocery stores, farms, factories, or any other enterprise necessary to develop the business side of the race. The National Baptist Convention, in this connection, stands for the complete development of the Negro as a man along all lines, beginning first with his religious life, and ending with the material, or business life. In these laudable objects we expect to have the sympathy and coöperation of all true men.

FOREIGN MISSION BOARDS.

The work of modern foreign missions is about a century old, while with us as a separate organization it is about twenty years old. And yet, the Son of God, who is an embodiment of missions, stood upon Olivet nearly nineteen hundred years ago and gave orders to his church to go into all the world and preach the Gospel to every creature, giving in connection therewith the blessed promise, "I am with you alway." If any one thing more than another should cause the church to repent, it is the neglect of foreign fields. It is my conviction that in proportion as the command to publish the Gospel to the heathen world has been obeyed, prosperity has been brought into our Christian homes.

We no longer need to apologize for the work being done through our Foreign Mission Board, for in the face of the many discouragements and unwarranted thrusts made at its methods and plans, it is doing a remarkable work for the Master in South Africa and elsewhere. It appears to be a providential thing that South Africa has been selected as the base of our missionary operations on the dark continent. Rev. R. A. Jackson, who, through the mediatorship of Rev. C. S. Morris, has resumed work under our Board, is proving to be an instrument of marvelous results in our African mission work. Even the natives look upon him as a God-sent man and believe him to be the one who is to lift them out of the pit of sin and ignorance. The Foreign Mission Board has been able this year to be more punctual in the payment of salaries than in previous years. This was very fortunate, owing to the fact that prices for food were very high on account of the British-Boer war. The officers of our Board have been faithful to the trust imposed upon them, and not only have sought the coöperation and support of all who believe in the work of missions, but have taken time to study it both as it relates to the heathen and to the people of this country. All the officers of the Board attended the great Ecumenical Conference of Foreign Missions, held in New York City from the 21st of April to the 2d of May, 1900, which meeting was an inspiration to them as well as to all who had the pleasure of attending it.

The Secretary of the Foreign Mission Board has not ceased at any time to call loud to the Baptists of this country to come up to the help of the Lord against the mighty. He has gone from city to city and from State to State, and has succeeded in creating an interest in foreign missions hitherto unknown to colored Baptists. I must urge, in this connection, that greater respect be given to the appeals sent out by our Foreign Mission Board, for it sometimes occurs that conditions arise on the field that require immediate relief, and as we have no invested funds, we must depend wholly upon the contributions sent up from our churches, associations, and conventions, to meet these conditions. The Board is endeavoring to raise before the close of the century, forty thousand dollars for its foreign work. This amount has been apportioned to the various States, according to the number of Baptists in them. We sincerely hope that the leaders in the various States will see to it that the amount allotted to be raised by their States, if not sent in already, will be forthcoming.

HOME MISSIONS AND PUBLICATIONS.

I confess that a special pride thrills me when I come to speak of our Home Mission Board, with its marvelous work of publication, partly because of the fact that it has undergone a greater degree of opposition and persecution than any of the Boards, and partly because of the material benefit it has been to the race. We do not conceal the fact that this Board has enjoyed a greater measure of prosperity than any of the rest, notwithstanding it has met with greater opposition. But since it has been so fully demonstrated that such an enterprise was a pressing necessity and the undertaking having proved a great success, we now venture to say that those who were its bitterest opponents will concede the wisdom of its beginning.

It was a hazardous undertaking, made, as it was, at the close of one of the most marvelous centuries since the dawn of creation, at a time when art, science, and literature were at their zenith and when the more advanced races were vying among themselves as to which could produce the best and most acceptable literature for the vast army of Christian readers. For a people only thirty years from slavery to undertake such a project was indeed perilous. As was expected, criticism came thick and fast, but our manager, a man who lays no claim to an education, was well prepared to receive all that came. And permit me to say that to his indomitable courage, coupled with his vast store of common sense, is due much of the success of that enterprise. He has lived to see the time already when many who were his severest critics are glad to acknowledge his superiority. The same may be said of the contributors to our periodicals, none of whom lay claim to perfection; nor do we claim for this Board that it produces a literature equal to the best, but we do claim it to be equal to any produced by our race and superior to that of any other race having only one generation of thirty years of advantages and opportunities in which to prepare for such work. Allow me to say, also, that as our increasing Baptist family sees more and more of this work and falls in to help it on, so will the work improve in literary taste and mechanical construction. When fourteen thousand Baptist Sunday schools, instead of nine thousand, as we now have, are honest, faithful patrons of our Publishing Board, we will be prepared to remove even the little objections which are now raised. In this connection, I wish to say to the Negro Baptists of the world and to those of this State in particular, that if you would occupy a place in the sacred history of to-day which is to be read by unborn generations, you will have to ally yourselves with these distinct and separate enterprises, fostered and managed by the race; otherwise, the passing of your life will be like the duration of a meteor or shooting star, while your fellows who have endeavored to leave a distinct heritage will be as fixed stars in the gaze of future generations. Every race must make and write its own history. The work of the Publishing Board stands for all there is in the Negro Baptist family so far as Christian literature is concerned, and we predict that before the close of the first decade of the twentieth century, all will be in line to encourage and support this marvelous undertaking.

In addition to the publication work, the Home Mission Board is supporting in part two missionaries in the extreme West, co-operating with State and district Boards in the employment of fourteen other missionaries and colporters, and aiding other feeble points with gifts of books and Bibles and other literature. I feel sure that the Board's report for the year just closed will show most gratifying results. We must do our part of the work on the Home field, and must not neglect to give the Bible to all who will accept it. To this end we are endeavoring to do a Bible work, which should be supported on Bible Day by the entire Negro Baptist family.

EDUCATIONAL BOARD.

The work allotted to this Board by the National Baptist Convention has been looked upon by many with a somewhat suspicious eye, owing to the fact that the educational work among the Negro Baptists has been largely looked after by the American Baptist Home Mission Society. But I want to say here and now that there need be no apprehension by any that it is the purpose of this Board to antagonize the work of the Home Mission Society. It is, however, the purpose of this Board to seek to strengthen or aid the schools owned and managed by Negroes themselves and to plan for the building and support of a National University by this Convention, and to encourage, if allowed to do so, the Home Mission schools. None among us are so ignorant as to think for a moment that the colored Baptists are able to support all the educational work necessary for the religious training of our people. During the past year this Board has been active in an effort to get the schools owned by the race to associate themselves for mutual protection and benefit. So far it has succeeded in getting quite a number of our best schools to enter into the confederation. These schools are to receive the moral support of the Convention and whatever financial aid it can give them. It is expected that in the next twelve months all the schools owned by the Negroes will join the federation, thereby bringing themselves in the same relation with the National Baptist Convention as they sustain to other societies, that they may receive such aid as the Convention may be able to give.

THE NATIONAL BAPTIST YOUNG PEOPLE'S UNION.

This new and heretofore untried department of our Convention work has been carried forward with a commendable degree of satisfaction and success. The work began with practically no money; but with faith in God and confidence in His people, the Secretary of this department has aroused interest in the work, and stirred the hosts of young Baptists to such activity as they never had during the progress of our great denomination. He has been loyal to every department of the Convention's work, advertising the same with a measure of success that was marvelous in the eyes of all who bore witness to his labors.

The work of organizing the young people has been pushed with unusual rapidity. Hundreds of local unions have been organized, many districts and States have been put in organic touch with the Board and made acquainted with its system of education and work. An effort has been made to make these societies helpful to the churches. The course of instruction outlined by the Board has been especially helpful in teaching the young people that the special work of their societies is to provide the essential drill ground for the unfolding of Christian doctrines, and to develop the young people of the churches in the responsibilities and activities of Christian life. Signs of the good work being done by this movement are seen and acknowledged by many of the leading pastors. The special effort of the Corresponding Secretary to raise an organizing fund of five thousand dollars is both timely and commendable. In view of the valuable assistance rendered pastors by this organization in the training and development of the latent and otherwise dormant forces under them, it is the imperative duty of every pastor to lend a strong helping hand in the effort to more thoroughly organize and systematize the work.

TRIBUTE TO THE LATE REV. E. K. LOVE, D. D.

In the midst of this address you will permit me to pause to say a word concerning one of our fallen heroes, one of the brightest stars in the ministerial galaxy. Rev. E. K. Love, D. D., of Georgia, who was an ardent supporter of our National Convention and its work, and who was preëminently the leader in his State and who also at one time occupied the chief seat in this Convention, passed from labor to reward on the 23d day of last April. The news of his death was like an earthquake shock to his friends throughout the country. Notwithstanding the fact that he was in ill health at the last meeting of our Convention, and was only able to come in at times and drop a word of advice and encouragement, it was not thought by many of his admirers that he would so soon be taken away. Men die, but principles never. His devotion to the principles of this organization was so strong that nothing but death could separate him from the work undertaken by it. But as his noble spirit looks down from the clouds, we would say to him that the cause which he so ably espoused and for which he laid down his life is still advancing. If I am correctly informed, he was standing at his post when the fatal arrow of death struck him down. "A veteran sleeping on his arms beneath the red cross shield." This Convention will doubtless adopt suitable resolutions and set apart a memorial page in the journal as a mark of the respect and esteem in which he was held.

WHAT OF THE FUTURE?

As a religious organization representing more than half of the Negro race in this country, and in view of the record the race has made in the last past thirty-five years, it is but appropriate to ask, What of the future? Before the question can escape from our lips, many discouragements rise up to face us and throw a shadow on the road ahead. But when we consider the past history of our country and the environments of the race, we may reasonably conclude that such things might be expected. Our race and people in America are, like the unwary waters of the mighty deep, impatient, irrepressible, and determined upon the amelioration of their condition. We do not condemn this spirit of anxiety in them, but we should bear in mind that only thirty-five years have passed since the march to a state of cultivated citizenship and high Christian motive was begun. We all deprecate the fact that conditions have arisen to darken the future of the black man in this country. We all regret that racial conflicts have taken place in any part of this glorious land, and that the spirit to disregard the laws of the country has grown in the last decade to marvelous proportions. But such disregard for the law does not represent the best element of our citizens or the true spirit of Americanism. Crime should and must be punished, and I would feel humiliated to hear any member of my race say one word in extenuation of the crimes alleged against persons who belong to the race, but I insist that the strong arm of the law is sufficient to mete out justice to all violators. But there is no doubt as to the fact that the utter disregard for law and order has produced a feeling of unrest all over the country, which has presented a serious problem to both the white and black races in the United States. This problem, however, is being considered in the counsel of both races by their wisest and best men, and it is my firm conviction that it will meet with satisfactory solution before another generation is passed. Many of our good and great men have suggested as a means to the solution of the problem rising out of the race conflicts such theories as African emigration, the industrial training of the Negro masses, colonization, etc. But it appears that none of the plans proposed meets the approval of a very large number of our people. The majority of the Negroes believe themselves to be American citizens by every right to which any can lay claim, and cherish the hope that pluck, energy, economy, and accumulation along material lines will eventually solve the problem. Racial prejudice can not be removed in a single generation, except in those cases where the religious nature dominates all others, and this, as you know, is a rare thing. What the black man can not understand is that for the first ten years after his emancipation, when he was least prepared for the enjoyment of his civil and political rights, he received these rights and the encouragement and apparent good will of all. But after having come in contact with the schoolhouse and the church, and begun to be more and more a man, there sprang up a unanimous action in the South to deprive him of those rights. There can not be the slightest doubt that many of the persons today who were born in slavery have improved every opportunity since their emancipation, to show themselves as men, and *nothing can come now to make them believe themselves less than men.* But having these things to face, is it not well to consider whether or not they are blessings in disguise? Do they not more and more tend to throw the race on its own responsibilities, and thereby establish the fact that it can be a race of resources? My brethren, these things mean to me that the Negroes are to be owners of farms, railroads, steamboats, factories, mills, banks, insurance concerns, dry goods stores, groceries; that we are to have grain dealers, cotton factors, and, in short, are to be actually associated with the business interests of the world. If we are permitted to judge the future by the past, so far as it relates to the race, it seems that nothing can be more hopeful than the future outlook of the Negro. When we take into account the outside agencies which God has at work in our behalf, coupled with the unprecedented efforts being put forth by the race and denomination, we will enter the twentieth century under conditions which to me are most encouraging. Our ministers and churches are far better prepared now than they have been at any time in the past to undertake great things for God. They are seeing the imperative demands being made upon them daily, for better citizenship, a better and more practical Christianity, than they have ever seen before. Better men, better prepared men, in every part of the country, are forging to the front in all our denominational work, and will not leave a stone unturned in convincing the world that while they have brought a majority of the Negro Christians into Baptist churches, they have the ability to utilize this mighty host to the glory of God and the uplift of fallen humanity.

In conclusion, permit me to thank you very sincerely for the hearty and loyal support which you have given to the objects of this Convention, under my administration. And as I go down from the exalted station as President of your great and grand organization, it is with the consciousness that I have striven to do my whole duty. I, perhaps, have not been able to please all the brethren all the time, but I have endeavored to be charitable to those who have differed from me, and am glad to say that my heart goes out in love for one and all with the earnest hope that the time will soon come when there can not be a single person of prominence found among us that can be used for the disintegration of our Baptist organizations. And finally, permit me to say, if there was ever a time when our race (or perhaps I would better say the people of the world) should draw near to God, and when we should draw near to each other, that time is now. We should bear with patience all the indignities heaped upon us, by those who have apparently lost all respect for the fundamental laws of our great country. And yet, we should contend with manly courage, in a Christian way, for every right enjoyed by any other people under the flag of our nation. But allow me to insist that our greatest hope for the future lies in the fact that "this gospel of the kingdom shall be preached in all the world for a witness unto all nations," for nothing short of the influence of that Gospel which was set in motion by the immaculate Prince of Glory, will bring on that time when there will be neither Jew nor Greek, bond nor free, but all will be one in Christ Jesus.

NINETEENTH ANNUAL ADDRESS OF E. C. MORRIS.

[Delivered before the Arkansas Baptist State Convention, Little Rock, Ark., November, 1900.]

Brethren, Co-laborers and Friends:

Again in life I have the distinguished honor of coming before you to present for your consideration my annual report as President of your Convention. For eighteen years, I have had the exalted privilege of occupying the same official relation in this grand body, that I occupy to-day. All of these years have been spent pleasantly, though crowded to overflowing with cares and responsibilities.

It is always a very pleasant thing to me to come to the annual meetings of our State Convention, for it is here that we meet those who have labored in different fields and hear them tell of their conflicts and of their victories achieved over the head of our adversary, Satan. Somehow or in some way, these meetings set before me the thought that at some period in the great future, God will call all his militant forces together for the final report and to dispense to each one the reward for faithful labors. I must congratulate you upon the wonderful achievements of the past which have been beyond our most sanguine expectations, and urge you to greater efforts in the future. You cannot be otherwise but proud of the peerless record you have made during the last twenty years, for you have risen from a small, inconsiderate State organization to be the greatest, grandest missionary and educational society of any single one of this great Union of States. It is also a source of pleasure to look back for the past eighteen years of our busy lives to the time when our scattered forces reunited in one Convention and have from that eventful time to the present marched steadily forward in unbroken phalanx defying evil-disposed men to tear us asunder. We have maintained in a very creditable way our missionary and educational work and have indeed by our unanimity of action forced our way to occupy the front rank in the great Negro Baptist family of the world. Nothing could be more gratifying to us than to be able to say that there is not the slightest token of dissension among us anywhere in our great State, and any effort on the part of any person or persons to create such divisions as have been characteristic of the Baptists of some other States, will prove futile. It seems as if an all-wise Providence has so united the Baptists of Arkansas from the Missouri line on the North to the Louisiana line on the South, from the Mississippi river on the East to the Lone Star State on the West, that no schemes or plans of finite beings can tear us asunder. It is true that we have not been able hitherto to get all of the latent forces in our State engaged in our work, but even these are not opposed to the progress which our organizations are making.

One of the most hopeful signs for the future of the Baptists is that the little jealousies that used to be entertained against the leaders on account of greed for office and notoriety have relegated themselves to the rear, and there is now a growing sentiment among our brethren everywhere to see who can do the most for the glory of God and the extension of his kingdom. This condition maintains not only in our state work but it is true also in our district conventions and associations. There is hardly a district in the State to-day which would retain a man as a moderator or leader who is not in hearty sympathy with all the work being done by the Baptists.

The marvelous period of prosperity which our country has enjoyed for the past years has been productive of great results in our work. Our associations, so far as I have been able to see, without a single exception, have made a marvelous increase in collections and the amount of other work accomplished by them, over any previous year. I feel sure that this session of our Convention will also close one of the most prosperous in the history of our organization. But in the wonderful successes which have attended our efforts, we should not overlook the fact that we have been aided by our white brethren both in and out of the state. The American Baptist Home Mission Society has been our constant friend in all the struggles of the past, and, so far, there is no indication that there will be any cessation of their beneficence according to our need. It is true that the aid which we have received from this society when compared with that given to other states is small. But it is in my judgment, far better for us that the gifts from the society were small, for while we were greatly aided by it (the Society) at the same time, we were made to understand that we had to assume the responsibility of carrying on our work ourselves. Therefore our usefulness has been made more practical and our own arms have been strengthened. As early as 1887, the Society came forward to help in our educational work, and has every year since then contributed something toward teacher's salaries, etc. We should not overlook the fact that it is by reason of the help we have received from these outside sources that we have been able to make the creditable showing which we can present today. Nor should we overlook the further fact that the white Baptists of our own State have been our true and tried friends in the great struggle we have made to build up our educational work. Not only have they given us financial aid, but they have given us the benefit of their strong moral influence. And this has been of incalculable benefit to us. These deeds of kindness on the part of our white brethren, North and South, will never be forgotten by the Negro Baptists of Arkansas. Speaking of the kindly acts of our white brethren brings to mind the fact that there has been considerable controversy concerning the matter of coöperation between the white and colored Baptists. And perhaps it is not out of place for us to make known our position in respect to that. We sincerely believe that Baptists of whatever race or nationality, are or should be a unit in Christian cooperation. But the differences of opinion which have found circulation, in my judgment, were caused by a failure on the part of the two wings of the denomination to understand each other as to the scope of the plans proposed for coöperation. It would be useless for me to say that coöperation means a work of co-partners, or workers together, in a given enterprise and pre-supposes a mutual respect of rights on the part of each for the other. Arkansas Baptists are for coöperation but are unalterably opposed to usurpation or absolutism in the affairs which should be mutually considered. There are no warmer hearts anywhere toward the Baptist societies among our white brethren than are found among the colored Baptists of Arkansas. But they are opposed to coöperation in name and not in reality. And it may also be said of them that where they feel themselves sufficiently strong to support any special feature of their work, without asking or receiving aid from others, it is their duty and inclination to do it and let the aid go to those who need it most urgently. They believe that this is not only right and proper, but it would be very wrong to receive aid to do a thing which they can do alone. It is perhaps possible that some friends could be found who would give enough money to buy all the grounds and put up all the buildings necessary for our college. But would it be the wisest thing for the Baptists of the State to accept such a gift if it were tendered them? Would not the acceptance of such a gift block the way to the development of the philanthropic spirit that is in us and which will be in our children, and thereby deprive the race of that practical experience to be gained by personal contact with such a work? In considering these great questions, we should never overlook the fact that we owe a duty to the more than sixty thousand Baptists in our State. These are to be developed and educated along all lines of Christian activity and there must be at hand a means for this development. Should our leaders step aside and permit others to conduct our missionary and educational work, it would at once remove the only opportunity, the only "open door" which we have set before us. It would be far better that we make no further advance in building and in getting ground for the next twenty years than to have paralyzed the opportunity of our churches to do educational and missionary work. The fact that we have used the opportunities given us has proved a wonderful lever in developing the activities and possibilities of our people, and in inspiring in them the unconquerable desire to carry the work begun in them to completion. When we compare the work of our

Convention for the past eighteen years with that of the first twelve years after its organization, we conclude that a special providence has guarded and directed our forces, and that he has made choice of the women and men who have been selected by our respective Boards to represent the cause both on the field and in the schoolroom. I am very glad to say that God has given to us men and women leaders in our work who have shown themselves willing to make any sacrifice necessary for the success of his cause. What is true of these men and women in our State organizations and institutions, is true also of those in our district organizations. In nearly every district in the State we have leaders and representatives in our associations and district schools who are men of honor and integrity and who are as loyal to our State work as if they had no district work on their hands.

Indeed, we may compliment ourselves on the almost perfect organic system which has been accomplished in the last eighteen years. There is scarcely a community in our great State that is not in touch with our State and national work. Our State Sunday School Convention, our Women's State Association, our State B. Y. P. U. Convention, nearly all of our district Sunday School Conventions and Associations have adopted as their paramount object the fostering of the Arkansas Baptist College and the support of Home and Foreign Missions. So popular has become the sentiment in favor of sustaining the college that a man dare not go before our people and speak against it.

The spirit of unity which has been so characteristic of the Arkansas Baptists for the last two decades has not been without results. It has challenged the admiration of the Baptists in all the states, and one brother writes me that it is amusing to him to see a State organization with two hundred and fifty thousand Baptists trying to keep up with the little Arkansas Convention with only sixty thousand. I have spent some time during the past year in the collection of such facts as would show what the Baptists of Arkansas are doing in the way of self-support. And, to my agreeable surprise, the reports show that the Negro Baptists of the State have collected in their various conventions and associations for missionary and educational work, above $18,000. These figures do not include all the collections made, but only cover the amount paid to State and district missionaries, the college and the other district schools and the amount contributed for foreign mission work. Then there are some district association in the State from which I have no report. A conservative estimate of the entire amount used for missionary and educational purposes would be about twenty-four thousand dollars raised by the Baptists in the State, or an average of about thirty-five per cent for each member. When we take under consideration the fact that a large number of our people have not yet been brought in personal contact with our work, these results are very gratifying indeed. But we should not overlook the fact that we have only made a beginning. We have simply laid the foundation of what is to be one of the grandest educational institutions in this country. Already the demands that are being made upon us are greater than we are able to fill. Our magnificent college building, which is used for every purpose of our school, including a dormitory for our girls, is running over, and yet there are others to come. And our young men have been holding on with a hope that some provision would be made for them and have been told that this meeting would provide means to purchase grounds with a view to putting up a young men's dormitory. We hope that they will not be disappointed. If there is anything that can appeal to the heart and conscience of Baptist men and women, it is the fact that our increasing denomination is showing a thirst for Christian education hitherto unknown. The very fact that we are building these grand and noble institutions and are supporting men to preach the gospel to the heathen and are operating a great publishing plant, which is reflecting the intelligence and zeal of our foremost men, for the propagation of our Baptist principles is attracting the attention of the world toward us as never before. We must not cease in our onward march, but in the language of Isaiah, we must enlarge the place of our tent and stretch forth the curtains of our habitation, strengthen our cords and strengthen our stakes. We should bear in mind that there is marching close behind us an almost countless army of young people who have allied themselves with this grand old Church of Christ, of John the Baptist, and the Apostles. They will soon mount upon the foundation which their fathers have laid and erect their own magnificent temples such as will recall the most enviable position which the sons of Ham occupied in the early history of the world. Don't despair of the young people; they are to be the history makers of the race, and will most surely reflect credit upon their fathers.

I desire in the conclusion of this address to say as I have said on many former occasions, that I thank you from the very depth of my heart for the loyal, warm-hearted, unflinching, manly, Christian support which you have given to our cause in this State and elsewhere under my feeble leadership. I rejoice in the fact that I have lived to see the day when the large number of Baptist preachers in Arkansas, whose greatest ambition was to make such a noise under what they called the holy tone as to excite the emotions of the people, have developed into an army of practical, Christian ministers, whose ideal is that Christ whom they will follow whithersoever he leadeth, and are willing to make any sacrifices necessary to place his cause above every other cause in the world.

ANNUAL ADDRESS AT THE CLOSING OF THE ARKANSAS BAPTIST COLLEGE.

[May 14, 1901.]

Mr. President, Ladies and Gentlemen: Seventeen years ago, with nothing but faith in God and with a courage that admits of no defeat, the Baptist State Convention, followed by a willing-hearted people, launched the craft of the now famous Arkansas Baptist College.

The first efforts for the school were apparently feeble and attracted little attention from outside sources. But beneath the small beginning lay an unconquerable faith which could not be turned from the plain path of duty by any discouragements that might arise. I desire to say to the honor of those who were the pioneers in this work (many of whom have finished their course and gone to their reward) that no selfish purpose or thought of personal gain ever entered their great minds. But, to the reverse, they labored that others might reap the reward. Very few, if any, who were prominent in the beginning of this work expected to live to see the magnificent accomplishments which we have to the credit of the denomination this day. Indeed, we have, after seventeen years of earnest work, what we had reckoned would be realized in fifty years. It is doubtless a source of great rejoicing to those of you who have been spared to see what great things the Lord hath done for us. Magnificent, indeed, is the history of this school, and it has, I believe, been directed by an all-wise Providence. As far back as 1880 the plans and specifications were drawn, by men, too, who had but little or no training in the higher branches of an education and no experience in the matter of school building. Some of you, perhaps, will recall the fact that the present speaker said then, that to found, build, and manage an institution of learning out of the voluntary offerings of a people who were very poor and only a few years from the slave pen, would be a greater work than to manage the affairs of a State whose revenues were collected by compulsory taxation. That remark inspired a desire in many of our pastors to show their ability to do such a work. We commenced by aiding young men to enter colleges in other States, that they might prepare themselves to take charge here when we had reached the place to have a school of our own. And be it said to the credit of the Negro Baptists of Arkansas, that the man who has for thirteen years been President of our school was among the first to be aided by them. That they made no mistake is evidenced by the fact that he has by his indomitable courage and keen foresight brought our school up through tears, trials, persecutions and fire, to be equal to the best in this beautiful Southland. Then, again, we have reason to rejoice in the fact that some of the men who seventeen years ago were buried, so to speak, in ignorance and superstition, are to-day, among the most prominent in our Church and school work, and they, too, have gained their prominence by reasons of having been students in the Arkansas Baptist College--some of them are graduates of a school which they helped to build. In all the trials and conflicts of the past, God has given us friends and the very best kind of friends--those who are friends for Jesus's sake. I mean that those who have aided us in the main have done so with no hope of reward except that which comes to all who seek to honor God by helping their brethren. Among that class of benefactors, I make bold to mention the American Baptist Home Mission Society which came to our aid with a gift of $1,000, and helped to inclose our first building, which unfortunately was destroyed by fire. Nor was that all. From 1877 down to the present day, it has cheerfully contributed amounts ranging from $600 to $1,500 per year on teacher's salaries, and we may add also that the white Baptist Convention of our own State has helped us nobly in furnishing a teacher for our ministers' class and by other kindness it has done. None of these friends will ever be forgotten, nor can their philanthropic deeds be separated from the work of our school.

I must not fail, however, to call the attention especially of the young people present to the sacrifices made by their fathers and mothers to make possible the brilliant scene which we have before us to-day. These grounds and buildings are the greatest evidence of their hope of a future. Not only is the hope in the future of the race in this country expressed by these, but they show that their hope reached beyond this transitory life. The preparations which they have made and are yet making for this and succeeding generations form a monument of no small proportions.

But, my friends, permit me to remind you that we have reached the most critical stage in our race's history--the most important period since the emancipation of our people from slavery. We have reached that point when the whole race is being put to the most crucial test in all the walks of life. I fear that too much is expected of us who have only been free for one generation, and I fear that the test at present is too severe, yet it must be passed. The best minds in our churches and schools have been worked up to their highest tension, trying to prepare the people of our race to meet the conditions which confront us at this day. The leaders fully realize that at this time, every impulse, every progressive idea, and every helpful influence must be brought into full play to preclude any reverse in the onward march which the race has been making for the last past thirty-six years. Every friend must be thanked, and asked to continue the helpful influences which they have wielded in our behalf. Having made such wonderful progress under past conditions and having come over into the morning of the twentieth century under such improved conditions, being surrounded with schools and churches, and having so many educated preachers and competent teachers, much more will be expected of us in the future. We will be expected to be better citizens, such as will not dodge the tax collector, no matter if we are discriminated against. We are to be better neighbors by owning our own homes, respecting and paying due regard for our neighbors' rights and possessions. Crime among our people must be lessened. Admitting that much of the crime charged and conviction obtained are by reason of the prejudice which finds a place in the breast of many of the other race, yet there is far too much crime among our people. There ought not be any; but since there is, the proportion is far too great. It devolves upon us to make the change. The other race can't, and many of them wouldn't if they could. The lessons of honesty, sobriety, and good citizenship are to be learned largely in our own schools. Without these foundation principles, not much can be looked for out of the race. (And I am sorry to say that these lessons are not taught in many of our homes.) The unwritten diploma of good citizenship and Christian bearing will be a testimony of far more value to you, of much more gratification to those who have reared and taught you than that which you receive to-day. If as you leave here it is with the determinate resolution to be men and women of integrity, of honor, whether sung or unsung, to make any necessary sacrifice to uphold the principles of virtue in you and to lend your lives for the service of mankind, it will be much more pleasing to your parents and teachers than the certificate you receive to-day acknowledging that you have completed the course as laid down in our school. The many irregularities which you will meet in life are not to be more powerful than you; neither are you to suppose that these can be erased by a single stroke by you. You are not to partake of them, but you are to strive in the proper way to correct them. "Resist the devil and he will flee from you." But your resistance must be genuine. It is a sad commentary upon the character of a young man or woman who goes out from school and succumbs to vice or immorality. It is his and her duty to modestly hold out against the tendency of a whole community, if that tendency is evil. The young man and woman from school must be the advocates of purity and right in every quarter, and must not for any cause surrender the ground occupied for these principles. Be serviceable, not complaining. Use your learning to lift up the people and not simply to show that you have it. Help to teach the people in private and in public the lessons which will raise the masses from their low estate; teach them the lessons which will help them to do away with the talk of the Negro's depravity; teach them by precept and example the lessons which will inculcate the habits of cleanliness, economy, decision. Aid them to learn better how to become friendly with the other race among whom they live. Be with the people. It is a dangerous presumption on the part of the school boy to consider that his way (because he is lettered) is to be high. The way of the really educated man is low. His life is dedicated to the service of his race, whether he chooses one profession or another. All the members of the race who are able to work must work for the race as well as for self. We are but pioneers of a race's destiny, no matter what may be our chosen profession, and every hand must be ready to do many things. The Negro race is yet burdened with some of the relics of slavery. The duty of parents to children, of children to parents, must be ever held up in the communities wherever there is one able to hold these duties up. Some cannot teach publicly, or deliver addresses (after this occasion) in public. But you can give what I am pleased to call abstract lessons. You can teach by conduct in public and in private. You can talk in private and always have an elevating conversation for those with whom you are speaking. You can without effort be noted as a reader of good books and magazines, which is one of the best signs of improvement that a young person can show after leaving the schoolhouse. The street corners must not be the young man's resting place. The house of gossip must not be the abode of the young woman. Occupy most of your time at work or study. Keep your surroundings clean. If you should choose to be a schoolteacher and not a carpenter, don't allow the fence around your place to become dilapidated for that reason, but take hold and fix it up, and don't allow the dirt to accumulate in your premises or in your home. Keep your eyes upon the inside habits of your life, for they shape character. Fix the little parts of the moral machinery and you regulate the larger parts; fix the little parts and the larger parts will give you no trouble.

I am not pessimistic as to the future of my race, but these words are spoken as a caution to such as believe that developments come by chance. I firmly believe in the possibilities of the race and I believe also that he that hath begun a good work in us will perform it; that God began the emancipation of our race, and that no power on earth can prevent its complete disenthralment. But in most of his dealings with men he has used human instrumentalities, and it is to this I wish now to call your attention.

First, He makes a way by which those he means to use shall be prepared for the work they are to assume. Secondly, He prepares them to do the work. It was so in the case of Moses, Joshua, Daniel, and the other prophets; it is so with us. The instruments which are doubtless to be used for the future development of our people are those who are being trained in our Christian schools. I repeat, much more will be expected of that class of trained leaders than was expected of the fathers. You must meet the responsibilities courageously and faithfully. The young men and women, boys and girls who will go forth from this place to-day, are to reflect upon their several communities the helpful influences which have formed the environment at school for the last eight months.

You should have decided already how you will try to make the old folks happy. You must not find fault with the domestics around home. If the food is not cooked as it has been here in this building, make no complaint and go into the kitchen yourself. By all means, let the young men lighten the burdens of their fathers by rising early and looking after the stock and cutting and hauling wood. Your coming here and your return to your home should mean that you know better how to work and have more pleasure in it. Those of you who are Christians--and I hope you all are--should be the most active persons in your churches as soon as you reach your homes. If you have not any money, gather a few flowers and present to your pastor. Be the first to get to the service and take part in the singing and other worship. Don't fail to show your appreciation of the sermon, notwithstanding the grammer in it may have been defective; and when it is over and the services are ended, tell your pastor how much you enjoyed the sermon and how glad you are to be once more at your home church. Never tell him how "different things are here" to what they are in the great city churches. But take hold and help to work up all necessary reforms.

And now to the class which has reached the point to commence education. Permit me on behalf of our Board of Trustees to congratulate you upon having completed the course prescribed by this institution. In doing so, you have honored both yourself and us, and you will, I trust, honor those who have spent so much time and patience with you to bring you up to this important point. You are now at the commencement of what we trust will be a most useful life. Your education will now begin as you go forth from this place to come in contact with the hard and knotty problems of life. The teachers' duty has been performed, the parents have done their duty, your duty now begins. How well you shall act your part remains to be seen. The little roll which you will receive to-day is a badge which may prove an honor or a disgrace to you in the years which are to come. May it be the former, and as you go out to mingle with the untrained and biased public, remember that you are the representatives of a board and faculty that have made untold sacrifices for your benefit.

Sermons, Addresses and Reminiscences and Important Correspondence

PRESIDENT'S ANNUAL ADDRESS.

[Delivered before the National Baptist Convention at Cincinnati, Ohio, September, 1901.]

Brethren of the Convention, Ladies and Gentlemen:

Since we last assembled in an annual meeting of this great missionary organization, we have seen the flickering light of a most marvelous century go out and have witnessed the advent of a new one, which we hope will be still more wonderful in achievement. In the century just passed our race in this country, so largely represented by you here to-day, occupied a very conspicuous place. For the first three-fifths of the nineteenth century the strong grasp of slavery was hard upon our people, while in the latter two-fifths we enjoyed the distinction of being freedmen. During the closing years of the nineteenth century our people were the object of sympathy and pity to the majority of the intelligent people of the world by reason of past conditions. But in this new century, which will determine the destiny of the race, very little sympathy need be expected more than that extended to other races. No matter what the conditions may be to deter us from an equal chance in the race of life, we will be expected to come up to the full measure of American citizenship, and to become the sculptors of our own destinies and fortunes.

I come before you to-day with the apprehension that you are not as fully impressed as you should be with the importance of your position as leaders, or of the great and difficult problems which you must face--and not only face, but successfully solve for the good of the whole people. Notwithstanding these apprehensions, I count it a rare privilege, as well as a pleasure, to be associated with those whom I know are deeply concerned in all that tends to lift up the race and make the nation better. Your very calling and the purposes which inspire this great assemblage set you forth as the highest court of earth, a court in which the presiding judge is the invisible, the immaculate Prince of Glory, who has predestined that the representatives of his church shall yet sit in equity upon all questions affecting the affairs of men in this world. And I venture to make the remark that only those who believe in and look forward to the complete triumph of Christian principles can realize that there is a satisfactory solution to the many vexed problems which confront the American people of this time. I do not conceal the fact that I (with perhaps many of you) have at times been very despondent. For we have looked as a race for equality of rights to the

Constitution of the United States and of the several States in this great Union, and it seems that each in turn has said, "It is not in me to secure your rights." We have turned to the different political parties and sought these rights and they have apparently declared, "It is not in us to give them." The great labor organizations in the country seem to say, "Your rights are not in our gift;" while the gigantic trusts seem to say, "We are powerless to aid you in getting a recognition of your rights upon the industrial field." But with all these discouragements, we still have an optimistic view of the situation: for Christ our Lord has said, "This Gospel of the kingdom shall be preached," and we know that when the Gospel of the Son of God shall be proclaimed by a hundred thousand divinely inspired men from a hundred thousand pulpits in this land, only one result can follow, namely, an acknowledgment of the Fatherhood of God and the brotherhood of man. But, my brethren, is it not reasonable to suppose that owing to past and present conditions, our race in this country must expect hardships of a longer period than hardships have already been borne. In my opinion, these conditions, to a large extent, are purposely brought on, that we may be more strongly united in all that tends to the uplift of our people.

We have come up to the beautiful Queen City of the grand State which has the honor of having given to the nation one of the most noble-hearted men that ever occupied the Executive Mansion at Washington, to report the work of the largest and most indomitable wing of the great Baptist family of the world. While we represent the Baptists in general, we represent in particular the nearly two million Negro Baptists. To me it is a very great day when we come together from ten thousand battle fields to make reports, to gather fresh inspiration and then return to the scenes of conquest determined to conquer or die.

The year has been filled with cares and increasing responsibilities. Nor has the path of duty been smooth all the way. As in former years, the conflicts have been fierce and long, and, much to our regret, a large portion of the opposition to our work has come from within our ranks. But we have endeavored to exercise great patience in dealing with those who seek the overthrow of our Convention. It is remarkably strange that men who lay claim to intelligence and faithfulness to the cause of Christ can be found who will attempt to break up and throw back into chaos an organization that has united the Negro Baptist family as nothing else could have done. Twenty years ago our people were like wandering sheep, and could only be known through the grace of those who had marshalled a few of them at the great centers in support of our denominational schools. The masses had not been touched. But now, since the organization and consolidation of our national bodies, there is scarcely a secluded spot in this great country where the influence of our work is not felt and recognized. And yet there are men in our own denomination who seek the overthrow of the Convention which has done so much for the race and for the cause of Christianity. Since we do not believe that such men can in any way do us serious harm, we will not refer to them any further in this connection, but will leave them to get their notoriety from those whom they deceitfully serve.

I am glad also to say that while the year has been one of conflict, the valiant host of Baptists, led on by capable Boards, have made progress, and the Boards will be able to report an increase of work done over any previous year. It is gratifying also to note that the interest in our work has increased steadily every year since the reorganization of our Convention. We have endeavored to live on peaceable terms with all men, but most especially with those of the household of faith. In addition to the co-operation entered into by and between the Executive Board of the Missionary Union and our Foreign Mission Board, our Home Mission Board has taken an advance step by entering into co-operation with the Home Board of the Southern Baptist Convention. The plans are similar to those agreed and operated upon by the Foreign Mission Boards, except that the Home Board of the Southern Baptist Convention prescribes the territory to be occupied by the missionaries under the joint appointment. The co-operation thus entered into leaves the way open for further co-operation between the remaining Boards of the National Baptist Convention and the Boards of our white brethren representing other features of the work carried on among our people, an opportunity which I hope our remaining Boards will not be slow in taking up.

The position of the National Baptist Convention on the matter of co-operation is being more favorably considered and understood by those who are the advocates of this system. Ere long the whole world will respect and honor the high stand you have taken for individuality in the great work of the denomination. Indeed, my brethren, the time has passed for the men of our race to lie idle and beg for alms. We must get up and act for ourselves, and that which we cannot do, God will give us friends to aid in doing.

Our Convention has demonstrated beyond all contradiction the ability of our leaders to plant and operate great business concerns and to manage great missionary systems. It has also proven to the world that our people are not too stupid to come up to the support of these enterprises when set forth by their leaders. It seems to be God's plan to have the descendants of Africa in this land remain a separate and distinct race of people. And I am sure it is not the desire of any intelligent Negro to have it otherwise. Now, since we are separate in nearly all matters, religious and secular, we would do well to begin now to contemplate and prepare for the time when black men must have absolute control of all the affairs of their denominational work--the time when the stronger brethren of the other race will be glad to be contributors or benefactors to the work carried on by their weaker brethren. Unlike other races, nearly all the leaders of our people are ministers. Our ministers are expected to stand for the people in nearly every avenue of life, even when the attention of the people is turned from religious to secular matters. The ministers are called upon to aid in the solution of every problem, and since this is true, I will say to you in the name and words of him who will yet rule the world in righteousness: "Be ye as wise as serpents, and harmless as doves." Do not let the upheavals of race prejudice and the enactment of proscriptive laws in many sections of the country unbalance you. The matter is in the hands of a higher power. For as surely as there is a God, and that he began forty years ago the emancipation of our race, so surely will he complete the emancipation begun. The process may seem slow to us, but in his own time will he bring on the complete disenthrallment of our people. There is much work ahead, and the leaders should be seeking and settling upon better and more improved methods of doing this work. The acquisition of the Philippine Islands by this country opens a new and favorable field for missionary work, and to me it is a star of hope for the black man of this country. All these peoples added to the millions already under the flag of our government, are to be trained under the highest type of civilization, and before the close of the present century they will have extended their influence to all the isles of the sea, and even Africa will have arisen from the dust and ashes of ignorance and superstition by the magic touch of these trained millions of her descendants and will take her place along side the other great powers of the world.

In our own march, amid the many persecutions heaped upon the race, I urge that you exercise great patience and then exhort your people to patience. Many of us expect far too much of the race in this day. Our demands are entirely too great. We are asking for fifty thousand first-class school teachers; twenty-five thousand pulpits are demanding educated and trained preachers; doctors, lawyers, statesmen and men of all classes of professions are demanded for the race, and only one generation has passed since the shackles fell from our limbs. The time we have been free is too short to have developed all these and at the same time accumulate from nothing a billion dollars' worth of property. My friends, I urge you to be encouraged. We have done well. The next generation will do far better. The foundation which has been laid will be of inestimable value to the race in its onward move. The church has taken an advance step in all that concerns the race's progress in this and other countries. It is preparing the way for the civilization of heathen lands by giving to them the Gospel of the Son of God. It is to this department of your work that I now desire to call your attention.

FOREIGN MISSIONS.

The unusual activity among the Baptists in the interest of our foreign work is the most hopeful sign of the future success of the race and denomination. Devotion to missionary effort, on the part of the churches, sets them forth as the direct representatives of the first and greatest missionary who said, "As my Father hath sent me, even so send I you." It is very gratifying to be able to say that we have suffered no diminution of effort in our foreign work, but, to the reverse, have made wonderful advancement. The force on both the home and foreign field, has been increased and the contributions have increased proportionately. Rev. E. B. Koti, who was present at the last meeting of our Convention, has returned to his post of duty in South Africa. Rev. L. N. Cheek, who was also present at the last meeting of our Convention, has been sent out by the Board to reinforce Brother Chilembwe at East Central Africa. These brethren went out in January and send back most encouraging reports. The work in South Africa under Rev. R. A. Jackson is progressing as rapidly as could be expected, considering the small amount of means that the Board has had to put into this work. As to the special details of the work of the respective stations, the Board will report.

When our hopes had been raised to the very highest point as to the future of our Liberian missions, the sad news was borne to us of the death of Rev. R. L. Stewart, who was, indeed, a hero in a cause which enveloped his whole being. His very sudden death was as much a surprise to us as it was a calamity to our work, he having a short time before reported his field in a most promising and encouraging condition. Then, to add to the sadness of the report, came also the news that his little daughter and the little African boy, Charlie, whom he was training for the mission field, were both left in London without any means of support, Brother Stewart having left them there in school on his return to Africa. His bereaved wife was not so much as permitted to look upon his face after his death, he having died in the interior and been buried by the natives. This information comes from Sister Stewart. Our Board, however, as soon as it was apprised of the condition there, at once set about relieving the situation as rapidly as means could be collected. And I understand that Sister Stewart has been paid in full the amount due her deceased husband.

There are other fields which are calling for help and the Board stands ready to heed the call as soon as the condition of the treasury will warrant it in doing so. So far as I have been able to learn, the co-operation between our Foreign Mission Board and the Missionary Union has proved entirely satisfactory, and has been a means of very great help to our work through the agency employed by the respective Boards. It is my most earnest desire that this spirit of amity may be kept alive between our great Baptist organizations, and that, instead of the relations becoming more strained, there will eventually be a mutual or fraternal feeling which will set forth all the Baptists throughout the world as one great army of the living God.

The Woman's National Baptist Auxiliary Convention, which was organized one year ago, has devoted most of its time, as I understand, to the work of foreign missions. The organization has met with very flattering success. Its work has been conducted largely by the Corresponding Secretary of the Board, who has been tireless in her efforts to arouse the Baptist women all over the country to greater activity in support of this work, for which she is to be commended. I am in hearty accord with the plan to to have our Baptist women do their work through a separate Board, but do not think it necessary that they should have a separate Convention. In my judgment, a better plan would be to have a Woman's Home and Foreign Mission Board chosen in the same manner in which all the other Boards of the Convention are chosen, and that they have separate and distinct headquarters from the headquarters of the other Boards, reporting annually to the Convention as do the others.

Each year's experience in mission work has added to the zeal and efficiency of the officers and members of our Foreign Mission Board, and the Convention may justly congratulate itself on having such an aggressive and wide-awake set of brethren to conduct the work on foreign fields. To me the outlook in this department is very hopeful and promises an abundant harvest.

HOME MISSIONS AND PUBLICATIONS.

I am glad to say that the Home Mission Board will be able to report such progress at this session of the Convention as will doubtless thrill the heart of every Baptist in the land. For some time the missionary efforts of this Board have been confined to the aiding of a few pastors in the West and the paying of a part of the salaries of missionaries in some of the older States and helping poor Sunday schools with grants of books and other periodicals. The remainder of the

Board's time and means has been given to the publication of Sunday School literature and other bookwork. But fortunately, the officers of our Home Board were called in conference with the representatives of the Home Board of the Southern Baptist Convention. The conference referred to was held at Chattanooga, Tenn., in November, 1990, at which plans of co-operation were agreed upon and subsequently ratified by the respective Boards. The plan provides for the appointment of two general missionaries by our Board who are to devote their entire time to the work on the home field, while the Home Board of the Southern Baptist Convention is to pay the salaries of these men. This co-operation has been sustained but a short time. It has been very helpful, however, and will enable our Home Mission Board to do more work in the future.

The growth in our publication work continues to be one of the marvels of the age. If you will pardon the comparison, I would say that the progress in our publishing work is much like that of the old servant who, as the story goes, was to stand at the wheel and hold the prow of the moving vessel between two certain stars while his master slept. When the master awoke, he shuddered to find that the stars were no where visible ahead. He remonstrated with his servant so jovial and jolly, shouting, "What have you done? We're off our course. Where are those stars?" But Sambo, the cool-headed servant, replied, "Law, massa, we's done passed dem stars lon' 'go!"

In 1896, our statistician, who was also the representative of the Sunday School work of the American Baptist Publication Society, told us that there were ten thousand Negro Baptist Sunday Schools in the United States. We set our compass upon these vast numbers, and if he will but open his eyes, we will inform him now that we have "done passed dem stars long 'go," and that now twelve thousand Negro Baptist Sunday schools buy their periodicals and other supplies from the counters of the National Baptist Publishing Board.

The President's attention has been called several times during the year to the severe criticisms which have been made against the management of our Publishing Board and to the further criticism brought against the President himself, to the effect that he knew of the "mismanagement of affairs," and was being paid to say nothing about it. The report was so ridiculous that at first we thought to pay no attention to it. But when we had been repeatedly addressed and interviewed by persons who were deeply concerned in the success of our publishing department, we then informed them that so far as our knowledge of the affairs extended, every charge made was malicious and had no foundation in fact. When asked why no reply was made to these charges, we invariably said, it would be a loss of time and means to stop a fast mail and express train making sixty miles an hour to scare a rat off the track. In this same connection let me say: So far as the President is concerned, all of his official acts are as open as a book and he invites, rather than objects, any criticism that may come--for the reason that if he has made any mistakes, he most earnestly desires to correct them for the good of himself and the denomination.

The President has visited the Publishing House several times during the year and recently spent a whole week there, and frankly confesses that the success of that enterprise has been a revelation. Instead of finding fault, it seems to me that every man who has one bit of race pride and who desires that the world shall know the good accomplished by the race through this medium would be glad to give his unqualified support to it. I say with some degree of modesty that no enterprise which has been pushed out upon the sea of public opinion has met with such signal success. The lashing waves which have beaten against the craft have only served to prove her seaworthy.

My brethren, we could not live to future generations without this or a similar enterprise. The best and greatest spirits that the race has produced are to be kept alive through this or a similar medium long after those noble spirits have gone to their reward. The literature produced by this and other publishing houses will be the photograph of the men and women who write and read it to be looked upon five hundred years hence. It will be a picture true to life, one which no other race could produce for us. But why should I labor hard to encourage you in your support of this department of our Convention's work, when you have already proven your loyalty to it. Let us now turn to another important feature.

THE EDUCATIONAL WORK.

The report of the Educational Board made to the Convention one year ago was one of the most inspiring that it has been our pleasure to listen to. In that report it was shown what the Negro Baptists were doing toward their own education. For several years an unintentional wrong has been done the Negro Baptists by publications which have purported to show the amounts given by them for their own development. I presume these reports were taken from statements by Boards which made no attempt at keeping accurately an account of the moneys paid in for the education of the Negro. It was, indeed, humiliating to read how little had been accredited to Negro Baptists for their own education, and if the figures could have been believed, it would have shown them as being very unworthy of the help which they received. Our Educational Board is endeavoring to ascertain the real amount paid by our people for their own education and we regret to say that notwithstanding these efforts, many of our schools and colleges are not reported yet. It seems that any man who is competent to be president of a Negro Baptist School would have enough race pride and love to report accurately to the Secretary of our Educational Board the full amount paid by our people for the support of their educational institutions. For in no other way can the truth in this respect be ascertained.

In my humble judgment, the work of the Educational Board is paramount to any other and should be so regarded by this Convention. If this be true, it is entirely out of the question to entertain, for a single moment, the idea that the Secretary of our Educational Board can do the work of his Board and, at the same time, serve in the capacity of a pastor.

B. Y. P. U. WORK.

This department has met with a reasonable degree of success. The work among the young people is yet in its experimental state, but its present rate of progress is prophetic of a bright and hopeful future. The work of organizing has been carried forward rapidly and successfully. The Corresponding Secretary has been diligent, earnest and aggressive in extending his plans of co-operation with State Conventions of the B. Y. P. U. into nearly all the States co-operating with this Convention. Pastors heretofore indifferent and inactive have become friendly to the work, and not a few of them have volunteered to organize local societies in their churches and otherwise encourage the movement. The young people have a more accurate and profitable understanding of the fundamental principles for which the organization stands and in furtherance of its primary objects, much work has been done by the various local, district and State organizations in support of all the claims of our great denomination. There has been marked advancement in the systematic study of the Bible, in the study on evangelical missionary movements, in the acquiring of a more extensive knowledge of Baptist history and doctrines and the steady increase of a love for missionary agencies throughout the world. Many of those who are engaged in educational and missionary work have learned to look to the B. Y. P. U. societies for help. And it is encouraging to state that they do not always look in vain. In addition to the general awakening that has come to our young people and the increased activities with which they have been stimulated, the Corresponding Secretary of the B. Y. P. U. Board has rendered heroic service to all departments of the work of this Convention. "The National Baptist Union," the young people's paper, has spoken for the interest of the Convention along all lines and, therefore, is entitled to the unanimous support of the denomination. I cannot close my remarks upon the work of this Board without urging you to consider how important it is to give encouragement to this, the youngest of our National Boards, with the hope of holding the host of young people to the doctrines which are so sacred to us.

IN MEMORIAM.

My brethren, I pause here to say that in the midst of a busy life filled with noble deeds, crowned with many honors justly won, Rev. Richard DeBaptiste, one of the pioneer members of this Convention, passed from the active scenes of battle to the still more active scenes of that bright and glorious city where the wicked cease from troubling and the weary are at rest. In the month of June just while looking over a contribution written by Dr. DeBaptiste for our "Convention Teacher," a telegram was brought into my office announcing his death. The sad news came like a clap of thunder from a clear sky. For a moment the report seemed incredible. But, alas! it was true. Another of our faithful comrades had been mustered out and gone home. His sterling qualities of true piety and noble manhood will ever remain with us to inspire greater courage in those who survive him.

> "If I must die, oh let me die
> In peace with all mankind,
> And change these fleeting joys below
> For pleasures more refined."

CONCLUSION.

Now, my brethren, in conclusion, permit me to say that my official relation with this Convention has increased my faith in the possibilities of my race. No greater people in heart lives upon the face of the earth, and while we have been kept under the smouldering heat of persecution for many years, the sparks of religious devotion and of loyalty to our nation and our nation's honor are beginning to come forth. Ere long the whole world will recognize in the Negro the very highest type of Christian manhood and citizenship which has only the Golden Rule as a guide; that never once thinks of arraying labor against capital or class against class, but that believes in the moral law as taught in the Bible and in the Declaration of Independence which has made this country great. Such a people will ever be needed to keep the scales balanced between man and man. Let me again remind you that we are living in a new age, an age which will not for a moment stop to consider the past or present condition of the race. Hence, we must assume at once our share of the responsibilities of maintaining the institutions of the country, both by precept and example. In the matter of church building, our people have become the example for all the other people of the world. We have done fairly well in establishing and maintaining Christian schools and have made some progress in the professions. But these are not enough. Our people are to be led into the business of commercial affairs of the country and into the industrial and agricultural pursuits, and in this, as in other matters, they must be taught by their ministers. Encourage the people to go into business and become noteworthy in commerce as well as in religion, thereby commanding the respect of all mankind.

And finally, let me thank you from the depths of my heart for the warm-hearted and loyal support you have given the objects of the Convention and for the confidence in me which you have repeatedly expressed. Let me assure you that whether in or out of official relationship to your Convention, while I have strength to lift my voice, it shall be for the highest development of the possibilities of my people along the lines of their distinctive work.

REMINISCENCES.

MANY incidents crowd into twenty years of active participation in the affairs of a great denomination. My first official relation with the denomination was in 1880, as Secretary of State Baptist Convention of Arkansas. After being installed as the recorder of the proceedings, our first effort was to take down as much of what was said and done as possible for one who could not write shorthand, hence much attention was attracted from those about us. We often heard the remark, "I tell you, mun, that's a smart fellow," or "Don't he shove a scandless pen?" Back in those days there were only a few competent men to fill the position of Secretary, hence that office was considered of more importance than the presidency, and even until now, with many of our people the art of good penmanship is termed education.

At one time while serving in the capacity of secretary, a serious dispute which had for several years divided the churches of the State, came up. A delegation of what we termed the dissenters, came to the regular convention under a truce, so to speak, and the chairman of the delegation, addressing the President, said: "Mr. Chairman, we are here, sir, to ask on what terms our Convention can be received into your honorable body." The President replied that if they desired it, he would appoint a committee to take the matter under consideration and talk over the terms with him and the committee could report to the Convention. This seemed to be satisfactory to all but one of the number, who insisted upon having the Secretary name the terms. By consent of the President, the Secretary rose and said: "Brethren, if you have been chosen as messengers from your respective churches to the regular Baptist State Convention, you have reached the place and the organization; pass your letters over to the Committee on Enrollment." The President ruled the Secretary out of order, and appointed a special committee, which committee and delegation failed to agree. The following year these same brethren came to the Convention and presented their letters in the usual way and were received without opposition. At that meeting the Secretary was elected President. It was not seldom that it could be heard, "I tell you, we ought not took dat man way fom dat table;" some would say, "Well, Brer Pres'dent, we'se lected yo' dar, but yo must keep yo eye on dem books." But fortunately, a very worthy and competent man has been kept in the Secretary's office all these years.

In those days it was a custom for churches to recommend persons to come before the Board of the Convention or association to be examined for ordination. These examinations were usually conducted by a committee appointed for that purpose. We recall an instance where a young man was sent up from his church, one of the deacons accompanying him. This deacon seemed exceedingly anxious that the young man should pass, as it was called. And while the committee was asking questions touching the doctrines and polity of the church and the young man seemed to be dumbfounded, the good deacon put in and said: "Brer Mod'rater, dat 'mittee is talkin' too high for ----; he's no edicated man." The moderator replied, "I will have the committee come down."

A short time after the Baptists of Arkansas undertook to do educational and missionary work and also to publish a weekly paper, the presiding officer was beseiged by educated young men for positions in their respective fields; hence he decided to make as a test of qualifications for these places the following: "Have you a pair of mud boots?" If the answer was no, then he would say: "You must get you a pair and go down to the river bottoms and see how many of the Baptist churches you can induce to come to the next meeting of the Convention." Only one of the many stood this test and went into the rural districts to help organize the work, and that man, after a brief period on the mission field, was called by his brethren to the Presidency of the Arkansas Baptist College, and has remained in that position for fourteen years.

When the educational work in Arkansas was first organized, the writer was elected to the Presidency of the school, which school was only on paper at that time. One of the first thoughts to come to his mind was that to be the President of a great Convention and at the same time fill the exalted station as President of a great school was an honor which demanded that the recipient be married and the head of a family. Accordingly he at once reopened correspondence with the lady whom he had chosen in his mind when only a youth, to be his companion, and was successful in gaining the hand and heart of Miss Fannie Ella Austin, of Fackler, Ala. The marriage took place in November, 1884. The local paper had this to say of it: "At the residence of the bride's parents, Fackler, Ala., Thursday, November 27, at 6 o'clock P.M., Rev. L. C. Roach officiating, Rev. E. C. Morris of Helena, Ark., and Miss Fannie E. Austin, of Fackler, Ala., were united in the holy bonds of wedlock. After the ceremony a grand reception was held, and the heartiest congratulations poured in on the happy couple. There were in attendance two hundred and twenty-seven guests which swelled the wedding crowd to an ovation. The contracting parties, accompanied by Mr. T. T. Morris, a brother of the groom, departed on the next day for Helena, Ark., stopping at Stevenson, Ala., and Tullahoma, Tenn., where they had relatives; then to Nashville and Memphis, arriving at Helena at 2 P.M., December 2, over the Iron Mountain railway. A grand dinner was given by Mrs. S. J. Caver the same afternoon in honor of the bride and groom. Dinner being over, the happy pair proceeded at once to their residence where they will be found in the future. Rev. Morris is the popular pastor of the Centennial Baptist Church and President of the Baptist State Convention of Arkansas. Mrs. Morris is a member of one of the oldest and most highly respected families of Fackler, Ala., and a very amiable and lovely young woman. The Epoch extends its warmest congratulations and best wishes for a long and happy life."

Nothing has added so much to the writer's success in life as the faithfulness and devotion of her who has willingly shared all his griefs and sorrows and has indeed been so very self-denying that the cause of God and the Baptists might go on, so far as we had to do with it. To us have been born eight children, five of whom are now living. Three are members of the Baptist Church and we are watching daily for the others to come in, which we feel sure they will do as soon as they are capable of exercising faith in the Lord Jesus Christ. Our second boy made a profession when he was about six years old. We thought it best to wait awhile before consenting that he should be baptized. The following year after his profession when a large number of young people were joining the church, I again approached him on the matter of his profession. His reply was: "I had religion last year, but you wouldn't let me keep it."

We have received many flattering compliments on the ease with which we have presided in the National Baptist Convention from such men as Drs. McVicar, Johnson, Griggs, Boyd, Parrish. Jones, and others. We have never been able to understand how the brethren have been so easily managed, especially when we recall some of the stormy scenes occurring during the administration of our able predecessors. But one incident comes to mind, which took place in 1890. Dr. Simmons, the President, being ill, the writer, who was one of the Vice Presidents, was called to preside. While trying to dispatch the business of the Convention, we noticed a brother who had several times made an effort to display his parliamentary knowledge, standing at a distance with--parliamentary guide behind him, with his fingers between the leaves. Having just made a ruling on a point of order raised by another, this brother called out: "Brother President, I want to ax you what manual you rules this convention by?" Quickly as could be thought, the reply went to him: "We go by Morris' Manual of Common Sense," to which the brother replied: "All right, we don't use that down here," and he sat down with a smile of embarrassment mingled with an expression of gratitude for the special information received, and has not given any trouble since as to parliamentary authority.

Some years ago a war broke out in Texas, which was borne all the way to the National Baptist Convention, and was the source of much confusion, for the reason that the two factions were almost equally divided, and each as aggressive as the other. There could be no agreement between them as to which party should represent the state on the various national committees. When we brought to face the situation, we suggested that Texas was large enough to form two states, and if no objection was raised, Texas would henceforward be given two members on each committee, one representing each faction. The suggestion was agreed to by the Convention and to our genuine embarrassment each of the Texas delegations accepted the solution, one delegate remarking: "Humph! that fellow can make a state at a word." This ended the feud in Texas so far as the National Baptist Convention was concerned.

During the heated discussion which was going on concerning the organization of a District Foreign Mission Convention, one good brother said to me: "You National Convention men are not going to attempt to hold your Convention in Richmond, are you?" I replied, "Yes, sir." Said he: "Virginia belongs to the District Convention." "But," I continued, "Virginia is in the United States, and not the United States in Virginia; and unless Virginia secedes from the Union, our National Convention will sustain the same relation to Virginia that it sustains to all the other states without interfering with any of her local or district affairs." Virginia did not secede.

PRESIDENT E. C. MORRIS OF THE NATIONAL BAPTIST CONVENTION ARRAIGNS HIS CRITICS.

Editor Christian Banner, Dear Sir and Brother:

Some time ago you called attention, in a brief editorial, to a charge brought against the President of the National Baptist Convention by the editor of the "Florida Evangelist." I did not wish to appear in public print as replying to such a glaring statement, hence, I wrote you a private letter. But I see "The Evangelist" in a recent number, makes the startling announcement that, "There is a disposition on the part of those at the head of the National Baptist Convention not to recognize as members of that body those who are not in favor of the National Publishing House." I desire to be charitable in all I may say, but for the life of me, I cannot see how any man, whether Christian or sinner, can, in the face of the facts so potent, make such a statement.

The editor of the "Evangelist" knows as well as any body that Rev. S. N. Vass, who is District Secretary for the South of the American Baptist Publication Society, was for two years an officer of the National Baptist Convention, and still, at the same time represented the Publication Society; he knows also that Brother Wm. H. Steward, a man honored and beloved by all of the members of the National Baptist Convention, has been Secretary of the Convention for many years and at the same time was, and is now, the Sunday School State Missionary of the Publication Society, and that his friendship and loyalty to the Society did not, in any way, effect his standing with the National Baptist Convention; and he knows further, that Rev. E. W. D. Isaac was at one time a strong opponent of the National Baptist Publishing House, and without any surrender of opinion or position on these questions, Brother Isaac was chosen Corresponding Secretary of the National B. Y. P. U. Board.

But why further fellow up the unmistakable evidence that no such prejudice as charged by the "Evangelist" exists in the officers of the National Baptist Convention? Still to be more personal, he says, "If it is known that a member is in favor of coeration with white Baptist Societies of the North, and that he believes in remaining loyal to the American Baptist Publication Society he is snubbed by the President of the National Baptist Convention, left off the program by the program committee, referred to in speeches, papers, reports, sermons, newspaper articles, as being untrue to his race, etc." It should not be a secret with one to favor co-operation. The President of the National Baptist Convention favors co-operation and makes no scruples in saying so, and would therefore, according to "The Evangelist," have to snub himself. But while he believes in co-operation he also believes that he should have a say as to plans and purposes set forth, in a matter in which he is expected to co-operate. The relations which persons sustain to other organizations have never been considered in the arranging of a program for the National meetings, and, as a result, the persons officially connected with all existing Baptist organizations have, from time to time, been on program. Fortunately the Board has always succeeded in getting some of the best men in the country to accept places on the program. It is not the good fortune of the President to hear all that is said at our National meetings. But of the speeches, papers and sermons which he did hear he is glad to say that they were all of a very high order--and so high that some things received no notice at all. This perhaps was wrong, for little things should not be overlooked.

I would not accuse the editor of the "Evangelist" of an attempt to deceive the people of his State and those on the outside who may chance to see his paper. But what can he mean, when he says that the officers of the National Baptist Convention give one who does not favor the Publishing House to understand, "that however much he may be in favor of the Foreign Mission work of the National Convention, he is not needed unless he is prepared to abuse and browbeat the Northern white Baptists and do all in his power to destroy the American Baptist Publication Society?" If the above words were directed to any particular person it would, perhaps, be better to leave them to torment the writer without any comment. But to accuse the National Baptist Convention of not wanting anybody as its members except such as are "prepared to abuse the Northern white Baptists" is indeed a serious charge, and perhaps, accounts for the fact that only two of our great white Baptist Societies were represented at Nashville by white messengers, notwithstanding all had been invited. No one knows better than the editor of the "Evangelist" that no such thing as abuse of the Northern white Baptists was ever heard in the National Baptist Convention.

We have no words of criticism to speak concerning the Lot-Cary Convention. If there is such a Convention, (and we believe there is) and it can do anything toward sending the Gospel to Africa, we would not urge a single objection. The Foreign Mission Board of the National Baptist Convention will do all that the Baptists of America will permit it to do in sending the Gospel through missionaries, to the heathen in Africa. But if the Baptists choose to send their means through another channel, who can hinder them? However, we do not believe that the Baptists of the country will turn away from a Board which has accomplished more in five years than was accomplished in fifteen years under the original design. Nor do we think the "Evangelist" was authorized to say that the "Lot-Cary Convention was organized to give the preachers and laymen who had been ruled out of the National Convention an opportunity to carry out the original design of the Convention."

We repeat that we have no fight to make on the Lot-Cary Convention and we do not agree with the editor of the "Evangelist" that it is composed of excluded members of the National Baptist Convention. But to the contrary, if we have been correctly informed, there are some of the very best men in our denomination connected with it; and the fact that they are good men will, in our humble judgment, lead them ere long to see that it will be to the best interest of the denomination to concentrate all of our efforts through one Board.

But there is no reason for one Board abusing the other. It might be well to say that the fact that the National Baptist Convention is fostering more than one enterprise, has not in any respect decreased its Foreign Mission work. Instead, the work has been increased every year since 1895, the time of the consolidation; also the States which are giving the greatest support to the Publishing House and other work of the National Convention also give the largest amount of money to the Foreign Mission work.

Indeed it appears to us that some of the Baptists, especially the "Evangelist" of Florida, have not yet opened their eyes on the marvelous progress made by the Negro Baptists of this country. Not only have they made wonderful progress in a material way, but their intellectual strength and the matchless decorum in their national meetings have challenged the admiration of the world. Wake up, Rip Van Winkle, and realize that you are in a progressive age.

December, 1899.

E. C. MORRIS.

NATIONAL BAPTIST CATECHISM.

INTRODUCTION.

This little catechism was written for the purpose of giving to the thousands of Baptists who do not have an opportunity of attending the annual meetings of the National Baptist Convention a chance to learn the objects, aims and purposes of that Convention, as it is represented by the respective Boards. It will serve also as a useful little handbook for those who attend these meetings as delegates, messengers, etc. It is hoped that the brief information here given will awaken a deeper interest among the people in the general work, to the end that the contributions from churches, Sunday schools, societies, etc., may be increased from year to year until our collections will respectively represent the large, and rapidly increasing membership in our churches. Already unusual activity is manifest in some sections, but until this spirit is generally diffused all over the country, the agitation of this work should be kept before the people. With best wishes for the success of our work and principles along all lines, I am,

Very truly yours,

E. C. MORRIS.

CATECHISM.

Question. What is the National Baptist Convention?

Answer. The National Baptist Convention is an organization composed of delegates from Baptist Churches, Associations, State Conventions, Missionary Societies, Baptist Young People's Unions, etc., etc., which meet annually for the purpose of hearing and considering the reports of Boards, Standing Committees and to receive the contributions sent up from local organizations or individuals, and to appropriate the same to the several causes represented by the Convention, or to such purpose as designated by the donors, and to plan for future work.

Q. Are all the Baptists in America represented by this organization?

A. No. The white Baptists have their own Church Societies. This Convention represents about one-third of all the Baptists in the world, and nearly all the colored Baptists. It claims a constituency of 1,687,000 communicants, 13,000 churches, and 12,000 ordained ministers.

Q. Are all the colored Baptists of America connected with the National Baptist Convention?

A. The New England Baptists have not united with the Convention, but they contribute to its objects and help support the African Mission Work. It is hoped that they will unite with the National Baptist Convention at its meeting in Boston this year.

Q. What gave rise to the organization of the National Baptist Convention?

A. The plan for such an organization was conceived in the brain of Rev. Wm. J. Simmons, D. D., LL. D., who gave as the object the "collection of statistics, and to consider the moral and intellectual growth of the denomination, and to bring them closer together for effectual work in the Master's kingdom."

Q. When and where was the Convention organized?

A. It was organized at St. Louis, Mo., in August, 1886, in the First Baptist Church. Dr. Simmons was elected President.

Q. Has the Convention met each year since its organization?

A. Yes. The meetings of the National Baptist Convention have been held at the same time and place of the Baptist Foreign Mission Convention from 1887 to 1895, when all the National organizations merged into one. The consolidation of the three great Conventions took place at Atlanta, Ga., in the Friendship Baptist Church.

Q. Did the consolidation of the three Conventions destroy the identity of the other two Conventions?

A. No. Each of the three Conventions as they formerly existed is now represented by Boards, which are chosen at the annual meetings by the respective State delegations, in the same manner that the officers of the Convention are chosen, and these hold their respective offices until their successors are elected and qualified. The officers of the Convention, and the vice presidents (one from each State) constitute one general Executive Board.

Q. Are the orders of the Convention binding upon the Boards, or are they to act independently of the Convention?

A. The Boards are created by the Convention, and cannot set aside any of its orders. Each of these Boards is required to make annual reports, hence all suggestions for changes would necessarily come before the Convention.

Q. Has each of the Boards a specific work, and is their work defined by the Constitution of the Convention?

A. Each Board has a specific work, but the work of the Home Mission and Educational Boards has not been as fully defined as that of the Foreign Mission Board. This is owing to the fact that the Constitution of the Convention is not complete, but it is understood that the Board is to prosecute the work of the Convention that it was created to represent.

Q. What is the aim, object and work of the Foreign Mission Board?

A. It is the object and aim of the Foreign Mission Board to create an interest among all the Baptists of America in Foreign Missions by continually urging upon them the "great commission," and to organize Missionary Societies in the churches, and to urge an observance of the special days set for missionary purposes, with a view to raising means to give the Gospel to the heathen in Africa, and elsewhere as Providence may direct.

Q. Have the Baptists done any work in foreign lands through this Board?

A. Yes. The Board began work on the West Coast of Africa, in 1881, and has kept missionaries continually on the field ever since. The work among the Vey tribe was interrupted by a war which broke out between the native tribes, and has not been permanently resumed among that people. The principle station now is at Cape Town, South Africa.

Q. How many missionaries have been sent out by this Board, and what are their names and residences?

A. There have been fourteen missionaries employed and sent to Africa by the Foreign Mission Board, others (natives) have been employed as interpreters and resident missionaries. The following named persons were sent from America: Rev. Samuel Cosby, N. C.; Rev. and Mrs. W. W. Colley, Rev. and Mrs. J. H. Presley, Rev. and Mrs. J. J. Coles, Va; Rev. H. McKinney, Rev. J. J. Diggs, Rev. E. B. Topp and wife, Miss.; Rev. J. O. Hays, N. C.; Rev. and Mrs. R. A. Jackson, Ark.

Q. How many of these missionaries are now living, how many dead, and how many are now on the field?

A. There are ten of the missionaries who were sent to Africa, living; Revs. Cosby and McKinney, and Sister J. H. Presley died in Africa, and Rev. J. J. Coles died in this country after he returned home from the field. Rev. R. A. Jackson and wife, and Rev. J. O. Hays are now on the field; besides these are Revs. R. T. Stewart, John Tule and John Thomas, recently employed. The two latter are native Africans.

Q. Where is the headquarters of the Foreign Mission Board, and who are the officers?

A. The headquarters of the Foreign Mission Board is at Louisville, Ky. Rev. J. H. Frank is chairman; S. E. Smith, D. D., Secretary; D. A. Gaddie, D. D., Treasurer; and Rev. L. G. Jordan, Corresponding or Field Secretary.

Q. What day has been designated by the National Convention as "Foreign Mission Day?"

A. The fifth Sunday occurring in each year has been designated "Foreign Mission Day," and it is the duty of the Foreign Mission Board to furnish a program for the use of all the Baptist churches on that day, the money raised to be sent to the Treasurer of the Board.

Q. What is the work and aim of the Home Mission Board?

A. The work and aim of the Home Mission Board is at present confined to the publication of Sunday school literature, but as its name indicates, its aim is to look after the mission work at home, and to co-operate with other agencies in building up the denomination in America.

Q. Is there not a society which has for years been engaged in the publication of Sunday school literature?

A. Yes, there are several such societies among the white Baptists, the principal one being the American Baptist Publication Society.

Q. Are not these societies among the white Baptists better prepared to publish Sunday school literature, and at lower prices than the Home Mission Board?

A. Certainly, some of them are very wealthy, and can employ the very best scholars to write for their periodicals, and can put their work out at such low prices as to make competition almost impossible. But while the Home Mission Board cannot compete in prices and may not for the present be able to compete in other respects with the older and wealthier societies, it will give employment to colored Baptists, thereby giving encouragement to capital and scholarship, which will eventually enable them to compete with other societies along all lines.

Q. Do the publication societies among the white Baptists give employment to colored Baptists?

A. Only as missionaries and colporteurs. The only place of prominence ever held was that of District Secretary. No colored men are employed as contributors, associate editors, clerks in book houses, etc., hence there is no incentive to aspire to, or prepare for such places.

Q. Are all the leading ministers among the colored Baptists in sympathy with the Publishing Board.

A. No. There are some who claim to honestly oppose the movement, but they are greatly in the minority. Nearly all the great men in the denomination are in sympathy with the Board, as they can see that this is the only way by which the acts and writings of the race can be preserved and transmitted to their posterity.

Q. What is the cost of the literature used in the colored Baptist Sunday schools?

A. The estimated cost of the literature used in colored Baptist Sunday school is $100,000 a year. This includes all kinds of periodicals.

Q. Does all of this vast sum go to any one of the older societies?

A. No. It is divided among all the publishing societies, some even use what is called non-sectarian literature. The largest amount goes to the American Baptist Publication Society, and the next largest to the Sunday School Board of the Southern Baptist Convention.

Q. Will the Home Mission Board get the patronage of the entire colored Baptist denomination?

A. Not at present, and perhaps never will be able to control the entire patronage, but they hope to secure at least half of all the patronage in the next two years. The fact that the success of the enterprise means employment, and the giving to the colored Baptists a place in religious history, which without it would be lost to them, will cause all the most thoughtful ones to support the movement.

Q. Where is the headquarters of the Home Mission Board and who are the officers?

A. The headquarters of the Home Mission Board is temporarily at Little Rock, Ark., the permanent location will be determined at the Convention which meets at Boston, in September, 1897. The officers of the Board are Rev. G. W. D. Gaines, Chairman; Prof. J. A. Booker, A. M., Secretary; Rev. J. P. Robinson, Treasurer; Rev. R. H. Boyd, D. D., Corresponding and Field Secretary.

Q. Why is the literature published at Nashville and the Board headquarters at Little Rock?

A. The Board appointed a Publishing Committee whose duty it is to publish the literature, and this Committee, after careful examination, found that the work could not be satisfactorily done at Little Rock, hence by consent of the Board the contract for the work was let to a Nashville firm.

Q. Where is the headquarters of the Educational Board and what are its duties?

A. The headquarters of the Educational Board is at Washington, D. C. The duties of the Board are many, but at present they are devoting their efforts to the publication of the *Baptist Magazine,* and the organization of the forces for effectual work along other lines. There are forty-four (44) schools run exclusively by colored Baptists, and the Board may at some day be able to so organize them and the Baptists in support of them, as to make each and all beneficiaries of the National Convention.

Q. Will the Educational Board attempt to interfere with the management of the Home Mission Society's Schools?

A. By no means; but rather encourage and support their efforts, for the simple reason, that the Home Mission Society has always recognized the colored Baptists as men, and has appointed and supported in positions of honor and trust many of our ablest men, not as missionaries only, but as college presidents, treasurers and secretaries.

Q. What can the Educational Board do to help the schools now owned and operated by the colored Baptists and the Society?

A. When these schools have become a part of the National Convention, and a system has been adopted to receive and disburse the gifts and bequests of philanthropists, it will encourage men in our own race, as well as others, to give, when they know that their gifts will be handled by a competent Board.

Q. Are the Baptist newspapers in sympathy with the National Convention in its work along these lines?

A. They are practically a unit in support of the objects and plans of the National Convention. They differ somewhat as to methods of procedure, etc. The fact that a Baptist Press Association was organized at the last Convention, and will meet in connection with the Convention in future, will make them practically a unit on the methods, etc., in future, as the editors of these papers are members of and help to shape the policies of the Convention.

Q. Is there a national organization of the Baptist women in the United States?

A. Yes, prior to the meeting of the St. Louis Convention there were two of these, but the consolidation of the National Convention, and the General

Association of the Western States and Territories left only one organization. They meet at the same time and place of the National Convention.

Q. Are women received as delegates, messengers, etc., in the National Convention on equality with the men?

A. Yes. There is no discrimination; they are given the same privileges as the men, and are put on the programmes, committees, etc.

Q. What about the Baptist Young People's Union? Is it a part of the National Convention?

A. The organization of the Baptist Young People's Union as an auxiliary of the National Convention was effected at St. Louis. The work of this organization has not as yet been defined by the Constitution, but a beginning having been made it is hoped that it will soon develop into a strong society.

The following comparative statistics of other denominations are taken in part from the Eleventh Census Report for 1890, and partly from authorized reports and estimates of the denominations given for that year:

U. S. CENSUS REPORTS FOR 1890.

African Methodist Episcopal	452,725
African Union Methodist Protestant	3,415
African Methodist Episcopal, Zion	349,788
Congregational Methodist	319
Colored Methodist Episcopal	129,383
Colored Cumberland Presbyterian	13,439

OTHERS ESTIMATED.

Colored members in Methodist Episcopal Church	100,000
Colored members in Protestant Episcopal Church	20,000
Colored members in Presbyterian Church	20,000
Colored members in Congregational Church	12,000
Colored members in Christian Church	25,000
Colored members in Roman Catholic Church	100,000
The Negro Regular Baptists numbered by the U. S. Census of 1890 in fifteen States and D. C.	1,362,140
The same year the States, etc., not included in U. S. Census Report, contained Colored Baptists	46,687
Making a total for 1890	1,408,827
Total Negroes in other denominations, including Roman Catholic Church	1,256,069
Majority Negro Baptists	182,758

Since the above was compiled and printed, the National Baptist Young People's Union Board has been constituted with headquarters at Nashville, Tenn. Rev. E. W. D. Isaac is the Corresponding Secretary.

IMPORTANT CORRESPONDENCE.

New York, February 5th, 1900.
E. C. Morris, D. D., President of the National Baptist Convention,
Helena, Ark.

Dear Brother:--I write you (not by the authority of the Executive Board of the American Baptist Home Mission Society, but on my own volition) this letter which I desire to have considered as tentative and preliminary to possible action by our Executive Board.

Since 1862, the American Baptist Home Mission Society has been engaged in prosecuting missionary and educational work in behalf of the Negroes in this country. I need not here refer to the character, quality, success or cost of that work. I may be permitted, however, to say that it has been a labor of love, having for its immediate practical end the uplift of an unfortunate people just emerging from bondage, and their preparation for independent American citizenship, and for self-directed service in the cause of the Redeemer. The work has appealed very strongly to the Baptists of the North, and the Society has to-day the same earnest interest and joy in it that it has had from the beginning. God has wonderfuly blessed it.

A GREAT CHANGE.

There has come about since 1862, a period of nearly forty years, a great change in the condition of your people--you number probably ten millions instead of four. The Baptists number probably one and three-quarter millions instead of four hundred thousand; a large body of your people have been educated in the schools founded and maintained for them by the Society, and in other institutions; many of your people have purchased their own homes and accumulated no inconsiderable amount of property, you have now your national organization for missionary and educational work, and some of your people are manifesting a laudable ambition to be independent and self-supporting. It has been the fervent hope and confident expectation of those who have heretofore given and labored for the advancement of your people through the agency of the American Baptist Home Mission Society, that the time would come when the Negroes would be able to do their own missionary and educational work. Personally, I believe most firmly in individualism, in church independency, in self-help, in manhood under whatever guise it appears. I have rejoiced at all manifestations among you of a spirit of self-reliance. It would afford me personally inexpressible pleasure if I could feel that the time had so speedily come when the Negro Baptists of this country could not only do their own missionary and educational work, but could lend a hand to their unfortunate brethren in Africa and in other benighted regions. In view, however, of the magnitude of the work and of the enormous financial burden which it involves, we have not felt that it would be wise to throw prematurely upon a people inexperienced and still impoverished, such responsibility. I am not sanguine enough to believe that the time has come for your convention to do more than make a beginning in this great work, but I hope the time has come for that.

Meanwhile the work of the American Baptist Home Mission Society has extended so as to embrace Puerto Rico and Eastern Cuba on the east and Alaska on the west; the vast throngs of immigrants from the old world are still pouring into the country and their religious needs appeal powerfully to the Society for missionary work among them; the religious condition of our great cities is forcing upon the Society year by year the consideration of its duty with reference to these centers of population. The needs of our work outrun our resources.

THE NATIONAL CONVENTION.

In view of these circumstances, it seems to me--and to my associates--that probably the time has come when we should ask the National Convention to assume a portion at least of the burden of missionary and educational work among your people.

First. Missionary Work: Chiefly from the lack of funds the Society is now doing no missionary work in Maryland, the District of Columbia and Western Virginia on the east, nor in Alabama, Mississippi, Florida, Louisiana and Texas on the south. Here is a vast field where a great missionary work ought to be in progress, and which is now being largely neglected, except such work as is being done by local organizations. The brethren in these States need the counsel, encouragement and help which ought to come to them through the aid of a great central organization. May I ask whether it might not be agreeable for the Society which you represent to undertake missionary work in the States named? If you feel that the work is too vast, too difficult, too costly for your body to undertake it all at once, could you not at least take a portion of it, and as you grow in strength and experience extend your operations further and further? Or, if by chance you should feel that the work suggested to you is not extensive enough, which I can hardly think probable, I think I am safe in saying that the American Baptist Home Mission Society will be very glad to relinquish to you other fields just so far and so fast as you are prepared to assume the responsibility of caring for them.

I strongly feel that the home missionary work here proposed to you is large in extent, important in character and urgent in its demands; and it ought to appeal, it seems to me, very strongly to you and your associates in the National Convention. I assure you that the officers of the Society will be very glad to give you any possible help by way of suggestions growing out of the Society's experience in such work for nearly forty years as you may desire to have.

Second. As to the Educational Work: The American Baptist Home Mission Society is concentrating its educational work chiefly on a few great centers--Richmond, Raleigh, Columbia, Atlanta, Nashville, Jackson and Marshall--where it has established and maintained magnificent institutions of learning which are growing year by year in efficiency, and which, having already accomplished a splendid service, are destined as the decades go by to do more and more in the preparation of noble men and women for leadership in the various walks of life. These schools, already very costly, are demanding year by year increasing expenditures, and if they are to endure and accomplish the full measure of their service, they must be liberally endowed. We have reason to hope and believe that in due course of time the patrons of the Home Mission Society who have already indicated so deep an interest in this work will, in response to our appeals, endow these institutions. We can hardly feel that your people in their present circumstances ought to undertake this stupendous work. Not less than $2,000,000 of endowment will suffice to properly care for and meet the needs of the institutions which I have mentioned. It is an open question still whether even the Society will be able to secure so large an amount. I am very certain that it cannot secure it unless it retains its responsibility for their management and continues to enjoy the confidence of its constituency. Any radical change in the management of these schools would necessarily tend to shake that confidence and to interrupt that flow of liberal contributions which is now the hope of these institutions. I feel, therefore, that it would be an act of unkindness to even suggest to you that your convention should assume the burden of supporting and endowing these central institutions. So long as the Society bears the financial burden it must be responsible for their administration.

There are, however, a number of important schools which are now owned and controlled absolutely by your people, having Negro Boards of Trustees and Negro Faculties, which the Society is aiding year by year as liberally as its funds will allow. It perhaps would be asking too much of your convention to ask you to assume the full oversight and care of even these schools. Most if not all of them are heavily in debt; none of them are properly equipped with buildings, libraries or apparatus and none of them have any endowments. Each of them requires more teachers and larger salaries, if they are to do satisfactory work. If your convention should undertake the entire supervision and nurture of these schools, it would become involved at once in a very heavy outlay and it might not find it easy to secure the money needed; and then, also, it is possible that some of the schools which have been so long under the care and fostering hand of the Home Mission Society would prefer to still look to it for superintendence, counsel and financial aid. I think I can assure you that so far as this Society is concerned it would be very glad to relinquish at once to your convention the entire oversight, support and endowment of these institutions.

There are also a number of schools--one in Virginia, one in Georgia, at least two in Texas, two in Mississippi, one in Arkansas and probably others--which are receiving no aid from the Society and to which the Society cannot extend aid.

PLAN SUGGESTED.

May I then be allowed to ask if it would not be possible for your convention to undertake educational work along some one or more of the following lines: (1) Could it not assume the superintendence and financial aid of any worthy schools now existing which at present are receiving no aid from this Society? (2) Could it not encourage the founding of other similar schools in regions where they are very greatly needed, and where none at present exist? (3) If this should not afford sufficient scope for your present resources, can you not aid those schools now under Negro control--such as the universities at Louisville and Selma, the colleges at Little Rock and Macon, and the academies and lower schools elsewhere that are so greatly in need of financial aid? (a) In the payment of their debts; (b) in the enlargement of their equipments; (c) in the increase of their faculties; (d) in the accumulation of endowments. It is asking a great deal of you even to consider so herculean a task as this, but possibly the magnitude of the burden might stimulate the host of Negro Baptists to some conception of their might if it were properly used. (4) There is still another line of work which I think might wisely be considered, and that is the raising of a fund year by year of several thousand dollars to be used in aiding worthy students, either by gift or loan, in prosecuting their studies. There are thousands of Negro young men and young women not in school to-day who would be there, doubtless, if they could have a little pecuniary assistance. There are numerous educational societies in the North, some of them covering a wide range of territory, engaged in this laudable work of providing beneficiary aid to students. This is a field almost wholly unoccupied among your people in the South.

If your convention is willing to undertake this educational work as suggested, either wholly or partially, you may feel very sure that the Home Mission Society will not only not stand in your way, but will surrender to you just as fast as you are able to assume the responsibility, all the educational work that you can possibly accomplish.

UNITED BUT INDEPENDENT WORK.

As I look upon the problem of religious destitution among your people and the urgent call for increased missionary and educational work in order that they may be prepared for the fierce conflicts of twentieth century life in America, I tremble for the future. It is one that calls for a united effort on the part of every lover of Christ, every friend of humanity and every patriot. As to the method of doing this work, let me say:

- 1. At present a large portion of it is being neglected, and as the Home Mission Society is unable for the lack of funds to include this work unless your convention comes to the rescue--so far as I can see--it will go undone, and multitudes of your people will perish in their sins or remain in ignorance and superstition for the lack of that friendly aid that might be extended to them by your convention. We can hardly feel that you will be satisfied with inaction and apathy in view of so urgent a call.
- 2. I can hardly believe that the need will be met by local zeal and liberality; there seems to be an urgent demand for that aid that can be given only through some great national organization; heretofore the Home Mission Society has been seeking to co-operate with State conventions and other local organizations because there did not seem to be in the field any great central national organization among you which was quite prepared to undertake the work.
- 3. In the present state of public sentiment among your people, particularly as voiced by a few men who seem to be held in high repute, with regard to the work of the American Baptist Home Mission Society, I do not feel warranted in even suggesting to you any form of co-operation between the National Convention and this Society.
- 4. I have therefore ventured to suggest to you that you undertake independent work, with the conviction that you will find the task growing upon your hands more rapidly even than you will find money with which to carry it on. But you can make a beginning, and undoubtedly accomplish a great deal for those for whom you labor, as well as for those of you who assume the burden of responsibility.
- 5. I think I may say for the Society, that while it would be glad to be relieved of the tremendous burden of this work, in order that it might give its strength and money to the West and to the cities, as well as to the islands of the sea; nevertheless the Society, I believe, will be willing, and even glad, to continue to render financial aid in the prosecution of the work which I have suggested to you--at least during its incipiency.

Sermons, Addresses and Reminiscences and Important Correspondence

I wish you would give this matter careful and prayerful consideration, and tell me how it presents itself to your mind. If the matter approves itself to your judgment and conscience, I shall be glad to bring it before the Executive Board of the American Baptist Home Mission Society for such formal action in the premises as may seem to the Board wise. What I have said is only in the way of suggestion. If it does not commend itself to your judgment, will you kindly outline such a scheme of new missionary and educational work, in addition to what it is now doing, as you think your convention would like to undertake, and also indicate the relation which the convention would like to have this Society assume toward it.

In conclusion, allow me to say that for several years the officers of the Home Mission Society have been zealously laboring, with some degree of success, to promote the largest co-operation between all branches, white and colored, North and South, of the great Baptist family, in behalf of missionary and educational work among your people. I am firmly persuaded that, perhaps, on the whole, this is the wisest policy to be followed, and I believe that if it could be fully understood by your people it would command their support; but the policy seems to be misunderstood, and the Society is subjected to criticism and the work is hindered. It is with a view of removing any possible cause of friction between any considerable body of intelligent men among you and the Home Mission Society that the above proposition is submitted to you. We are brethren of a common faith, children of the same Father, folowers of the same Christ, and having before us the same great high and noble purpose, and animated by the same Christian motives. There should be no difference between us; no antagonism. The Society which I represent seeks only to promote the Redeemer's Kingdom and to render that help to your people which they need and desire, and I trust that there may be such an understanding between the people represented by your organization and those represented by this, and there shall be, if not co-operation, at least harmony and friendliness in independent work.

Hoping to hear from you at an early day, I am.

Fraternally yours,

(Signed) T. J. MORGAN, Corresponding Secretary.

Helena, Ark., February 9th, 1900.
Rev. T. J. Morgan, LL. D., Corresponding Secretary American
Baptist Home Mission Society,
111 Fifth Avenue, New York City.

Dear Brother:--Your esteemed letter of the 5th instant, reviewing the work of the American Baptist Home Mission Society, and suggesting plans for the further conduct of the work by it and the National Baptist Convention, is now before me.

In reply to same would say that I have read it with deep solicitude and care, and unhesitatingly subscribe to all you say relative to the great work of the Society among the Negroes for nearly forty years of the past. It is hardly possible to do justice in words to the very marvelous work of love which has been accomplished by the Society for the Negroes of this country. The best evidences are in the men and women who have been trained in the schools supported by it. It is a well known fact that a large per cent of the literary and religious advancement of the race is due to the philanthropic deeds of Northern friends, which aid has been conveyed through such channels as the Home Mission Society. The Negroes know this, and are, without an exception, thankful for all that has been done in their behalf.

A very noteworthy change has come about in the last forty years. Indeed, a new generation is now upon the stage, many of whom have had excellent advantages, and much of those advantages came through the American Baptist Home Mission Society as one of the Lord's instrumentalities in lifting up a race which had been so long in bondage. And the fact that schools have been founded and supported for that race accounts, in a great measure, for the material prosperity of the race, which I think, when reported by the eleventh census, will astonish the civilized world. But, notwithstanding that the race has made great progress in the accumulation of homes and other property, it is far from being able to assume the entire responsibility of supporting the educational and missionary work necessary for the continued advancement of the Negro Baptist family, which, in all probability, will number nearly 2,000,000 by the close of the century. I too, would be exceedingly glad if the day had come when the Negro Baptists were able to maintain all the schools and missionary work among them, and then to show their deep gratitude to those who had helped them by helping others. As for self-help in relation to the question: (1) experience has taught that only those who attempt to help themselves ever become men of determined, consecrated will, capable of planning and executing noble purposes in life; (2) it is, indeed, in my opinion, a runious thing for another to help a man or a set of men wherein his or their self-help will suffice the purpose desired; and just in proportion as the more unfortunate are unable to provide themselves with the necessary means for their progress, should they be assisted by others able to render the assistance.

Now, as to the reference made in your letter to the National Baptist Convention, would say that I speak only as an individual, and express myself freely and conscientiously upon the matters which have greatly agitated some of our people and perhaps some of the friends of the Society at the North. You say that you are "not sanguine enough to believe that the time has come for your (National Baptist) convention to do more than make a beginning in this great work, but I hope the time has come for that." In view of the strained relations which has existed between the American Baptist Home Mission Society and some of the local or State organizations, one would infer that you believe that the National Baptist Convention is in some way responsible for the friction existing. I wish to say that the National Baptist Convention has not at any time or in any way desired to antagonize the educational or missionary work of the American Baptist Home Mission Society, and does not dersire to do so, so far as my knowledge of its purposes extends. I think that the policy and objects of the National Baptist Convention have been greatly misunderstood.

The constitution of the Convention, like that of the Society which you so ably represent, clearly sets forth the object of the Convention. Hitherto the Missonary efforts have been confined to the preaching of the Gospel in Africa Cuba and a few stations in the United States of America. It has not sought to enter any field already supplied. It has not attempted to do any educational work except to adopt plans looking to the establishment of a national university somewhere in the United States. It has also undertaken to do a publication work which has proved to be a wise experiment and a marvelous success. What you say about the large number of immigrants pouring into the country from the old world is a matter which we have given some consideration, but the Convention has not as yet felt itself able to contribute to the very deserving and urgent needs of these new comers without impairing the work already begun by it. I am sure that should your Board ask the National Baptist Convention to assume a portion of the burden of carrying on the missionary and educational work of the Society, it would be given the consideration and respect that such a proposition deserves. But I would give it as an individual opinion that the Convention would not be justified in assuming the responsibilities outlined in your letter. In the States which you name and in which you say the Society is doing no missionary work, and yet "a vast field where a great deal of missionary work ought to be in progress," and in answer to the question, if it might not be agreeable for the Society which I represent to undertake missionary work in the States named, would say, individually, I am of the opinion that with the possible exception of one of the States named, the people of those States are fully able to support their own missionaries. They perhaps could not properly support their educational institutions. But these, like all other educational institutions, should have access to and the notice of (through regularly organized channels) the philanthropists of the North and East.

If the Negroes of the South are in need of help in their educational work--and they are--and the Home Mission Society is to assume a part of that work, and the National Baptist Convention a part, and the money for the support of these is to be given by the friends of the Negroes at the North, then each of these societies should stand in the same relation to these friends. But I do not deem such a course advisable or desirable, for I have implicit confidence in the management of the Home Mission Society, and would much prefer that it continue its work as now constituted, and that the Negro Baptists foster the work which they have constituted, and as they become able, enlarge their work, which will be augmented by the aid of the Home Mission Society. In thirty years more, perhaps the local State organizations will be able to assume further responsibility of caring for the work. I repeat here that in the States named, with proper organization, there is a sufficient number of Negro Baptists to give enough for effective missionary work.

I do not question the wisdom of the Society in concentrating its educational operations at Richmond, Raleigh, Columbia, Atlanta, Nashville, Jackson and Marshall, but it seems to me that it would be a serious mistake if the Society should decide to devote its entire efforts at Negro education at the centers. I think a better plan would be to continue to support all the schools now owned by it and help as many more owned by the Negroes as its resources will permit.

NO CHANGE OF METHOD ASKED FOR.

I hope you will not believe for a single moment that the National Baptist Convention is asking for a change in the management of the Home Mission schools. If any such demands have been made, they are local and do not represent the National Baptist Convention. The Negro Baptists form a large percentage of the constituency of the American Baptist Home Mission Society, and I know of no demand for a change of the management of the schools, except from a few individuals. I firmly believe that the Negro Baptists ought to build and support schools of their own. Such a course is necessary for their liberal development in educational matters. But there should be no friction between them and the Home Mission Schools, and in those States where the Negroes own and operate schools I think that the entire people should be encouraged to give their financial aid to said institutions, by both the Home Mission Society and the State organization, while the better equipped schools should receive the moral support of all State organizations.

The schools now owned and controlled by the Negro Baptists are the best evidences of what the Negro is capable of doing for himself. As a matter of course, they are not equal in many respects to the Home Mission schools, but they are the unmistakable evidences of the progress of the race, and should be given aid and encouragement from all Baptist Societies.

I need not take up the matter of the National Convention's assuming jurisdiction of the schools referred to in your letter in this wise as I have already stated about the scope of the Convention's work, except to say that these schools ought to and can get a liberal aid from their respective States. You perhaps know that the National Baptist Convention has not appealed to its Northern friends for aid in educational or missionary work, and would have no just cause to do so as long as the work is so succesfully carried on by the Home Mission Society. I feel justified in making the statement, however, that the Convention would look with favor upon any proposition made to it by the Home Mission Society to render aid in the settlement of any local differences that may exist between the Society and the Negroes in their educational work. I feel fully impressed with the great responsibilities which will engage the best thought of our leading men in preparing the vast army of Baptists to meet the demands of the twentieth century. I agree with the sentiment that the exigencies of the hour call for a concentration of the efforts of every lover of Christ and every friend of humanity. And this condition will come about when the respective societies fully understand one another.

FRATERNAL RELATIONS.

The reference which you make to a "few men," and who, you seem to think, voice the sentiment of the Negro Baptists, I respond to thus: The voice of those "few men" is only the voice of those few men, and perhaps represents the local sentiment where they live. While I heartily approve of the desire of Negroes to own and control enterprises of their planting and have given encouragement to such, I do not think it at all necessary that the operation of such enterprises should be a means of strained or unfriendly relations between the friends of such and the American Baptist Home Mission Society. Indeed, my dear sir, when all the efforts of the Negroes have been exerted in their own behalf, and the great societies of the North have done all they can to help them, there will still be much more to be done. You say you would like for me to indicate the relation which the Convention would like to have the Society assume to it. If the foregoing does not fully set forth an answer, I would say that we could not ask it to assume any other relation than that which it sustains to all the great Baptist organizations. As to the matter of co-operation, I have frequently expressed myself as being favorable to such a scheme. But I am not sure that I could fully approve the plans as they now exist, and am not competent to give a definite opinion, as I have not observed the plans in practical operation, except in so far as we have co-operation in the payment of teachers' salaries in this State, and that has proved very satisfactory. But I would suggest that if the Society desires to continue its plan of co-operation in the South a conference of the leaders in all those states to be affected by the plan be called at some central point, and let them and the Society's representatives agree upon such plan as all can heartily subscribe to.

In conclusion, I wish to say that I very much appreciate the free and open manner in which you write upon these matters which are of vital interest to me and my people. And I assure you again that there is no antagonistic spirit in the National Baptist Convention against the American Baptist Home Mission Society. We are, indeed, brethren of one common faith, and our destiny is one: and I am thankful to Almighty God for what He hath done through such instrumentalities as your great Society for me and my people. Moreover, I shall endeavor to work for harmony and friendship between all existing Baptist organizations North and South.

With very best wishes for your continued prosperity in the great work intrusted to your care, I am

Very truly yours,

E. C. MORRIS.

[From "The Christian Banner," Philadelphia, Pa.]

Last week we published the letter of Dr. Morgan to Dr. E. C. Morris. This week we publish Dr. Morris' reply to this letter. The reply speaks for itself and will be read with interest by the many readers of the "Banner." The letter will do much good in helping to bring about a better understanding between the Home Mission Society and Negro Baptists. We are sure that there is not much consolation in Dr. Morris' letter for the few extremists in our Baptist ranks, and down in their hearts they are disagreeing with him, but the great majority of Negro Baptists agree with him almost in full. It is very fortunate for the National Baptist Convention to have such a man as Dr. Morris as its President at this time when men in our ranks are making war on all who don't agree with them in fighting the very agency and men who have helped to make the way for the liberty, education and the great progress of the race along all lines. We can hope for a peaceful and amicable settlement of all differences in our ranks and the removing of all misunderstandings between Negro and white Baptists with such men as Dr. Morris at the head of affairs.

Palestine, Tex., October, 1896.
Rev. E. C. Morris, D. D.,
President National Baptist Convention,
Helena, Ark.

Dear Brother:--I am now planning to meet our Home Mission Board on the 6th of November, at Little Rock, Ark. I have been very busy ever since the adjournment of our Convention at St. Louis trying to get matters in shape so that I might devote my whole time to the work of the Home Board. I have not had much encouragement; in fact, I have been advised by friends that the step which I am about to make is a very dangerous one, and that I would not be able to get a support out of the work of the Home Mission Board. But since I have accepted to assume the responsibilities of the office of Secretary, I am willing to lay my life on the altar for the success of the enterprise which we are about to undertake. You are aware that you have been chosen as editor in chief, and I would suggest that you begin to look over the country to select a competent staff. I shall expect you also to see what arrangements you can make with any publishing house to do our work, as it will perhaps be some time before we can do it ourselves. I am in correspondence with a few publishing houses which have made bids upon the work as I have outlined it to them, that will be an agreeable surprise to you. Please write to Brother Gaines and have him get every thing ready for the meeting on the 6th.

Yours,

R. H. BOYD.

Helena, Arkansas, October 13, 1896.
R. H. Boyd, D. D.,
Palestine, Texas.

Dear Brother:--Your esteemed favor of recent date is now before me and has been read with pleasure. In reply to same would say that I am glad to find you so sanguine of success in the matter of our proposed publishing house. I have not receded one iota from the position occupied four years ago upon this question. Indeed, my faith in the justice and ultimate success of such an enterprise grows stronger each day.

In the matter of correspondence looking to some kind of arrangement with those publishing houses already established, would say that I wrote Dr. C. O. Boothe several days ago and requested him to write Dr. Rowland and ascertain what arrangements could be made with the Publication Society. Dr. Boothe wrote Dr. Rowland, and I have the letter's reply which came in to-day's mail. I am sorry to say that he does not speak favorably of the arrangements which we had hoped could be made with the Society; and Dr. Boothe seems to have weakened in that he suggests that a conference of the leaders be held before any further steps be taken. While I have great respect for the opinions of both the brethren named, we cannot afford to be influenced by such suggestions. Our duty is plain: it is to get out a series of Sunday school matter by January 1st, 1897. This duty has been imposed by the National Baptist Convention, and cannot be set aside by us or even by the Home Mission Board. I have but one regret in connection with this work and that is, that the Board chose me to be the editor of the periodicals to be issued. Under ordinary circumstances, I would by no means accept the position; but since it is dangerous to "swap horses in the midst of the stream," I will hold on this year, at least. You need have no fears about a support, or what the outcome of the enterprise will be. Of the million and half Negro Baptists in this country, enough of them will be found favorable to the movement to give a ready support to our publishing concern and insure success from the beginning. I have great faith in my people, and as great patience with their imperfections, and am sure that God is in this movement and will keep it and those who foster it. God willing I will meet you at Little Rock on the 6th prox.

Very truly yours,

E. C. MORRIS.

"DR. E. C. MORRIS FAVORS THE NEGRO PUBLISHING HOUSE PROJECT."

Editor "Christian Banner:"

It cannot be other than interesting to read the discussion going on in the "Christian Banner" among such men as Drs. Phillips, Rowland and Johnson, and also the strong editorial comments on these discussions. It is not my object to get into this discussion by writing this letter; but simply to express an opinion as one of the interested parties. The subject is not one which was sprung a few days ago. It has been a matter before the National Baptist Convention for several years. In 1893, I had the distinguished honor of being appointed to read a papaer before that august assembly in the city of Washington, D. C., upon "The Demand for a Negro Baptist Publishing House." Judging from the hearty approval given to the ideas there advanced, there is doubt in my mind that such an enterprise is sure to be set on foot in the near future. I believe that most of the prominent leaders among us are in sympathy with the movement; but none of them are willing to disturb the peaceful relations that exist between us and the white Baptists of the country. Therefore, they are "making haste slowly." There are a great many "calamity-howlers" among us--men with pessimistic views, who cannot see anything but destruction in such a movement; hence, much patience must be exercised in order to convince them that we do not mean to pull down our neighbor's fence by splitting rails to build one around our little farm. There will be sure to come some competition between our work and that of our neighbor; but competition is not opposition, and our white brethren will not so regard it when they see the fruits of such an enterprise. In arguing this question before the

National Convention, we took the ground that such an enterprise was needed for race employment.

It cannot be successfully denied that some of the ablest and most scholarly men among us are forced to occupy very menial positions or seek employment in some other field, by reasons of the fact that they cannot get the employment to which their attainments entitle them. We must begin to set a premium on our church connection, and show to the world that while it costs something materially to be a Baptist, it is worth something materially to be a Baptist. We are in duty bound to show to the thousands of young people who are yearly crowding into our churches, that we will at least reciprocate their confidence by preparing a way by which they may learn how to become bookmakers, clerks, superintendents, managers, etc. What greater heritage can we leave our children than the well-laid plans of an enterprise that will give employment to hundreds of the best young men and women in the denomination? This matter however, cannot be accomplished in a year, nor in half a dozen years; but the foundation may be laid by this generation and the building erected by the next.

Dr. Phillips in a letter referring to your editorial says, "The spirit of your editorial is right. I agree with all you say;" and then adds, "I believe it a waste of time, and will be for some time to come;" thereby expressing a doubt as to the success of such a course. I cannot understand how that time spent in doing a thing that is right can be wasted. As a matter of course, we cannot hope to be able to compete successfully with societies of ripe experience in any short time. But our people will not be able to criticise the books of others until they learn to write and critcise their own productions. I do not wish to go on record as favoring the establishment of a publication society on the ground that we are getting the proper recognition; but on the ground that such an enterprise is needed for race employment, race development, a bequest to our posterity and as a business enterprise.

I have no unkind words for the American Baptist Publication Society, for all are agreed that it is one of the greatest religious organizations in the world. But the birth of another such society will not cause it to die or famish. The wonderful sacrifices which this great friend has made for the intellectual advancement of the race is a legacy left us by them, with the understanding, no doubt, that we would not always be begging for alms. If any have been healed, let them arise and go forward and help others. If the Publication Society has made mistakes, they have only done what we are sure to do.

Dr. Rowland, in his letter replying to Dr. Phillips, attempts to show that the Society is doing the best it can do for the colored people. No one is in a better position to know this than Dr. Rowland; and yet this is not a reason why we should not attempt to do something for ourselves. As to the amount of money spent annually with the Society by the colored Baptists, that cuts no figure in the matter under discussion. I admit that the Society's interest would be fostered by a broader recognition of our leading men, and that it would be simple justice to place some of the branch houses under the management of competent Negro Baptists; but all of this will not supplant the necessity for a publishing house by the Negroes themselves. The absolute necessity for such an enterprise will remain so long as there is such a thing in this country as our "colored brethren." We admit that our Publication Society has not been as ready to recognize merit and ability in the colored Baptists as our Home Mission Society; for they have half a dozen Negro presidents in their colleges and no doubt would gladly put in others if the conditions required it. And so far as I have been able to learn, the results are as satisfactory as those under white presidents.

But in any event let us have peace. Let us go forward and build up new enterprises, being careful not to overburden ourselves, avoiding, by all means, entangling alliances with all other Christian organizations. I have implicit confidence in the great Negro Baptist family in this country, and believe that all the money needed to foster such an enterprise will be forthcoming as soon as the plans are properly laid.

Very truly yours,

E. C. MORRIS.

Helena, Ark., Jan. 27, 1895.

Raleigh, N. C., June 7th, 1901.
Rev. E. C. Morris, D. D.,
Helena, Ark.

Dear Brother:--I found it not possible to come to Memphis at the time I had hoped, and hence could not come to see you much to my regret. I send you herewith for your consideration some articles of co-operation I wish to suggest to you. Of course some one must make the start, and I am sure I should like to see such approved; and I for my part, and also the Society, will do as we agree. These articles will meet the approval of our Society. Will you kindly let me know whether you approve same. Is it not possible for us to cast aside little differences and work in closer co-operation?

Your truly,

S. N. VASS.

- 1. That the Publication Society and the National Baptist Publishing Board each continue to publish literature as at present.
- 2. That nothing be said or done or intimated by the representatives of either that will reflect upon the other, or prejudice the people against either, whether through correspondence or in public addresses, but that each adhere to the policy of presenting its own claims upon merit and resting the case with the people.
- 3. That the next session of the National Baptist Convention adopt a resolution similar to the one long ago passed by our white brethren of the Southern Baptist Convention, in which the Convention will pledge itself not to regard as disloyal to the Convention those organizations among Negro Baptists that still use the literature and books of the Publication Society, and observe its fixed missionary and Bible days.
- 4. That the National Convention also recommend each local district, State and General Baptist organization to adopt in good faith a similar resolution throughout the entire country.
- 5. That at our national, state and district and local gatherings, the Convention recommend that equal time and opportunity be allowed the representatives of both the Publication Society and the National Baptist Publishing Board to lay their cause fairly before the people.
- 6. That upon the ratification of these articles of agreement in their present form or in such shape as can be mutually agreed upon, that the parties to the compact be requested to affix their official signatures as evidence of good faith, *i. e.,* the Secretaries of the Publication Society and the Board.

Helena, Ark., June 10th, 1901.
Rev. S. N. Vass, D. D., District Secretary American Baptist Publication Society, Raleigh, N. C.

Dear Brother:--This letter will acknowledge receipt of yours of the 7th inst., in which you enclose a series of suggestive resolutions, setting forth your idea of a suitable plan by which the American Baptist Publication Society and the Publishing Department of the Home Mission Board of the National Baptist

Convention might enter into co-operation, to which I would say that I cannot speak for our Home Mission Board in this matter without an unpardonable assumption on my part. Hence, whatever I may here say may be taken only to represent my personal views:

To the first suggestion, would say that the two societies will doubtless continue to publish literature as at present, since there is no visible sign that they will do otherwise.

To the second: I deny that anything has ever been said by any person authorized to represent our Board, against the good name of the American Baptist Publication Society. But to the reverse, it has always been held up by our representatives as one of the great Baptist societies of the world. I admit, however, that much has been said concerning persons who have misrepresented the Publication Society; and yet, in every case of which I know, it was a statement of facts to rebut these misrepresentations. Hence, when the war on our Board ceases, there will be nothing but the kindliest brotherly feeling toward the Society by the Negro Baptists of the country.

To the Third: In view of the past efforts of the Publication Society's representatives on the field at the disintegration of the National Baptist Convention, and believing as I do that the National

Page 174

Baptist Convention is a necessity for the development of the Negro Baptist Christians, I could not consent to give any influence to a resolution which would accomplish the very thing that the Publication Society's representatives have tried to do but failed. Then, again, there is a very appreciable difference between the relation which the Southern Baptist Convention sustained to the American Baptist Publication Society at the time that resolution to which you refer was adopted and the relation which the National Baptist Convention sustains to the American Baptist Publication Society. Would say, also, that for the National Baptist Convention to assume by resolution or otherwise to instruct or advise those Negro Baptist Churches which do not affiliate with the Convention, would be a repudiation of your idea expressed some time ago of the New Testament teaching of church independence, and no one believes more than I do in that teaching.

To the Fourth. Here may be applied all that is said with reference to the third suggestion, and also may be added the following quotation from Scripture: "Study to be quiet, and to do your own business."

To the Fifth. Until some better and more modified connection of amity has been effected by the action of the official Boards of the two societies, I cannot see that our society can do other than recommend that your society's representatives be accorded the same courtesies shown all other fraternal messengers. Beyond that, I do not see what cause these representatives should seek to have in our meetings.

To the Sixth. Since I do not agree to any of the foregoing suggestions made in your draft of resolutions, there need be no reply to the sixth.

Referring to the last paragraph in your letter, would say that I think it is possible to "set aside the little differences and work in closer co-operation," but not upon the series of resolutions which you suggest to be passed by the National Baptist Convention which is only one involuntary party to the difference. And the co-operation in which I believe will be accomplished only by the simple will and act of setting aside the unprofitable differences and each of the organizations in question attending strictly to its own affairs. For, in my opinion, each performing faithfully and well the work in his own sphere will be co-operating to duty's extent in advancing the Master's kingdom.

BIOGRAPHICAL SKETCH.

[Written for the "Preachers' Magazine" by R. M. Caver.]

E. C. Morris, D. D., was born in Murray County, Ga., May 7, 1855. He, as well as his parents, was a slave and remained in bondage until liberated by the success of the Union arms over the Confederate. His first breath of freedom was drawn in May, 1864, when, with his parents, he left the old plantation and moved to Dalton, Ga., a distance of eight miles. He received only a common school education, owing to the fact that his father died before he reached his majority, but by close and careful study at home and the observation of current affairs, his storehouse of information is such as very few men of his advantages have. He was converted and entered upon the work of the Gospel ministry in 1874. In the year 1877, he moved to Helena, Ark., his present place of residence. He accepted the degree of Doctor of Divinity conferred by the faculty of State University, Louisville, Ky.

Dr. Morris is noted for his ability to organize and to direct in matters of public concern, and his advice is ardently sought by all his constituency. He has organized educational, missionary, and literary publishing interests. In 1884, he organized and set in motion what is now the Arkansas Baptist College, an institution which is the pride of the people of the State. For sixteen years he has been chairman of the Board of Trustees of the above-named institution. One of the highest positions which Dr. Morris holds is that of President of the National Baptist Convention, the largest deliberative body of Negroes in the world. He has filled this position continually since 1894. He is also editor in chief of "The Convention Teacher."

He was called to the pastorate of the Centennial Baptist Church, of Helena, Ark., in 1879, and has held that position down to the present day. He is held in the highest esteem by the people of his community, both white and black, and is a great help to his people even in the way of business advice, and partly in consequence of this the colored people of his community are of the thriftiest class.

He is earnest, decisive and unassuming. He realizes that he is a public servant, that leadership is a task, and proceeds with the conviction that it is a duty to him just as following is a duty to many.

BIOGRAPHICAL AND OTHERWISE.

BY THE AUTHOR.

My public career began twenty-five years ago, with my election to the pastorate of the Centennial Baptist Church of Helena, Ark. At that time I was only twenty-one years of age, and the church had a membership of twenty-five. When quite young, my highest ambition was to be pastor of some good church, and beyond that I had no desire for leadership or prominence. But by the uncompromising determination of the people hitherto, it has been impossible to evade the task of leadership in nearly all things with which it has been my privilege to be personally connected. Shortly after the beginning of my pastoral career, the demand for an associational organization of the Baptist churches in the section where was located the faithful little flock over the which the Holy Ghost had made me overseer, was imperative.

Strange as it was, all eyes seemed to rivet upon the humble pastor of Centennial Baptist Church for leadership in this matter of associational organization. With a desire to please my Heavenly Father and to advance his kingdom on earth, I consented to do the best I could with the aid of a few devout brethren who had determined upon such an organization. In obedience to the popular command, we went to work and organized what is known as the Phillips, Lee and Monroe County Baptist Association, and for twenty-two years the brethren composing this grand body have unanimously looked for counsel or advice in all the work of the association, to the same humble source to which they looked in the beginning of the organization of that body. It may be said to the credit of this association that it is, perhaps, the only one in the United States that requires the churches each year to send up money for Home and Foreign Missions, for educational work and all the other work of the denomination. It is indeed and in truth a missionary organization.

My first meeting with the Baptist State Convention of Arkansas was in 1880, and at this session of the Convention I was chosen as Secretary and was re-elected the following year; but in 1882, I was chosen President of the Convention and have been kept in that position for nineteen consecutive years. One of the most satisfactory and highly valuable legacies to the claim of the writer is that he enjoys the confidence and esteem of all the Baptists of the State. At the time of my election to the Presidency of the Arkansas Baptist State Convention, there was a membership in the State of only thirty thousand, and there was not a single educational institution in the state operated by colored Baptists. But now they have a membership of seventy thousand, five high schools and one college. The college is located at Little Rock, the capital of the State, and stands second to no school for the training of the colored youth of the South. The denomination in the State has also a printing plant worth five thousand dollars and sends out a weekly paper (now the "Baptist Vanguard," but formerly the "Arkansas Times"), which is equal to the best denominational journal in the country. The management and editing of this paper started nineteen years ago, was the first effort of the writer at journalism. In attempting to found and build the Arkansas Baptist College, we were not ignorant of the fact that the task was a weighty one, and knew that for awhile it would seem unavailing toward the great end before us. But my cohorts and I relying upon the truth and spirit of the adage, "Where there is a will there is a way," proceeded with a view of spending a lifetime at the great task, not expecting to live long enough to see even the main building of the institution completed, but rather urged our associates and followers that we would do a marvelous work to buy and pay for the ground and lay the foundation of a great school out of our scanty means for the next following generation to build upon. Unlike most of our people who have built up educational institutions since the Civil War, we decided that instead of begging the means from the good white people of the North, who had given so much for like causes, we would endeavor to buy and build from the means given by our own people, thereby giving ourselves a practical knowledge of such a work and that would be an inspiration to those who are to follow. And in a large measure we have succeeded, having received only one thousand dollars from the American Baptist Home Mission Society for building purposes. It is due that Society, however, to say that it has been our constant friend and has given each year liberally to aid our Board in paying teachers' salaries. The amount of work which was laid out to do in fifty years has been done in seventeen, and now, from past demonstrations, the comparatively few Baptists in our State Convention challenge the colored Baptists of any State in the Union to compete with them in the amount of work accomplished each year for the denomination at home and abroad. But these great accomplishments are not the work of any one man or two, but are the result of united action on the part of the leaders all over the State.

During the first years of my pastoral life, very close attention was given to the local work of the church, and every interest of the people, so far as could be known, was carefully studied and looked after until the entire congregation became to look to the pastor for advice in all matters of a public character. No concern was ever felt about a support by this pastor; but having looked after their every interest, the church in turn looked after his. This church is one of the strongest in the State, and agrees each year to give as much for the various causes of missions and education as is necessary to sustain a competent pastor. The church having succeeded in coming up to be one of the foremost in the state under my pastoral guardianship, and having been chosen President of the State Convention. I felt that no expression of higher regard remained for me, and there was no desire on my part for greater notoriety. But the Lord willed that I should labor on, and in this light have all the public expressions of confidence reposed in me been received. Hence, in 1894, when our National Conventions were assembled at Montgomery, Ala., the presidency of the Foreign Mission Convention of the United States was placed upon me. The work of the Convention had almost ceased to receive the hearty support of the churches, and it was with a feeling of reluctance mingled with humility, that I yielded to the insistence of the brethren to accept the position of President, which had been tendered by an almost unanimous vote, and, indeed, was only influenced to take up such responsibility with the understanding that I would not be required to continue in said position after the first year. The entire time between the meeting at Montgomery, in 1894, and the one at Atlanta, in 1895, was devoted to the reorganization of the work. In this effort, the officers of the Convention had, as in other matters, the hearty co-operation of our brethren.

The meetings at Atlanta, in 1895, merged all the Baptist organizations into one Convention to be known as the National Baptist Convention. At this time I was again called to the presidency of the consolidated body and have been re-elected each year since that time, although contrary to my expressed intention, and accepted the position more as a duty than an honor. The plan adopted by the Convention, by which the work of the denomination was to be conducted by Boards, originated in the same minds which conceived the idea of the great National Convention and has proven a wonderful success. While the president has been only ex officio connected with the Boards which sprang into existence at the time of the Atlanta consolidation, he has devoted most of his time to the work which they represent. He has been officially connected with the Publishing Board since its organization, as editor of the Convention series of periodicals. Indeed, long before the colored Baptists had undertaken to do a publishing business, he advocated in public and in private the establishment of such an enterprise. With that end in view, he was appointed to read a paper before the National Convention which met in Washington, D. C., in 1893, which paper was ordered published and distributed.

When the plans were being laid to carry out the order of the National Baptist Convention respecting the publishing business, the matter of correspondence was put upon the writer, while Dr. R. H. Boyd looked after the other business. No attempt will be made in this chapter to give even an outline of the marvelous success which has come to the publishing department of the denomination. It may be said, however, that the beginning of this enterprise brought forth a storm of opposition from many who had been prominent in the affairs of the Convention. But we endeavored to deal charitably with all who opposed the effort and this conservative course has won over nearly all the Negro Baptists to the support of the enterprise. The rapidity with which the colored Baptists have developed since the consolidation of the several conventions is indeed wonderful and is owing largely to the unanimity which has characterized the entire brotherhood from Maine to California, and from the Lake to the Gulf, and is an irrefutable argument of what can be accomplished by united action. In the midst of the prosperity and success which came to our cause by reason of our union and the approval of a kind Providence, the greatest personal joy lies in the fact that we have had, so far as we have been able to learn, the entire confidence and support of those who are the leaders in the work.

In public matters aside from denominational work, a very great draught has been made upon my time. The first call of this kind was in 1881, when the position as one of the directors of the city public school was kindly tendered me. I served this position three years, declining a second nomination. In 1884, I was chosen as alternate delegate at large to the National Republican Convention, which nominated James G. Blaine for President; in 1892, was chosen without opposition a delegate from the first district of Arkansas to the Convention which nominated Benjamin Harrison for President; and again, in 1900, delegate from the first district of Arkansas to the Convention which nominated William McKinley a second time for President. Notwithstanding the fact that my hands have been full of religious work for all these years, I have found time to be at and a member of every Republican Convention held in the State for the last past twenty years. I have never been with that class who hold that ministers of the Gospel should have nothing to do with politics; indeed, I believe that they should interest themselves in all public questions, and while not bidding for office, should exert their influence in favor of good men for public service. I have never had a desire to hold a political office, but gave way to the pressure brought to bear by friends to become a candidate for Recorder of Deeds for the District of Columbia, in 1897, and finally consented to make a formal application which was supported by hundreds of personal endorsements, as well as the endorsement of the State and congressional committees of the party in my State. A few endorsements are hereafter given which are humbly regarded as a far richer treasure than the office could have been, had the appointment been made in my favor.

E. C. M.

Little Rock, Ark., February, 1897.

His Excellency, Hon. Wm. McKinley, President U. S. A., Executive Mansion, Washington, D. C.

Esteemed Sir:--I beg to call your attention to the candidacy of Rev. Dr. E. C. Morris for Recorder of Deeds in the District of Columbia. Dr. Morris is a man of ardent party faith and excellent business qualities. He is also President of the National Baptist Convention, which has the largest constituency of colored people in this whole country. Should you see fit to appoint him to that position, you would not only show recognition of personal merit based on business ability and party faithfulness, but you would also gratify the hearts of one million seven hundred thousand church members, all of whom are admirers of your personal leadership and devotees to the political party whose standard you bear.

Yours respectfully,

Jos. A. Booker, President Arkansas Baptist College.

Chattanooga, Tenn., February, 1897.

His Excellency, Hon. Wm. McKinley, President United States, Washington, D. C.

Dear Sir:--As the Rev. Dr. Morris is presented to me, I am sure he is a very worthy man and I commend him to your favorable consideration.

Very truly yours,

H. CLAY EVANS.

Cane Springs, Kentucky, February, 1897.

To Whom it May Concern:

I know of no man better fitted to represent the interests of the colored people of the country than E. C. Morris, of Arkansas. As to party service and devotion and that patriotism that makes for the welfare of the nation, he merits high recognition. His appointment as Recorder of Deeds for the District of Columbia, will, in my opinion, give general satisfaction to all classes. I know him to be highly efficient, trustworthy and prompt in execution.

Respectfully submitted,

C. H. Parrish, President Eckstein Norton University.

Philadelphia, Pa., February, 1897

Hon. Wm. McKinley, President of the United States.

Dear Sir:--As editor of a national paper that represents a large constituency who have been in all these years, to my knowledge, loyal to the principles of the grand old Republican party, I want to add my unqualified endorsement of E. C. Morris, of Helena, Ark., to the many that have come to you, for the position of Recorder of Deeds in the District of Columbia. He is one of the most eminent colored citizens of this country and is in every way qualified to fill the position. His appointment would meet the hearty approval of the great majority of colored voters of this republic. Hoping to have your favorable consideration of this request, I am,

Yours truly,

G. L. P. Taliaferro, Editor of "The Christian Banner."

Normal, Alabama, February, 1897.

Hon. Wm. McKinley, President of United States, Washington, D. C.

Sir:--Please permit me to say that Rev. E. C. Morris, D. D., of Arkansas, who applies to be appointed Recorder of Deeds for the District of Columbia, is one of the most prominent and beloved men of the South, indeed, I may say, of the United States. He is in every way qualified for the position, and his appointment would meet with general approval. The recognition of the Negroes of the South can be most effectually manifested by the recognition of Mr. Morris.

With high respect, I am,

W. H. COUNCILL.

New Orleans, La., Feb. 2nd, 1897.

Hon. Wm. McKinley, President Elect United States, Washington, D. C.

Dear Sir:--The appointment of Rev. E. C. Morris of Helena, Ark., to the position of Recorder of Deeds for the District of Columbia would please exceedingly many of the best Afro-American citizens throughout the entire country. He is a man of such splendid abilities and high moral worth that we can speak of him with pride. This letter expresses the desire of the best Negro element among us. Thanking God for your election and praying for you as you are about to assume the responsibilities of the presidency, I am,

Your humble servant,

Alexander S. Jackson, Ex-Receiver of Public Moneys at New Orleans (under appointment from President Harrison).

1316 Arabella St., New Orleans, La., Feb. 12, 1897.

Hon. Wm. McKinley, President United States of America.

Dear Sir:--Dr. E. C. Morris of Helena, Ark.; President of the National Baptist Convention, whose constituency represents 1,687,000 persons, is put forward by his friends in various parts of the country as a candidate for the Recordership of Deeds in the District of Columbia. Knowing him to be a man of ability and integrity and of exalted Christian character, I take pleasure in endorsing him for the position, assured that, if he is appointed, he will perform his duty with scrupulous fidelity.

Very truly,

S. T. CLANTON.

St. Louis, January 27th, 1897.

To His Excellency, President Wm. McKinley, Executive Mansion, Washington, D. C.

Dear Sir:--This is to certify that I have been personally acquainted with the Rev. Dr. E. C. Morris, of Helena, Ark., who is an applicant for Recorder of Deeds for the District of Columbia, for several years. I believe him to be thoroughly competent to fill the position which he seeks at your hands. He is a staunch Republican and has been always known to use his influence for the success of the "Grand Old Party," especially during the last Presidential campaign. He is President of our National Baptist Convention of the United States of America and is held in high esteem by the one and one-half million communicants of the great Negro Baptist family of America. I heartily endorse the Rev. Dr. Morris for the above mentioned position, feeling confident that he will faithfully discharge his duties creditably should you see fit to appoint him to the said position.

Yours respectfully,

J. L. COHRON.

Seguin, Texas, February 22nd, 1897.

To President Wm. McKinley, U. S. A.

Honored Sir:--Rev. E. C. Morris, D. D., of Helena, Ark., is a candidate for Recorder of Deeds. We regard Dr. Morris as one of the ablest men of our race in this country. In the first place he is a scholar, well informed. Secondly, he has splendid executive ability. This is observed the more pointedly when it is remembered that he is the President of the greatest religious organization in this country, numbering over one and a half million members as well as President of the same religious body in his own State (Arkansas). This shows what abundant and explicit confidence is placed in him. Thirdly, he is strictly honest, sound in morals, and a polished gentleman all round. His appointment would be hailed with universal satisfaction by his own people, regardless of religious sect or creed and by the Republican party, whose cause he has so earnestly espoused these years and especially in the recent campaign where an effort was made to ditch the government. We go so far as to say that the institution of the country, of this people, would rejoice to know that such a worthy and meritorious citizen was appointed Recorder of Deeds.

Very truly yours,

DAVID ABNER, JR.
Delegate to National Republican Convention, St. Louis, Mo.,
and member of Campaign Committee of Texas.

Nashville, Tenn., Feb. 25, 1897.

Hon. Wm. McKinley, Canton, Ohio.

Dear Sir:--I have known E. C. Morris, of Helena, Ark., for many years. I know him to be an honest, upright and Christian gentleman, and in every way qualified to fill the position to which he aspires.

S. P. HARRIS, Attorney at Law.

Darien, Ga., February 19, 1897.

To whom it may concern:--I know of no man among all American Negroes whose selection as Recorder of Deeds by President McKinley would give more satisfaction than the choice of Dr. E. C. Morris, of Arkansas. He is in every way eminently qualified for the office, and would fill it with great credit to himself and the entire satisfaction of the people.

E. M. BRAWLEY,
Ex-President National Baptist Convention.

Helena, Ark., March 5th, 1897.

To the President:--Dr. E. C. Morris, of this city, has resided here for twenty years, and I have known him well ever since he came here. It affords me pleasure to say, that during that time I have always found him as a man, as a citizen and as a Republican, doing his whole duty. Any position he aspires to he is capable of filling, and as a representative of the colored race, he stands high. His integrity is second to none and his ability is well known to me. Any favor extended to him will be a well merited recognition to one worthy of it.

Yours very respectfully,

Jacob Trieber, Attorney at Law.

Pensacola, Fla., March 12, 1897.

To His Excellency, Hon. Wm. McKinley, President U. S. A., Washington, D. C.

My Dear Sir:--I notice in the newspapers that Dr. E. C. Morris, of Helena, Ark., is an applicant for Recorder of Deeds for the District of Columbia. I take great pleasure in endorsing him for the same. I have known Mr. Morris for several years. He is held in high esteem by his own race as well as by the other race. I know of no one applying better qualified for the place than Dr. Morris, and whose appointment would give more general satisfaction to the colored people of the whole country. His service and loyalty to the Republican party as a party leader is acknowledged by all who know him. His open letter published throughout the country just prior to election inspired hope in the Republican ranks and did invaluable service.

Very respectfully yours,

G. W. RAIFORD.

"It seems that it is the usual custom of Presidents to appoint some man outside of the District, Recorder of Deeds for the District of Columbia. Among the many names mentioned in connection with this position is that of Rev. E. C. Morris, D. D. We are of the opinion that there is no man in this country more eminently fitted for this position than Dr. Morris. He is an American that will honestly and faithfully discharge his duties, and the noble exponent of Republican principles in whom the best interests of the party have always found an advocate. The appointment of Dr. Morris would be a just recognition of honor, merit, fidelity and ability."--*Weekly Herald, Eufaula, Ala.*

Louisville, Ky., April 10, 1897.

To The President:

I desire to add my unqualified endorsement to the application of E. C. Morris, of Helena, Ark., for appointment of Recorder of Deeds, Washington, D. C. I do this in no perfunctory way, for I think that in point of capacity, integrity and executive ability, that he is equal in every respect to discharge the duties of this office to the entire satisfaction of its patrons, the people and yourself. He is in all respects a representative Republican and has always been earnest, zealous and effective in presenting its claims and working for its principles. I think beyond doubt he has the largest personal following of any man of his class and is exceptionally fortunate in being able to both make and retain the friendship of those with whom he comes in contact.

Dr. Morris is an editor, a scholar and a leading spirit in all popular movements among the people, and his appointment will give general satisfaction. In his own State he is beyond question the foremost man of his race, and is always among its delegates to the National Republican Convention. His appointment will not only be gratifying to them, but to many who reside in other States.

Respectfully,

WM. H. STEWART,
Editor "American Baptist" and President National Press Association.

DIRECTORY.

For the benefit of those who may choose to put a copy of this book in their libraries, we have compiled a long list of names of ordained ministers, giving their post office addresses. These addresses are taken largely from the Baptist Year Book, published by the American Baptist Publication Society, and are as nearly correct as is possible to get them. It is a feature which will prove an invaluable aid as a reference, and will give an idea as to the clerical strength of the Negro branch of the denomination. As no separate account is taken of the Negro ministers in the Northern States, it is difficult to obtain their names and addresses; but, the names of those who have been most active in our national work are given.

Sermons, Addresses and Reminiscences and Important Correspondence

- **ALABAMA**
  - Abercrombie, L., Abercrombie.
  - Adams, D. S., Bessemer.
  - Adams, H. Orrville.
  - Adams, W. D., Columbus, Miss.
  - Adarine, P. A., Gadsden.
  - Adkins, R. A., Wetumpka.
  - Agnew, J. B., Covin.
  - Alexander, H., Greensboro.
  - Alexander, L. A., Elyton.
  - Alford, P. D., Bladen Springs.
  - Alford, Robt., Bruceville.
  - Allen, R., Flora.
  - Alston, J. A., Northport.
  - Anderson, A. S., Claiborne.
  - Anderson, I. P., Pine Hill.
  - Anderson, J. A., Brierfield.
  - Anderson, N. P., Birmingham.
  - Anderson, W. M., Whitesburg.
  - Andrews, R. D., Milton.
  - Anthony, E. W., Rayland.
  - Anthony, F. M., Wylan.
  - Archer, M. M., Opelika.
  - Archibald, J. C., Bridgeville.
  - Armstead, C. A., Panther.
  - Arobouski, Jas., Hayneville.
  - Atty, J. T., Memphis.
  - Atwood, B. H., Trussville.
  - Autry, J. A., Repton.
  - Baker, H. R., Tuscumbia.
  - Baker, J. A., Speed.
  - Barnes, S., Bughall.
  - Barnett, L. C., London.
  - Barton, J. P., Talladega.
  - Baskin, W. B., Farmersville.
  - Beauford, S. M., Gadsden.
  - Battle, A. A., Anniston.
  - Beck, A., Camden.
  - Beck, Elias, Canton Bend.
  - Beck, F. A. E., Old Spring Hill.

- Beckwith, H., Oakland.
- Belser, S. L., Birmingham.
- Benson, Young, Chuncula.
- Berry, R., Fort Payne.
- Bibb, A. A., Jennifer.
- Bibb, B., Mongomery.
- Bibb, W. T., B. D., Bessemer.
- Billingslea, A., Marion.
- Bishop, B., Griffin.
- Blakley, Wm., Union Springs.
- Blankenship, J. A., Attalla.
- Boatright, B., Gainesville.
- Boatwright, J. B. S., Gainesville.
- Booth, C. O., D. D., Hollywood.
- Bostick, I., Rutherford.
- Boyd, D., Gees Bend.
- Bowden, P. T., Selma.
- Boyd, W. L., Five Points.
- Bradford, W. C., Tuscaloosa.
- Bragg, H. C., Hamburg.
- Brawley, F. J., Leighton.
- Brazele, W., Fayette.
- Brent, G. W., Fayette.
- Brewton, G. W., Alexandria.
- Bridges, L. W., Millport.
- Brince, J., Linden.
- Broaden, W., Sumterville.
- Brock, A. A., Dudleyville.
- Brooks, G. J., Birmingham.
- Brooks, N., Pickensville.
- Brown, A. B., Huntsville.
- Brown, J., Carrollton.
- Brown, J. A., Talladega.
- Brown, L., Epes.
- Brown, M., Tuscaloosa.
- Brown, R. E., Selma.
- Brown, S., Boligee.
- Brown, T., Rehoboth.
- Brumby, J. H., Wadsworth.
- Bruton, G. W., Alexandria.

Sermons, Addresses and Reminiscences and Important Correspondence

- Bryant, L., Selma.
- Bryant, M. C., Warsaw.
- Burnett, S., Boligee.
- Burt, J. M., Burney.
- Burton, H., Collinsville.
- Butler, J. B., Oakland.
- Byers, M., Livingston.
- Byrd, S., Camden.
- Gaddell, P. C., Columbiana.
- Cade, H. C., Anniston.
- Calloway, L. W., Fort Deposit.
- Campbell, A., Kings Landing.
- Campbell, D. B., Powderly.
- Carlton, E. L., Chunchula.
- Carrall, D. C., Independence.
- Carter, S. C., Old Springhill.
- Carter, W. C., Auburn.
- Cary, H., Tilden.
- Catton, J. C., Calera.
- Cephas, Geo. W., Mobile.
- Chandler, F. C., Birmingham.
- Chapman, F. A., Flint.
- Charles, A., Clayhill.
- Chatman, J., Reeltown.
- Chisholm, J. J., Opelika.
- Clark, H. C., Opelika.
- Clark, J. D., Ehren.
- Clarke, Wm., Jones Switch.
- Clay, A., Jones Switch.
- Clay, A. C., Blount Springs.
- Cleveland, A. D., Whatley.
- Cobb, Frank.
- Cochran, P., Jr., Orrville.
- Coleman, D. C., Brookwood.
- Coleman, D. M., Crumtonia.
- Coleman, W. T., Selma.
- Collins, A. C., Hazen.
- Connor, W. T., Madison Station.
- Conyer, S. M., Thompson.
- Cook, C., Sylacauga.

Sermons, Addresses and Reminiscences and Important Correspondence

- Cook, W. P., Tuscaloosa.
- Cotton, J. C., Attalla.
- Cottrell, Peter, Greensboro.
- Cowles, F. H., Milstead.
- Cox, C., Grovehill.
- Cox, J., Sylacauga.
- Cranford, H. J., Horse Creek.
- Cranford, R. W., Notasulga.
- Crawford, C., York Station.
- Crawford, J. C., Northport.
- Critz, A., Madison Station.
- Crowley, A. M., Iron City.
- Cummins, H., Notasulga.
- Cunningham, B. C., Garden.
- Cunnigham, C. C., Carrollton.
- Cunningham, J. W. T., Carrollton.
- Cunningham, M. H., Talladega.
- Curry, C. C., Attalla..
- Curry, J. C., Fort Deposit.
- Daniel, H., Masillon.
- Daniel, J., Lawrenceville.
- Daniels, A., Sherman.
- Darby, A., Fayettevile.
- Davis, A., Florence.
- Davis, C. J., Selma.
- Davis, C. M., Flint.
- Davis, G., Whitesburg.
- Davis, John, Carrollton.
- Davis, J. P., Opelika.
- Davis, Lewis, Clay Hill.
- Davis, R. L., Samantha.
- De Jarnette, P., Verbena.
- De Yampert, A. W., Talladega.
- De Yampert, E. W., Birmingham.
- De Yampert, R. Z., Augustine.
- Dial, R., Sumterville.
- Dinkins, S. C., D. D., Selma.
- Dixon, T., Tuscaloosa.
- Doak, H. E., Calera.
- Donald, R., Pratt City.

Sermons, Addresses and Reminiscences and Important Correspondence

- Dorsey, N. D., Sweetwater.
- Douglass, T. L., Gadsden.
- Dozier, G. D., Judson.
- Easom, A. R., Huntsville.
- Eason, J. H., D. D., Anniston.
- Eaton, Jas., Cedarville.
- Echols, P. B., Auburn.
- Echols, W. C., Gold Hill.
- Edwards, A. J., Benton.
- Edwards, R. D., Eutaw.
- Ellington, M., Fort Davis.
- Ellis, H. L., New Decatur.
- Ellison, L. V., Birmingham.
- English, K., Talladega.
- Etheridge, R., Boiling Springs.
- Fancher, P., Longview.
- Farley, C. H., Pratt City.
- Farley, R. T., Hull.
- Fennerson, O. F., Jemison.
- Fikes, A. J., Pratt City.
- Finch, A. H., Luggsville.
- Fisher, C. L., D. D., Birmingham.
- Flood, T. J., Greensboro.
- Flournoy, M. A., Troy.
- Forbes, W. S., Grandbay.
- Ford, H., Berlin.
- Ford, J., Whatley.
- Forkner, S., Livingston.
- Fort, Jas., Pickensville.
- Foster, Dennis, Hull.
- Foster, J. A. S., Belle Sumter.
- Foster, L. P., Selma.
- Foster, R. F., Deatsville.
- Franklin, S., Mount Meigs.
- Frazier, A. L., Auburn.
- Frazier, J. L., Mobile.
- Freeman, J. H., Oakville.
- Gaines, F., Gallion.
- Gaines, S. M., Huntsville.
- Gardner, J. B., East Lake.

- Garlington, H. J., Camphill.
- Garlington, J. H., Judson.
- Garner, D. D., Stringer.
- Garner, I. H., Thompson.
- Garrett, J. M., Myrtlewood.
- Garth, J. M., Crowton.
- George, S., Pinehill.
- Gibson, H., Montgomery.
- Gilchrist, P., Letohatchee.
- Glasscock, J. K., Fayette.
- Glover, B. C., Siddonsville.
- Glynn. Geo. R., Columbiana.
- Goeter, W. Y., Judson.
- Goldsby, T. B., Selma.
- Goodgame, J. W., Talladega.
- Goodwin, J., Speed.
- Goodwin, G. O., Shelby.
- Grant, E., York Station.
- Graves, R., Bangor.
- Gray, J. B., Cusseta.
- Grayson, D., Minter.
- Green, H. G., Tuscaloosa.
- Green, L. A., Livingston.
- Green, L. J. Florence.
- Green, Simpson, Notasulga.
- Green, W. M., Dayton.
- Gresham, D., Verbena.
- Griffin, D. L., Sulligent.
- Griffin, J. A., North.
- Gunn, S. Q., Lafayette.
- Hall, J. R., Abbeville.
- Hall, O. H., Roxanna.
- Hall, R. N., Irondale.
- Hall, S. M., Smithfield.
- Hall, W. R., Bartonville.
- Hallin, M. H., Society Hill.
- Hamilton, T., Forkland.
- Hampton, Jas., Leighton.
- Handy, C. H., Gallion.
- Handy, E., Bethel.

Sermons, Addresses and Reminiscences and Important Correspondence

- Hansley, A., Verbena.
- Hardwick, J. L., Cedar Bluff.
- Harrell, A. J., Marion.
- Harton, G. W., Arden.
- Hart, M. H., Camp Hill.
- Hatcher, J., Orrville.
- Hawkins, E. A., Sizemore.
- Hawkins, H. L., Verbena.
- Hawthorne, L., Avondale.
- Hawthorne, N., Gravella.
- Hayes, B., Columbiana.
- Heard, T. H., Selma.
- Heath, C. R., Welsh.
- Henderson, A. J., Roxanna.
- Herring, P. T., Hartsells.
- Herring, R. V., Falkville.
- Hicks, J. P., Eufaula.
- Hightower, D., Jemison.
- Hill, J. Whatley.
- Hinton, R., Pickensville.
- Holloway, W. H., Thomas.
- Holmes, J., Mount Union.
- Holt, L. R., Thompson.
- Hood, G. W., Ehren.
- Hood, J. D., Gregory.
- Hooks, M. J., Decatur.
- Hopkins, C. H., Birmingham.
- Hopson, A. R., Coal Valley.
- House, J. Y., Dead Level.
- Howard, H., Pickensville.
- Howard, Jas., Pickensville.
- Huckabee, W. H., Newbern.
- Hughes, S. W., Mt. Vernon.
- Hughley, F. M., Opelika.
- Hughley, L. M., Notasulga.
- Hughley, M. H., Opelika.
- Hume, J. H., Smithsonia.
- Hunter, J. H., Faunsdale.
- Hunter, R. B., Horse Creek.
- Hurston, A., Notasulga.

- Hurston, James, Mary.
- Huston, J. W., Sunny South.
- Hutchins, P. S. L., Newbern.
- Hutchinson, R. L., Livingston.
- Ingraham, R., Sepulga.
- Irwin, M., Shorterville.
- Jackson, A., Opelika.
- Jackson, A. C., Birmingham.
- Jackson, B., Mumford.
- Jackson, Delmar, Tuscaloosa.
- Jackson, J., Sweetwater.
- Jackson, M., Harris.
- Jackson, M., Mitchell Station.
- Jackson, T. J., Sylacauga.
- James, L. D., Birmingham.
- James, V. B., Avondale.
- Jelks, F., Attalla.
- Jemison, J. H., Birmingham.
- Jenkins, S. W., Fort Deposit.
- Jennings, J. B., Shelby.
- Jeter, G. W., Milstead.
- Jett, J. C., Goshen.
- Johnson, F., Portland.
- Johnson, G. B., Courtland.
- Johnson, O., Sunny South.
- Johnson, P. J., Union Springs.
- Johnson, W. W., Corbin Hill.
- Jones, A. J., Deatsville.
- Jones, G. M., Selma.
- Jones, H., Commerce.
- Jones, J. R., Mulberry.
- Jones, L. A., Childersburg.
- Jones, M. T., Orion.
- Jones, P. J., Phifer.
- Jones, S., Union Springs.
- Jones, Wilson, Whitehall.
- Jones, W. J., Salem.
- Jordan, J. W., Forkland.
- Jordan, P., Talladega.
- Karm, John, Montgomery.

- Keller, R. H., Woodlawn.
- Kenard, J. J., Gainesville.
- Kendrick, J. H., Rockford.
- Kennedy, F. R., Anniston.
- Kennedy, Wm. M., Selma.
- Kerley, N., Lebanon.
- Key, B. M., Somerville.
- Kimbrough, F., Ornall.
- Kimbrough, P., Pinehill.
- Kimbrough, W. M., Kings.
- King, B., Leighton.
- Knight, A. J., Montgomery.
- Knight, J. C., Phifer.
- Knight, Thos., Finchburg.
- Knox, J., Bethany.
- Koonce, E. L., Headland.
- Lane, E. D., Florence.
- Langston, Y. P., Shorterville.
- Latham, R. J., Pine Hill.
- Lathon, S. T., Branchville.
- Lawson, J. A., Alberta.
- Lee, A., Brookside.
- Levi, H. E., Courtland.
- Lewis, Geo., Mobile.
- Lewis, H., Fayetteville.
- Lewis, R. L., Waverly.
- Lewis, R. T., Waverly.
- Lewis, S., Ensley City.
- Lockett, R., Dixons Mills.
- Long, C. L., Bladen Springs.
- Looney, L. J., Fayetteville.
- Love, D., Milton.
- Lowe, G., Livingston.
- Lowry, M. C., Troy.
- Luny, D., Wythe City.
- Mack, Geo., Sumterville.
- Mackey, W. T., Lafayette.
- Maddox, D., Loachapoka.
- Maddox, Jno., Fayette.
- Maddox, J. D., Eufaula.

- Maddox, R. E., Oneonta.
- McEwen, Jas., Birmingham.
- McAlpine, W. H., D. D., Montgomery.
- McIntosh, M., Octagon.
- McKenny, G., Montgomery.
- McKerson, J., Demopolis.
- McLine, D. C., Sylvan.
- Madison, S. M., Repton.
- Madison, Wm., Uniontown.
- Madison, Wm., Jr., Selma.
- Mallory, B. M., Childersburg.
- Mallory, C. A. J., Childersburg.
- Marbury, Randall, Goodwater.
- Martin, A., Union Springs.
- Martin, H., Blackman.
- Martin, J. A., Uniontown.
- Massey, H., Keener.
- Matthews, E., Mobile.
- Matthews, J. W., Forkland.
- Matthews, S. M., Ozark.
- Matthis, C. C., Flint.
- May, B., Livingston.
- McCall, S. B., Snow Hill.
- McConnell, M., Claiborne.
- McCord, C. S., Selma.
- McCreary, R., Herbert.
- McDonald, D. A., Decatur.
- McEwen, A. N., Mobile.
- McLinn, Wm., Prattville.
- McCurdy, R. V., Felix.
- McNeal, L. W., Alexander City.
- Megginson, A. L., Thomasville.
- Megginson, A., Thomasville.
- Merrill, M. C., Fort Deposit.
- Merritt, D. R., Sylacauga.
- Merritt, J. M., Brookside.
- Michael, Z., Evergreen.
- Middleton, H. H., E. Gadsden.
- Miller, M. E., Gadsden.
- Miller, Wm., Attalla.

- Milton, Wm., McLendon.
- Mimms, G. W., Notasulga.
- Mimms, Wm., Independence.
- Minard, B., Olney.
- Mitchell, H. W., Whatley.
- Mitchell, L. B., Ozark.
- Mitchell, O. M., Stroud.
- Mixon, D. S., Burnsville.
- Mixon, E. P., Burnsville.
- Mixon, H. W., Thomasville.
- Mixon, J., Selma.
- Mixon, J. H., Jones Switch.
- Mixon, R. C., Shelby.
- Moncrief, W. M., Oxanna.
- Moore, E. M., Union Springs.
- Moore, G. W., Society Hill.
- Moore, J. F., Leeds.
- Morgan, T. H., Chunchula.
- Morris, John, Montgomery.
- Morris, Rich., Claiborne.
- Moseley, J. A., Tuscaloosa.
- Moseley, T., Tasso.
- Moseley, W. M., Glendale.
- Moses, D. C., Franconia.
- Moss, A., Yantley.
- Moss, B., Hayneville.
- Moss, C. E., Loachapoka.
- Moss, E. E., Notasulga.
- Moss, H., Notasulga.
- Moss, J., Thaddeus.
- Moss, S., Notasulga.
- Motley, D. L., Independence.
- Mott, H., Reeltown.
- Munds, W. M., Anniston.
- Murphey, R. B., Springville.
- Myer, S. C., Tyler.
- Myles, M. L., Equality.
- Myree, J. W., Selma.
- Nall, J. P., Davis Creek.
- Nall, Y. R., Hico.

Sermons, Addresses and Reminiscences and Important Correspondence

- Nash, G. R., Aldrich.
- Nash, T., Central Mills.
- Neal, L., Providence.
- Nelson, K., Coalburg.
- Niblet, W. L., Neals Mills.
- Nichols, A. W., Calera.
- Nichols, J., Greenville.
- Nickerson, Jas., Taylorsville.
- Nolls, Y. B., Fayette.
- Norris, I., Berlin.
- Northcross, W. E., Tuscumbia.
- Nunn, E., Autaugaville.
- Oden, A. J., Vine Hill.
- Oden, M. C. B., Beaver Valley.
- O'Harra, Henry, Columbia.
- Ousley, C., Wadsworth.
- Owen, A. J., Moulton.
- Owen, W. C., Birmingham.
- Owens, A. F., Mobile.
- Owens, H., Lafayette.
- Owens, O. W., Helena.
- Page, J. S., Lockville.
- Page, R., Tuscaloosa.
- Page, S., Tuscaloosa.
- Parker, J. C., Milton.
- Parker, T. M., Brierfield.
- Parks, G. W., New Castle.
- Pater, W. C., Lincoln.
- Paterson, L. S., Mary.
- Payne, R. T., Calhoun.
- Peel, J. A., No. Birmingham.
- Peoples, A., Plantersville.
- Peoples, H. W., Vine Hill.
- Peterson, B. H., Tuskegee.
- Peterson, Jas., Eufaula.
- Pettiford, W. R., D. D., Birming-
- Phillips, Z. P., Pikeroad.
- Pickett, Esau, Selma.
- Pierce, Wm., Boligee.
- Pinson, A. D., Whitney.

Sermons, Addresses and Reminiscences and Important Correspondence

- Pleasant, W. E., Mitchell Station.
- Pollard, I. M., Notasulga.
- Pollard, R. T., A. B., Selma.
- Poole, Frank, Reeltown.
- Pope, P., Pratt City.
- Potts, C. R., Notasulga.
- Potts, D. A., Notasulga.
- Prentice, D. L., Brookside.
- Prentice, J. H., Aldrich.
- Prewitt, G. H., Samantha.
- Prewitt, J. O., Samantha.
- Price, Cato, Verbena.
- Pritchett, J. M., Ellison.
- Pugh, W. J., Grove Hill.
- Rabb, J. R., Mary.
- Ragland, A. W., Marion.
- Rand, B., Oakland.
- Reddick, Wm., Newbern.
- Reed, A., Rescueville.
- Redd, C. D., Whistler.
- Revees, S. M., Montgomery.
- Richardson, A. B., Stafford.
- Richardson, C. C., Mobile.
- Richardson, J. C., Activity.
- Richardson, Wm., Demopolis.
- Richey, R. R., Pickensville.
- Richmond, S. R., Society Hill.
- Riley, J. P. O., Gadsden.
- Robertson, C. M., Benton.
- Robertson, J. R., Wilsonville.
- Robinson, C. L., Thomasville.
- Robinson, M., Boligee.
- Robinson, S. M., Decatur.
- Rogers, E., Faunsdale.
- Roots, E. W., Ehren.
- Ross, M. M., Opelika.
- Roundtree, H., Deatsville.
- Russell, R. W., Axle.
- Salmons, A. D., Bridgeville.
- Salmons, D. C., Olney.

- Sanders, L. M., Roxanna.
- Sanders, S. D., Avondale.
- Saunders, Austin, Tuscaloosa.
- Sapp, G. D., Birmingham.
- Savage, D., Mumford.
- Sawyers, W. S., Calera.
- Schell, R. T., Eufala.
- Scott, A. A., Woodlawn.
- Scott, J. R., Selma.
- Session, A. L., Coffeeville.
- Sewel, D. M., Birmingham.
- Shannon, I., Brooklyn.
- Sharp, W. L., Dunkling.
- Sharpley, Robt., Massey.
- Shaw, J., Linden.
- Sheppard, E., Jefferson.
- Sheppard, D., Evergreen.
- Sherman, L. E., Troy.
- Shields, E. W., Linden.
- Shorter, F., Clayton.
- Simmon, J. D., Orrville.
- Simon, H., Mt. Vernon.
- Simpson, Green, Notasulga.
- Simpson, I. T., Opelika.
- Sims, H. P., Stone.
- Sims, D. C., Horsecreek.
- Sistrunk, N. S., Tuskegee.
- Slaughter, W. D., Camp Hill.
- Simedley, C. C., Welsh.
- Smith, E., Brundidge.
- Smith, Emanuel, Mobile.
- Smith, G. W., Tuscalosa.
- Smith, H., Livingston.
- Smith, J. H., Faunsdale.
- Smith, J. H., Tallassee.
- Smith, W. D., Memphis.
- Snoden, A., Elmore.
- Somerville, S., Stone.
- Spruil, W. B., Garden.
- Starlworth, A., Betts.

Sermons, Addresses and Reminiscences and Important Correspondence

- Stallworth, E. L., Sepulga.
- Stallworth, A. J., Sunday.
- Stallworth, W., Tincie.
- Stokes, A. J., D. D., Montgomery.
- Steindack, L. S., Birmingham.
- Stephens, C. J. Coatopa.
- Stephens, H., Scotts Station.
- Stephens, J. M., Attala.
- Stephens, Wm., Uniontown.
- Stewart, J. H., Birmingham.
- Stith, J., Columbia.
- Stratman, W. S., Selma.
- Swindall, A. L., Wetumpka.
- Swindall, Jno. W., Sykes Mills.
- Tait, P. A., Burnt Corn.
- Tate, P., Ashville.
- Tate, W. P., Selma.
- Taylor, B., Tuscaloosa.
- Taylor, H., Hilton.
- Terry, C. C., Roanoke.
- Thomas, A., Coatopa.
- Thomas, E., Lyon.
- Thomas, Irwin, Tuscaloosa.
- Thomas, Isaac, Cottondale.
- Thomas, J. D., Opelika.
- Thomas, J. T., Salem.
- Thomas, J. T., Atmore.
- Thompson, H. S., Birmingham.
- Thompson, I. S., Dayton.
- Thompson, M. J., Mobile.
- Thompson, T. J., Old Spring Hill.
- Thompson, Wm., Woodland.
- Thompson, W. T., Flint.
- Thornton, C. H., Aberfoil.
- Thornton, J. H., Selma.
- Tod, P. T., Five Points.
- Thompkins, Jas., Stone.
- Thompkins, W. M., Sherman.
- Toney, S., Montgomery.
- Townsend, W. J., Birmingham.

- Travis, S. G., Betts.
- Tremier, E. K., Neals Mill.
- Troupe, A., Town Creek.
- Turner, D. G., Talladega.
- Turner, W. C., Sylvan.
- Turpin, R., Girard.
- Tyler, M., D.D., Lowndesboro.
- Tyson, E. B., Choctaw Corner.
- Underwood, M., Milton.
- Upshaw, D., Tuskegee.
- Vassar, R. D., Orrville.
- Vaughn, M. B., Crawford.
- Vincent, A. J., Goodwater.
- Vogle, R. H., Birmingham.
- Walker, A. G., Siddon.
- Walker, Job, Clanton.
- Walker, H. G., Thompson.
- Walker, R. J., Demopolis.
- Walker, T. W., Birmingham.
- Walker Wm. Avondale.
- Wallace, C. W., Demopolis.
- Walker, W. L., Tilden.
- Wallace, E. L. M., Wilsonville.
- Walton, A., Tuskegee.
- Ware, Wm., Hoffman.
- Warren, L., Leighton.
- Washington, R. B., Selma.
- Washington, B. J., Old Spring Hill
- Washington, E. S. T., Gordo.
- Washington, G., Barlow Bend.
- Washington, J. H., Birmingham.
- Washington, J. J., Girard.
- Watkins, A., Rogersville.
- Watkins, F. W., Tuscumbia.
- Waytes, W. J., B. D., Marion.
- Webb, B. L., Tuskegee.
- Webb, G. W., Eufaula.
- Wells, L. W., East Lake.
- West, N. H., Calera.
- Wettles, S., Sunny South.

- Whatley, H. W., Whiteplains.
- White, B. W., Mt. Sterling.
- White, T. W., Rescueville.
- White, Y. R., Selma.
- Wilburn, W. W., Caldwell.
- Wilhite, J. Q. A., Birmingham.
- Wilhite, R. W., Massey.
- Wilhite, W. A., Massey.
- Williams, Antony, Chastang.
- Williams A. D. Perdue Hill.
- Williams, C. W., Claiborne.
- Williams, D. W., Tombigbee.
- Williams, Frank, Pratt City.
- Williams, J. A., Putnam.
- Williams, T. A., Burkville.
- Williams, J. W., Havana.
- Williams, L. D., Hoffman.
- Williams, M. G., Greenville.
- Williams, R., Eustis.
- Williams, T., Eutaw.
- Williams, W. H., Wilsonville.
- Williamson, J. A., Judson.
- Willingham, I., Gainesville.
- Wilson, James, Riley.
- Wilson, J. E. A. Pratt City.
- Winston, N., Gainesville.
- Winston, J. S., Gainesville.
- Witherspoon, J. W., Randolph.
- Womack, A. L., Selma.
- Wood B. L., Alco.
- Wood, R. T., East Lake.
- Woolen, P. Woodlawn.
- Woody, T. W., Lafayette.
- Wright, E., Boligee.
- Young, C. Y., Tuskegee.
- Young, G., Livingston.
- Young, Wm., Safford.
- Youngblood, C., Indian.
- Youngblood, F., Childersburg.
- Youngblood, G., Bruceville.

ARKANSAS

- Abernathy, J. H., Brinkley.
- Adams, R. A., Baxter.
- Adway, C. A., Carmel.
- Allen, J. C., Millville.
- Alexander, B. W., N'th Little Rock.
- Alexander, S., Trenton.
- Allen, G., Red Store.
- Allen, J. C., Corner Store.
- Allen, S. A., Morrell.
- Allen, W., Galloway.
- Allen, W. H., Dermott.
- Allen, Wm., Searcy.
- Allen, --, Barefield.
- Alston, M. H., Blytheville.
- Anderson, A. L., Peters.
- Anderson, D., Hollywood.
- Anderson, T. P., Redemption.
- Anderson, Z. H., Prescott.
- Archie, A. M., New Lewisville.
- Armour, W. M., Gilmore.
- Arnette, G. E., Wynne.
- Auglin, H. C., Pearla.
- Austin, J. A., Pine Bluff.
- Author, T., Marvell.
- Avant, L. E., Forrest City.
- Baccus, A. B., Madison.
- Bailey, I. G., Pine Bluff.
- Baker, B. G., Pine Bluff.
- Baldwin, L. H., New Lewisville.
- Ballentine, I. K., Beebe.
- Bankhead, J. M., Pine Bluff.
- Banks, H. C., Sardis.
- Barber, J. H., Luxoria.
- Barnes, J. H., Hampton.
- Battle, J. C., Pine Bluff.
- Barrett, W. E., Vincent.
- Barrett, W. M., Vincent.
- Barrow, S., Lee.
- Bass, L. M., Horatio.

Sermons, Addresses and Reminiscences and Important Correspondence

- Bell, A., Dermott.
- Bell, J. C., Forrest City.
- Bennett, J. R., Hot Springs.
- Benton, J. B., Hope.
- Bentley, C., Coffee Creek.
- Berry, M., Lagrange.
- Beverley, E. L., Searcy.
- Beverley, G. W., Snapp.
- Blackwell, L. A., Weldon.
- Blake, J. A., Princeton.
- Blakely, Wm., Helena.
- Bledsoe, E. D., Brinkley.
- Blount, E., Scanlan.
- Blue, L. W., Walnut Lake.
- Boatright, P. B., England.
- Bolden, J. B., Pine Bluff.
- Booker, J. A., D. D., Little Rock.
- Booker, J., Kedron.
- Booker, W. W., Luna Landing.
- Booth, H., Arkadelphia.
- Bowles, A. E., Poindexter.
- Boyd, J. C., Woodson.
- Boyland, G. D., Julius.
- Bradley, H., Yorktown.
- Bradley, Wm., Taylor.
- Brewer, J. N., Higginson.
- Brewer, S. B., Alma.
- Brewster, A. Stephens.
- Brice, J. E., Helena.
- Brinkley, H. B., Pettus.
- Brooks, F. M., Carlisle.
- Brooks, D., Pine Bluff.
- Brown, B., Marianna.
- Brown, B. J., Magnolia.
- Brown, C. B., Marianna.
- Brown, G. W., Julius.
- Brown, H. B., Plumerville.
- Brown, H. B., Okolona.
- Brown, H. E., Grand Lake.
- Brown, J. B., Arkadelphia.

- Brown, J. L. J., Magnolia.
- Brown, J. W., Marianna.
- Brown, R. B., Garland City.
- Brown, W. H., Surrounded Hill.
- Bryant, Ben B., Camden.
- Bryant, C. B., Garland City.
- Bryant, E., Jersey.
- Bryant, F. O., Pine Bluff.
- Bryant, M. C., Fareman.
- Bryant, R. E., Marianna.
- Bumpas, A. J., Chapel Hill.
- Bunn, G. W., Pine Bluff.
- Burnett, P. B., Wynne.
- Burrough, L. W., Thornton.
- Burroughs, R. B., Pettus.
- Burt, D. W., Becks Spur.
- Burton, S. R., Hillsboro.
- Burton, H. B., New Lewisville.
- Bush, D., Yorktown.
- Butler, M., Ethel.
- Butler, M., Sleeth.
- Butler, A. B., Rocky Comfort.
- Cade, H. C., Camden.
- Cain, J. C., Corner Stone.
- Caldwell, H. C., Texarkana.
- Caldwell, M. V., Colt.
- Campbell, W. H., Hickman Bend.
- Canaday, E. C., Red Store.
- Canada, L. C., Walnut Lake.
- Cannon, A., Carson Lake.
- Cannon, J. C., Fay.
- Cannon, S. L., Marianna.
- Carey, C. H., Prescott.
- Cesar, W. B., Arkadelphia.
- Chandler, A., Holly Grove.
- Chatman, T. C., Brinkley.
- Claiborn, R. B., England.
- Clark, H. C., Drewton.
- Clark, W., Moro.
- Cole, A., Dardanelle.

- Coleman, J. C., Colona.
- Collins, S. C., Mayflower.
- Collins, Wm., Collins.
- Cotton, L., Hopefield.
- Cotton, L. B., Altheimer.
- Cowan, O. C., Luxoria.
- Cornelius, E., Little Rock.
- Craig, T. C., Wilmot.
- Craig, Wm., Little Rock.
- Crawford, D. J., Camden.
- Crawford, J T., Clarkson.
- Criner, E., Lunette.
- Critz, R. W., Higginson.
- Cuff, C., Calhoun.
- Cuff, Tom, Magnolia.
- Cummings, P., Magnolia.
- Cummings, S. J., Magnolia.
- Curry, A. G., Wheeling Springs.
- Curry, M. C., Mandeville.
- Dandridge, E., Lambertsville.
- Dargan, E., Conway.
- David, J. W., Turner.
- Davis, D. D., Lonoke.
- Davis, J. S., Garland City.
- Davis, J. W., Turner.
- Davis, L. D., Pendleton.
- Davis, R. N., Tillar.
- Davis, Wm., Little Rock.
- Dean, J. B., Red Fork.
- Dean, S., Fort Smith.
- Deloney, J. J., Hot Springs.
- Dillahenty, B. A., Cerro Gordo.
- Dixon, A. D., Lewisville.
- Dixon, A. F. D., Jericho.
- Dixon, Thos., Helena.
- Dockery, B. D., Marche.
- Dockery, S. B., Falcon.
- Donerson, R., Conway.
- Donnell, Geo., Poplar Grove.
- Donnell, J. B., North Creek.

- Dooley, F. C., Center Ridge.
- Dooley, T. J., Center Ridge.
- Dorch, M., Trenton.
- Dorn, C. L., Malvern.
- Douglass, S. D., Walnut Lake.
- Drake, R. H., Grayson.
- Duffin, J., Marion.
- Durham, F., Blouse.
- Edwards, N. E., Grand Lake.
- Edwards, S. E., Bald Knob.
- Edwards, W. A., Pine Bluff.
- Ellerson, S. E., Altheimer.
- Elliot, M. E., Osceola.
- Ellis, D. C., Lambertsville.
- Ellis, G. T., Pendleton.
- Ellis, J. H., Little Rock.
- Ewing, C., Helena.
- Exsome, C. L., Morrillton.
- Farmer, D. G., Park Place.
- Faulkner, J., Harwood.
- Fielding, D., McCrory.
- Fields, A., Marvell.
- Fleshman, J. F., Ashvale.
- Ford, J. W., Plumerville.
- Fort, C. W., Live Oak.
- Fountain, W. T., Little Rock.
- Franklin, H. H., Pendleton.
- Franklin, J. T., Richmond.
- Freeman, I. G., Little Rock.
- Gaines, G. W. D., Little Rock.
- Galbert, A. W., Locust Bayou.
- Gatewood, P. G., Beebe.
- Gardner, G. H., Pastoria.
- Garner, M., Dublin.
- Garrison, P. A., Violet.
- Gaskins, I. D., Elliot.
- Gatlin, A. B., Three Creeks.
- Gholston, G. G., Colt.
- Gibson, W. B., Monticello.
- Giddens, C. M., Prescott.

Sermons, Addresses and Reminiscences and Important Correspondence

- Gill, A., Locust Bayou.
- Gibson, E., Pine Bluff.
- Goff, J. W., Jakajones.
- Goldsbury, Wm., Barton.
- Goodwin, H. G., Tremont.
- Goodwin, R. G., New London.
- Gordon, M. F., Ozark.
- Gorman, J., Rosston.
- Grant, W. L., Pine Bluff.
- Gray, W. E., Galloway.
- Green, E., Fordyce.
- Green, J. W., Carlisle.
- Green, Wm., Widener.
- Griggs, J. A., Mandeville.
- Gross, A., Baxter.
- Grove, D. B., Little Rock.
- Grundy, H., Jericho.
- Guy, R. W., Jonesboro.
- Guyler, L. R., Columbus.
- Hale, I. J., New Lewisville.
- Hall, D., Clear Lake.
- Hall, J. W., Carlisle.
- Hammond, J. H., Jericho.
- Hardin, S. P., Lake Village.
- Hardner, J. W., Haynes.
- Hardy, B. J., Texarkana.
- Harper, C., Pine Bluff.
- Harper, M. I., Concord.
- Harrell, Wm., Rocky Comfort.
- Harris, J. M., Texarkana.
- Harris, N. P., De Ann.
- Harshaw, J., Hickory Plains.
- Haskell, R., Linwood.
- Hatchett, P., Little Rock.
- Hawkins, I. H., Arkadelphia.
- Hawkins, M., Springfield.
- Hawthorne, A. W., Junction City.
- Hayes, M., Conway.
- Hayes, N. H., Plumerville.
- Hayes, R. H., Plumerville.

- Hayes, B. H., Redemption.
- Hayward, L. J., Pine Bluff.
- Haywood, B. F., Richmond.
- Heggins, Wm., Turner.
- Henderson, F. H., Arkansas Post.
- Henderson, S. E., Forrest City.
- Henderson, W. H., Woodson.
- Henry, A. J., Scotts.
- Henry, G. H., Carmel.
- Herington, Robert, Junction City.
- Hester, G. W., Grand Lake.
- Hill, N. H., Little Rock.
- Hill, R. H., Dumas.
- Hill, R. H., McCrory.
- Hill, W. H., Forrest City.
- Hillard, T. P., Texarkana.
- Hilton, E. W., Dermott.
- Hinton, J. H., Baxter.
- Hoke, J. H., D. D., Little Rock.
- Holland, N. H., Gaines Landing.
- Holmes, W. A., Helena.
- Holmes, W. H., Red Fork.
- Holt, J. H.
- House, J. H., Plumerville.
- Houston, C. H., Scotts.
- Huggins, W. D., Poplar Grove.
- Humble, W. A., Palarm.
- Humphrey, J. D., Brinkley.
- Hunt, L. H., Dexter.
- Hunt, W. H., Conway.
- Hunter, J. H., Clinton.
- Hunter, N. H., Hydrick.
- Jackson, A. J,. Junction City.
- Jackson, L., Osceola.
- Jackson, L. Y., Pine Bluff.
- Jackson, Wm., Palestine.
- Jarrett, Wm., Coffee Creek.
- Jamison, J. R., Plumerville.
- Jeffries, J. S., No. Little Rock.
- Jeffries, R. W., Moro.

Sermons, Addresses and Reminiscences and Important Correspondence

- Jeffery, C. I., McGehee.
- Jenkins, B. J., Helena.
- Jenkins, ., Damascus.
- Jimmerson, N. J., Eight Miles.
- Johnson, A. D., Brinkley.
- Johnson, A. W., Beirne.
- Johnson, C., Pecan Point.
- Johnson, H., De Queen.
- Johnson, I. J., Helena.
- Johnson, J. S., Fairfield.
- Johnson, S. J., No. Little Rock.
- Johnson, T. J.
- Johnson, W. F., Cummins.
- Johnson, W. F., Park Place.
- Johnson, W. H., Ozan.
- Johnson, W. P., Scotts.
- Jones, C. W., Southland.
- Jones, F. L., Arkadelphia.
- Jones, H. M., Holly Grove.
- Jones, J. J., Texarkana.
- Jones, J. S., Wabbaseka.
- Jones, J. J., Columbus.
- Jones, M., Clarendon.
- Jones, M. J., Douglass.
- Jones, R. B., Holly Grove.
- Jones, S. J., Chidester.
- Jones, T. J., Grayson.
- Jones, W. B., Ladd.
- Jones, W. J., Augusta.
- Jordan, D. L., Oak Forest.
- Jordan, H. J., Monticeno.
- Kale, Jno., Helena.
- Keeble, J. A., Devalls Bluff.
- Kegler, James, Butler.
- Keith, R. H., Carmel.
- Kellogg, G. L., McAlmost.
- Kemp, J. C., Lansing.
- Keyes, C. H., McGehee.
- Kimbrew, S., Pine Bluff.
- King, O. R., Little Rock.

Sermons, Addresses and Reminiscences and Important Correspondence

- Kirkland, H., Sunnyside.
- Knowles, P. A., Little Rock.
- Knox, G. B., Center Ridge.
- Knox, J. E., B. S., Little Rock.
- Knox, P. B., Center Ridge.
- Konints, M., Richmond.
- Lacey, A. A., Gillett.
- Lacey, T. A., Southbend.
- Ladell, J. S., Conway.
- Lawson, R., Little Rock.
- Lawson, T. L., England.
- Leak, A., Sunnyside.
- Lee, J. M., Clarendon.
- Lemley, T. H., Atkins.
- Lewis, G. W., Greer.
- Lewis, W. L., Germantown.
- Linsey, D. L., Pine Bluff.
- Linsey, H., Formosa.
- Littlejohn, J., Marianna.
- Lockett, R. W., Stuttgart.
- Love, F. F., Pendleton.
- Lovelace, W. F., Wynne.
- Lowe, G. W., Holly Grove.
- Lowe, J. P., Magnolia.
- Lyons, J. W., Luxoria.
- Madden, S. M., Mound City.
- Madison, K. G., St. Charles.
- Marshall, C., Wabbaseka.
- Martin, R. C., Cypert.
- Massey, Wm., Marianna.
- Matlock, E. T., Roe.
- Matthews, H. L., Hamburg.
- Matton, J. M., Seyppel.
- McCamey, J. M., Garland City.
- McClelland, A., Lakeport.
- McClelland, R. B., Rocky Comfort.
- McCoy, J. C., Stamps.
- McCoy, S. M., Pine Bluff.
- McDaniel, I. S., Lick Mountain.
- McDaniel, M. D., Reedville.

Sermons, Addresses and Reminiscences and Important Correspondence

- McGillen, R., Julius.
- McKay, M., Tiller.
- McKinney, S. M., Germantown.
- McKinsey, S. H., Spring Creek.
- McLemore, M. W., Plumerville.
- McLemore, O., Pural.
- McLin, D. V., Vernon.
- McMillan, H. M., Little Rock.
- McMillan, H. R., Cotton Plant.
- McNeal, G. L., Kedron.
- McNeely, M., Clinton.
- McSpringer, M., Forrest City.
- Meadowes, H., Kedron.
- Menser, J. C., Hillsboro.
- Meux, C. S., Nodena.
- Middlebrook, A. M., Pine Bluff.
- Miller, A. H., Helena.
- Miller, A. J., Harwood.
- Miller, A. S., Dexter.
- Miller, H., Menifee.
- Miller, J. M., Forrest City.
- Mitchell, D. J., Helena.
- Mitchell, James, Fort Smith.
- Mitchell, J. S., Camden.
- Mitchell, R. A., Plumerville.
- Moore, B. F. H., Sweet Home.
- Moore, B. J., Sarassa.
- Moore, J. M., Fulton.
- Moore, L. C., Hyde Park.
- Moore, M. C., Rocky Comfort.
- Moore, M. W., Plummersville.
- Moore, N. W., Morrillton.
- Morgan, C. W., Winchester.
- Morgan, J. J., Wynne.
- Morris, C. M., Spring.
- Morris, E. C., D. D., Helena.
- Morton, L., Tucker.
- Moseley, R. E., Augusta.
- Moseley, S. A., Pine Bluff.
- Moss, L. G., Colona.

- Moss, R. M., Prescott.
- Moultry, W. M., Widener.
- Murphey, T. J., Louann.
- Neasley, J. H., Corner Stone.
- Nelson, D. J., Parkdale.
- Nelson, I. S., Van Buren.
- Nelson, J. M., Helena.
- Nelson, J. N., Colesboro.
- Netherland, C. L., Fayetteville.
- Newsome, T. F., Clifton.
- Nichols, E. D., Tucker.
- Nightengale, D., Hot Springs.
- Norphleet, D. Pine Bluff.
- Norris, N. L., Poplar Grove.
- Norton, J. M., Batesville.
- Odom, S. S., Brinkley.
- O'Neal, G. L., Randall.
- Otey, Wm., Marianna.
- Owens, H., Marianna.
- Owens, J. M., Augusta.
- Owens, M., Little Rock.
- Paradise, J. W. S., Palestine.
- Parks, Wm., Morrillton.
- Patterson, F. K., Little Rock.
- Patterson, R. W., Mount Holly.
- Patton, W. D., Park Place.
- Paxton, J. P., Kress City.
- Payne, J., Turner.
- Payne, W. S., Ethel.
- Pearce, L., Curtis.
- Pennington, W. P., Emmet.
- Percy, J. P., Ashvale.
- Pettis, H. C., Marianna.
- Pettis, R. S., Grady.
- Petty, J. D., Seyppel.
- Phillips, Jas., Crocketts Bluff.
- Pitts, I. L., Goodwin.
- Polk, R. P., Forrest City.
- Pope, R., Dardanelle.
- Powell, N., Palarm.

Sermons, Addresses and Reminiscences and Important Correspondence

- Price, S. P., Hannaberry.
- Proffitt, M., Helena.
- Pugh, P., Lake Village.
- Pumphrey, M. P., Scotts.
- Rand, J., Douglass.
- Ratcliffe, B., Gaines Landing.
- Reason, M., Altheimer.
- Redd, C., Olden.
- Redic, A., Little Rock.
- Reed, Job, Eldorado.
- Reed, R., Dermott.
- Reed, Wm., Winchester.
- Reeves, T. M., Stuttgart.
- Reeves, Wm., Wynne.
- Reeves, Z. R., Hope.
- Rexter, Wm., Seyppel.
- Rhodes, F. R., Buena Vista.
- Rhumph, A. R., No. Little Rock.
- Richard, D., Dermott.
- Richards, A., Junction City.
- Rideoute, R. M., Portland.
- Right, T. A., Dean.
- Riley, T., Pinnacle Springs.
- Ritter, E. W., Portland.
- Roberson, J. T., Toledo.
- Roberson, T. A., Shuler.
- Roberts, S. J., Beulah.
- Robinson, A. R., Lagrange.
- Robinson, E. B., Helena.
- Robinson, F. R., Carmel.
- Robinson, J. P., Little Rock.
- Robinson, L., Lagrange.
- Robinson, N. A., Jefferson.
- Robinson, N. E., Lake Village.
- Rogers, J. C., Pine Bluff.
- Rogers, L., Plummersville.
- Rogers, T. S., Gregory.
- Rogers, Wm., Blanton.
- Roland, J. L., Crawfordville.
- Roland, W. E., Jericho.

Sermons, Addresses and Reminiscences and Important Correspondence

- Rose, A., Bardstown.
- Ross, D. R., Little Rock.
- Ross, J. A., Cooper.
- Rowan, S., Pine Bluff.
- Ruben, S. J., Mannings.
- Runyan, H., Glennville.
- Sandefur, G. S., Wheeling Springs.
- Sandefur, T. S., Guerdon.
- Sanders, J. S., Scotts.
- Sanders, M. S., Pine Bluff.
- Scott, D. C., Spring Creek.
- Scott, J. S., Rocky Comfort.
- Scott, J. T., Sunnyside.
- Screws, T. W., Arkansas City.
- Sears, P. W., Sherman.
- Sharp, C. C., Jefferson.
- Sharp, G. M., Magnolia.
- Shad, D. S., Helena.
- Shelby, G. M., Scanlan.
- Short, S. L., Trenton.
- Shull, J. H., Camden.
- Shull, J. W., Louann.
- Simpson, D., Van Buren.
- Sims, J. H., Wampoo.
- Sims, S., Wampoo.
- Smalls, W. S., Lansing.
- Smith, A. S., Richmond.
- Smith, A., Hensley.
- Smith, E. S., Rison.
- Smith, G. S., Fordyce.
- Smith, J. A., Millwood.
- Smith, M. S., Arkadelphia.
- Smith, N. B., Fordyce.
- Smith, S., Pine Bluff.
- Smith, Wm., Oakdale.
- Smith, W. W., Reydell.
- Spight, J. A., Pine Bluff.
- Springer, M. C., Palestine.
- Starks, J. H., Vandale.
- Stackhouse, E. L., Helena.

- Steel, A. J., Scotts.
- Steel, Jas., Scotts.
- Stevenson, A. G., Crowder.
- Stevenson, H. W., Randall.
- Stevenson, W. S., No. Little Rock.
- Stewart, Wm., Mandeville.
- Stout, J. W., Ashvale.
- Stuckey, J. S., Hope.
- Suggs, J. M., Forrest City.
- Swanagan, D. N., Wittsburg.
- Sykes, R. M., Jonesboro.
- Taffe, B. T., Rocky Comfort.
- Talley, S. T., Osceola.
- Tatum, A. T., Summerville.
- Taylor, G. W., Scanlan.
- Taylor, H. M., Holly Grove.
- Taylor, J M., Little Rock.
- Taylor, O. T., English.
- Taylor, T. G., Marvell.
- Thomas, I. G., Hazen.
- Thomas, M., Fay.
- Thomas, R. T., Fulton.
- Thomas, S. L., Humphrey.
- Thomas, Wm., Pendleton.
- Thompson, E. G., Baucum.
- Thompson, J. N., Forrest City.
- Trent, E. D., Washington.
- Trezevant, G W., Morrillton.
- Turner, J., Lagrange.
- Turner, I. W., Trenton.
- Turner, S. P., Horsehead.
- Turner, S. T., Ware.
- Utterback, H. D., Edmondson.
- Van Pelt, L. J., Fort Smith.
- Vaughn, C., Solgohachi.
- Vaughn, M., Pine Bluff.
- Wade, A. W., Pine Bluff.
- Walker, G. L., New Gascony.
- Walker, H., Conway.
- Walker, L. E., Lufra.

- Walker, L. O., Carmel.
- Walker, R. B., Kenyon.
- Walker, T. W., Helena.
- Walker, Wm., Sweet Home.
- Wall, H., Millwood.
- Walters, T. W., Helena.
- Warren, G. H., Newport.
- Washington, G. B., Earle.
- Washington, G. W., Peters.
- Washington, G. W., Plummersville.
- Washington, G. W., Sherrill.
- Washington, N. R., Kingsland.
- Watkins, P., Palarm.
- Watson, N. C., Marvell.
- Welch, C. W., Okolona.
- Western, H., Texarkana.
- Westmoreland, H. W., Brinkley.
- Wheat, B. L., Palmer.
- White, B. J., Varner.
- White, F. K., Little Rock.
- White, S. C., Van Buren.
- Whitehead, K., Wabbaseka.
- Whittington, C. H., Fort Smith.
- Whitlow, B. W., Malvern.
- Wilkerson, J. W., Jericho.
- Wilkins, C., Corner Store.
- Williams, A. L., McGehee.
- Williams, A., North Creek.
- Williams, C. A., Tillar.
- Williams, C. H., Linwood.
- Williams, E. C., Helena.
- Williams, E. D., De Ann.
- Williams, E. W., Winchester.
- Williams, F., Purel.
- Williams, G. P., Lamberton.
- Williams, G. W., Eldorado.
- Williams, H. W., Clarendon.
- Williams, J. D., Forrest City.
- Williams, L., Camden.
- Williams, N., Chip.

- Williams, O. E., Texarkana.
- Williamson, G. W., Desarc.
- Wills, H. W., Pendleton.
- Wilson, F. W., Rawlison.
- Wilson, H., Houston.
- Wilson, J., Carmel.
- Wilson, J. W., Southbend.
- Wilson, P. D., Little Rock.
- Wilson, R. W., Pine Bluff.
- Wilson, Wm., Marvell.
- Winfrey, C. F., Toltec.
- Wise, C. W., Texarkana.
- Wise, J. W., New Lewisville.
- Woods, C. R., Dob.
- Woods, J. W., Newcastle.
- Woods, Wm., Alma.
- Woodson, H., Lake Village.
- Woolfork, C. A., Gethsemane.
- Woolfork, J. S., Gethsemane.
- Woolfork, S. L., Altheimer.
- Wright, S. L., Rocky Comfort.
- Wright, T. W., La Grange.
- Wymbs, J. W., Crawfordsville.

DISTRICT OF COLUMBIA.

- Alexander, S., Washington.
- Berkeley, G. H., Washington.
- Brooks, W. H., D. D., Washington.
- Brooks, W. T., Washington.
- Brown, B. M., Washington.
- Catlett, A. H., Washington.
- Champ, C. R., Washington.
- Clark, J. T., Washington.
- Cole, G. W., Washington.
- Dent, J. C., Washington.
- Dillard, Jno., Washington.
- Dillard Noah, Washington.
- Epps, J. E., Washington.

Sermons, Addresses and Reminiscences and Important Correspondence

- Gaines, J. W., Washington.
- Gaskins, Madison, Washington.
- Gibbons, Wm. P., Washington.
- Hayes, Peter, Washington.
- Harold, J., Anacostia.
- Holmes, R. L., Washington.
- Hored, W. H., Washington.
- Howard, W. J., Washington.
- Jackson, Andrew, Anacostia.
- Jackson, Wm., Washington.
- Johnson, Robert, Washington.
- Johnson, W. B., D. D., Washington.
- Lamkins, S. C., Washington.
- Lee, Geo. W., D. D., Washington.
- Lee, J. H., Washington.
- Lewis, Peter, Washington.
- Lott, A. A., Washington.
- Loving, J. I., Washington.
- Matthews, J. W., Washington.
- McGoins, Geo. Washington.
- Miller, Shelton, Washington.
- Morris, Daniel, Washington.
- Morton, J. T., Washington.
- Nelson, S. J. R., Washington.
- Peyton, R. V., Washington.
- Phillips, Bartlett, Washington.
- Pratt, Arthur, Washington.
- Robinson, J. E., Washington.
- Robinson, J. H., Washington.
- Robinson, W. J., Washington.
- Shields, A. W., Washington.
- Stewart, Philip, Washington.
- Taylor, Jesse A., Goodhope.
- Taylor, Jno. A., Washington.
- Taylor, R., Spencerville, Md.
- Thomas, A. S., Washington.
- Waller, Washington, Washington.
- Warren, Wm., Washington.
- Waters, W., Washington.
- Wilbanks, Alex., Washington.

Sermons, Addresses and Reminiscences and Important Correspondence

- Willis, Edwards, Washington.
- Winston, J. H., Washington.
- Yancey, Jer., Washington.

FLORIDA

- Anderson, A. A., San Mateo.
- Anderson, J. W., Gainesville.
- Anderson, Paul, Jacksonville.
- Anderson, P. R., Belleview.
- Anderson, W. A., Palma Salo.
- Asia, H. S., Palatka.
- Banks, James, Pensacola.
- Bell, W. M., Palatka.
- Bennett, C., Bradentown.
- Best, E. B., White Springs.
- Blackshear, Jas., Greenwood.
- Blackwell, J. R., Belleview.
- Bowers, Geo., Pensacola.
- Boyd, D., McMeekin.
- Bradley, F. B., Ocala.
- Brawley, E. M., D. D., Palatka.
- Brewer, C., Sanford.
- Brice, W., Gulf Hammock.
- Bridgeman, F. B., Crawford.
- Bristow, T., Belleview.
- Brown, A. F., Fernandina.
- Brown, A. J., Gainesville.
- Brown, D. H., Ocala.
- Brown, J. H., Arcadia.
- Brown, O. D., Reddick.
- Brown, S. B., Martin.
- Broxy, G W., Waukeenah.
- Bryant, G. B., Waukeenah.
- Bryant, M. B., Whitney.
- Buntley, A. B., Lumberton.
- Butler, A. J., Lake Como.
- Butler, P. J., Thomasville, Ga.
- Butler, Thos., Callahan.

Sermons, Addresses and Reminiscences and Important Correspondence

- Cain, F. C., Martin.
- Carter, A., Apalachicola.
- Castleberry, S., Pensacola.
- Clark, J. C., Montague.
- Coleman, G. C., St. Augustine.
- Colson, L., Sarasota.
- Cook, A. C., Jacksonville.
- Cook, Wm., St. Augustine.
- Criswell, W. H., St. Nicholas.
- Crivillier, L. W., Blitchton.
- Dacosta, H. B., Jacksonville.
- Dancey, F., Archer.
- Davidson, W. M., Pensacola.
- Davis, J. A., McMeekin.
- Davis, J. D., Stanton.
- Davis, W. H., Waycross, Ga.
- Dozier, E. L., Jacksonville.
- Dudley, Andrew, Greenwood.
- Dukes, G. H. G., Jacksonville.
- Ealy, J. S., Palmbeach.
- Edwards, W. J., Jacksonville.
- Ellis, R., Greenwood.
- Ellison, N. W., Belleview.
- English, R. S., Ocala.
- Evans, J. J., Madison.
- Evans, M. W., Jacksonville.
- Faulks, F. H., Tampa.
- Finlayson, J. F., Ashville.
- Flemming, H. M., Fernandina.
- Fleming, S., Lake Ogden.
- Frazier, W., Jacksonville.
- Garvin, A., Madison.
- Gilbert, B., Greenwood.
- Gilbert, M. W., Charleston, S. C.
- Glymph, T. A., Cincinnati, Ohio.
- Glymph, Z., Ocala.
- Goodwin, B. F., San Mateo.
- Griffin, L. C., Bellview.
- Hagan, A., Shady.
- Harkenson, J. B., Daytona.

- Harper, H., Brooksville.
- Harris, V. G., Chaires.
- Hart, Geo., Melrose.
- Hayes, A., Greenwod.
- Henderson, P. H., Citra.
- Hill, G. J., Jacksonville.
- Hines, David, Greencove Springs.
- Hinton, John, Perry.
- Hinton, N. T., Cocoa.
- Holy, C. H., New Smyrna.
- Holman, H., Tampa.
- Hurston, John, Eatonville.
- Hutchinson, Jas., Fernandina.
- Hyman, E. W., Dunnellon.
- Isham, Ephraim, Pensacola.
- Jackson, I. J., St. Augustine.
- Jackson, P. P., Apalachicola.
- Jackson, S. H., San Mateo.
- James, A. L., Madison.
- James, P. R., Lakeland.
- Jameson, John, Jacksonville.
- Jelks, H. J., Fernandina.
- Jenkins, S. Q., Palatka.
- Johnson, D. W., Jacksonville.
- Johnson, L. W., Kendrick.
- Johnson, W. M., Wildwood.
- Jones, Ezekiel, Rochelle.
- Jones, E. C., Longwood.
- Jones, H. F., Pensacola.
- Jones, J. A., Gainesville.
- Jones, W. W., Rochelle.
- Kelker, J. Jr., Pensacola.
- Kelley, E., Yallaha.
- Kemp, R., Fernandina.
- Kemp, W. H., Welaka.
- Kilpatrick, C., Tallahassee.
- King, J. W., West Palmbeach.
- King, N. W., Horney.
- Lake, J. B., Bartow.
- Lancaster, F. W., Fernandina.

- Lancaster, T., Jacksonville.
- Lang, Lewis L., Stagepond.
- Lee, C. N., Jacksonville.
- Leonard, Wm., Lloyd.
- Lewis, H., Belleview.
- Lewis, John, Pensacola.
- Lloyd, I. N. L., Grasmere.
- Long, Sandy, Campbellton.
- Long, W. R., Monticello.
- Lorrick, Eph., Jacksonville.
- Luke, Q. H., Jacksonville.
- Lundy, C., Morriston.
- Martin, F. D., Greenwood.
- Martin, G. W., Greenwood.
- Mason, J. T., Pensacola.
- Matthews, J. H., Fort White.
- McClendon, G. W., Bartow.
- McCoy, A. C., Orange Park.
- McCray, A. G., Fort White.
- McDaniel, Peter, Live Oak.
- McGee, Jas., Bostwick.
- McIntosh, C. M., Tampa.
- McKinney, Geo., P., Live Oak.
- Means, A., McIntosh.
- Mickerson, D. A., Lamont.
- Middleton, C. A., Jacksonville.
- Miles, F., Greenwood.
- Mills, W B., Fernandina.
- Mobley, Morris, Brooksville.
- Moore, P. A., Jacksonville.
- Moore, W. L., Madison.
- Morris, N. J., Tampa.
- Mullins, W. M., Pensacola.
- Nance, J. L., Blitchton.
- Newman, J. H., Jacksonville.
- Nobles, J. Jacksonville.
- Norman, A. M., Tallahassee.
- Peacher, B. F., Crystal River.
- Pelham, W. H., Edgar.
- Peppers, F., Palatka.

Sermons, Addresses and Reminiscences and Important Correspondence

- Perkins, W. P., Archer.
- Peterson, Abner. Fernandina.
- Philyaw, D. W., Floral City.
- Pinkney, J. E., Tallahassee.
- Pinkston, M. S., Palatka.
- Posey, J. W., Gainesville.
- Powers, E. L., Greencove Springs.
- Raiford, G. W., D. D., Pensacola.
- Reed, D. L., Bagdad.
- Reese, J. B., Tarpon Springs.
- Reid, E. R., Lakeland.
- Ritchie, A. N., Sparr.
- Roberts, J. E., Baldwin.
- Roberts, Y. A., Palatka.
- Robertson, Edmund, Archer.
- Robinson, G. W., Jacksonville.
- Robinson, H. P., Mt. Dora.
- Robinson, James, Jacksonville.
- Robinson, L. N., Palatka.
- Robinson, M. T., York.
- Robinson, N. W., Titusville.
- Rosier, D. W., Milton.
- Ross, Jas. G., Pittsburg, Pa.
- Sanford, J. W. M., Wildwood.
- Saunders, S. S., St. Augustine.
- Savage, C., Palmetto.
- Scarboro, L. N., Palatka.
- Schofield, J. M., Johnson.
- Scott, C. J., Orlando.
- Scurry, J. B., Drifton.
- Shambley, Geo., Orange Springs.
- Shivery, R. E., Gainesville.
- Simmons, E. F., Gainesville.
- Simmons, J. H., St. Augustine.
- Simmons, W. A., Levyville.
- Smith, C. J., Greencove Springs.
- Smith, E., Blitchton.
- Smith, Osborne, Jacksonville.
- Somers, P. S., Leesburg.
- Spark, S., Lake City.

- Spencer, J., Tallahassee.
- Stewart, M., Ocala.
- Strow, D., Monticello.
- Sumpter, M. J., Callahan.
- Taylor, A., Stanton.
- Taylor, A. F., Esmeralda.
- Taylor, B. J., Sparr.
- Taylor, J. T., Marianna.
- Thomas, P., Jacksonville.
- Thomas, R., Key West.
- Thomas, R. W. H., Pomona.
- Thomas, W. H., Welaka.
- Thompson, B. W., Lake City.
- Thompson, C., Lake City.
- Thompson, W., Brooksville.
- Tillman, G. B., Aucilla.
- Timmons, A., Brooksville.
- Trammell, J. M., Jacksonville.
- Tucker, A. W., Kendrick.
- Tuggles, W. H., Jacksonville.
- Tutson, L. S., Melrose.
- Vann, W. D., Jacksonville.
- Vaught, C. M., Jacksonville.
- Waldron, J. Milton, Jacksonville.
- Walker, A., Edgar.
- Walker, L. W., Clayton.
- Wallace, S., Gainesville.
- Walton, Richard, Archer.
- Washington, L., Brooksville.
- Washington, R. W., De Land.
- Waters, A. W., Blitchton.
- Watson, J. S. P., Jacksonville.
- Welch, A. R., Gainesville.
- Welch, P., Gainesville.
- West, W., Gainesville.
- White, Arthur, Spring Park.
- White, M., Edgar.
- Wilkerson, S., Ocala.
- Wilkerson, W. A., Flemington.
- Williams, H. C., Jacksonville.

- Williams, N. B., Miami.
- Williams, P., Chaseville.
- Williams, R., Jacksonville.
- Williams, T. H., Stanton.
- Williamson, D. A., Jacksonville.
- Wilson, B. F., Blitchton.
- Wilson, C. L., Keysville.
- Wright, B. F., Jacksonville.
- Yates, Handy, Jacksonville.
- Yeoman, P., Sanford.
- Young, E. D., Jacksonville.

GEORGIA

- Abrams, A., Augusta.
- Adams, D., Montezuma.
- Adams, M. A., Dublin.
- Adams, S., Okapilco.
- Alexander, Hugh, Garlandville.
- Alexander, J., Mobley.
- Alexander, S., Forsyth.
- Alexander, Wm., Unionpoint.
- Allen, A. J., Cuthbert.
- Allen, C. J., Sparta.
- Allen, C. L., Luther.
- Allen, G. M., Allentown.
- Allen, R. T., Culverton.
- Allen, T. M., Marietta.
- Amie, A. J., Newnan.
- Anderson, Brown, Dublin.
- Anderson, H. H., Newnan.
- Anderson, Wm. H., Savannah.
- Andrews, P., Gresston.
- Arline, Enoch, Ethel.
- Ash, E., West Point.
- Atkinson, O., Brunswick.
- Austin, H., Milledgeville.
- Austin, M. H., Lakepark.
- Avery, Amos, Pennington.

- Avery, R., Mt. Zion.
- Bailey, F., Valdosta.
- Baker, Henry, Warrenton.
- Banks, G. A., Corinth.
- Barber, A. B., Flovilla.
- Barnes, C. H., Bradley.
- Barnes, G., Augusta.
- Barnes, H., Handy.
- Barnett, Wm., Winterville.
- Barrett, R. B., Albany.
- Barrow, D., Sandersville.
- Bateman, J. H., Savannah.
- Batey, J. B., Hagan.
- Batey, J. M., Augusta.
- Battle, J., Louisa.
- Beard, C. B., Stockton.
- Beasley, S. P., Stateline.
- Beasley, T. H., Wadley.
- Beauford, S., Waycross.
- Beavers, A. J., Carrollton.
- Beavers, J. C., Lithia Springs.
- Beckham, L., Leary.
- Bell, A., Griffin.
- Bell, A., Jr., Bogart.
- Bell, A. J., Stephens.
- Bell, C., Macon.
- Bell, J., Marshallville.
- Bell, Marshall, Watkinsville.
- Benn, H., Godfrey.
- Bennett, H. R., Newnan.
- Bennett, S., Perry.
- Benson, J., Bullards.
- Benton, T., Eatonton.
- Berrien, W. B., Savannah.
- Berry, J. B., Cedartown.
- Bessant, W. B., Waynesboro.
- Bibbs, R. D., Harlem.
- Bicker, E. E. S., Atlanta.
- Bigsbee, E., Brunswick.
- Bines, J. H., Perkins Junction.

- Black, J. W., Lagrange.
- Black, M. H., Dalton.
- Blake, Richard, Bartow.
- Blalock, H., Atlanta.
- Blanchard, A. S., Harlem.
- Bloom, E., Macon.
- Blow, Frank, Cornucopia.
- Boddie, M. B., Lagrange.
- Bolden, J. M., Atlanta.
- Boles, M., Atlanta.
- Bond, D. B., Marietta.
- Bond, L., Savannah.
- Bones, C., Bradley.
- Booker, D. S., Augusta.
- Booker, D. V., Lovelace.
- Borders, J. B., Macon.
- Bostick, L., Fort Valley.
- Bowen, H., Walden.
- Bowers, J., Macon.
- Boyd, R., West Point.
- Bracy, D. C., Buckhead.
- Bradley, H. A., Savannah.
- Branham, C., Everett Station.
- Brantly, S. H., Hawkinsville.
- Brawley, E. M., D. D., Darien.
- Briggs, Geo. W., Augusta.
- Briggs, H., Quitman.
- Bright, J. F., Cartersville.
- Brightharp, C. H., Milledgeville.
- Brightwell, J. H., Maxeys.
- Brinkley, Jacob, Gibson.
- Brittian, David, Rocky Mount.
- Brittian, G. W. P., Winterville.
- Broughton, J. A., Augusta.
- Brown, A., Eastman.
- Brown, Cyrus, Atlanta.
- Brown, C. R., Bartow.
- Brown, E., Browns Crossing.
- Brown, Geo., Savannah.
- Brown, G. W., Berner.

- Brown, H. C., Harlem.
- Brown, J. B., Ousley.
- Brown, J. S., Montezuma.
- Brown, R., Macon.
- Brown, S. R., Forsyth.
- Brown, ... H., Valdosta.
- Brown, W. M., Atlanta.
- Bryan, A. L., Edgewood.
- Bryan, J. C., Brunswick.
- Bryant, E. B., Cochran.
- Bryant, H., Macon.
- Bryant, I., Guyton.
- Bryant, P. J., Atlanta.
- Bryant, P. R., Kirkland.
- Bryant, S. O., Kiokee.
- Bugg, Turner, Harlem.
- Bunn, J. M., Dawson.
- Burge, H. A., Woodstock.
- Burgess, S. B., Perry.
- Burke, H., Pennington.
- Burke, M., Burroughs.
- Burney, J. B., Hemphill.
- Burrus, R. S., Avalon.
- Burson, R. H., Atlanta.
- Bush, J. B., Barnesville.
- Bussey, Turner, Harlem.
- Butler, A. A., Guyton.
- Butler, Geo., Washington.
- Butler, G. B., Buckhead.
- Butler, P. J., Walthourville.
- Butler, S. B., Riceboro.
- Butler, T. M., Adamspark.
- Butler, Thos., St. Marys.
- Byrd, G. S., Smithville.
- Byrd, M., Atlanta.
- Byrd, S. L., Culverton.
- Cain, G., Kathleen.
- Callaway, J. R., Penfield.
- Cameron, R. C., Atlanta.
- Campbell, G. J., Rosier.

Sermons, Addresses and Reminiscences and Important Correspondence

- Campbell, M. C., Stevens Pottery.
- Campbell, M. F., Quitman.
- Campbell, R. C., Lithia Springs.
- Cantrell, W. R., Dougherty.
- Capers, C. H., McIntyre.
- Carlton, L., Athens.
- Carmichael, T. S., Sharpsburg.
- Carr, T. C., Milledgeville.
- Carson, J., Reynolds.
- Carswell, T., Coolspring.
- Carter, A. R., Appling.
- Carter, E. R., Atlanta.
- Carter, Josiah, Hephzibah.
- Carter, M. C., Leesburg.
- Carter, R., Barnesville.
- Carter, Sylvanus, Americus.
- Cash, P. L., Madison.
- Center, J. C., Lithonia.
- Chandler, C., Lowell.
- Chapman, P., Macon.
- Chester, Geo., Arlington.
- Childs, J. H., Macon.
- Chislum, J. J., Lagrange.
- Charlk, J. H., Jesup.
- Clark, A., Munnerlyn.
- Clark, J., Newnan.
- Clark, R. T., Augusta.
- Clay, H. C., Lovelace.
- Clay, O. C., Turin.
- Clayton, A. L., Sparta.
- Cobb, A., Buckland.
- Cobb, T. W., Stockton.
- Cobb, W. C., Georgetown.
- Cochran, R. B., Cochran.
- Cochran, Sam'l, Rutledge.
- Cole, Wm., Chamblee.
- Coleman, G. H., Macon.
- Collins, A. J., Clyattville.
- Collins, Benj., Ohoopee.
- Combs, C. H., Thomson.

Sermons, Addresses and Reminiscences and Important Correspondence

- Combs, Wm., Philomath.
- Coney, Zebulon, Dublin.
- Conley, Aaron, Sandersville.
- Conner, G. W., Drone.
- Conner, S. P., Garfield.
- Cook, S. M., Gresston.
- Cooper, A. Augusta.
- Cooper, J. F., Girard.
- Copeland, S., Unity.
- Corbett, Isham, Irwinton.
- Corbin, Israel, Reynolds.
- Cornelius, A., Fitzpatrick.
- Cornelius, S., Bullards.
- Cost, R., Madison.
- Costin, R., Thomasville.
- Crawford, D. D., Americus.
- Cray, G. L., Baxley.
- Culbertson, M. C., Lagrange.
- Culbertson, S., Lagrange.
- Culbreath, A. S., Smithonia.
- Culpepper, J. C., Warrenton.
- Cummings, E. C., Macon.
- Curtis, A. H., Irwinton.
- Daggett, A., Augusta.
- Daniel, U., Cartersville.
- Daniels, E. S., Camilla.
- D'Antignac, A. L., Noah.
- Darden, John, Milledgeville.
- Davenport, A. R., Point Peter.
- Davis, F. R., Albany.
- Davis, J. B., Thomasville.
- Davis, J. S., Atlanta.
- Davis, Jonah, Milledgeville.
- Davis, J. R., Lockhart.
- Davis, R. D., Watkinson.
- Davis, W. J., Lagrange.
- Dawson, J. W., Lavilla.
- Decatur, I. C., Atlanta.
- Denmond, H. D., Grady.
- Dennard, M., Gardi.

Sermons, Addresses and Reminiscences and Important Correspondence

- Dennard, P., Elko.
- Dias, E. C., Athens.
- Dickerson, D. E., Millen.
- Dillard, G. S., Crawford.
- Dixon, Madison, Augusta.
- Dixon, N. P., Cuthbert.
- Dixon, Valentine, Griffin.
- Dodd, M. A., Alphraretta.
- Dodson, S. T., Belton.
- Dolger, J. E., Thomaston.
- Dominick, Wm., Turin.
- Dooly, F. C., Ironrock.
- Dooly, J., Warrenton.
- Douglass, Wm., Lagrange.
- Downs, J. B., Ellabell.
- Dozier, G., Atlanta.
- Dozier, J. E., Thomaston.
- Drake, J. W., Darien.
- Drake, S. W., Brunswick.
- Drew, S. L., Marietta.
- Drew, Wm., Marietta.
- Drinks, E. V., Dexter.
- Drisley, D. T., Blythe.
- Du Bignon, J. H., Barnesville.
- Dunlap, A. C., Downing.
- Dunn, B. B., Woodville.
- Dunn, C. G., Dawson.
- Dunn, W. H., Augusta.
- Durham, B., Macon.
- Durham, J., Jeffersonville.
- Durham, J. J., Savannah.
- Dwelle, Geo., H., Augusta.
- Dyson, C. D., Thomasville.
- Early, R. H., Lagrange.
- Edwards, J. W., Louisville.
- Edwards, Lewis, Dixie.
- Edwards, N. M., Whitehouse.
- Elder, W. H., Tallapoosa.
- Ellington, A., Elder.
- Ellis, Alex., Savannah.

- Ellis, C. J., Camilla.
- Epkins, I., Lakepart.
- Ethel, H., Harrison.
- Evans, Cyrus, Atlanta.
- Evans, G. N., Crawfordville.
- Evans, J., Athens.
- Evans, E. A., Augusta.
- Evans, F. E., Tallapoosa.
- Evans, S., Madison.
- Evans, Thos., Raysville.
- Everett, G. B., Waycross.
- Fallon, I., Sterling.
- Fambro, J. Y., Madison.
- Fann, P., Fort Valley.
- Farmer, J. F., Atlanta.
- Farmer, J. W., Atlanta.
- Farmer, S. T., Carrollton.
- Farmer, J. W., New Rome.
- Felder, H. L., Perry.
- Findley, D. V., Maxeys.
- Fireall, J. B., Pennick.
- Fisher, E. J., Atlanta.
- Flagg, J. W., Walker Station.
- Fleming, J. W., Savannah.
- Fleming, Wm., Winterville.
- Flewellen, E., Corinth.
- Flowers, A., Newnan.
- Flunell, B., Hickorygrove.
- Forney, M. A., Thena.
- Forsyth, C. F., Westlake.
- Foster, Lewis, Augusta.
- Foster, P. T., Bolingbroke.
- Franklin, J. W., Dublin.
- Frazer, Luke, Dupont.
- Freeman, A. B., Senoia.
- Fuller, Handy, Barnett.
- Fullwood, Jas., Irwinton.
- Garmon, T., Perry.
- Garner, G. H., Pearson.
- Garner, Thos., Athens.

Sermons, Addresses and Reminiscences and Important Correspondence

- Garvin, D. J., Smiley.
- Gary, A., Augusta.
- Gary, T. A., Ousley.
- Gibbs, R. S., Augusta.
- Gibson, J. R., Augusta.
- Gibson, M., Kathleen.
- Gifford, J., Dublin.
- Gilyard, W. M., Augusta.
- Glasscock, Peter, Augusta.
- Glover, Aaron, Shadygrove.
- Glover, S. G., Arlington.
- Goldman, W. H., Waynesboro.
- Goodrum, A., Elgin.
- Goodrum, A. G., Stark.
- Goodwin, G. A., Atlanta.
- Gordon, H., Westlake.
- Gordon, J. D., Louisville.
- Gore, J. W., Chipley.
- Goudy, E., Statenville.
- Grady, R. D., Burns.
- Graham, J. M., Rome.
- Grant, A. T., Halcyondale.
- Grant, H., Savannah.
- Grant, P. T., Patterson.
- Graves, G. E., Brunswick.
- Gray, Wm., Savannah.
- Green, B. J., Waycross.
- Green, Jas., Savannah.
- Green, J. W., Covington.
- Green, O. C., Ellaville.
- Green, P., Wadley.
- Green, S., Lagrange.
- Green, T. G., Matthews.
- Greenway, W. R., Decatur.
- Griffin, A., Hephzibah.
- Griffin, G. W., Savannah.
- Griffin, S. G., Waco.
- Griffith, T. J., Avalon.
- Griswold, J. J., Newnan.
- Groover, T. W., Iric.

- Gross, R., Bainbridge.
- Guilford, H., Ellabell.
- Gullins, D. G., Atlanta.
- Gullins, G. W., Macon.
- Guin, G. W., Midville.
- Hairston, J. W., Luthersville.
- Hall, H., Macon.
- Hall, J. R., Macon.
- Hall, J. H., Midville.
- Hall, P. H., Edy.
- Hall, S. H., Valdosta.
- Hamilton, H. B., Savannah.
- Hamler, M., McDonalds Mill.
- Hammock, T. M., Temple.
- Haralson, C. H., Sasser.
- Hardin, Alonzo, Decatur.
- Hardin, L. J., Davisboro.
- Hardin, N., Waynesboro.
- Harman, R. A., Louisville.
- Harper, J., Ohoopee.
- Harris, J. W., Eastman.
- Harrison, H., Ethel.
- Harrison, M. W., Bayview.
- Hart, N. A., Pembroke.
- Hart, M. W., Warrenton.
- Harvey, A. L., Decatur.
- Harvey, B. T., Atlanta.
- Harvey, G. B., Woodstock.
- Hassell, R., Macon.
- Hawkins, H. W., Rocky Ford.
- Hawkins, P. M., Atlanta.
- Hawthorne, L. A., Kiokee.
- Hicks, J. W., Roundoak.
- Hightower, R., Carrollton.
- Hightower, W. H., Eatonton.
- Hill, S. H., Albany.
- Hill, Wm., Drybranch.
- Hill, W. W., Athens.
- Hilliard, Geo., Greens Cut.
- Hillman, G., Whiteplains.

- Hinsman, J. M., Villa Rica.
- Hinton, S., Stone Mountain.
- Hollingshead, H., Sandypoint.
- Holmes, C. G., Rome.
- Holmes, Wm. E., Atlanta.
- Homes, G. E., Oliver.
- Hopkins, G. W., Norcross.
- Hornsby, T. J., Augusta.
- Horton, Henry, Athens.
- Horton, J. H., Athens.
- Howard, B. J., Athens.
- Howard, E., Macon.
- Hubert, M., Pride.
- Hudson, A., Savannah.
- Hudson, F., Lakepark.
- Hughes, Allen, Dublin.
- Hughes, J. T., Lightfoot.
- Hughes, M., Johnston Station.
- Hull, S., Monroe.
- Hunter, A. H., Norcross.
- Hunter, Green, Gainesville.
- Hunter, Peter, New Providence.
- Hutchins, W. H., Centerville.
- Irby, J. S., Savannah.
- Irvin, E., Hardaway.
- Ivey, R., Evans.
- Jackson, H., Savannah.
- Jackson, A. J., Barnett.
- Jackson, B. J., Savannah.
- Jackson, D. V., Leesburg.
- Jackson, Geo., Macon.
- Jackson, Henry, Augusta.
- Jackson, Nathan, Unionpoint.
- Jackson, R. J., Savannah.
- Jackson, S. J., Swainsboro.
- Jackson, Thornton. Unionpoint.
- Jackson, Wm., Metcalf.
- Jackson, W. J., Ector.
- Jacob, A., Davisboro.
- James, A. J., Thomasville.

Sermons, Addresses and Reminiscences and Important Correspondence

- James, L. H., Savannah.
- Jenkins, P. J., Augusta.
- Jenkins, E., Mobley.
- Jenkins, J., Wadley.
- Jenkins, P. W., Savannah.
- Jenk, M., Orchard Hill.
- Jennings, J. N., Octavia.
- Jennings, W. J., Augusta.
- Johnson, A., Savannah.
- Johnson, B., Warrenton.
- Johnson, E., Crawfordville.
- Johnson, E. G., Stanley.
- Johnson, E. P., Atlanta.
- Johnson, E. W., Athens.
- Johnson, Gad S., Macon.
- Johnson, G. T., Walker Station.
- Johnson, G. W., Crawfordville.
- Johnson, N. A., Leesburg.
- Johnson, P. L., Camilla.
- Johnson, P. P., Grovetown.
- Johnson, R., Milledgeville.
- Johnson, Robt., Watkinsville.
- Johnson, L., Philomath.
- Johnson, Wm., Cedartown.
- Johnson, W. C., Waycross.
- Johnson, W. G., Macon.
- Jones, B., Albany.
- Jones, C. O., Atlanta.
- Jones, E., Quitman.
- Jones, G. W., Kiokee.
- Jones, H., Harlem.
- Jones, Isham, Statenville.
- Jones, John J., Albany.
- Jones, J. N., Americus.
- Jones, Jas., M., Iric.
- Jones, Jerry M., Rocky Ford.
- Jones, J. N., Flint.
- Jones, R., St. Marys.
- Jones, R. M., Kiokee.
- Jones, Wm., Norcross.

Sermons, Addresses and Reminiscences and Important Correspondence

- Jones, W. L., Atlanta.
- Jordan, A. J., Forsyth.
- Jordan, Benj., Dawson.
- Jordan, D. J., Dawson.
- Jordan, Wm., Liberty Hill.
- Joyner, M., Hawkinsville.
- Justice, B., Devereaux.
- Keith, B., Brunswick.
- Keith, E. D., Canton.
- Keith, O. T., Carronton.
- Kellam, J., Stephensville.
- Kelley, E., Norcross.
- Kelly, R., Mobley Pond.
- Kelsey, A. P., Bartow.
- Kent, M., Sylvania.
- Kidd, John, Sandycross.
- Killings, J. W., Milledgeville.
- King, A., Twiggsville.
- King, C. T., Louisville.
- King, R. D., Lagrange.
- King, Stepney, Parnell.
- Kitchens, Y., Agricola.
- Klugh, D. S., Augusta.
- Knight, C., Leliaton.
- Lacy, Thos., Augusta.
- Lacy, W. H., Greens Cut.
- Ladson, P., Martinez.
- Lamar, H., Milledgeville.
- Lamb, R. J., Quince.
- Landman, P. H., Savannah.
- Lane, G. W., Millen.
- Lane, H. C., Waynesboro.
- Lane, P., Lagrange.
- Lane, R., Millen.
- Langston, Perry, Woodville.
- Lanier, C., Excelsior.
- Lanier, F., Collins.
- Law, Edward, Rays Mills.
- Lawrence, C. L., Wadley.
- Lawson, J. W., Augusta.

- Lawson, R., Hollywood.
- Layson, O. C., Eatonton.
- Leak, S., Boston.
- Lee, S. B., Cork.
- Leary, E., Macon.
- Lemons, J. F., Oakley Mill.
- Leonard, Lewis, Dixie.
- Level, J., Newnan.
- Lewis, Geo., Macon.
- Lewis, J., Athens.
- Lewis, J. L., James.
- Lewis, R., Augusta.
- Linert, P. P., Waynesboro.
- Linsley, J. J., Lagrange.
- Linton, F., Baxley.
- Lockett, H., Macon.
- Lockett, T., Brunswick.
- Lockhart, C., Metasville.
- Locklin, B. J., Monroe.
- Love, W. L., Grantville.
- Lovett, S. J., Statesboro.
- Lovett, W. H., Millray.
- Lowe, Richard, Athens.
- Luke, G. W., Lagrange.
- Lundy, Albert, Macon.
- Luper, G. L., Marietta.
- Mack, A., McBean Depot.
- Mackey, Reuben, Doyle.
- Maddox, I., Lawrenceville.
- Maddox, J., Senoia.
- Maddox, M. J., Savannah.
- Major, P. J., Waynesboro.
- Manley, C. J., Waycross.
- Mann, A. S., Duluth.
- Marchman, C., Atlanta.
- Marcus, R., Macon.
- Marcus, Samuel, Bullards.
- Marshall, J., Evens.
- Martin, D., Madison.
- Martin, G. W., Atlanta.

- Mathis, A. A., Atlanta.
- Matthis, F. B., Cochran.
- Maxwell, A., Marietta.
- Maxwell, J. R., Savannah.
- McAllister, P., Newnan.
- McArthur, G., Forsyth.
- McCall, N. G., Dublin.
- McCloud, W. A., Wadley.
- McConnell, T. B., Doctortown.
- McCoy, A. C., Franklin.
- McCoy, G. K., Enongrove.
- McCrary, G. W., Jewels.
- McCrary, J. C., Cork.
- McCrary, M. P., Valdosta.
- McCray, J., Forsyth.
- McFarland, A., Walker Station.
- McGarrity, H. J., Royston.
- McGowan, I. J., Harlem.
- McGriff, S., Surrency.
- McGuire, M. C., Atlanta.
- McHorton, D., Augusta.
- McIntosh, A., Atlanta.
- McJunkin, D. F., Royston.
- McKeever, Thos., Boston.
- McKinne, A. R., Elberton.
- McNatt, Thos., Savannah.
- McNeal, S. A., Columbus.
- McTier, D., Baxley.
- Mead, J. M., Stone Mountain.
- Melson, C. C., Enongrove.
- Merrien, P. M., Louisville.
- Merritt, J. M., Albany.
- Michael, J. M., Svlania.
- Mifflin, P. R., Darien.
- Miller, G. C., Darien.
- Miller, G. W., Morven.
- Mills, L., Macon.
- Mims, C., Macon.
- Minter, G. W., Covington.
- Minter, W. W., Munnerlyn.

- Mitchell, A. F., Flatcreek.
- Mitchell, C. M., Carrollton.
- Mitchell, C. T., Gracewood.
- Mitchell, Esau, Patten.
- Mitchell, G. B., Forsyth.
- Mitchell, H. M., Cedartown.
- Mitchell, K. D., Ailey.
- Mitchell, R. J., Patten.
- Mitchell, S., Moreland.
- Mitchell, S. M., Atlanta.
- Mitchell, W., Athens.
- Mitchell, Wm., Brunswick.
- Mobley, P. M., Hogansville.
- Monroe, J. M., Camilla.
- Monson, R., Americus.
- Moody, J. P., Newnan.
- Moore, B. W., Gardi.
- Moore, M., Washington.
- Moore, M., P., Dawson.
- Morgan, Henry, Augusta.
- Moreland, W. S., Cork.
- Morris, C., Warrenton.
- Morris, J. H., Baxley.
- Morton, Jas., Watkinsville.
- Moseley, A., Smiley.
- Moseley, B. B., Albany.
- Moseley, D. A., Albany.
- Murden, A. B., Athens.
- Murden, D., Woodville.
- Murphy, I. M., Atlanta.
- Murray, A., Crawford.
- Neely, J. F., Newnan.
- Nevells, J. W., Surrency.
- Newby, R., Cornucopia.
- Newell, J. W., Moreland.
- Newsom, J. J., Quitman.
- Newton, B. E., Bolingbroke.
- Noble, C. J., Augusta.
- Norris, H., Wood.
- Norris, I. V., Senoia.

- O'Brien, S., Kiokee.
- Odom, A. T., Albany.
- Odom, Frank, Milledgeville.
- Olley, Wm., Parnell.
- Owens, Henry, Augusta.
- Owens, H. H., Augusta.
- Owens, S., Grantville.
- Owens, S., Louisa.
- Overstreet, W. W., Captola.
- Pace, Edmond, Atlanta.
- Parker, Calvin, Philomath.
- Parker, J. A., Atlanta.
- Parks, B. S., Toomsboro.
- Parkston, E., Howard.
- Partee, Y., Bairdstown.
- Paschal, J. P., Waycross.
- Paschal, T., Decatur.
- Pate, A., Culverton.
- Pate, W. H., Walthourville.
- Patrick, F., Macon.
- Payne, A., Cochran.
- Phillips, M. P., Albany.
- Phillips, Wm., Atlanta.
- Philpot, A. J., Newnan.
- Pierce, Andrew, Athens.
- Pierce, L. D., Tyty.
- Pinkston, J. A., Claxton.
- Pitman, H. G., Americus.
- Pitman, J. S., West Point.
- Pitman, P. C., Cork.
- Pitman, T., Albany.
- Pitts, S. P., Louisville.
- Poe, L., Milner.
- Poindexter, J. G., Rome.
- Ponder, M. P., Forsyth.
- Porter, Jackson, Montezuma.
- Ports, H. P., Alexander.
- Powell, J., Halcyondale.
- Powers, A. C., Winterville.
- Poythress, A. S., Owensbyville.

Sermons, Addresses and Reminiscences and Important Correspondence

- Pratt, H., Covington.
- Price, D., Barnesville.
- Prior, A., Waynesboro.
- Proctor, A. P., Macon.
- Proctor, C., Bartow.
- Proctor, S., Forsyth.
- Price, S. P., Grady.
- Pritchett, M. O., Corinth.
- Ranear, B. H., Savannah.
- Rayford, C., Powelton.
- Rayford, Jos., Statenville.
- Rayford, W. M., Milledgeville.
- Raymond, R., Dixie.
- Reese, C., Mountville.
- Reese, Jas., Bath.
- Reid, A. D., Hawkinsville.
- Reid, Chas. C., Mesena.
- Reynolds, D., Social Circle.
- Richards, A., Milledgeville.
- Richards, R., Athens.
- Richardson, D., Sterling.
- Richardson, J., Laurens Hill.
- Richardson, N., Laurens Hill.
- Richie, N., Locust Grove.
- Ridgeway, Lemuel, Monroe.
- Riggins, J. C., Atlanta.
- Ringer, M. L., Lagrange.
- Roberts, H., Haides.
- Roberts, A. M., St. Marys.
- Roberts, B. J., Sheffield.
- Roberts, E., Sylvania.
- Roberts, S. C., Brunswick.
- Robertson, G. R., Midville.
- Robey, H. G., Eatonton.
- Robinson, A., Atlanta.
- Robinson, J., Bremen.
- Rogers, Julius, Darien.
- Rogers, I. R., Greensboro.
- Rooks, A., Culloden.
- Rosier, S. D., Augusta.

Sermons, Addresses and Reminiscences and Important Correspondence

- Ross, J. M., Eatonton.
- Rozzell, E. J., Brunswick.
- Ruff, Frank, Rutledge.
- Rug, T. J., Wisdoms Store.
- Russell, J. T., Wadley.
- Russell, Wm., Augusta.
- Samuel, W., Oconee..
- Samuels, M. F., Appling.
- Sanders, Geo., Camilla.
- Sanders, J. A., Mobley.
- Sanders, R., Camilla.
- Sanders, S., Bairdstown.
- Sapp, J. M., Alexander.
- Sapp, S., Alexander.
- Scott, B. J., Hartwell.
- Scott, E. L., Quitman.
- Scott, J. M., Hawkinsville.
- Scott, J. S., Weisman.
- Scott, W., Albany.
- Scott, W. J., Balton.
- Sellers, Henry, Dixie.
- Sewell, Chas., Moreland.
- Shannon, G. W., Milner.
- Shell, M., Griffin.
- Siffrage, R. C., McDonalds Mill.
- Simmonds, F. M., Covington.
- Simms, J. M., Savannah.
- Sims, D., Maxeys.
- Sims, J. H., Athens.
- Sims, Lafayette, Aonia.
- Sims, S. F., Lula.
- Sims, T. H., Newnan.
- Sims, W. M., Enongrove.
- Simpkins, J. B., Cuthbert.
- Simpson, C., Americus.
- Slayman, G. S., Modoc.
- Slayton, G. W., Jr., Crawford.
- Smith, A., Newnan.
- Smith, Alex., Athens.
- Smith, A. W., Newnan.

- Smith, C. W., Lexington.
- Smith, D. A., Newnan.
- Smith, H. M., Crawford.
- Smith, Isaac, Newnan.
- Smith, J. A. J., Gennie.
- Smith, J. C., Waco.
- Smith, J. H., Welcome.
- Smith, J. W., Macon.
- Smith, O., Elberton.
- Smith, R., Lagrange
- Smith, R. B., Lutherville.
- Smith, R. D., Antioch.
- Smith, S. S., Buckhead.
- Smith, Wm., Bremen.
- Smith, W. C., Bartow.
- Smith, W J., Newnan.
- Smith, W. L., Carrollton.
- Snelling, R. S., Macon.
- Solomon, H. S., Kathleen.
- Solomon, J. A., Pippin.
- Solomon, L., Cuthbert.
- Spann, C. M., Louisville.
- Spann, N. S., Midville.
- Spann, R., Louisville.
- Spearing, J. R., Evelyn.
- Spence, J., Camilla.
- Staley, A. S., Americus.
- Stanfield, A. L., Buckhead.
- Stark, Pleasant, Lexington.
- Stephen, C., Grantville.
- Stephen, J. T., Solomon.
- Stevens, T., Sparta.
- Stevens, W., Lilburn.
- Stewart, York, Butler.
- Stinson, H., Atlanta.
- Stokes, C., Handy.
- Stokes, W. J., Newnan.
- Storgen, G. W., Franklin.
- Story, Wm., Newnan.
- Stovall, A. J., Athens.

Sermons, Addresses and Reminiscences and Important Correspondence

- Stovall, Isaac, Maysville.
- Streeter, J. T., Atlanta.
- Strong, J. S., Americus.
- Styles, H. S., Marietta.
- Styles, W. H., Thebes.
- Sutton, S. P., Ola.
- Swain, J. W., Macon.
- Swan, G. W., Palmetto.
- Swanson, B., Lagrange.
- Sweet, A. B., Blackcreek.
- Sweetwine, M., Brunswick.
- Tanner, J. T., Hogansville.
- Tarver, W. F., Quitman.
- Taylor, G. L., Thomasville.
- Taylor, J. T., Whigham.
- Taylor, M., Dames Ferry.
- Taylor, R., Mitchell.
- Taylor, S. T., Eatonton.
- Taylor, Wm., Vienna.
- Thomas, D. A., Macon.
- Thomas, F. M., Forsyth.
- Thomas, James, Martinez.
- Thomas, J. H., Savannah.
- Thomas, S., Devereaux.
- Thomas, W. M., Peachtree Park.
- Thompson, A. G., Oneida.
- Thompson, F. T., Savannah.
- Thompson, J. A., Tennille.
- Thompson, N. T., Culverton.
- Thornton, M. L., Greensboro.
- Thrasher, E. T., Atlanta.
- Thurman, S. M., Jackson.
- Tilman, P., McIntosh.
- Tilman, W. H., Atlanta.
- Tooks, A., Fort Valley.
- Trimble, C., Dames Ferry.
- Trimble, R. T., Tallapoosa.
- Trowbridge, A. T., Sandersville.
- Tucker, Marcus, Westpoint.
- Tuggle, W. H., Atlanta.

Sermons, Addresses and Reminiscences and Important Correspondence

- Turner, Henry, Lyneville.
- Turner, Pete, Lyneville.
- Turner, T. E., Macon.
- Turnipseed, W. H., Stockbridge.
- Upshaw, G. W., Pinelog.
- Vandegriff, J. P., Boston.
- Veal, C. T., Watkinsville.
- Vest, H., Grantville.
- Vincent, H., Statham.
- Watkins, W., Stilesboro.
- Walker, E., Americus.
- Walker, James, Savannah.
- Walker, J. W., Savannah.
- Walker, N., Millen.
- Walker, P., Augusta.
- Walker, S. C., Augusta.
- Walker, S. M., Claxton.
- Walker, T. W., Wrightsville.
- Wallace, G. W., Unionpoint.
- Wallace, M. W., Millen.
- Walton, B., Covington.
- Ward, G. W., Toland.
- Ward, G. W., Jr., Forsyth.
- Ward, P., Siloam.
- Ware, A. N., Metasville.
- Warner, Geo. W., Savannah.
- Warner, N. W., Americus.
- Washington, D. W., Naylor.
- Washington, E. W., Augusta.
- Washington, F. E., Burroughs.
- Washington, G., Machen.
- Washington, G. H., Albany.
- Washington, Jas., Shadyville.
- Waters, D., Savannah.
- Watkins, P. W., McBean Depot.
- Watson, C. H., Locust Grove.
- Watson, J. E., Worthville.
- Watson, W. B., Cork.
- Watts, Jos., Forsyth.
- Way, Henry, Hawkinsville.

- Weaver, J. W., Waynesboro.
- Weaver, P. G., Carrollton.
- Weeks, Simon, Montezuma.
- Weems, S., Louisville.
- West, H., Grantville.
- Weston, W. L. P., Savannah.
- Whitaker, Jno., Augusta.
- White, A. W., Thomasville.
- White, C. W., Pennick.
- White, E. V., Thomson.
- White, H. W., Atlanta.
- White, W. J., D. D., Augusta.
- White, W. J., Cedartown.
- White, W. W., S. Atlanta.
- Whitefield, A. B., Wrightsville.
- Whitehead, Duncan, Greens Cut.
- Whitehead, G. W., Sardis.
- Whitehead, J. W., Augusta.
- Whitfield, J. W., Dawson.
- Whitfield, W. C., Collins.
- Whitfield, W. H., Waynesboro.
- Whitlock, D. J., Nankin.
- Whitmore, J. B., Augusta.
- Whitmire, N. H., Savannah.
- Wilkerson, E., Senoia.
- Wilkerson, N., Greens Cut.
- Wilkes, F. B., Eatonton.
- Wilkins, C. S., Augusta.
- Wilkinson, P. W., Owensbyville.
- Williams, A., Barnett.
- Williams, A. W., Atlanta.
- Williams, Chas., Augusta.
- Williams, H., Frazier.
- Williams, James, Augusta.
- Williams, J. C., Barnesville.
- Williams, J. M., Daisy.
- Williams, J. W., Augusta.
- Williams, R., Perry.
- Williams, Robert, Macon.
- Williams, W., Athens.

- Williams, Wm., Macon.
- Williamson, N. B., Albany.
- Willis, T. W., Frankville.
- Wilson, A., Baileys Mills.
- Wilson, A. W., Augusta.
- Wilson, D. B., Walker Station.
- Wilson, G. W., Savannah.
- Wimberly, W., Cochran.
- Wimbish, D. J., Greenville.
- Winn, S. A., McIntosh.
- Winters, J., Cedartown.
- Wood, M. C., Enongrove.
- Woods, E. L., Chamblee.
- Woods, S., Belair.
- Woodbright, J., Damascus.
- Woodbright, J. W., Albany.
- Woodward, F. W., Forsyth.
- Wooten, Robt., Dames Ferry.
- Wright, D., Quitman.
- Wright, J. W., Dixie.
- Wyatt, Sam'l, Shadydale.
- Wynn, Henry W., Summit.
- Wynn, J., Tippettville.
- Wynn, W. B., Garfield.
- Young, G. T., Wadley.
- Young, H., Godfrey.
- Young, J. T., Augusta.
- Young, M., Boston.
- Young, W., Pennington.

INDIAN TERRITORY.

- Alexander, J., Wagoner.
- Balks, J. R., Berwyn.
- Brewer, Samuel, Fort Gibson.
- Brown, T. S. E., Ardmore.
- Campbell, R. G., Muldrow.

- Cartwright, R. A., So. Canadian.
- Crawford, S. T., Purcell.
- Darrington, H. E., Berwyn.
- Elliott, Wm., Fort Gibson.
- Ford, R., Tahlequah.
- Gaston, L., Direct Texas.
- Hall, G. W., Berwyn. [Texas.
- Hambleton, W. M., Garretts Bluff,
- Harris, J. W., Vian.
- Hill, R. H., Garretts Bluff, Texas.
- Johnson, R., Redland.
- Johnson, S. J., Pawpaw.
- Jonas, L., Manard.
- Kernals, Joseph, Muscogee.
- Lyons, C. C., Colbert.
- Monday, M., Braggs.
- Moore, A. J., Stringtown.
- Neal, P. R., Ardmore.
- Pannell, R. C., Berwyn.
- Peter, B. R., Berwyn.
- Ransom, S. M., Marietta.
- Ross, L. T., Tahlequah.
- Rowe, Jesse, Vinita.
- Smith, Thomas, Cado.
- Solomon, Samuel, Muscogee.
- Starr, L. S., Tahlequah.
- Stephens, Wm. W.,, Muldrow.
- Tanner, R. E., Garretts Bluff, Tex.
- Temple, George, Hanson.
- Terrell, S. B., Burneyville.
- Vann, G. A., Tahlequah.
- Ware, E. E., Wynnewood.
- Washington, R. W., Vian.
- White, T. J., Lehigh.

KANSAS

- Anderson, --, Kansas City.
- Blake, W. S., Olathe.

- Burdette, G. W., Lawrence.
- Brown, G. W., Lawrence.
- Banks, R. P., Junction City.
- Banks, W. P., Leavenworth.
- Brown, James, Oskaloosa.
- Braunigan, Wm. R., Bogue.
- Berry, B. F., Weir City.
- Baker, G. N., Topeka.
- Cox, Robt., Salina.
- Childers, A. B., Paola.
- Copeland, M. L., Wichita.
- Coleman, J. A., Coffeeville.
- Clayborne, E. W., Ottawa.
- Davis, John, Dunlap.
- Davis, O., Holliday.
- Dudley, J. L., Fort Scott.
- Durden, Frank, Parsons.
- Dunn, James, Hutchinson.
- Ewing, T. H., Leavenworth.
- Fairfax, A., Parsons.
- Frazier, H. F., Wichita.
- Farley, John, Sedan.
- Grant, W. L., Kansas City.
- Garnett, W. H., Newton.
- Green, E. P., Kansas City.
- Greene, T. W., Mound City.
- Hickman, D., Hill City.
- Hardy, W. R., Wichita.
- Harris, Jessie, Leavenworth.
- Henderson, G. P., Leavenworth.
- Jones, D., Kansas City.
- Jones, C. H., Garnett.
- Jamison, A. D., Kansas City.
- Jackson, S., Wathena.
- Johnson, J. J., Oswego.
- Johnston, R. J., Great Bend.
- Jones, M. S., Garden City.
- King, John, Boner Springs.
- King, J. S., Cherokee.
- Lee, S. M., Bogue.

- Merritt, W. H., Dunlap.
- McNeal, Geo., Kansas City.
- Morrow, J. D., Yale.
- Olden, G. D., Topeka.
- Price, J. W., Emporia.
- Pollett, W. H., Emporia.
- Plummer, H. V., Kansas City.
- Payne, D. D., Humboldt.
- Pierce, T. E., Girard.
- Pierce, A. C., Girard.
- Richardson, J. R., Kansas City.
- Richey, J. E., Frankfort.
- Rainy, J. H., Hutchinson.
- Rainy, G. D., Burlingame.
- Rhodes, Frank, Hiawatha.
- Robinson, N. C., Oswego.
- Rogers, A. J., Yale.
- Scott, H. W., Ottawa.
- Skinner, P. D., Lawrence.
- Stoner, E. C. N., Topeka.
- Smith, C. O., Hutchinson.
- Smothers, Wm., Atchison.
- Teal, Chas, Coffeyville.
- Turner, Reason, Wichita.
- Taylor, W. B., Galena.
- Thomas, D., Edwardsville.
- Thomas, James, Salina.
- Thomas, H., Pittsburg.
- Tutt, C. G., Valley Falls.
- Van Leu, J. H., Wichita.
- Voorhies, A. L., Topeka.
- Wilson, A. E., Kansas City.
- Watson, G. W., Manhattan.
- Watson, G. W., Burlington.
- Wright, J. A., Eudora.

KENTUCKY

- Adams, Joseph, Calhoun.

Sermons, Addresses and Reminiscences and Important Correspondence

- Adams, J. F., Atoka.
- Adams, R. S., Lexington.
- Akens, H., Henderson.
- Alexander, P., Louisville.
- Allen, H. C., Adairsville.
- Allen, M., Louisville.
- Allen, Wm., Lexington.
- Allen, W. C., Franklin.
- Allensworth, J., Hopkinsville.
- Amos, H., Earlington.
- Anderson, E. J., Georgetown.
- Anderson, J. B., Lexington.
- Anderson, D., Louisville.
- Arnett, C. H., Roberts.
- Bailey, J. E., Earlington.
- Bailey, R. T., Nebo.
- Baily, L., Bowling Green.
- Baker, C. C., Bonnieville.
- Baker, H. C., Winchester.
- Baker, W. S., Paducah.
- Barker, R., Corydon.
- Black, W. B., Cynthiana.
- Blanton, J. D., New Concord.
- Bigbee, C. P. M., Newport.
- Blakemore, C. D., New Castle.
- Blackburn, J. L., Bagdad.
- Blewett, J., Bowling Green.
- Brown, H., Rileys.
- Brown, J. J., Greensburg.
- Brown, O. M., Edmonton.
- Brown, G. W., South Carrollton.
- Brown, J. P., Providence.
- Brown, R., Lawrenceburg.
- Brown, J. B., Louisville.
- Brown, William, Bloomfield.
- Browning, James, Bevier.
- Brock, John, Georgetown.
- Brockman, John, Winchester.
- Bright, T., McKinney.
- Buckler, L. T., Campbellsville.

Sermons, Addresses and Reminiscences and Important Correspondence

- Blewitt, P. W., South Union.
- Barlow, P. B., Prices Mill.
- Britt, L. D., Brownsville.
- Brevard, A., Columbus.
- Burnsides, J. K., Lancaster.
- Blanton, J. B., Tharp.
- Buckner, R., Dezarn.
- Buckner, T., Lexington.
- Bush, G. B., Lexington.
- Butler, R. B., Lexington.
- Butler, T. R., Waddy.
- Breckenridge, R., Louisville.
- Bush, Thomas, Centerville.
- Bolling, G. W., Elizabethtown.
- Braddock, G. W., Bandana.
- Broaddus, T. H., Richmond.
- Caldwell, N., Scotts Station.
- Campbell, G. W., Hopkinsville.
- Campbell, M., Gordonsville.
- Campbell, R., Erlanger.
- Canada, A., Shelbyville.
- Canada, G. W., Keene.
- Clark, W. E., Henderson.
- Claybrook, A., Owensboro.
- Collins, James, McHenry.
- Cross, J. C., Mt. Sterling.
- Chinn, J. W., Yarnallton.
- Childs, M., Cicero.
- Coleman, I., Woodlake.
- Claypool, H., Bowling Green.
- Carpenter, H. D., Bowling Gren.
- Carpenter, H. C., Woodburn.
- Craighead, J. W., Louisville.
- Clay, E., Louisville.
- Clark, Calvin, Paducah.
- Clark, J. W., Nicholasville.
- Calamese, J. W., Paris.
- Caldwell, J. M., Smithfield.
- Carter, J., Hustonville.
- Cross, P. W., Stowers.

Sermons, Addresses and Reminiscences and Important Correspondence

- Chrice, R., Bandana.
- Cleaver, D., Leitchfield.
- Caulder, A. L., Junction City.
- Childress, W., Hopkinsville.
- Coleman, W., Versailles.
- Coleman, S., Washington.
- Conn, N. L., Franklin.
- Clark, William, Prices Mill.
- Carter, B., Smiths Grove.
- Cowan, L. W., Montevista.
- Cowherd, E., Greensburg.
- Cowherd, W. P, Saloma.
- Crenshaw, D. W., Cadiz.
- Crenshaw, S. W., Edmonton.
- Dabney, Robert, Cadiz.
- Darden, G. W., Montgomery.
- Davis, D. D., Paducah.
- Davis, C., Harrodsburg.
- Durett, O., D. D., Hickman.
- Durett, P. R., Woodville.
- Duncan, R., Bloomfield.
- Dodd, L. H., Covington.
- Dunlap, L., Springfield.
- Darbland, W. D., Clinton.
- Diggs, C. D., Fulton.
- Diggs, Peter, Madisonville.
- Dickerson, W., Cadiz.
- Dixon, D. F., Bowling Green.
- Dixon, John, Bonnieville.
- Dixon, J. T., Booneville.
- Dorsey, G. W., Corydon.
- Dupee, James, Campbellsville.
- Debo, H., Paducah.
- Dudley, S., Burlington.
- Douglass, E., Lexington.
- Douglass, C. D., Lexington.
- Drain, G. W., Hartford.
- Dunlap, M., Bells Station.
- Duncan, James, Lexington.
- Ealey, J. H., Elkton.

Sermons, Addresses and Reminiscences and Important Correspondence

- Earle, R., Diggersburg.
- Edmonds, A., Henderson.
- Embry, C., Millian.
- Evans, D., Hickman.
- Elliot, G. W., Henderson.
- Engham, J., Seymour.
- Elkins, J. T., Keene.
- Ephraim, J., New Vernon.
- Ewing, Jilson, Dycusburg.
- Faulkner, T. M., Louisville.
- Faulkner, W. G., Clinton.
- Fentress, C. A., Rockcastle.
- Fields, G. H., Barboursvile.
- Fishback, C., Winchester.
- Fishback, C. G., Bowling Green.
- Fishback, C. J., Louisville.
- Fishback, E. T., Frankfort.
- Fisher, G. M., Hopkinsville.
- Fish, G. W., Altamont.
- Fisher, J., Franklin.
- Fisher, W., Danville.
- Flemming, J. J., Hopkinsville.
- Foston, D. H., Owensboro.
- Foster, W. M., Kuttawa.
- Frances, C. R., Casky.
- Frances, D. C., Richmond.
- Francis, S. L. M., Bardstown.
- Frank, J. H., Louisville.
- Fronk, J. A., Mt. Sterling.
- Fry, J. H., Louisvile.
- Fuller, I. Lexington.
- Gaddie, D. A., D. D., Louisville.
- Gaddie, G. R., Saloma.
- Garner, M., Chilesburg.
- Garnett, J., Glasgow.
- Garnett, K., Pinchem.
- Garrett, B. J., Hopkinsville.
- Glover, W. E., Paducah.
- Goggins, R., Somerset.
- Goode, J., Bandana.

- Goodloe, G. S., Perryville.
- Goodloe, S. Q., Perryville.
- Gordon, H. H., Earlington.
- Graham, P., Sonora.
- Graves, A. G., Lexington.
- Green, A. J., Harrodsburg.
- Greenwade, G., Linton.
- Greenwade, J., Bennettstown.
- Gregory, R., Wickliffe.
- Gant, G. T., Lexington.
- Hall, W. B., Pewee Valley.
- Hallowell, Thos., Princeton.
- Hambleton, F. L., Middleboro.
- Hampton, A. S., Corniff.
- Hampton, F. G., Louisville.
- Hampton, G. W., Anchorage.
- Harding, J., Russellville.
- Harper, W. O., Winchester.
- Harris, A. W., Midway.
- Harris, T. H., Lexington.
- Hart, W. F., Maysville.
- Hawkins, J. W., Paducah.
- Hazelwood, G., Silver Lake.
- Henderson, J. H., Lexington.
- Henry, G. H., Barren Plains.
- Henry, N., Hopkinsville.
- Hensley, A., Switzer.
- Hicks, J., Louisvile.
- Hightower, J. H., Louisville.
- Hines, B. J., Louisville.
- Holloway, L. C., Lexington.
- Holmes, R. E., Lawrenceburg.
- Howard, A., Bowling Green.
- Hunter, J. D., Fredonia.
- Hurt, Geo., Columbia.
- Ingram, J., Uno.
- Irwin, R. D., Lexington.
- Jackman, P. H., Columbia.
- Jackson, B. J. M., Reeds Station.
- Jackson, J. I., Georgetown.

Sermons, Addresses and Reminiscences and Important Correspondence

- Jacobs, C. M., Louisville.
- Jacobs, J., Harrods Creek.
- Jacobs, W. H., Prospect.
- Jenkins, M. S., Gracey.
- Johnson, J., Cynthiana.
- Johnson, T. J., Washington.
- Johnson, W., Hickman.
- Johnson, W. M., Louisville.
- Jones, S., Canton.
- Jones, W., Sebree.
- Jones, H. W., Owenton.
- Kane, G. W., Milburn.
- Kennedy, P. H., Henderson.
- Kimberly, W. H., South Carrollton.
- King, Henry, Washington.
- King, S. T., Murphysville.
- Kirby, J. H., Hobsons Store.
- Kirby, J. S., Princeton.
- Kirkwood, H. S., Manitou.
- Lackey, E. W., Barren Forks.
- Lackey, M., Somerset.
- Lackey, J. W. Stanford.
- Ladd, J. E., Cerulean.
- Ladd, Thos., Cadiz.
- Lampkins, I., Millville.
- Lasley, R. H., Allensville.
- Leavel, S. J., Cadiz.
- Leavell, W. H., Princeton.
- Lewis, C. M. C., Bonnieville.
- Lewis, H., Bradenburg.
- Lewis, J., West Point.
- Lewis, J. H., Paris.
- Lewis, J. H., Greenburg.
- Lewis, J. W., Louisville.
- Livers, F. Owenton.
- Locke, S. P., Owensboro.
- Logan, J. M., Stanford.
- Long, Jno., Paducah.
- Loving, G. D., Louisville.
- Lucas, E., Crittenden.

- Mack, S., Shelbyville.
- Mack, T. H., Franklin.
- Majors, C. N., Henderson.
- Majors, L. C., Pembroke.
- Majors, P. S., Hartford.
- Majors, Z. T., Hopkinsville.
- Malone, C., Hopkinsville.
- Mars, E. P., D. D., Louisville.
- Marshall, C. N., Henderson.
- Marshall, C. N., Pinckard.
- May, J. H., South Carrollton.
- Mayfield, J. M., Nicholasville.
- McClellan, B. G., Louisville.
- McCray, Jesse, Hopkinsville.
- Merrifield, A., Louisville.
- Mitchell, R. H. C., Harrodsburg.
- McCutcheon, J. J., Mayfield.
- McFarland, J., Hibbardsvile.
- McFarland, P., Helena.
- McNairy, B., Cadiz.
- McRidley, W. H., D. D., Cadiz.
- Milam, J., Mayfield.
- Mitchell, R., D. D., Frankfort.
- Murrell, O. G., Horse Cave.
- Murrell, P., Glasgow.
- Moran, J. S., Harrisonville.
- Miller, J. B., Lancaster.
- Miller, I., Paytontown.
- Miller, G. B., Richmond.
- Miller, H., Burgin.
- Mills, James, Gresham.
- Moore, G. M., Lexington.
- Moore, J. M., Franklin.
- Moore, G. W., Campbellsville.
- Moore, E. M., Garrettsburg.
- Moore, S. T., Central City.
- Moore, John, Hopkinsville.
- Moreland, J. F. K., Lawrenceburg.
- Murphy, C. J., Eminence.
- Matthews, J T., Glasgow.

- Moran, J., Glasgow.
- Morton, William, Hopkinsville.
- Moseley, M. M., Hopkinsville.
- Motheral, W. L., Cayce.
- Myers, William, Russellville.
- Neal, J., Canmer.
- Nelson, O. A., Maysville.
- Norton, H. J., Altamont.
- Nutter, H., Paris.
- Offutt, E. T., Louisville.
- Offutt, H. C., Franklin.
- Offutt, William, Pensod.
- Orendorf, B., Schochoh.
- Overall, C. C., Louisville.
- Overall, R. H., Campbellsville.
- Owsley, J., Somerset.
- Parks, H., Brassfield.
- Parks, John, Berea.
- Parrish, C. H., D. D., Louisville.
- Patton, J. C., Louisville.
- Patterson, H., Pittsburg.
- Paterson, P. P., Stowers.
- Posey, L. S., Henderson.
- Posey, L., Henderson.
- Perdue, J. H., Louisville.
- Polk, J. K., Versailles.
- Pierson, N., Smith's Grove.
- Prewitt, S. H., Owensboro.
- Proctor, A. C., Owensboro.
- Price, J., Covington.
- Price, W. J. M., Ashland.
- Polk, H. D., Henderson.
- Payton, W. H., Richpond.
- Price, C., Hopkinsville.
- Pettis, P. W., Bennettstown.
- Pool, W. H., Hardinsburg.
- Powers, W. H., Mayslick.
- Polk, C. D., Corydon.
- Purce, C. L., D. D., Louisville.
- Quarles, R., Paris.

- Rapier, G. W., Rome.
- Ratcliff, L. B., Earlington.
- Ray, J., Winchester.
- Reed, B. R., Owensboro.
- Reed, E. W., Louisville.
- Reed, John, Paradise.
- Reed, Wm., Buechel.
- Rice, D. A., Campbellsville.
- Riley, J., Louisville.
- Reed, T. R., Berea.
- Reed, G., Paris.
- Reynolds, R., Lagrange,
- Rhodes, I. H., Louisville.
- Russell, A. A., Shelbyville.
- Russell, E. E., Louisville.
- Robb, C. H., Princetown.
- Rollins, B. S., Winchester.
- Rouse, W. T., Franklin.
- Richardson, W. R., Louisville.
- Sadler, H., Depoy.
- Sailes, I., Lexington.
- Samuels, A. M., Pembroke.
- Samuel, W., Jetts Station.
- Sands, C. H., Louisville.
- Shrewsberry, Wm., Utica.
- Silvey, W. T., Providence.
- Slayden, J. H., Dawson.
- Skaggs, B. F., Dezarn.
- Stone, C. W., Bloomfield.
- Stone, G. N., Gadberry.
- Scott, Jacob, Shepherdsville.
- Scott, G. E., Louisville.
- Slaughter, J. R. G., Danville.
- Seales, D. W., Georgetown.
- Shobe, L., Smith's Grove.
- Shobe, M. B., South Union.
- Shobe, L., Chalybeate Springs.
- Smith, E., Barren Forks.
- Smith, S. S., Ambrose.
- Smith, S. E., D. D., Owensboro.

Sermons, Addresses and Reminiscences and Important Correspondence

- Smith, J. O., Lexington.
- Smith, A., Clinton.
- Smith, I. N., Bandana.
- Smith, G. T., Kuttawa.
- Smith, J., Turners.
- Smith, L., Bryantsville.
- Smith, J. W., Louisville.
- Smith, S., Goose Creek.
- Smith, G.W., Whitesville.
- Smith, T. L., Greenville.
- Smith, A., Hopkinsville.
- Smother, C., Versailles.
- Starks, L. W., Greenville.
- Shearer, S., Stanford.
- Strauss, R., Maysville.
- Sleet, M., Mitchellsburg.
- Spencer, G. C., Chilesburg.
- Starks, Y. W., Settles.
- Swope, L., Bryantsville.
- Swope, M., Davistown.
- Talbott, J., Ford.
- Tapp, J. F., Uniontown.
- Taylor, R., Whitewood.
- Taylor, F. T., Adairville.
- Tribble, R., Elizabethtown.
- Thompson, G. H., Leitchfield.
- Tinsley, O., Danville.
- Toliver, W. L., Williamsburg,
- Turner W. L., Russellville.
- Tyler, J. W., Puducah.
- Tilford, G. H., Lexington.
- Thompson, W. D., Kirkville.
- Towns, W., Herndon.
- Tyler, M. W., Allensville.
- Tull, J. C., Willmore.
- Turpin, H. C., Danville.
- Utley, A., Harrodsburg.
- Valentine, J., Garrett.
- Vaughn, C. C., Russellville.
- Vaughn, C. T., Hopkinsville.

Sermons, Addresses and Reminiscences and Important Correspondence

- Venable, G., Franklin.
- Vinegar, P., Lexington.
- Walker, A., Flemingsburg.
- Walker, P., Corydon.
- Ward, G. W., Louisville.
- Watkins, W., Robards.
- Watson, H., Livermore.
- Watts, Fred., Richmond.
- Watts, S. M., Paytontown.
- Watts, W. W., Sadieville.
- Weaver, J. M., Newstead.
- Weathers, R., Zoneton.
- Webster, H. B., Paris.
- Welsh, G. W., McKenney.
- Wilson, A. H., Gresham.
- Whallen, S., Anchorage.
- White, W. T., Knoblick.
- White, J. H., Camp Knot.
- Williams, E., Hopkinsville.
- Williams, A., Bowling Green.
- Williams, N., Georgetown.
- Williams, J. D., Louisville.
- Williams, B., Sacramento.
- Williams, E. P., Mayfield.
- Wheeler, W. W., Hodgensville.
- Wheeler, J. T., Sharpsburg.
- White, W. R., Independence.
- Wills, B., Arlington.
- Wills, G. W., Olmstead.
- Whitesides, R. P., Russellville.
- Willis, T. J., Leitchfield.
- Wilson, J., Kensee.
- Wood, J. E., Danville.
- Wood, W. B., Elizabethtown.
- Woodford, J. C., Becknerville.
- Wright, W. W., Sulphur.
- Young, P. M., Lexington.
- Young, S. P., D. D., Lexington.
- Young, Wm., Lexington.
- Young, William, Louisville.

- Young, Wm., Elkton.

LOUISIANA.

- Abit, Nat., Homer.
- Adam, S., Shreveport.
- Adams, J. W., Donaldsonville.
- Albert, Prince, Baldwin.
- Ambrose, S. J., New Orleans.
- Anderson, E., Thibodeaux.
- Anderson, John, Cottonport.
- Anderson, Levi, St. James.
- Armstead, Geo., Napoleonville.
- Armstrong, Geo., Lobdell.
- Aubert, J. P., Houma.
- Banks, E. D., Jeanerette.
- Baptiste, John, Algiers.
- Barnes, A. L., Liberty Hill.
- Bell, W. D., Vidalia.
- Belt, T. J., Rhoda.
- Benjamin, M., Mansura.
- Bennett, B., Keachie.
- Berry, T. S., Thibodeaux.
- Bird, Geo., Baton Rouge.
- Blount, A. R., Natchitoches.
- Bolden, J. B., Monroe.
- Bolding, Wm. H., New Orleans.
- Boon, J. M., Shreveport.
- Boyd, C. W. J., Opelousas.
- Boyd, Alex., Hamburg.
- Boyd, E., Bordelonville.
- Boykin, Chas. S., Shreveport.
- Bradford, Wm., New Orleans.
- Bragg, S. B., Pisgah.
- Brice, Cyrus, Monroe.
- Brooks, G. W., Delta.
- Brooks, Lucius, Carrollton.

Sermons, Addresses and Reminiscences and Important Correspondence

- Brooks, Robt., Baton Rouge.
- Brown, Burnett, New Orleans.
- Brown, G. W., Shreveport.
- Brown, H., Thibodeaux.
- Brown, H. B. N., Alexandria.
- Brown, John, New Orleans.
- Brown, Thomas, Darrow.
- Brown, Wm., Shiver.
- Bryant, Stephen, New Orleans.
- Burton, S. R., Farmerville.
- Butler, A. R., Arnaudville.
- Butler, Geo., New Orleans.
- Canfield, L. W., Shreveport.
- Canty, Adam, Donaldsonville.
- Carpenter, I. J., St. Joseph.
- Carter, G. W., Houma.
- Carter, I. A., Shreveport.
- Carter, J. M., Mansfield.
- Carter, Nelson, Monroe.
- Cass, Lewis, New Orleans.
- Casimier, G. C., St. Martinsville.
- Clabon, S. C., Shreveport.
- Claiborne, J. C., New Orleans.
- Clanton, S. T., D. D., New Orleans.
- Clark, I. J., Montague.
- Climons, G. R., Patterson.
- Clayton, William, Cloutierville.
- Cobb, D. C., Gretna.
- Coleman, Edmund, Gretna.
- Coleman, H. D., Berwick.
- Coleman, P. D., Delhi.
- Coleman, Robert, New Orleans.
- Columbus, Thomas, New Orleans.
- Cooke, F. H., Vidalia.
- Cooper, S., Ruston.
- Conn, G. C., Lake Providence.
- Cornelius, I. W., Baton Rouge.
- Cotton, H. C., Belle Alliance.
- Costan, S. A., Hamburg.
- Craig, James, Algiers.

Sermons, Addresses and Reminiscences and Important Correspondence

- Cummings, R., Jeanerette.
- Curtis, I., New Orleans.
- Dabner, Archie, Monroe.
- Dade, J. W., Moscow.
- Daggs, Joseph, Donaldsonville.
- Darrington, W. P., Monroe.
- Davidson, F. J., New Orleans.
- Davis, C. W., Washington.
- Davis, D. C., Videlia.
- Delly, C., Unionville.
- Delly, F. F., Ruston.
- Delly, G. B., Unionville.
- Dickerson, W. R., New Orleans.
- Diggs, P. H., Clarenton.
- Dowell, John, St. Joseph.
- Downs, J. W., New Orleans.
- Duncan, D. W., Opelousas.
- Duncan, H., Monroe.
- Edwards, Jas., Lafourche.
- Ellis, E., Houma.
- Epp. Thomas, Alexandria.
- Ewell, Richard, Paincourtville.
- Fleming, John H., Algiers.
- Flood, A. B., Delhi.
- Flynn, R. H., Shreveport.
- Foster, H. C., New Orleans.
- Franklin, S. R., Cottonport.
- Foster, Joseph, Baton Rouge.
- Frazier, Robert, Algiers.
- Fuller, J. J., Kingston.
- Gaither, S. G., Lake Providence.
- Gales, W. M., Big Bend.
- Gardner, C., Monroe.
- Gettridge, M., New Orleans.
- Gill, Jesse, New Iberia.
- Gipson, S. M., Arcadia.
- Gipson, W. S., Athens.
- Goff, Charles, Zachary.
- Gomez, Martin, Donaldsonville.
- Governor, A. C., Zachary.

- Gray, J. W., Franklin.
- Gray, Wm., Shiloh.
- Green, Henry C., New Orleans.
- Green, M. H., Convent.
- Green, P., Alexandria.
- Green, S. H., Lake Providence.
- Greenup, W. W., Bayou Sara.
- Greggs, M., New Orleans.
- Gross, Wesley, Mahnville.
- Gurst, M. A., Natchitoches.
- Guice, Samuel, Frogmore.
- Hall, Benjamin, Monroe.
- Hall, George, Franklin.
- Hamilton, L., Port Hudson.
- Hamilton, William, Monroe.
- Harris, A., Franklin.
- Harris, Rufus, Mt. Colin.
- Harroll, A. H., St. Joseph.
- Harrison, A. W., Shreveport.
- Harvey, C. H., Jr., Ruston.
- Harvey, S., Simsboro.
- Haywood, L., Simmesport.
- Hawkins, J. L., Ellendale.
- Hawthorne, A. W., Junction, Ark.
- James, Gabriel, Vacherie.
- Jefferson, Thomas, Rayville.
- Jennings, P., Pugh.
- Johnson, A., Bastrop.
- Johnson, E., Longbridge.
- Johnson, Henry, St. Martinsville.
- Johnson, H. C., Smoke Bend.
- Johnson, J. W., New Iberia.
- Johnson, Wm., Simmesport.
- Johnson, Wm., Jr., Houma.
- Jones, A. W., English Turn.
- Jones, Edmund, Algiers.
- Jones, F. L., Homer.
- Jones, J. J., Monroe.
- Jones, Morris, Olivia.
- Jones, Simon, Gretna.

Sermons, Addresses and Reminiscences and Important Correspondence

- Jones, Sylvester, Albermarle.
- Keels, S. L., Ruston.
- Kelly, Jacob, Frogmore.
- Kernall, E., Vidalia.
- Kent, J., Lake Providence.
- King, Charles, Alexandria.
- King, R. C., Trinidad.
- Langman, E. S., Lafourche.
- Labou, J. T. B., Baldwin.
- Large, C., New Iberia.
- Lawrence, R., Shreveport.
- Leonard, J. H., Berwick.
- Lewis, Adams, Raccourci.
- Lewis, B. S., D'Arbonne.
- Lewis, T., Baton Rouge.
- Livingston, J. B., New Iberia.
- Malone, R. D., Arcadia.
- Manning, S., Downsville.
- Marks, John, New Orleans.
- Marshall, H., Lafarche Crossing.
- McCall, A., Tallulah.
- McComo, S. L., Houma.
- McDaniel, I. J., Henderson.
- McKay, J. P., Berwick.
- Means, J., Arnaudville.
- Mellon, P. P., Gibsland.
- Merritt, C., Thibodeaux.
- Merritt, G. W., New Orleans.
- Milburn, Charles, New Orleans.
- Miller, Z., Franklin.
- Mitchell, Jack, Jackson.
- Mitchell, W., Abbeville.
- Moore, J., Dubberly.
- Moore, Monroe, Minden.
- Moore, R. B., Liberty Hill.
- Morrison, Harmon, Port Hudson.
- Morrison, Robert, Plaquemine.
- Murphy, Walker, Monroe.
- Murray, Allen, Crawford.
- Muse, S., Paincourtville.

Sermons, Addresses and Reminiscences and Important Correspondence

- Nance, S. D., Baton Rouge.
- Nixon, H. W. F., New Orleans.
- Oliver, A., Jr., Morgan City.
- Orlage, A. P., New Orleans.
- Parker, Albert, Olivia.
- Paul, Matt., Liberty Hill.
- Payne, J. M., Patterson.
- Payne, L., St. Joseph.
- Perrie, S., Charlieville.
- Perrow, Benjamin, Coushatta.
- Pierce, H. P., Ruston.
- Pollard, I., Houma.
- Rainey, Wm., Gray.
- Randall, Joseph, Alexandria.
- Rankins, A. A., Point Coupee.
- Raphael, J. S., Natchitoches.
- Reese, C. D., Houma.
- Rhodes, T. J., Thibodeaux.
- Richardson, P., Jeanerette.
- Rideau, D., Houma.
- Rideau, Villenau, Washington.
- Roberts, C. L., Cheneyville.
- Roberts, P. A., Kings.
- Roberts, W., Moreauville.
- Robbins, J. R., Patterson.
- Rochaw, J. A., Pattonville.
- Rochelle, J. C., New Iberia.
- Royster, Jefferson, Jonesville.
- Ruffin, N., New Orleans.
- Sapp, C. S., Arcadia.
- Schackey, Charles, New Orleans.
- Scott, A. S., Lake Providence.
- Scott, B. T., St. Joseph.
- Scott, E. B., Rayville.
- Shafer, A., St. Joseph.
- Shelton, C. S., Furrh.
- Sherman, A., West Monroe.
- Simon, L. C., Opelousas.
- Simmons, C., Columbia.
- Simmons, E., Columbia.

- Simms, E. D., New Orleans.
- Small, I., Raccourci
- Smith, A., Baton Rouge.
- Smith, A. L., Odenburg.
- Smith, A. M., Iberia.
- Smith, Ben, Antioch.
- Smith, C., Lake Providence.
- Smith, E., Shiver.
- Smith, Lorenzo, Fairmount.
- Smith, S., Longwood.
- Smith, S. T., Houma.
- Smith, Wm., Franklin.
- Smothers, M., Zachary.
- Spiles, M., New Orleans.
- Squire, L., Zachary.
- Stemley, Green, Redfish.
- Stephens, J. M., Lamourie Bridge.
- Steward, Bush, Franklin.
- Stewart, E., Kenner.
- Stewart, I. H., New Orleans.
- Stewart, W. H., Sparta.
- Talbert, James, New Orleans.
- Taylor, A., Raccourci.
- Taylor, Belt, Thibodeaux.
- Thomas, Israel, Alexandria.
- Thomas, W. H., Houma.
- Thompson, F., Dulac.
- Thompson, Henry, Houma.
- Thompson, J. H., Houma.
- Thornton, Edw., New Orleans.
- Torrey, J. C., Lake Providence.
- Tyson, W., D'Arbonne.
- Vincent, M., Donaldsonville.
- Wagner, Andrew, New Orleans.
- Walker, J., Napoleonville.
- Walker, P., Thibodeaux.
- Washington, G. B., Ruston.
- Washington, J. W., New Orleans.
- Washington, S. G., Arrandville.
- Welch, T. L., Houma.

Sermons, Addresses and Reminiscences and Important Correspondence

- Whaley, J. D., Homer.
- White, C. W., Arcadia.
- White, J. W., Evergreen.
- White, N., Ashley.
- White, William, Frogmore.
- Whiteley, W., New Orleans.
- Wiley, Philip, Gretna.
- Williams, Charles, Plaquemine.
- Williams, F. L., New Orleans.
- Williams, Geo., Simsboro.
- Williams, G. W., Longbridge.
- Williams, Hannibal, Baton Rouge.
- Williams, J., Shreveport.
- Williams, J. W., Lake Providence.
- Williams, L. A., Sicily Island.
- Williams, Levi H., Morgan City.
- Williams, M. M., Alexandria.
- Williams, O., Tallien.
- Wiliams, Rich, Evergreen.
- Williams, Samuel, Baton Rouge.
- Williamson, J., Shreveport.
- Wilson, A., New Orleans, B.
- Wilson, C. H., Ruston.
- Wilson, D. J., New Orleans.
- Wilson, John, Morgan City.
- Winfield, N., Goldman.
- Woods, B., Moreauville.
- Wright, C., Amite City.
- Wright, T., Thibodeaux.
- Wyatt, J. H., Tallulah.
- Young, J. M., New Orleans.
- Young, David, New Orleans.
- Young, William, Alexandria.
- York, N., Shreveport.
- Zenn, Willis, Port Hudson.

Sermons, Addresses and Reminiscences and Important Correspondence

MARYLAND.

- Alexander, W. M., Baltimore.
- Allen, J. C., Baltimore.
- Baylor, W. H., Baltimore.
- Brown, A., Baltimore.
- Callis, A. B., Baltimore.
- Crockett, S. S., Cumberland.
- Hall, F. G., Hyattsville.
- Jackson, R. J., Crisfield.
- Johnson, Harvey, D. D., Baltimore.
- Mack, D. G., Baltimore.
- Minkins, A. E., Baltimore.
- Reid, G. H., Annapolis.
- Scott, J. W., Baltimore.
- Waller, G. R., Baltimore.
- Ward, R. B., Doncaster.
- Williams, F. R., Baltimore.
- Wilson, J. F., Crisfield.
- Wormley, S. S., Baltimore.

MISSISSIPPI.

- Adams, M. C., West Point.
- Alexander, G. W., Pershire.
- Allen, C. H., Port Gibson.
- Allen, T. H., Pickens.
- Alston, R. B., Cockrum.
- Anderson, E. H., Hernando.
- Anderson, R. C., Pickens.
- Anderson, J. H., Vicksburg.
- Austin, H. S., Lawshill.
- Avant, J. C., Como Depot.
- Bailey, R. P., Pine Valley.
- Banes, H. W., Russell.
- Banes, S. R., Russell.
- Bartlett, A., Benoit.
- Barrett, Jno. H., Pelahatchee.
- Battle, R., Trinity.

Sermons, Addresses and Reminiscences and Important Correspondence

- Bell, A., Winona.
- Bell, A. B., Winona.
- Bell, E. F., Water Valley.
- Bell, R. P., Pine Valley.
- Bell, S. P., Pine Valley.
- Bell, B. R., Vicksburg.
- Bellmaster, A., Green Grove.
- Berry, A. B., Columbus.
- Billups, A., Trimcane.
- Blewett, J. D., West Point.
- Bolden, B., Helms.
- Bolton, A. B., Greenville.
- Booker, C. H., Avondale.
- Bims, P., Washington.
- Bowen, H. W., Durant.
- Boykin, J. G., Winona.
- Bozeman, J. O., Whynot.
- Bradley, S. A., Hazelhurst.
- Bradley, W. S., Warrenton.
- Brandt, A. B., Pheba.
- Brown, A. J., Vicksburg.
- Brown, S. S., Sataria.
- Brown, T. G., Cleveland.
- Bryant, L. W., Bluella.
- Buchanan, C. A., Kosciusko.
- Burnett, A. B., Siloam.
- Burnett, G. W., Pelahatchee.
- Butler, J. B., Coldwater.
- Butler, S. S., Yazoo City.
- Byas, J., Valley Park.
- Campbell, A. C., Winona.
- Cade, J. C., Arcola.
- Calvert, J. C., Stanton.
- Cannon, A. H., Ittabena.
- Carington, E. E., Avondale.
- Carter, A. C., Yazoo City.
- Carter, J. H., Hollandale.
- Chappman, H. C., Newton.
- Christmas, J. N., Kingston.
- Clayton, D., Victoria.

Sermons, Addresses and Reminiscences and Important Correspondence

- Cleveland, D. B., Vicksburg.
- Coleman, J. C., Cobb Switch.
- Colins, A. H., Mastodon.
- Connelly, Henry, Coldwater.
- Cook, W. C., Trinity.
- Cooper, A. D., Hazelhurst.
- Crawford, A. M., Forest.
- Cunneghan, E. M., Magnolia.
- Crossgrove, Jas., Natchez.
- Custard, C. R., Vicksburg.
- Davenport, A., Stanton.
- Davis, B. J., Kosciusko.
- Davis, D. C., Natchez.
- Davis, E., Como Depot.
- Davis, Willis, Natchez.
- Delaware, S. J., Yazoo City.
- Delone, L. D., Hickory Grove.
- Demas, R. W., Gloster.
- Dembly, L. E., Vidalia.
- Diggs, C. W., Ben Lomond.
- Diggs, J. J., Ben Lomond.
- Donald, L. W., Newton.
- Drake, F., Stanton.
- Drake, Alex., Pine Ridge.
- Duke, S. M., Columbus.
- Echols, W. S., Wallhill.
- Edmondson, M., Alpika.
- Egerton, B. W., Commerce.
- Evans, J. J., Hernando.
- Evans, P. S., Magnolia.
- Falkner, P. F., Penn.
- Fears, G. W., West Point.
- Fenton, J. C., Columbus.
- Ferrell, R. D., Greenville.
- Foster, H. C., Vicksburg.
- Frisby, P. E., Cannonsburg.
- Garrison, M., Burdette.
- Gaunn, S. F., Swiftwater.
- Gayles, G. W., Greenville.
- George, G. W., Alligator.

Sermons, Addresses and Reminiscences and Important Correspondence

- Gibbons, Wm., Rosedale.
- Gillespie, W. C., Starkville.
- Gilliam, J. S., Leland.
- Gordon, J. W., Toomsuba.
- Gordon, P., Toomsuba.
- Graham, W. F., Corinth.
- Green, G. P., Bentonia.
- Greene, M. J., Ingleside.
- Gregory, R. S., Tyro.
- Griffin, I. G., Redbanks.
- Griffin, J. O., Greenville.
- Griffin, Wm., Gunnison.
- Hall, Wm., Carey.
- Hamilton, A. A., Vicksburg.
- Hardy, A. A., Barland.
- Hardy C. L., Pineville.
- Harkins, J. H., Wintersville.
- Harper E. L., Winona.
- Harper J. H., Artesia.
- Harris, A., Senatobia.
- Harris, D., Fasonia.
- Harris, W. H., Newton.
- Hawkins, J. H., Winterville.
- Hayes, J. E., Whynot.
- Henderson, R. H., West Point.
- Hendricks, J. E., Canton.
- Henry, J. H. C., Natchez.
- Hicks, J. W., Vicksburg.
- Higgins, W. H., Raymond.
- Hightower, Wm., Round Lake.
- Hill, A. M., Como Depot.
- Hill, S. C., Belzonia.
- Hines, L. H., Montpelier.
- Hodges, A., Artesia.
- Hodges, S., Sessumsville.
- Holland, Wm., Jr., Cobb Switch.
- Holloway, S., Garlandville.
- Hubbard, G. E., Lauderdale.
- Hudson, G. H., Glenville.
- Humphries, G. B., Mayhews Station.

- Hunter, C. P., Natchez.
- Jackson, J. E., Pheba.
- Jackson, Owen, Coldwater.
- Jernagan, W. H., Okolona.
- Jinkins, I., Briers.
- Johnson, A., Starkville.
- Johnson, A. J., Jackson.
- Johnson, A. M., Vicksburg.
- Johnson, C. P., Clinton.
- Johnson, H. E. W., Senatobia.
- Johnson, P. A., Crawford.
- Johnson, P. J., Coffeeville.
- Johnson, R. J., Cannonsburg.
- Johnson, S., Torrence.
- Johnson, S. H., Hollywood.
- Johnson, V. S., Bolton.
- Johns, D., Vicksburg.
- Jones, E. P., Greenville.
- Jones, J. J., Forest.
- Jones, T. A., Hattiesburg.
- Jordan, S. A., Brookhaven.
- Jordan, T. L., West Point.
- Keen, J. A., Battlefield.
- Kelly, J. K., Chatham.
- Killens, R., Golden.
- Knight, J., Yazoo City.
- Lambert, J. C., Calhoun.
- Layton, H., Winona.
- Lee, L. S., Meridian.
- Lewis, D., Natchez.
- Lewis, D. J., Starkville.
- Lewis, J. A., Artesia.
- Lewis, J. M., Columbus.
- Little, T., Sardis.
- Long, P. W., Torrance.
- Lowe, C. H., Port Gibson.
- Lowe, H. H., Port Gibson.
- Lyde, J., Penn.
- Lyles, G. W., Forest.
- Lyman, H. C., Jackson.

Sermons, Addresses and Reminiscences and Important Correspondence

- Marr, M., Wallhill.
- Marten, T. L., Greenville.
- Martin, C. M., Greenville.
- Martin, S. P., Grenada.
- Mays, A., Cedar Bluff.
- McAlster, A. D., Aberdeen.
- McCook, E. M., Como Depot.
- McGray, C., Vicksburg.
- McCraven, Wm., Bolton.
- Mickey, D. M., Cary.
- Middleton, J. E., Vicksburg.
- Middleton, Wm., Natchez.
- Miles, P. M., Artesia.
- Minor, S. D., Crystal Springs.
- Mission, J. M., Columbus.
- Mitchell, D. C., New Hope.
- Montgomery, J. S., Carpenter.
- Moore, J. H., Harmonton.
- Moore, Wm., Canton.
- Morris, A. C., Steens, Creek.
- Murphy, A. T., Clarksdale.
- Murphy, R., Indianola.
- Neeley, H. M., Starkville.
- Nettles, R., Agency.
- Nichols, H. H., Brunswick Point.
- Nichols, S., Decatur.
- Nicholson, W. W., Shuqualak.
- Owen, S. M., Mhoon Valley.
- Patton, C. S., Como Depot.
- Patton, J. F., Singleton.
- Payne, J. H., Carolina.
- Payne, C. R., Coffeeville.
- Person, J. R., Looxahoma.
- Person, S. L., Coffeeville.
- Peyton, J. J., Water Valley.
- Phillips, G. P., Midnight.
- Pleasant, J. S., Greenville.
- Pleasant, W. S., Hazlehurst.
- Pope, Wm., Shelby.
- Price, B. P., Columbus.

- Price, J. J., Vicksburg.
- Pringle, P., Russell.
- Ramsey, L. A., Como Depot.
- Rankin, Wm., Homewood.
- Rasberry, T. R., Palo Alto.
- Ray, Wm., Natchez.
- Reid, R. H., Newton.
- Rhodes, J. C., Battlefield.
- Rivers, S. A., Meridian.
- Roane, W., Natchez.
- Roberts, A. M., Coffeeville.
- Robinson, I. J., Dudleys.
- Robinson, A. G., Bolton.
- Rose, F., Vicksburg.
- Rucker, P. C., Cannonsburg.
- Rucks, K., Vicksburg.
- Ruffin, D., Bonita.
- Sanders, H. E., Artesia.
- Saulsbury, B. S., Starksville.
- Scott, H. W., Edwards.
- Scott, G. P., Rolling Fork.
- Scott, E. H., Natchez.
- Scott, J. W., Stoneville.
- Simmons, C., Okolona.
- Simpson, J. M., Winona.
- Sims, D., Vicksburg.
- Sims, R. T., Canton.
- Sims, W., Meharis.
- Smith, John, Natchez.
- Smith, S. T., Keenan.
- Smith, J., Natchez.
- Smith, Z. P., Senatobia.
- Snodgrass, A. D., Westside.
- Spencer, H., Amory.
- Spratley, O. O., Aberdeen.
- Stamps, C. T., Edwards.
- Spencer, J. H., Pheba.
- Stewart, J. W., Prairie Point.
- Stitt, Wm., Sardis.
- Strother, N. S. W., Doloroso.

- Suggs, A., Water Valley.
- Tatum, J. A., Montrose.
- Tarrance, Chas., Coffeeville.
- Taylor, D. S., Greenville.
- Taylor, J. T., Midway.
- Taylor, T. C., Jackson.
- Taylor, W. A., Byhalia.
- Teague, A., Holly Springs.
- Temple, R. J., Natchez.
- Thomas, A. T., Arcola.
- Thomas, P., Yazoo City.
- Thompson, A., Coldwater.
- Thompson, J. H., Crawford.
- Thompson, H. M., Okolona.
- Thompson, P. H., Kosciusko.
- Thornton, J. H., Leland.
- Topp, E. B., Jackson.
- Triplett, E. H., Westside.
- Tucker, S., Rio.
- Turner, A., Artesia.
- Turner, J. H., Newton.
- Turner, S. M., Regenton.
- Turnipseed, S. T., Columbus.
- Tyler, D., Cannonsburg.
- Walker, D. S.,
- Walker, J. H., Stanton.
- Walker, H. W., Cedarbluff.
- Walker, J. C., West Point.
- Wallace, E. W., Columbus.
- Wallace, N. W., Greenwood.
- Ward, C. A., Goodman.
- Ward, G. W., Duncan.
- Ware, W., Waterford.
- Washington, J. W., Waverly.
- Watson, H., Brooksville.
- Watson, S. P., Oak Smith.
- White, E. D., Cary.
- White, G. W., Coahoma.
- White, J. W., Stoneville.
- Whitley, L., Chatham.

- Whiting, W. H., Watsonia.
- Whitehead, B. F., Toomsubia.
- Wilkins, A., Coldwater.
- Williams, F. P., Natchez.
- Williams, I. C., Yazoo City.
- Williams, S. D., Senatobia.
- Williams, S. W., Starkville.
- Willis, R., Greenville.
- Wilson, A. L., Rio.
- Wilson, D. W., Muldrow Station.
- Wilson, E. W., Yazoo City.
- Wilson, G. R., Port Gibson.
- Wilson, J., Carey.
- Wilson, J. F., Senatobia.
- Wilson, M. W., Coffeeville.
- Woods, S. P., Manana.
- Yancey, I., Coffeeville.
- Young, H. L., Winona.
- Young, J. C., Winterville.
- Young, J. H., Reganton.
- Young, J. D., Starkville.
- Young, S. D., Natchez.
- Young, T. G., Senatobia.
- Zuber, J. D., Kosciusko.

MISSOURI.

- Adams, Jesse, Carthage.
- Adkins, R., Kansas City.
- Alexander, E. W., St. Louis.
- Allen, M., Kansas City.
- Alphine, P., St. Louis.
- Anderson, S. P., St. Louis.
- Anthony, A. L., Poplar Bluff.
- Armistead, James, St. Louis.
- Bacote, S. W., Kansas City.
- Bates, F., Belton.
- Bell, B. J., Kirkwood.
- Blake, W. S., Carthage.

- Bly, G., Pierce City.
- Boggs, P. G., St. Louis.
- Bond, O. D., Neosho.
- Botts, J. W., Meadeville.
- Botts, W. F., Moberly.
- Botts, W. P., Neosho.
- Bouey, H. N., Macon.
- Bowen, William, St. Louis.
- Boyd, G. W., Kansas City.
- Branigan, William, Joplin.
- Brooks, W. P., Moberly.
- Brown, G. W., Kansas City.
- Brown, W. H., Bainbridge.
- Brown, W. J., St. Louis.
- Buchanan, G. A., Kansas City.
- Burnham, E., Cedar City.
- Burris, J. R. A., Weston.
- Burton, H. J., Jefferson City.
- Carter, W. D., Minneapolis, Minn.
- Carter, W. L., South St. Joseph.
- Caston, J. T., Fulton.
- Caves, J., Lexington.
- Chears, S., Boonville.
- Chinn, G. C., Macon.
- Clark, G. W., Louisiana.
- Clark, E., Linneus.
- Clark, E., Chillicothe.
- Clay, M. L., Carrollton.
- Clemmons, G. C., St. Louis.
- Clinton, R. M., Clinton.
- Cohron, E. M., St. Joseph.
- Cohron, J. L., St. Louis.
- Cole, E. C., St. Louis.
- Cole, R. H., St. Louis.
- Collins, J. M., St. Louis.
- Collins, M. C., Spring Valley.
- Cox, M. C., St. Louis.
- Dibrell, J. M., St. Louis.
- Diggs, J. S., Columbia.
- Dorsey, G. W., Sedalia.

Sermons, Addresses and Reminiscences and Important Correspondence

- Dorsey, J. S., Springfield.
- Douglas, B. L., Mexico.
- Dunbar, R. D., Sedalia.
- Dupree, W., St. Louis.
- Edwards, T. J., Higginsville.
- Elionth, M. A., So. Sedalia.
- Emery, G. E., Neosho.
- Ewing, T. H., Kansas City.
- Finney, J. D., Clark.
- Fitts, J. W., Independence.
- Garnett, G., Carthage.
- Garnett, W. A., Carrollton.
- Garrett, J. H., Jefferson City.
- Glasgow, J., Dalton.
- Goins, J., Richmond.
- Gordon, J. W., Clinton.
- Green, D. D., Lagrange.
- Green, E. D., Lagrange.
- Green, J. M., Kansas City.
- Grey, R. J., Kirkwood.
- Griffin, B. J., Edgewood.
- Guthrie, B. J., Weston.
- Harris, Z. P., St. Louis.
- Hawkins, J. B., Shelbina.
- Hawkins, J. J., Mt. Leonard.
- Hawkes, J. B., Sedalia.
- Hayes, J. G., Mexico.
- Helm, J. H., Hannibal.
- Henderson, T. H., Macon.
- Higgins, C. W., Slater.
- Homesley, J. H., Lexington.
- Horton, H., Plattsburg.
- Howard, R. E., Chillicothe.
- Hunter, Walker, St. Louis.
- Jackson, C. H. M., St. Louis.
- Jackson, G. N., Macon.
- Jackson, J. P., Bevier.
- Jefferson, Thomas, St. Louis.
- Jenkins, N. S., Clarksville.
- Jennings, J. H., Mexico.

Sermons, Addresses and Reminiscences and Important Correspondence

- Johnson, A. B., St. Louis.
- Johnson, H. F., Charleston.
- Johnson, Z. H., Springfield.
- Jones, C. H., Lebanon.
- Jones, F., Glencoe.
- Jones, H. S., Wentzville.
- Jones, James, Wentzville.
- Jones, W. M., Higginsville.
- Jones, W. P. T., St. Louis.
- Lane, Lewis, St. Louis.
- Lawton, C. J., Independence.
- Lewis, A. M., Salisbury.
- Lewis, H. S., Kansas City.
- Lewis, S., Brookfield.
- Lias, Alex., Pacific.
- Long, W. H., O'Fallon.
- Love, S. A., St. Louis.
- Lucas, R. A., St. Louis.
- Martin, Edward, Granby.
- Martin, N., St. Louis.
- Martin, William, Nevada.
- McCoy, J. I., Maryville.
- McDaniel, H. C., Laclede.
- McDowell, C. R., St. Louis.
- McKamey, William, Mexico.
- McKinney, F., St. Louis.
- Miller, A. M., Rocheport.
- Mills, I., Kansas City.
- Mitchell, T. M., St. Louis.
- Morton, E., Gronly.
- Morton, H., Plattsburg.
- Morton, I., Wentzville.
- Mudd, J. M., Tipton.
- Oden, J. H., St. Louis.
- Parks, P. L., Belmont.
- Pearman, J. T., Palmyra.
- Pickett, S., Kansas City.
- Polk, W. D., Glasgow.
- Powell, J. W., St. Louis.
- Redd, O. T., Macon.

- Reed, J. F., Brunswick.
- Reed, H., Bonfils.
- Reeves, J., St. Clair.
- Richardson, J. R., Lexington.
- Roy, Harrison, St. Louis.
- Rucks, K., St. Louis.
- Salter, W. P., Kansas City.
- Saunders, G. D., Brunswick.
- Saunders, M., Montserrat.
- Saunders, Scott, Kansas City.
- Sawyers, D. S., Chillicothe.
- Scott, A. S., Lebanon.
- Scruggs, E. L., Macon.
- Shores, N. W., Union.
- Sibley, J., Fernridge.
- Sime, W., Carthage.
- Slatter, W. S., St. Louis.
- Smith, G. W., Huntsville.
- Smith, H., Boonville.
- Smith, J. L., Hartville.
- Smith, S. S., Springfield.
- Smith, T. L., Columbia.
- Stewart, F. K., Bonfils.
- Strother, R. H., Richmond.
- Swancy, J. S., Carrollton.
- Sydnor, R. H. C., St. Louis.
- Taswell, J. T., Carrollton.
- Taw, A. W., Rocheport.
- Taylor, R., Columbia.
- Thomas, G. C., St. Louis.
- Thomas, J., St. Joseph.
- Thompson, A. J., Mt. Vernon.
- Thompson, Mark, Macon.
- Thornley, J. T., Plattsburg.
- Trickler, William, Lexington.
- Tucker, J. E., Smithton.
- Turner, H. W., St. Louis.
- Valentine, Wesley, Shelbina.
- Vaughn, H. C., Moberly.
- Vernon, R. M., Nevada.

- Wadlington, B. F., Bridgeton.
- Ward, T. T., Higginsville.
- Washington, D., Parkville.
- Watson, R., Kansas City.
- Watts, G. W., Dewitt.
- Watts, L. S., Armstrong.
- West, G. W., St. Louis.
- West, W. A., Lagrange.
- White, H. H., Paris.
- Wiggans, C. W., Fulton.
- Wiggins, J. D., Harrisonville.
- Williams, J., Kirkwood.
- Williams, R. H. D., St. Louis.
- Wilson, Silas, Boonville.
- Winer, W. M., Fairville.
- Wright, J. A., New Palestine.
- Yancey, A., St. Louis.
- Young, J. W., Mexico.

NORTH CAROLINA.

- Abbott, J. P., Salisbury.
- Alexander, L. J., Wise.
- Alderman, W. H., Teacheys.
- Allen, Lewis, Brookston.
- Alston, B., Henderson.
- Alston, G. W., Salisbury.
- Alston, H. B., Rausoms Bridge.
- Alston, I., Warrenton.
- Alston, J. B., Littleton.
- Alston, L. B., Warrenton.
- Alston, O. B., Enfield.
- Alston, Preston, Panacea.
- Alston, S. G., Ringold.
- Alston, W. G., Ita.
- Alston, Wyatt, Ringold.
- Andrews, W. H., Idaho.
- Anderson, David, Bowmans Bluff.
- Anderson, S., Wilmington.

Sermons, Addresses and Reminiscences and Important Correspondence

- Anderson, W. H., Garysburg.
- Arnold, Isaac, Coldraine.
- Arrington, J. H., Halifax.
- Arrington, M. T., Hilliardston.
- Askow, W. A., Como.
- Atkinson, G. W., Sand Bluff.
- Atkinson, S., Whitville.
- Austin, Boston, Garysburg.
- Auterbridge, W., Tarboro.
- Avery, D. J., Raleigh.
- Bailey, A., Brevard.
- Baker, C., Oaklette, Va.
- Baker, G. W., Kinston.
- Baldwin, C. C., Pittsboro.
- Baldwin, G. W., Mapleton.
- Barrett, J. S., Old Store.
- Beam, M., Gastonia.
- Bell, E. J., Burgaw.
- Bell, J. J., Roister.
- Bennett, J., Grantsboro.
- Bennett, T., White Store.
- Berry, Zion H., Elizabeth City.
- Best, D. T., Clinton.
- Billups, C. M., Lewiston.
- Bizzle, C. S., Angle.
- Black, A., Emma.
- Blackman, S., Silas Creek.
- Blake, E. B., Raleigh.
- Blake, R. E., Raleigh.
- Blakeney, J. B., Monroe.
- Blanks, J. J., Lumberton.
- Blanks, J. W., Rosier.
- Blevens, J., Jefferson.
- Blount, Geo., Washington.
- Blount, W. A., Washington.
- Bogan, J. B., Monroe.
- Boone, A., Jackson.
- Boone, W. H., Hallsville.
- Boone, C. C., Winton.
- Bowman, V. R., White Store.

- Boyd, Daniel, Broadie.
- Boyd, B. H., Matthews.
- Boyd, W. H., Vaughn.
- Broadie, J. H., Monroe.
- Brewer, G. W., Monroe.
- Brewer, Jos., Garysburg.
- Bridges, B., Metal.
- Brinkley, A., Snowhill.
- Brock, Z. P., Pates.
- Brown, A. N., Apex.
- Brown, C. S., Winton.
- Brown, D. P., Lenoir.
- Brown, Geo., Leiston.
- Brown, G. W., Monroe.
- Brown, H., Littleton.
- Brown, Jas., Margarettsville.
- Bron, L., Littleton.
- Brown, M., Halifax.
- Brown, M. W., Apex.
- Brown, Peter, Whitakers.
- Brown, S., Rose Hill.
- Brown, S. L., Old Store.
- Bryant, J. L., Brunt.
- Bryant, W. A., Fort Barnwell.
- Buchanan, Wm., Wilmington.
- Bullock, G. O., Henderson.
- Bullock, Lester, Lyons.
- Bullock, O., Manson.
- Bunting, A. R., Wilmington.
- Burgess, A., Arcola.
- Burgess, J. H., Arcola.
- Burwell, Jeff., Kittrell.
- Burwell, T. H., Kittrell.
- Butler, W. L., Monroe.
- Bynum, C. H., Apex.
- Caldwell, J. H., Chapel Hill.
- Call, T. M., Tarheel.
- Cameron, F. C., Tarheel.
- Campbell, D., Lansing.
- Capps, Chas., Belvidere.

Sermons, Addresses and Reminiscences and Important Correspondence

- Carey, J. H., Shelby.
- Carelock, G. M., Monroe.
- Carr, A., Rose Hill.
- Carr, H., Rose Hill.
- Carroll, R. C., Goldsboro.
- Cartright, C. M., Edenton.
- Carver, G., Roxboro.
- Chatham, Henry, Wilson.
- Chavis, Jas., Hutchinson Store.
- Chavis, Jordan, Lumberton.
- Christmas, M., Warrenton.
- Clanton, S., Vaughan.
- Clark, Benj., Lewiston.
- Clark, Erasmus, Allison.
- Clark, Freeman, Palmyra.
- Clark, J. T., Washington, D. C.
- Cobb, W. A., Harrellsville.
- Coggin, W. R., Jackson Creek.
- Cole, E. H., Chapel Hill.
- Collins, T. M., Hampton, Va.
- Cook, H. T., Wake Forest.
- Cooper, A., Windsor.
- Council, T. M., Tarheel.
- Cousins, D. N., Allensville.
- Cousins, J. H., Gaston.
- Covington, A., Rockingham.
- Covington, R., Rockingham.
- Cowan, W. C., Taylors Bridge.
- Cowan, W. T., Taylors Bridge.
- Cowper, E. C., Sparta.
- Cozart, J. R., Berea.
- Craig, M. H., Salisbury.
- Craig, P., Waxaw.
- Craig, R. H., Columbia.
- Crenshaw, R. C., Whitakers.
- Crosby, J. O., Salisbury.
- Croslin, J., Prospect Hill.
- Culley, W. H., Havelock.
- Curney, Samuel, Beaufort.
- Crumpler, J. L., Robin Hill.

Sermons, Addresses and Reminiscences and Important Correspondence

- Daniel, D. T., Halifax.
- Davis, Adams, Lumber Bridge.
- Davis, F. M., Wilson.
- Davis, G. W., Magnolia.
- Davis, H. V., Rocky Mount.
- Davis, J. F., Polkton.
- Davis, S. A., Washington.
- Davis, S. P., Grimesland.
- Day, J. W., Mt. Tirzah.
- Deston, Benjamin, Warrenton.
- Devaughan, D. D., Alpine.
- Devaughan, S., Harrells Store.
- Devaughan, Wm., Wilmington.
- Deveraux, V., Tillery.
- Dew, J. W., Goldsboro.
- Dickson, J. P., Grassy Creek.
- Dixon, Benj., Ridgeway.
- Dixon, K., Leasburg.
- Dockery, S. W., Maxton.
- Dorsett, J. H., Castle.
- Downing, H. W., Plymouth.
- Dudley, W. M., Newport.
- Dunham, N. B., Cedar.
- Dunlap, C., Wadesboro.
- Dunston, A. S., Hertford.
- Dunston, J. H., Morrisville.
- Earkette, Thomas, Palmyra.
- Earley, D. W., Aulander.
- Eaton, A. P., Henderson.
- Eborne, Thomas, E., Palmyra.
- Edwards, T. B., Raleigh.
- Ellerbee, Wm., Raleigh.
- Elliot, L. T., Cisco.
- Ellis, A., Waco.
- Ellis, C., Falling Creek.
- Ellis, G., Linwood.
- Ellison, W., Hillsboro.
- Ellison, E. S., Falkland.
- Evans, Jas., Orton.
- Evans, T. S., Morehead City.

Sermons, Addresses and Reminiscences and Important Correspondence

- Erkett, T., Grimesland.
- Farrow, E. F., Tarboro.
- Fason, L. E., Monroe.
- Faulk, J. A., Hertford.
- Faulkner, E., Marshallville.
- Felton, Samuel, Edenton.
- Fennell, J. L., Rose Hill.
- Fenner, Sandy, Halifax.
- File, R. L., Salisbury.
- Filyaw, B. H., Wilmington.
- Fisher, C. J. W., Raleigh.
- Flock, H., Barnardsville.
- Fleming, J. A., Elizabeth City.
- Fletcher, G. W., Austin.
- Flood, A. T., Greenville.
- Floyd, T. J., Shelby.
- Fogg, P. P., Epsom.
- Foreman, H., Pantego.
- Forney, W. W., Gold Hill.
- Freeman, G. E., Powellsville.
- Fuller, J. A., Oxford.
- Fuller, T. O., Memphis, Tenn.
- Galloway, Peter, Leakesville.
- Garrett, J. G., Leicester.
- Gardiner, J. L., Macon.
- Garirs, J. M., Lewiston.
- Gatlin, Simeon, Grifton.
- Gibbs, C. W., Enfield.
- Gibson, C. W., Qualley.
- Gibson, J. F., Saxon.
- Gilmore, Nathan, Edonia.
- Goodwin, J. W., Belvidere.
- Gore, G. W., Vineland.
- Grady, G. W., Lanes Creek.
- Grady, T., Hillsboro.
- Graham, Jno., Heathville.
- Graham, S., Pollocksville.
- Grant, Julius, Harrellsville.
- Gratton, Jno., Fayetteville.
- Graves, A. G., Yanceyville.

Sermons, Addresses and Reminiscences and Important Correspondence

- Graves, Peter, Ruffin.
- Gray, Wm., High Point.
- Green, A. J., Henderson.
- Gregg, S. D., Oakville.
- Gregory, Wm., Ridgeway.
- Griffin, G. D., Elizabeth City.
- Grimes, J., Hamilton.
- Grinton, R., Dellaplane.
- Hackney, C. D., Chapel Hill.
- Hackney, L. H., Chapel Hill.
- Hairston, J. D., Winston.
- Hairston, T. H., Winston.
- Hall, J. H. S., Washington.
- Hall, H. H., Scotland Neck.
- Hall, P. T., Raleigh.
- Hampton, S. W., Monroe.
- Hanna, A., Concord.
- Hardick, W. S., Pollicksville.
- Hardin, W. H., Stice.
- Hardy, W., Aurora.
- Hare, P., Winston.
- Hargrove, J. D., Lexington.
- Harper, B., Essex.
- Harper, B. H., Lagrange.
- Harper, S., Ransoms Bridge.
- Harrell, J. D., St. Paul.
- Harriford, W. N., Wentworth.
- Harris, J. C., Oxford.
- Harris, W. H., Oxford.
- Harris, J. R., Henderson.
- Haris, James, Falkland.
- Harris, R. H., Roxboro.
- Harrison, W. H., Pelham.
- Hart, W. F., Wilmington.
- Hartman, C., Linwood.
- Hasty, B., Ansonville.
- Hauser, C. H., Yadkinville.
- Hawkins, J. A., Letha.
- Hawkins, M. F., Ingleside.
- Hawkins, M. T., Louisburg.

Sermons, Addresses and Reminiscences and Important Correspondence

- Hawkins, S. S., Salisbury.
- Hayden, W. D., Burlington.
- Hays, L. H., Pactolus.
- Haynes, Willis, Hallsboro.
- Heck, J. J., Brookston.
- Heck, J. R., Broadie.
- Hemphill, B. F., Hendersonville.
- Hemphill, C. W., Vernon.
- Hemphill, R. A., Rutherfordton.
- Henderson, C. J., Brookston.
- Henderson, S. S., Greensboro.
- Henderson, Wm., Henderson.
- Herbert, G. W., Hayesville.
- Hicks, Jno., Goldsboro.
- Hicks, S., Weldon.
- Hicks, T. B., Williamsboro.
- Hill, Andrew, Lota.
- Hill, B. B., Reidsville.
- Hill, J. G., Scotland Neck.
- Hockadeay, F. M., Weldon.
- Hodge, Luke, Elizabethtown.
- Hogan, J. W., Rosier.
- Hogans R. H., Asheville.
- Hoggard, R. W., Winston.
- Holden, J. H., Youngsville.
- Holden, Lewis, Wake Forest.
- Holland, G. W., Winston.
- Hood, G. L., Lagrange.
- Hopkins, B. F., Creedmore.
- Holley, P. H., Ahoskie.
- Holley, T., Mt. Gould.
- Horne, D., County Line.
- Houston, K. T., Mt. Olive.
- Howard, W. H., Idalia.
- Howell, W. M., Tarboro.
- Hunt, D., Acton.
- Hunter, S., Shelby.
- Huntley, Jos., Goodman.
- Hurst, C., Wrightsville.
- Hyman, A., Hill.

Sermons, Addresses and Reminiscences and Important Correspondence

- Hyman, H. W., Pactolus.
- Huffman, R. T., Wilmington.
- Ivey, A. W., Littleton.
- Jackson, A. J., Halifax.
- Jackson, D. M., Rockingham.
- Jacobs, Jesse, Clinton.
- Jacob, King, Rich Square.
- Jarvis, J., Jamesville.
- Johnson, A., Kings Mountain.
- Johnson, A. L., Yanceyville.
- Johnson, Caleb, Asheville.
- Johnson, Caesar, Raleigh.
- Johnson, D., Winstead.
- Johnson, D. G., Pleasant Grove.
- Johnson, E., Scotland Neck.
- Johnson, G. W., Kernersville.
- Johnson, J., Littleton.
- Johnson, John, Newbern.
- Johnson, J. M., Rose Hill.
- Johnson, P. J., Scotland Neck.
- Johnson, R. J., Lemay.
- Johnson, R. R., Garner.
- Johnson, W. A., Mt. Energy.
- Jones, A., Charlotte.
- Jones, Allen, Wilsons Mills.
- Jones, A. A., Raleigh.
- Jones, A. E., Spring Hope.
- Jones, D. M., South Mills.
- Jones, H. C., Chapel Hill.
- Jones, L. S., Sanford.
- Jones, Isaac, Cresswell.
- Jones, Jas., Warrenton.
- Jones, J. J., Chapel Hill.
- Jones, R. B., Method.
- Jones, R. P., Littleton.
- Jones, S., Gibson Mills.
- Jones, Wm., Apex.
- Jones, W A., Raleigh.
- Jones, W. A., Mill Creek.
- Jordan, W. H., Scotland Neck.

- Joseph, H., Polkton.
- Joyner, E., Wilmington.
- Joner, J. J., Potecasi.
- Kennedy, A. T., Washington.
- Ker, A. D., Faison.
- King, O., Hendersonville.
- Kirby, E. D., Chapel Hill.
- Kirk, J. A., Wilmington.
- Knight, S. P., Edenton.
- Knotts, S. M., Monroe.
- Kornegay, W. B. F., Willard.
- Laskin, S., Wilmington.
- Larkin, S. C., Long Creek.
- Latta, J. M., Red Mountain.
- Lawson, C. C., Washington.
- Lawson, R. P., Roxboro.
- Leake, W., Ansonville.
- Lee, A., Charlotte.
- Lee, H., Burgaw.
- Lenox, B. J., Drews.
- Lewis, A., Charlotte.
- Lewis, J. G., Oxford.
- Linn, D. H., Concord.
- Linsey, Saul, Arden.
- Lipscomb, E. H., Asheville.
- Little, W., Mangum.
- Locklear, A. D., Moss Neck.
- Locklear, Gilbert, Lowe.
- Long, F. A., Greensboro.
- Love, F., Hycotee.
- Lyles, J. D., Fayetteville.
- Lynch, J. J., Bowmans Bluff.
- Lyon, J. H., Berea.
- Lytle, I. D., Marshville.
- Macafee, T., Leicester.
- Mainor, W. R., Clinton.
- Majors, J. W., Fair Plains.
- Maloy, H. M., Goldsboro.
- Maloy, P. F., Grensboro.
- Marable, T, N., Clinton.

Sermons, Addresses and Reminiscences and Important Correspondence

- Mason, E. M., New Hil.
- Massey, R. B., Monroe.
- Matthewson, M. D., Tarboro.
- Mayer, C. H., Hargrove.
- Mayo, C., Oxford.
- Mays, J., Littleton.
- McCall, J. M., Tarheel.
- McCray, T. H., Monroe.
- McDaniel, T. W., Enfield.
- McDonald, H. C., Lumber Bridge.
- McDonald, J. J., Grays Creek.
- McGruder, H., Estelle.
- McIntire, H., Laurenburg.
- McKellars, Jas., Lumberton.
- McMillan, A., Curtis.
- McMillan, Peter. St. Pauls.
- McNeil, H. S., Clarkton.
- McPherson, Jno., Columbia.
- Mebane, A., Plymouth.
- Melvin, L., Cedar Creek.
- Miller, S. J. A., Biddleville.
- Mincey, S. L., Wilson.
- Mills, J., Old Fork.
- Mills, H., Deavers.
- Mitchell, A., Wake Forest.
- Mitchell, B., Windsor.
- Mitchell, Jackson, Powellsville.
- Mittman, L. T., Mt. Airy.
- Montgomery, D. M., Dallas.
- Moore, D. J., Rosendale.
- Moore, Eli, Durham Creek.
- Moore, G. W., Raleigh.
- Moore, Henry, Risden.
- Moore, I., Littleton.
- Moore, J. C., Shelby.
- Moore, Nicholas, Wallace.
- Moore, S. L., Wilmington.
- Moore, W. D., Durham Creek.
- Moore, W. H., Kerrs.
- Morris, G. R., Newbern.

Sermons, Addresses and Reminiscences and Important Correspondence

- Morris, J., Marion.
- Morris, H. W., Apex.
- Morrison, L. N., Whiteville.
- Morrison, M., Vineland.
- Morrison, Thos., Newhill.
- Moye, L. W., Newbern.
- Murray, R. C., Burgaw.
- Neal, R. C., Clayton.
- Nelson, A. P., Greensboro.
- Nelson, J. R., Asheville.
- Nevils, T. D., South Gaston.
- Newkirk, T., Odessa.
- Nesome, S. G., Suffolk.
- Nicholas, Elias, Plymouth.
- Nixon, J., Wilmington.
- Norman, M. W. D., Elizabeth, City.
- Norris, T. B., Lumberton.
- Nunnelly, J. L., Concord.
- Oats, J. P., Stubbs.
- Outlaw, H., Avoca.
- Overby, L. R., Oxford.
- Pladgett, A., Collinsville.
- Pair, H., Shotwell.
- Parham, E. F., Wentworth.
- Parker, A., Potecasi.
- Parker, J. R., Woodland.
- Parker, Thos., Burgaw.
- Parks, F., Felts.
- Parks, V. A., Dellaplane.
- Paterson, Jerry, Wilmington.
- Patterson, J. G., Falling Creek.
- Pattillo, W. A., Oxford.
- Packston, John, Edenton.
- Pearsall, E., Pikeville.
- Peebles, H., Jackson.
- Pegues, A. W., Raleigh.
- Perry, Amos, Youngsville.
- Perry, G. B., Durham.
- Perry, G. W., Raleigh.
- Perry, Jos., Raleigh.

- Perry, Joshua, Winston.
- Perry, L. H., South Mills.
- Peters, C. C., Gaston.
- Peterson, B. P., Raleigh.
- Peterson, H., Kelleys.
- Pettiford, S. B., Guilford College.
- Petty, G. W., Wilkesboro.
- Phason, L. E., Monroe.
- Pierce, J. A., Franklinton.
- Pierce, Luke, Windsor.
- Pitchford, M., Littleton.
- Pitts, E. L., Hamilton.
- Plummer, T. J., Macon.
- Powell, J. E., Elm City.
- Powell, R. P., Webster.
- Powars, I. M., Wallace.
- Poteat, D. A., Big Falls.
- Price, A. T., Shotwell.
- Pugh, Simon, Spring Hope.
- Quick, H. J., Rockingham.
- Ragland, L. C., Mill Creek.
- Randolph, E. E., Hobbsville.
- Ransom, J. M., Littleton.
- Ransom, M. C., Oxford.
- Ratliff, Jos., Deep Creek.
- Rawls, J. C., Palmyra.
- Ray, S. W., University Station.
- Ray, Wortham, Red Mountain.
- Reavis, W. B., Oxford.
- Redfearn, A., Lanes Creek.
- Redman, Jno., Felts.
- Reed, Wm., Murfreesboro.
- Reynolds, E., Coleraine.
- Rice, E., Spring Hope.
- Richardson, G. R., Tarheel.
- Richmond, Cary, Hycotee.
- Roberts, N. F., Raleigh.
- Robertson, N., Abbottsburg.
- Robins, B. F., High Point.
- Robinson, A. R., Grimesland.

Sermons, Addresses and Reminiscences and Important Correspondence

- Robinson, J. J., Smithfield.
- Rogers, H. C., Oxford.
- Rhyne, U. S. G., Dallas.
- Ross, M. R., Elams.
- Royalls, R., Kelleys.
- Royster, Wm., Oxford.
- Rountree, Henry, Stokes.
- Roundtree, N. C., Beaufort.
- Ruffin. A. R., Tarboro.
- Russell, E. G., Ridgeway.
- Russell, J. J., Littleton.
- Sales, Wiley, Asheville.
- Sanders, Cato, Clayton.
- Sanders, W. P., Clayton.
- Sansom, Wm., Moss Neck.
- Satterfield, A. R., Roxboro.
- Satterwhite, R. B., Wingwood.
- Saulter, D. S., Raleigh.
- Saunders, H. D., Smithfield.
- Saunders, J. C., Wiggins X Road.
- Scarborough, Alex., Fayetteville.
- Scarborough, J., Wilson.
- Scott, D. S., Newbern.
- Shadd, D. L., Monroe.
- Sessoms, T. S., St. Johns.
- Sharp, Thos., St., Pauls.
- Sharp, W. P., Harrellsville.
- Shaw, W. H., Littleton.
- Sheets, D., Burningtown.
- Shepard, A., Charlotte.
- Shepard, R., Oxford.
- Sherrer, R. F., Sweetwater.
- Sherrill, J. A., Doolie.
- Shuford, W. S., Mt. Holly.
- Sills, J. S., Tarboro.
- Simmons, S. A., Durham.
- Sinclear, Simeon, Lumberton.
- Snow, C. T., Abbotsburg.
- Sledge, J. B., Pollocksville.
- Smith, A. A., Mt. Olive.

- Smith, A. W., Taylorsville.
- Smith, C., Leasburg.
- Smith, C., Scotland Neck.
- Smith, C. R., Big Rock.
- Smith C. S., Faison.
- Smith, E. E., Fayetteville.
- Smith, H. T., Wilmington.
- Smith, Jos., Morganton.
- Smith, J. M., Deavers.
- Smith, L. T., Fair Plains.
- Smith, R., Blue Wings.
- Smith, R., Wiggins X Roads.
- Smith, S. W., Folsom.
- Smith, Wm., Wilmington.
- Snider, J., Hannersville.
- Snider, N., Poplar Hill.
- Sommerville, C. C., Charlotte.
- Sommerville, M. T., Warrenton.
- Spaulding, J. A., Elkton.
- Spears, C., Mt. Olive.
- Spells, J., Wilmington.
- Spencer, S. S., Newbern.
- Spicer, W. H., Wilmington.
- Spruell, Miles, Newbern.
- Stamper, G., Cedar Creek.
- Stamper, L. B., Louisburg.
- Stanfield, T. Y., Roxboro.
- Stanfield, W. H., Durham.
- Staten, D. A., Goldsboro.
- Stokes, D. S., Castalia.
- Stough, A. D., Webster.
- Stroud, A., Cary.
- Stuart, W. H., Massey.
- Sumner, A. L., Warsaw.
- Sydney, C. F., Leasburg.
- Sykes, B. K., Dunn.
- Tate, J. W., Clinton.
- Taylor, C., Clinton.
- Taylor, D. W., Polkton.
- Taylor, J. A., Gaston.

Sermons, Addresses and Reminiscences and Important Correspondence

- Taylor, J. L., Green Hill.
- Taylor, J. M., Creedmoor.
- Taylor, L. C., Franklinton.
- Terry, F. R., Hightower.
- Thomas, C., Wilsons Mills.
- Thomas, Jno., Louisburg.
- Thomas, S., Burlington.
- Thompson, A. H., Lumberton.
- Thompson, E. M., Lumberton.
- Thompson, Jonah, Lewiston.
- Thompson, J. J., Lewiston.
- Tranaham, Geo., Abbotts Creek.
- Troxler, S., Gibbonsville.
- Tucker, Dan, Raleigh.
- Tucker, W. T., Clinton.
- Underwood, C. T., Clinton.
- Urrends, J., Tarboro.
- Vass, S. N., Raleigh.
- Vincent, A. B., Raleigh.
- Wade, S., Roxboro.
- Wadkins, O., Lumber Bridge.
- Walden, R. I., Henderson.
- Walker, J. R., Calhoun.
- Ward, N., Scotland Neck.
- Warren, Spencer, Hightowers.
- Washington, D., Enfield.
- Washington, H., Charlotte.
- Waters, C. B., Wilmington.
- Watkins, N. W., Rose Hill.
- Watts, R. B., Wilkesboro.
- Way, G. M., Nicholsons Mills.
- Webb, R. D., Center Grove.
- Wellein, Jas., Goldsboro.
- West, Henry, Afton.
- White, C. J., Windsor.
- White, G. H., Weldon.
- Whitaker, Isaac, Enfield.
- Whiteside, R. F., Burnsville.
- Whitted, A., Hillsboro.
- Whitted, J. A., Raleigh.

- Whitted, J. M., Cedar.
- Wilburn, A., Trinity College.
- Wilburn, S. S., Trinity College.
- Wiggins, W. H., Tarboro.
- Wilkins, C., Moss Neck.
- Wilkins, F. W., Enfield.
- Williams, B. N., Fair Bluff.
- Williams, B. W., Hub.
- Williams, C. G., Hamilton.
- Williams, D., Roxboro.
- Williams, D. R., Arcola.
- Williams, Green, Shotwell.
- Williams, Geo., Register.
- Williams, J. C., Woodland.
- Williams, J. H., Leasburg.
- Williams, L. W., Black Creek.
- Williams, N., Hulls X Roads.
- Williams, R. W., Hamilton.
- Williams, S. L., Blackmans Mills.
- Williams, Thos., Williamston.
- Williams, T., Taylors Bridge.
- Williams, W., Hamilton.
- Williamson, C. H., Raleigh.
- Williamson, V., Clinton.
- Wilson, Eli, Bakersville.
- Wilson, R., Purley.
- Wilson, R. E., Blanche.
- Wilson, S., Turkey.
- Wilson, T. H., Avoca.
- Winn, W., Mt. Carmel.
- Witherspoon, S. H., Charlotte.
- Wolfe, L. W., Matthews.
- Wood, J. W., Weldon.
- Woodward, W. H., Rockingham.
- Woodward, W. T. H., Littleton.
- Wooten, N. D., Clarkton.
- Wooten, R. A., Register.
- Worlds, J. J., Raleigh.
- Worley, R. M., Webster.
- Wyche, A. B. J., Henderson.

Sermons, Addresses and Reminiscences and Important Correspondence

- Yancey, Paul, Durham.
- Yokin, Thomas, Hobgood.
- Young, J. A., Ingleside.
- Zollicoffer, Chas., South Gaston.
- Zollicoffer, T., South Gaston.

SOUTH CAROLINA.

- Aaron, A., Camden.
- Adam, S., Donalds.
- Adams, S. H., Weston.
- Alexander, J. F., Lydia.
- Alexander, W. M., Rich Hill.
- Allen, J. O., Greenville.
- Alston, A., Summerville.
- Alston, J., Charleston.
- Anderson, C. H., Allendale.
- Anderson, H. C., Anderson.
- Anderson, Wm., Septus.
- Bacot, A. R., Society Hill.
- Baker, B. H., Grahamsville.
- Baker, J. R., Greenwood.
- Barksdale, D. C., Laurens.
- Barmore, A., Rileys.
- Baskin, J. N., Pleasanthill.
- Bass, B. B., Cheraw.
- Baylor, R. W., Columbia.
- Belk, L., Lancaster.
- Bell, A., Beech Island.
- Bell, H. A., Winnsboro.
- Bell, J. W., Port Royal.
- Benton, Eli, Longtown.
- Benjamin, C. P., Winnsboro.
- Bennett, W. K., Cheraw.
- Bentley, D. A., Moffettsville.
- Berry, K., Camden.
- Bibbs, B. B., Crosshill.
- Blakeny, D. D., Tradesville.
- Boyd, J. H., Aiken.

- Boykin, J. W., Camden.
- Boykin, M., Camden.
- Bracy, R. B., Lewiedale.
- Bright, P., Edisto.
- Brockington, I. P., Darlington.
- Brown, A. B., Goethe.
- Brown, D., Seneca.
- Brown, E H., Williamston.
- Brown, J., Frogmore.
- Brown, Jas., Salters Depot.
- Brown, J. H., Union.
- Brown, L., Lancaster.
- Bryant, J. B., Bordeaux.
- Burkett, J. C., Meeting Street.
- Bush, Wm., Ellenton.
- Butler, A. E., Boykins.
- Butler, J. C., Summerville.
- Byrd, Wm., Leeds.
- Bythewood, D. W., Beaufort.
- Cade, A. L., Bordeaux.
- Caldwell, B. W., Newberry.
- Callaham, P. W., Newberry.
- Carmichael, W. O., Orangeburg.
- Carolin, Jno., Tradesville.
- Carolin, W. J., Taxahaw.
- Carter E., Baldock.
- Carroll, R., Columbia.
- Chaney, J. J., Greenville.
- Chestnut, Wm., Camden.
- Chisholm, S. C., Salkehatchie.
- Chisholm, Wm., Shester.
- Cobb, B. B., Monterey.
- Cole, I. W., Sheldon.
- Coleman, A. C., Abbeville.
- Coleman, G. C., Hawthorne.
- Collier, A., Clark Hill.
- Cowan, P., Duewest.
- Craig, W. G., Townville.
- Crawford, A. C., Anderson.
- Crawford, G. W., Greenwood.

Sermons, Addresses and Reminiscences and Important Correspondence

- Crawford, J. Y., Lancaster.
- Crockett, R. H., Vanwyck.
- Cummings, A., Ellenton.
- Daniels, J. C., Columbia.
- Daniels, J. S., Honea Path.
- Dart, J. L., Charleston.
- Davis, N., Feasterville.
- Davis, Wm., Tradesville.
- Davison, I., Ravenels.
- Dawkins, S., Union.
- Deans, J. D., Ninety-six.
- Diggs, T., Catchall.
- Dixon, G. W., Petigru.
- Doe, A., Grahamville.
- Donaldson, H., Eden.
- Donaldson, S. J., Abbeville.
- Dorn, F., Monetta.
- Dow, R. C., Camden.
- Dow, T. S., Antioch.
- Drake, J. P., Cheraw.
- Drayton, G., Aiken.
- Dunbar, A., Beaufort.
- Dunbar, A. P., Columbia.
- Duncan, H., Fort Motte.
- Duron, Jno., Flatrock.
- Dutch, R., Lowndesville.
- Earl, G. W., Loopers.
- Earle, B. B.
- Edwards, Henry, Dacusville.
- Edwards, J., Greenville.
- English, A., Taxahaw.
- Evans, J. W., Jr., Greenwood.
- Fair, J., Robertsville.
- Faust, J. W., Denmark.
- Featherstone, L., Chester.
- Fennell, I. H., Early Branch.
- Foster, M. A., Union.
- Franklin, C. S., Greenwood.
- Frazier, J. T., Verdery.
- Fuller, A. A., Travelers Rest.

Sermons, Addresses and Reminiscences and Important Correspondence

- Fuller, H. B., Anderson.
- Gaither, D. D., Liberty Hill.
- Gaither, R. D., Killgo.
- Gant, S., Allendale.
- Gardenhire, E., Meriwether.
- Gardenhire, L. G., Meriwether.
- Garner, T. H., Goethe.
- Gassaway, E. V., Anderson.
- Gibbs, C., Spartanburg.
- Gibbs, T. C., Sumter.
- Gilbert, G. W., St. Albans.
- Gilbert, M., Mannville.
- Gilbert, M. W., Charleston.
- Giles, F. G., Greenville.
- Gilmore, J. A., Verdery.
- Gilmore, T. S., Rockhill.
- Glenn, R. D., Anderson.
- Glover, E. M., Winnsboro.
- Glover, W. J., Eutawville.
- Gooding, Jos., Ruddell.
- Goodson, A. G., Congaree.
- Goodwin, C. T., Greenwood.
- Goodwin, G., Liberty Hill.
- Goodwin, J. B., Congaree.
- Goodwin, W. C., Verdery.
- Gordon, D. W., Sheldon.
- Graham, C. J., Ridgeway.
- Graham, J. D., Newberry.
- Grantham, P., Sumter.
- Green, C. S., Plantersville.
- Green, W. W., Beaufort.
- Gunter, F., Congaree.
- Hall, M. P., Rockhill.
- Ham, E., Timmonsville.
- Ham, H. A., Mullins.
- Ham, I., Timmonsville.
- Hamilton, A. P., Beaufort.
- Hampton, T., Orangeburg.
- Hampton, W., Dale.
- Hancock, R. W., Phoenix.

Sermons, Addresses and Reminiscences and Important Correspondence

- Hanry, H., Orangeburg.
- Harmon, J. E., Sumter.
- Harriott, F. H., Magnolia.
- Harriott, R., Camden.
- Harris, Clark, St. Albans.
- Haynes, P., Columbia.
- Haynes, R. J., Summersville.
- Henegen, S., Key.
- Hill, A., Hamburg.
- Hill, H., Parksville.
- Hill, R., Almeda.
- Holland, C. F., Aiken.
- Holloway, J. W., Greenwood.
- Hood, W. D., Ridge Spring.
- Hopkins, O. H., Kershaw.
- House, J. J., Lancaster.
- Hunter, Albert, Easley.
- Hunter, M., Rembert.
- Ingram, Wm., Taxahaw.
- Jackson, J. C., Winnsboro.
- Jackson, J. C., Anderson.
- Jacobs, B., Columbia.
- James, S., Sumter.
- Jefferson, P. W., Pineville.
- Jenkins, G., Grahamville.
- Jenkins, I., Charleston.
- Jenkins, L. W., Forreston.
- Jenkins, S., Weston.
- Jennings, A. E., Copes.
- Johnson, Edw., Seminole.
- Johnson, H. N., Port Royal.
- Johnson, J. C., Varnville.
- Johnson, L., Camden.
- Johnson, S. J., Yemassee.
- Jones, A. L., Williamston.
- Jones, B. W., Johnston.
- Jones, C., Society Hill.
- Jones, E. S., Cantey.
- Jones, I. B., Anderson.
- Jones, L. L., Lanford Station.

Sermons, Addresses and Reminiscences and Important Correspondence

- Jones, Robert, Camden.
- Jones, R. S., Allendale.
- Jones, S., Sheldon.
- Jones, S. J., Anderson.
- Jones, T., Ridgeland.
- Jones, T. L., Charleston.
- Jones, W. P., Fairforest.
- Jumper, A. C., Camden.
- Kelly, A., Mossy.
- Kenner, R., Ridge Spring.
- Kenner, R. W., Meriwether.
- Kirkland, B. R., Seminole.
- Kirkland, G., Orangeburg.
- Land, J., Wilksburg.
- Lawton, C. L., Robertsville.
- Lawton, M. E., Dale.
- Lee, J. M., Camden.
- Leak, J. W., Crosshill.
- Lewis, A. B., Pendleton.
- Lewis, S., Neva.
- Lide, J. D., Darlington.
- Lillie, H., Lancaster.
- Lindsay, B. R., Anderson.
- Lindsay, G. M., Duewest.
- Lineberger, B. F., Kershaw.
- Lomax, B., Mayesville.
- Long, J. M., Union.
- Loman, W. M., Hopkins, Turnout.
- Mackey, D. M., Drycreek.
- Mackey, J. T., Robertsville.
- Maddox, J. S., Donaldsville.
- Marant, H., Rembert.
- Marshall, J. F., McCormick.
- Mattison, W. L., Williamston.
- Mauldin, B., Moscow.
- Mays, J. C., Reevesville.
- Mazyck, E. T., Trial.
- McBride, D. M., Vance.
- McCoy, J. L., Charleston.
- McElrath, T., Cashville.

Sermons, Addresses and Reminiscences and Important Correspondence

- McElwee, H. F., Pendleton.
- McGirt, G. W., Camden.
- McIntosh, J. W., Rileys.
- McIntosh, S. T., Abbeville.
- McKissic, E. R., Stoker.
- McNeill, T. N., Ridgeway.
- Meachem, D. W., Woodlawn.
- Melton, F., Chesterfield.
- Middleton, J. M., Beaufort.
- Mills, G. F., Spartanburg.
- Mills, H. P., Spartanburg.
- Mims, T. M., Greenville.
- Moore, G. T., Lowndesville.
- Moore, M., Reedy River Factory.
- Moore, S. L., Grenville.
- Moragne, M W., Verdery.
- Morgan, G. A., Edgefield.
- Morris, P. L., Abbeville.
- Morris, W. H., Graniteville.
- Nix, N. C., Orangeburg.
- Oliver, S., Storeville.
- Owens, S., Mullins.
- Page, M. B., Greenville.
- Palmer, S. W., Union.
- Parker, A. I., Orangeburg.
- Parker, W. R., Fair Play.
- Pawley, J. C., Charleston.
- Perkins, S. A., Kershaw.
- Peterson, W. M., Cleora.
- Phillips, J. G., Aiken.
- Pinckney, B. W., Beaufort.
- Pinson, J. A., Greenville.
- Poinsett, D., Frogmore.
- Prince, F. W., Bennettsville.
- Prince, M. P., Blenheim.
- Pringle, P., Jordan.
- Quilian, J. P., Timmonsville.
- Rapley, C. J., Abbeville.
- Ravennah, E. J., Gillisonville.
- Reed, E. B., Cummings.

- Reed, Elymas, Cheraw.
- Reese, E. D., Pendleton.
- Reid, D., Cantey.
- Rice, R. D., Lees.
- Richards, D., Liberty Hill.
- Richardson, J. J. B., Osborn.
- Ridgedell, E. R., Port Royal.
- Robert, G. W., Liberty Hill.
- Robertson, Jno., Aiken.
- Robertson, S. R., Meriwether.
- Robinson, A. R., Greenville.
- Robinson, J. A., Charleston.
- Robinson, J. J., Greenville.
- Rogers, E., Greenville.
- Rogers, J. E., Wellford.
- Rose, S., Tenmile.
- Rosey, A., Phoenix.
- Rouse, A. V., Greenwood.
- Rucker, R. B. Greenwood.
- Ruff, S., Blythewood.
- Salters, R. B., Salters Depot.
- Samuel, Wm., McCormick.
- Sanders, E., Beaufort.
- Sanders, W. S., Bennettsville.
- Saxon, F., Fairfax.
- Saxon, G., Blackville.
- Scott, A. N., Ninetysix.
- Scott, James, Gadsden.
- Screven, S. S., Grahamville.
- Shropshire, J., Kilgo.
- Simmons, J., Dean.
- Simmons, M. F., Beaufort.
- Simmons, B. W., Frogmore.
- Simmons, R. N., Belton.
- Simons, I. W., Columbia.
- Singleton, W. L., Dunbarton.
- Smart, C., Gifford.
- Smith, D., Early Branch.
- Smith, J., Westminster.
- Smith, J. C., Early Branch.

Sermons, Addresses and Reminiscences and Important Correspondence

- Smith, S. H., St. Matthews.
- Smith, T., Peeples.
- Spell, J. P., Aiken.
- Spencer, Peter, Anderson.
- Starks, J. J., Seneca.
- Starks, N., Kirksey.
- Steel, F. S., Vanwyck.
- Stephenson, L. S., Blackstock.
- Stewart, A., Duewest.
- Stewart, Jno., Walhalla.
- Stewart, Wm., Seminole.
- Streator, A. J., Cheraw.
- Sullivan, S., Greenville.
- Sumter, I., Beaufort.
- Sutherland, W. S., Pickens.
- Talley, Isaac, Marietta.
- Taylor, E. T., Walhalla.
- Taylor, I., Camden.
- Taylor, J. L., Columbia.
- Taylor, S. P., Sumter.
- Taylor, W., Congaree.
- Taylor, W. T., Cantey.
- Terrell, E., Anderson.
- Thomas, G., Ridgeway.
- Thompson, J. S., Eutawville.
- Thompson, P. M., Anderson. [out.
- Thompson, W. M., Hopkins Turn-
- Thurman, F. W., Colliers.
- Timms, R., Chester.
- Tobin, J. C., Greenville.
- Toland, W., Greenville.
- Tucker, W. A., Petigru.
- Turner, B. W., Verdery.
- Turner, Wm., Richland.
- Vant, H. N., Orangeburg.
- Wade, F. D., Lancaster.
- Wadkins, J. B., Port Royal.
- Wainwright, W., Orangeburg.
- Walker, A., Equality.
- Walker, Cato, Equality.

- Walker, Jas., Greenville.
- Walker, J. H., Greenwood.
- Walker, Jas., S., Central.
- Wallace, F. R. Newberry.
- Wallace, J., Union.
- Wallace, W. R., Orangeburg.
- Ware, M., Pliny.
- Warren, P., Midway.
- Washington, A. W., Orangeburg.
- Washington, D. C., Frogmore.
- Washington, D. E., Frogmore.
- Washington, F. J., Williamston.
- Washington, J. E., Woodville.
- Watkins, H., Belton.
- Watkins, S., Jackson.
- Watson, C. W., Silver.
- Watson, G. W., Clinton.
- Watson, J. A., Seneca.
- Watson, P. P., Beaufort.
- Webb, C., Abbeville.
- White, E. D., Rock Hill.
- White, E. S., Chester.
- Whitehead, C., Columbia.
- Wiggins, Harrison, Seneca.
- Wiggins, Henry, Seneca.
- Williams, B. W., Jacksonboro.
- Williams, E. W., Clinton.
- Williams, J., Donoho.
- Williams, J. B., Buckhead.
- Williams, J. W., Batesburg.
- Williams, L. A., New Market.
- Williams, M. S., Beaufort.
- Williams, R., Seneca.
- Williams, S., Beaufort.
- Williams, T. J., Camden.
- Williams, W. L., Ridge Spring.
- Williams, W. M., Charleston.
- Williford, J. M., Level Land.
- Williford, J. O., Moscow.
- Willingham, M., Hardeeville.

Sermons, Addresses and Reminiscences and Important Correspondence

- Wilson J. R., Columbia.
- Witherspoon, Wm., Lancaster.
- Woodward, W. H., Cheraw.
- Wright, W. M., Fairfax.
- Wyman, R. C., Crockettville.
- Youmans, H. Y., Grays.
- Young, S., Varnville.

TENNESSEE.

- Abernathy, S., Pulaski.
- Adams, C. W., McLemoresville.
- Adams, J., Toulon Landing.
- Alderson, Eli, Santa Fe.
- Alexander, A. J., Richardson.
- Allen, Jeff., Lagrange.
- Allen, J. A.
- Alston, S., Atoka.
- Alston, W. H., Burleson.
- Anderson, A. B., Chattanooga.
- Anderson, Jeff., Bells Depot.
- Anderson, William, Middleton.
- Anthony, J. T., Creevy.
- Archer, W. L., Kerrville.
- Armstrong, Jas., Lagrange.
- Armstrong, S. W., Riceville.
- Austin, E. A., Brownsville.
- Baker, C. Woodlawn.
- Baker, R. Clarksville.
- Baldwin, G., Rossville.
- Barnhill, G. W., Lexington.
- Bartlett, A. L., Memphis.
- Bass, B. J.
- Bates, C. C., Pikeville.
- Baugh, J. B., Martin.
- Bangus, J. B., Columbia.
- Bell, C. H., McCains.

- Benton, G. W., Murfreesboro.
- Bills, R. H., Hickory Valley.
- Blackwell, J. B., Brunswick.
- Blanton, J. D., Dover.
- Blew, A., Bartlett.
- Borders, N. D.
- Bowen, G. P., Wildersville.
- Bowers, J. C., White.
- Bowers, Titus, Middleburg.
- R. H. Boyd, D. D., Nashville.
- Boyd, E. D., Springfield.
- Bradley, J. C., Memphis.
- Branch, G. W., Eads.
- Branch, R., White.
- Branden, H. H., Roberson Fork.
- Brandon, D. T., Oakville.
- Bransford, J. S., Newbern.
- Brantley, A. Orchard Knob.
- Breedlove, Geo.
- Brooks, Bass. Flat Gap.
- Brown, A. R., Brunswick.
- Brown, Harrison, Brownsville.
- Brown, H. H., Roberson Fork.
- Brown, J. P., Henderson.
- Brown, L. R., Memphis.
- Brown, S., Milligan.
- Bryant, G. W.
- Burdine, E., Powells.
- Burt, M., Ooltewah.
- Cade, J. D.
- Caldwell Jas., Godwin.
- Callaway, H. C., Hickory Valley.
- Callon, L., Memphis.
- Carmen, L., Hartsville.
- Carpenter, L. C., Jackson.
- Carter, E. C., Memphis.
- Carter, R., Bellbuckle.
- Chaffin, N., Carters Creek.
- Chapman, S., Denmark.
- Chenault, S., Sideview.

- Chilton, A., Flippin.
- Chilton, H. B., Jackson.
- Chilton, J. W.
- Chrisman, J., Memphis.
- Chrisman, N. H., Palestine.
- Churchwell, J. C., Clifton.
- Clark, C. H., D. D., Nashville.
- Clark, G., Paris.
- Clark, U., Randolph.
- Clark, W. M., Blanche.
- Clemmons, H. E., Collierville.
- Clemmons, Jno., Knoxville.
- Coburn, J., Canadaville.
- Colbert, J.
- Colman, A., Pinewood.
- Colman, M., Fruitland.
- Coleman, S. K., Martin.
- Collier, R. H., Dickson.
- Collier, Wm., Paris.
- Collins, S., Clarksville.
- Connell, J., Saulsbury.
- Contz, A., Springfield.
- Cotton, I., Germantown.
- Crier, J., Woodstock.
- Crocker, J. W., Orlinda.
- Crosby, Jas. C., Nashville.
- Cross, A. B., Nashville.
- Cross, J. M., Eads.
- Cross, P., Erin.
- Crutcher, N. C., Murfreesboro.
- Culp, J., Sydneytown.
- Curran, A. G., Dyersburg.
- Dawson, J. H., Jackson.
- Dennis, E. F., Clarksville.
- Dennis, P. D., New Providence.
- Dickerson, B., Mason.
- Dillard, D., Sideview.
- Dixon, J. D., Castalian Springs.
- Dobson, J. D., Cairo.
- Dobson, Wyatt, Fayetteville.

- Dunlap, S., Springfield.
- Dupree, W., Brownsville.
- Earls, L., Knoxville.
- Easly, P., Chattanooga.
- Edmondson, Lot, Columbia.
- Edwards, H., Nashville.
- Eldridge, W. S., Orchard Knob.
- Ellington, W. S., Nashville.
- Ellis, H., Clarksville.
- Elrod, Wm., Lagrange.
- Evans, D., Covington.
- Evans, Jas., Tibbs.
- Evans, Jas. R., Milan.
- Evans, Wm., Carolina.
- Everett, R. L., Johnsonville.
- Fennick, W. P., Castalian Springs.
- Fields, E. N., Braden.
- Fields, G. H., Gallaway.
- Fields, W. D., Kingston.
- Fifer, E., Brighton.
- Flagg, O. B., Carolina.
- Flennory, Wm., Memphis.
- Fonnville, J. A., Martin.
- Foster, N.
- Foster, T. A., Cottage Grove.
- Foster, R. B., Como.
- Fowler, S., Nashville.
- Franklin, John, Madison.
- Freman, A. H., Martin.
- Freeman, R., Denmark.
- Frierson, B., Columbia.
- Fulgum, G. W., Bolivar.
- Fulton, A. F., Howell.
- Fulton, J. H., Brownsville.
- Gadsberry, N., Knoxville.
- Gaines, S. H., Glenloch.
- Garlington, J. H., Hixon.
- Garrett, S., Germantown.
- Gassaway, H., Lick Creek.
- Gibbs, L., Henderson.

Sermons, Addresses and Reminiscences and Important Correspondence

- Gilbert, M. W., Bodenham.
- Giles, G. S., Keeling.
- Gillespie, H. C., Memphis.
- Gilmore, J. S., Columbia.
- Glass, J. S., Martin.
- Gleaves, S., Hendersonville.
- Grant, B. F., Etna.
- Gray, S. W.., Memphis.
- Greer, J. H., Bristol.
- Gregory, John, McKenzie
- Gray, A., Augustus
- Griffey, H., Lyles
- Guy, G. W., Bond
- Hall, A. L., Memphis
- Hall, B. F., Dickerson
- Hall, J. H., Chattanooga
- Hall, W. G., Crescent
- Hanley, H. W., Jackson (ville
- Hansborough, E. E., McLemores
- Harding, J. H., Nashville
- Harris, H. G. Martin
- Harris, H., Memphis
- Harris, J. M., Chattanooga
- Harris, P., Eads
- Harrison, R., Memphis
- Harrison, W. E., Humboldt
- Hart, Jesse, Middleburg
- Hastings, T. H., Saulsbury
- Hathorn, E., Covington
- Haynes, J. R., Columbia
- Haynes, Wm., Nashville
- Hazelrigg, J. W., Knoxville.
- Henderson, J. H., Rutherford
- Henry, G. H., Barren Plain (nace
- Hicks, Jas. E., Cumberland Fur-
- Hicks, Wm., Knoxville
- Hill, G., Lebanan
- Hill, H., Brownsville.
- Hill, J. H., Grand Junction.
- Hillsman, J. H., Murfreesboro

Sermons, Addresses and Reminiscences and Important Correspondence

- Hogan, J. H., Chattanooga
- Hogan, R., Lucy
- Holloway, M., Memphis
- Holmes, S., Organs X Roads
- Holmes, T. H., Wallings
- Hood, W. W., Chattanooga
- Hope, I. J., Chattanooga
- Howard, D. T., Paris
- Howard, F., Clarksville
- Howard, R. R., Knoxville
- Hugely, Benj., Trenton
- Hunt, S. J., Memphis
- Hunt, W. R., Grand Junction
- Hurd, W. H., Memphis
- Hurt, A. D., Nashville
- Hutchinson, C. H., Trezevant
- Hutchinson, H. N., Chattanooga.
- Ingham, J. H., Andrew Chapel
- Isaac, E. W. D., Nashville
- Isom, S., Memphis
- Ivins, S., Columbia
- Jackson, D. B., Dayton
- Jackson, E. D., Tabernacle
- Jackson, B. J., Memphis
- Jeffries, D. J., Andrew Chapel
- Jett, J. F., Powell Station
- Johnson, A. J., Canadaville
- Johnson, C. H., Bristol
- Johnson, S. H., Columbia
- Johnson, L. J., Franklin
- Johnson, W. J., Paris
- Jones, C. H., Fulton
- Jones, D. V., Brunswick
- Jones, D. W., Somerville
- Jones, J. J., Ensley
- Jones S. T., McCains
- Jones, T. J., Nashville
- Jones, W., Philadelphia
- Jones, Wesley, Keeling
- Jones, Wm., Cuba

- Jones, W. C., Adams Station
- Jones, W. M., Bryson
- Jordan, J. C., Humboldt
- Jordan, J. H.
- Jordan, W. A., Jackson.
- Kendall, B., Buchanan
- Kendall, R., Paris Landing
- Kennedy, H. K., Columbia
- Kenney, A. O., Nashville.
- Kincaid, J. J., Humboldt
- Kilcrease, M. C., Lanton
- King, T. M., Chattanooga
- Lacy, G. W., Toulon
- Langster, J.
- Lanier, W. F., Somerville
- Lawrence, E. M., Nashville
- Leathers, J. J., Bond
- Lee, J., Pocahontas
- Lee, J. L., Memphis
- Leftwich, H. F., Elizabethtown
- Lewis, A. L., New Providence
- Lincoln, E. J., Prospect Station
- Long, P., Jackson
- Looker, J. W., Increase.
- Love, A., Chattanooga
- Love, R. J., Pulaski
- Lynch, E. L., Madison
- Lytle, J. E., Concord
- Manney, A., Nashville
- Marshall, J., Jackson
- Martin, M., Memphis
- Martin, Wm., Memphis
- Mason, J. M., Nashville
- Materson, D., Knoxville
- Matthews, J. P., Eads
- May, J. H., Clarksville
- McClellan, S. V., Trenton
- McClendon, S. C., Madisonville.
- McClure, C. C., Morristown
- McCrosky, A., Felker

- McDaniel, A. R., Lagrange
- McDonald, D. L., Bolivar.
- McDonald, G. W. J., Fayetteville.
- McGee, L., Fosterville.
- McKinney, W. J., Bethel
- McMichael, Wm. J., Memphis
- McVey, David, Paris
- Meals, D., Pulaski
- Meredith, H., Memphis.
- Merritt, C. M., Clarksville
- Metcalfe, H., Clarksville
- Miles, C., Pulaski
- Miles, D., Memphis
- Miller, J. B., Lewisburg
- Milligan, H., Orlinda
- Mimms, S., Cedar Hill
- Mitchell, J. B., Martin
- Mitchell, J. E., Hartsville
- Mitchell, J., Brunswick
- Mitchell, J. W.
- Mitchum, A., Germantown
- Moody, A., Brownsville
- Moore, C., Jackson
- Moore, Geo. W., Columbia
- Moore, R., Granberry
- Moorman, Fred., Williston
- Morgan, J. W., Jackson
- Morgan, Wm., Memphis
- Morgan, W. F. H., Memphis
- Morris, O. R., Bells Depot
- Murrell, A.
- Neal, H.,
- Nelson, G. W., Millington
- Nelson, H. W., Toulon
- Nichols, A. B., Memphis.
- Norman, R., Collierville.
- Northcross, J., Fruitland.
- Northcross, J. Fruitland
- Nunelly, J. L., Cottage Grove
- Oglesby, E., Hughes

Sermons, Addresses and Reminiscences and Important Correspondence

- Olden, ., Mason
- Owen, H. C., Brownsville
- Page, Robt., Nashville
- Parham, R., Sharon
- Parker, W. P. McMinville
- Parks, W. G., Knoxville
- Patrick, A. P., Moscow
- Patterson, L., Memphis
- Patterson, Luke, Pleasant View View
- Payne, J. Orlinda
- Peeples, Hollis, Milan
- Perdue, B. B., Baker
- Perkins, A., Clarksville
- Perkins, N., Clarksville.
- Petty, R. J., Memphis
- Phillips, G., Elizabethtown
- Phillips, H., Nashville
- Poe, J. T., Loanoke.
- Poore, John, Pocahontas
- Poter, A., Nashville
- Powell, A. P., Lexington
- Price, S. R., McLemoresville
- Pruatt, F., Hickory Valley.
- Quinn, P., Bulls Gap
- Reason, Wm., Randolph
- Redman, F.
- Reed, L., Memphis
- Reid, J. W., Daisy
- Reynolds, M. C., Oliver Springs
- Richardson, S. Richardson
- Riggins, H., Decherd (Landing
- Riley, M. F., Columbia
- Robertson, R., Canadaville
- Roberts, A., Riceville
- Roberts, Wm., White
- Robinson, J., Memphis
- Robinson, Jas., Bolivar
- Robinson, Simon, Woodstock
- Ruffin, J., Whitepine
- Russell, W. R., Dayton

Sermons, Addresses and Reminiscences and Important Correspondence

- Rust, J. R., Martin
- Rutherford, G. R., Brunswick.
- Sales, J. J., Chattanooga
- Sammons, G. W., Jordan Springs.
- Sanders, J. B., Memphis
- Sanderson, R., Columbia
- Scott, D. S., Chattanooga
- Scott, E., Germantown
- Scott, J. S., Turnersville
- Scott, Prince, Clarksville
- Searcy, T. J., Memphis
- Sholer, C. C., Columbia
- Shaw, P. S., Fowlkes
- Sherman, David, Chattanooga
- Siler, M., Loudon
- Skillon, M. C., Pulaski
- Smith F. K., Chattanooga
- Smith, H., Carolina
- Smith, H. C., Brownsville
- Smith, T. P., Good Springs
- Spratlin, J. B., Memphis.
- Spurlock, W. H., Madison
- Stamps, F. M., Nashville
- Stewart, E., Hughes
- Stokes, W. H. C., Memphis
- Stone, A., Paint Rock
- Stone, B. F., Union City
- Story, T. J., Shelbyville
- Strong, B. G., Antioch
- Stubblefield, T. H., McMinnville
- Stubbs, J. S. Wartrace
- Sutton, A. A., Brownsville
- Swaggerton, T. A., Newport
- Swan, G. G., Glen Alice
- Swayne, H. C., McKenzie
- Tall, Jas., Sibley
- Taylor, H. D., Franklin
- Taylor, Jerry, Hillsboro
- Taylor, M., Glimp
- Taylor, O. E., Jackson

Sermons, Addresses and Reminiscences and Important Correspondence

- Terry, B., Stanton Depot
- Terry, L. Saulsbury
- Thomas, B. T. Clarksville
- Thomas, F., Memphis
- Thompson, A. R., Mill Spring
- Thompson, J. B., White Pine.
- Thompson, S., Nashville
- Tillman, W. H., Chattanooga
- Toll, A. J., McKenzie
- Toomey, L., Kingston
- Townsend, D. A., Winchester
- Townsend, D. W., Winchester
- Tracely, M.
- Trimble, L., Winchester
- Tubberville, Henry, Martin
- Turner, E. L., Lagrange
- Turner, --., McMinnville
- Tyson, C. P., Pinson
- Tyson, Jas., St. Elmo
- Utterback, H. C., Memphis
- Vaughan, M., Clarksville
- Vertress, P., Gallitin
- Vinegar, Jas., Bolivar
- Walker, C. W., Rose Hill
- Walker, O. T., Brownsville
- Wallace, J. C. Grand Junction
- Ward, T.
- Ware, A. A. Plum Point
- Warefield, A., St. Bethel
- Warren, J., Fruitland
- Washington, G. L., Nashville
- Washington, J. W., Cedar Hill.
- Washington, S., Dante
- Washington, L. W., Johnson City.
- Webb, W. T., Jackson
- White, A., Godwin.
- White, A. L., Bolivar.
- White, M. C., Pulaski.
- White, M., Gallaway.
- Whitehead, N. J., Chattanooga.

- Williams, A. W., Alexandria.
- Williams, E., Gold Dust.
- Williams, J. W., Milan.
- Williams, L. W., Memphis.
- Williams, T., Plum Point.
- Williams, Wesley, Santa Fe.
- Wills, R., Obion.
- Wilson, A. W., Nashville.
- Wilson, L. H., Pocahontas.
- Wimberly, A. B., Clarksville.
- Woods, J. B., Memphis.
- Woods, R. L., Huntingdon.
- Woods, S. H., Huntingdon.
- Woodson, G. P., Milan.
- Woodson, W., Grand Junction.
- Wright, A., Cedar Hill
- Wright, J. W., Kingston.
- Wyatt, M. Benton.
- Young, W. B., Ripley.

TEXAS.

- Adams, P., Jasper.
- Alexander, D. C. L., Waco.
- Alexander, H. C., Kilgore.
- Alexander, L., Creek.
- Alexander, Nestor, Waco.
- Allen, E. A., Brenham.
- Allen, L., Waskam.
- Allen, M., Meridian.
- Ames, R. Harrisburg.
- Anderson, C. C., Henderson.
- Anderson, Jack, Flatonia.
- Anderson, J. A., Marlin.
- Anderson, P., Pittbridge.
- Anderson, R. B., Forney.
- Anderson, R. San Antonio.
- Andrews, R. A., Anderson.
- Archer, T., Hempstead.

Sermons, Addresses and Reminiscences and Important Correspondence

- Armstrong, E. A., New Waverly.
- Armstrong, M., Flatonia.
- Ayers, A. T., Gainesville.
- Bailey, J. W., Pirle.
- Balay, W. L., Dallas.
- Baldwin, John, Wharton.
- Baldwin, M. C., Paris.
- Baldwin, R., Liberty.
- Baldwin, S., Liberty.
- Ball, W. B., D. D., Seguin.
- Baptist, J. H., Longview.
- Barber, Galveston.
- Barefield, C. B., Tabor.
- Barnes, E., Towson.
- Barnes, R. R., Longview.
- Bass, A., Lagrange.
- Bass, N., Lagrange.
- Beck, S., Marshall.
- Beckham, Nelson, Jefferson.
- Beckham, Wm., Austin.
- Bedford, S. B., Wilderville.
- Bell, S. B., Fort Worth.
- Bell, J. W., Bastrop.
- Benson, T. T., Brazoria.
- Berryman, Z. T., Fiskville.
- Biggins, D. G., Ennis.
- Birch, I. B., Houston.
- Birdwell, Thomas, Jasper.
- Bivens, A. B., Bellville.
- Black, B., Gainesville.
- Black, R., Garneld.
- Blain, J. W., eede.
- Blair, D., Brazoria.
- Blake, L. W., Greenville.
- Bland, I., Waco.
- Blandford, E., Blooming Grove.
- Blue, E., Milwood.
- Bonner, A. P., Grapeland.
- Booker, George W., Houston.
- Boone, A. L., Lagrange.

- Boulding, J. B., Caldwell.
- Boulding, W. T., Austin.
- Bowens, W. W. Eureka.
- Boyd, F., Tyler.
- Boykin, H., Eagle Lake.
- Bradford, M. H., New Berlin.
- Bradley, J., Patterson.
- Branch, E. H., Brenham.
- Brooks, Austin, Brookeland.
- Brooks, Y. B., Fort Worth.
- Brown, G. T., Rusk.
- Brown, J., Alto
- Brown, R. E., Gonzales.
- Brown, S., Sandypoint.
- Brown, S. B., Cameron.
- Brownrigg, J. Clarksville.
- Bryant, J. B., Rockdale.
- Buckley, R., Mt. Pleasant.
- Bugg, R. T., Scottsville.
- Burditt, D., Austin.
- Burrel, D. B., Hearne.
- Burton, I. B., Giddings.
- Burton, R., Foster.
- Butler, C. M., Overton.
- Butirell, G., Quitman.
- Buyton, D. W., Orange.
- Caesar, A. E., Stellar.
- Calhoun, C. W., Wharton.
- Caldwell, F. C., Round Rock.
- Caldwell, H. C., Texarkana.
- Campbell, I. L., Austin.
- Capers, A. C., Jonesville.
- Carlton, F., Weimar.
- Carrington, A., Austin.
- Carroll, J., Fort Worth.
- Carson, J. H., Jewett.
- Carter, A. B., Fairfield.
- Carter, B. W., Smithville.
- Carter, J. M., Kingsbury.
- Carthan, A. E., Manor.

Sermons, Addresses and Reminiscences and Important Correspondence

- Chadburn, F. H., Gatesville.
- Chambers, C., Mt. Pleasant.
- Chappell, J. D., Giddings.
- Charles, Wm., San Antonio.
- Christian, B., Longview.
- Churchill, R., Humble.
- Claiborne, M. C., Dallas.
- Clark, Daniel, Seguin.
- Clark, Geo., Round Rock.
- Clark, J. W. Hempstead.
- Clark, P. C., Henrietta.
- Clark, S. M., Elgin.
- Clem, J. C., Oyster Creek.
- Clifton, J. C., Franklin.
- Coats, G. E. O., San Antonio.
- Cobb, S., Waco.
- Coffee, G. W., Trinity.
- Cole, S. W. R., Galveston.
- Cole, T. W. C., Golden.
- Coleman, C. L., Ferris.
- Coleman, Isaac, Colony.
- Coleman, R. C., Cameron.
- Collier, P. H., Houston.
- Collins, F. D., Columbus.
- Collins, H., Cottongin.
- Collins, H. C., Groesbeck.
- Collins, I., St. Hedwig.
- Collins, T. T., Austin.
- Collins, W. R., Webberville.
- Conaley, C., San Marcos.
- Conily, B. Chapel Hill Hill.
- Conley, E. M., Chapel Hill.
- Conley, John, Jefferson.
- Connell, J. C., Richmond.
- Conner, W. M., Paris.
- Cook, H. C., Brownsboro.
- Cooper, A. C., Ferris.
- Cooper, R. C., Steeles Store.
- Cooper, T. B., Kellyville.
- Corr, M. C., Ida

335

- Craft, A., Bastrop.
- Crawford, A. W., Speegieville.
- Crawford, J. C., Golden.
- Creame, L., Greenville.
- Crenshaw, B. J., Winona.
- Crockett D., Eagle Lake.
- Crouch, R. T., Thurber.
- Cruise, I., Lavernia.
- Cullars, J. C., Sulphur Springs.
- Culver, W. R., Sherman.
- Cumming, R. Columbia.
- Curlin, M., Greenville.
- Curry, G. C., Seguin.
- Curry, R. C., Sherman.
- Dailey, T. W., Marshall.
- Dallas, G. W., Clarksville.
- Daniels, B., Gainesville.
- Daniels, F., Giddings,
- Daniels, J. D., Walters.
- Darlington, H. E., Canton.
- Davenport, Jas., Dimebox.
- Davis, Alexander, Seguin.
- Davis, B. Buffalo.
- Davis, Dallas, Riddleville.
- Davis, F. G., McKinney.
- Davis, J. D., Milano.
- Davis, J. J., Fairfield.
- Davis, S., Ennis.
- Davis, S. M. C., Rockdale.
- Davis, T., Whitewright.
- Davis, W. W., Fort Worth.
- Denman, A., Winchester.
- Dennis, J. A., Waco.
- Denson, N. T., Marlin.
- Dibrell, N., Seguin.
- Dickson, W. L., Dallas.
- Diggs, J. H., Calvert.
- Diggs, P., Calvert.
- Dillon, S. W., Commerce.
- Dilworth, J., Gonzales.

Sermons, Addresses and Reminiscences and Important Correspondence

- Douglas, G., Milano.
- Dowsby, R., Mexia.
- Duke, R., Seguin.
- Dukes, G., Fiskville.
- Dunbar, J. B., Hearne.
- Dupree, A. D., Sherman.
- Eaton, M., Stone City.
- Edgar, F. E., Fiskville.
- Ellis, J. E., Hempstead.
- Ellis, J. M., New Berlin.
- Ellis, S. W., Brenham.
- Ellis, W., Wheelock.
- Evans, R. B., Courtney.
- Fennell, W., Seguin.
- Field, F. T., Barnum.
- Fields, T. J., Nacogdoches.
- Finnell, L. B., Tyler.
- Finnell, M., Woodville.
- Flournoy, G. B., Coke.
- Floyd, S., Fayetteville.
- Flurnoy, M. F., Clarksville.
- Fortson, T. J., Tyler.
- Fountain, M., Cleburne.
- Fowler, H., Sulphur Springs.
- Francis, S. H., Houston.
- Francis, R. B., Wills Point.
- Freeman, W. M., Houston.
- Fuller, G., Austin.
- Fuller, Wm., Austin.
- Furlough, D., Palestine.
- Gaines, J. H., Houston.
- Gaines, M., Giddings.
- Gaines, T. T., Calvert.
- Garland, A., DeKalb.
- Garland, H. E., Ravenna.
- Garvin, A. G., Ravenna.
- Gibson, J., Fiskville.
- Gilmore, Jas., Calvert.
- Golden, I. S., Hearne.
- Goode, D. A., Voxpopuli.

Sermons, Addresses and Reminiscences and Important Correspondence

- Gordon, A. A., Hearne.
- Gorman, J., Sulphur Springs.
- Graham, Jos., Elysium.
- Granger, R. A., Marshall.
- Grant, J., Ravenna.
- Grant, J. G., Lagrange.
- Grant, J. M., West Point.
- Grant, R. A., Burton.
- Green, Geo. G., Bastrop.
- Greer, G. W., Marlin.
- Griffin, A. G., Mineola.
- Griggs, A. R., D. D., Dallas.
- Griggs, E. M., Palestine.
- Groves, B. H., Austin.
- Gustor, S. G., Howth.
- Guyton, W. H., Lyons.
- Haines, James, Austin.
- Hale, H., Woodlawn.
- Hall, B. J., Houston.
- Hall, J. H., Galveston.
- Hampton, C. N., Paris.
- Hardeman, Fred., Austin.
- Hardeman, W. D., Ennis.
- Hareway, G. W., Jewett.
- Harges M. W., Littig.
- Harrel, G., DeKalb.
- Harrelson, D., Eagle Lake.
- Harris, A., Franklin.
- Harris, C. C., Austin.
- Harris, D. C., Hallsville.
- Harris, Edmund, Waelder.
- Harris, G. W., Prairie Lea.
- Harris, James, Dallas.
- Harris, John, Patterson.
- Harris, L. M., Augusta.
- Harris, M., Crockett.
- Harrison, G., Elysium.
- Harrison, M., Victoria.
- Harrold, J. H., Calvert.
- Hart, G., Nacogdoches.

Sermons, Addresses and Reminiscences and Important Correspondence

- Harvey, J. W., Wharton.
- Hawk, Thos., Spanish Camp.
- Hawkins, D., Houston.
- Haynes, M., Jewett.
- Hazeley, Wm., Hearne.
- Heiskell, C. H., Rockdale.
- Henderson, F., Navasota.
- Henderson, S. E., Houston.
- Hendon, I. M., Houston.
- Hill, A. L., Hallsville.
- Hill, G. W., Longview.
- Hill, L., Jonesville.
- Hill, N. H., Austin.
- Hill, P. W., Marshall.
- Hill, W. D., Denison.
- Hogan, J. T., Bastrop.
- Holder, J. H., McGregor.
- Holloway, A. J., Gladewater.
- Holmes, A., Seguin.
- Holmes, C. W., Navasota.
- Holmes, Geo., Sulphur Springs.
- Holsten, S., Bosqueville.
- Hood, G. T., Palestine.
- Hooks, F., Hooks.
- Hopkins, W. T., Wolfe City.
- Horn, S. H., Buffalo.
- House, D. D., Marlin.
- Houston, O. J., Sulphur Springs.
- Howard, J., Pleasanton.
- Howard, S., Marshall.
- Hoyl, S. M., Dallas.
- Hubbard, M. L., Manor.
- Hubbs, A., Galveston.
- Hughes, P. H., Emory.
- Humber, R. H., Branchville.
- Hunter, A., DeKalb.
- Hunter, J. W., Eagle Pass.
- Hunter, L. J., Montgomery.
- Hurd, J. H., Marshall.
- Hurd, M., Austin.

- Hysaw, P. H., Fort Worth.
- Ilsley, L., White.
- Ingram, Eli, Tenn. Colony.
- Inman, R., San Antonio.
- Irwin, Moses, Waco.
- Jackson, D., Tyler.
- Jackson, D. W., Warda.
- Jackson, H. W., Hearne.
- Jackson, J. A., Jones Prairie.
- Jackson, J. B., Caldwell.
- Jackson, M. F., Bethel.
- Jackson, N. A., Sulphur Springs.
- Jackson, W. M., Denison.
- James, E. M., Calvert.
- James, G. W., Cuero.
- James, J. J., Navasota.
- Jenkins, D., Richmond.
- Jernigan, S. J., Elysian Fields.
- Johns, C. J., Atlanta.
- Johns, T. J., Tunis.
- Johnson, A., Austin.
- Johnson, A., San Antonio.
- Johnson, A. J., Brenham.
- Johnson, A. L., Manor.
- Johnson, B., Longstreet.
- Johnson, B. J., Long Branch.
- Johnson, J. H., Austin.
- Johnson, J. J., Whitehouse.
- Johnson, L. L., Lavernia.
- Johnson, T. B., Henderson.
- Jones, C., Corsicana.
- Jones, H. Y., Elderville.
- Jones, John, Pritchett.
- Jones, L. K., Webberville.
- Jones, Prince, Fort Worth.
- Jones, S., Hughes Springs.
- Jones S. J., Clay.
- Kelly, C., Corsicana.
- Kelly, H. A., San Antonio.
- King, A. L., Hearne.

- King, S., Cuero.
- Lampkin, M., Waelker.
- Lawrence, G., Wharton..
- Lawrey, N. M., Chapel Hill.
- Lawson, J. A., San Antonio.
- Lawson, J. R., Navasota.
- Lee, A. L., Coldspring.
- Lee, B. H., Littig.
- Leflall, O. B., Deberry.
- Lemon, H., Winona.
- Lenox, A. B., Detroit.
- Lewis, Geo., Sulphur Springs.
- Lewis, James, Howth.
- Lewis, M., Luling.
- Lewis, S. L., Cottongin.
- Lewis, Wm.
- Liggins, Wm., St. Elmo.
- Light, F. L., Houston.
- Lillie, Bowie, Hempstead.
- Lilly, J. L., Richmond.
- Lister, J., Ennis.
- Litman, G. L., Calvert.
- Lloyd T. L., Kosse.
- Locket, M. D., Coltharpe.
- Love, C. B., Atlanta.
- Love, J. J., Austin.
- Lyons, Sandy, Austin.
- Mack, M., Brazoria.
- Mack, S. H., Brazoria.
- Mackey, E. D., Mackiesville.
- Mackey, L. W., Rockdale.
- Martin, A., Caney.
- Martin, C. B., Paris.
- Martin, J. J., Smithville.
- Mason, J. M., Lyons.
- Mason, R., Clarksville.
- Massey, Lewis, Calvert.
- Massey, Wm. Navasota.
- Matlock, F., San Augustine.
- Matthews, F., Jeddo.

- Maxfield, Samuel, Giddings.
- Maxwell, W., Marlin.
- Mayo, J., Sevenoaks.
- Mayes, J. M., Tatum.
- Mayes, P. J., San Marcos.
- McBride, J., Independence.
- McConnell, B., Brenham.
- McConney, B., Giddings.
- McCowan, B. H., Brenham.
- McCowan. C. M., Bellville.
- McDonald, A. J., Webberville.
- McFadden, S. A., Austin.
- McFarland, A. L., Jasper.
- McGee, R. D., Garden Valley.
- McGriff, P. R., Weimar.
- McIntosh, F., Paige.
- McIntyre, A., Seguin.
- McIntyre, S., Tyler.
- McKenzie, J., Mt. Pleasant.
- McKinney, D., Denison.
- McNorton, H. F., Clarksville.
- McPherson, C. L., Navasota.
- McQueen, L., San Marcos.
- Melton, G. A., Reilly Springs.
- Mickles, G., Spanish Camp.
- Miles, E. L., Hearne.
- Miller, F. N., Scottsville.
- Minor, S. M., Myers.
- Mitchell, S. M., Thorndale.
- Mitchell, T. H.., Williamsburg.
- Mitchem, M. B., Greenville.
- Moore, A. M., Marshall.
- Moore, J., Marlin.
- Moore, M. J., Tazewell.
- Morgan, A., Tracy.
- Morris, W. K., Tunis.
- Morrow, J. D., Dallas.
- Moss, A. W., Gainesville.
- Murphy, A. C., El Paso.
- Nance, D. B., Oyster Creek.

- Neal, C., Honeygrove.
- Neal, W., Farris.
- Nelson, A., Taylor.
- Nelson, G. O., Omen.
- Newman, H. T., San Marcos.
- Newsom, I. S., Fulshear.
- Nicholson, E. G., Tunis.
- Nix, Wm., Longview.
- Nixon, P., Mt. Vernon.
- North, Albert, Austin.
- North, F. B., Austin.
- Northington, P. A., Navasota.
- Norwood, A. D., Gonzales.
- Norwood, E. I., Austin.
- Norwood, J. S., Galveston.
- Norwood, L., Cameron.
- Oliyer, A., Hillsboro.
- Oliver, L., Ladonia.
- Orange, J. S.
- Orviss, G. P., Prairie Plains.
- Page, A., Richmond.
- Pardee, Z. D., Dallas.
- Parker, J. M., Waco.
- Parker, J. P., Houston.
- Parker, S., Eureka.
- Patrick, B. P., Madisonville.
- Patrick, C. H., Crockett.
- Patterson, J., Kerrville.
- Patterson, J. H., Marshall.
- Paynes, S., Hempstead.
- Perkins, E.
- Perpener, O. E., Cuero.
- Perrin, J. L., Honeygrove.
- Pettis, O. P., Cookville.
- Pipkin, S. M., Centennial.
- Pitts, C. T., Austin.
- Pope, H. B., Stone City.
- Pope, T. B., San Antonio.
- Pounds, J. B., Owlet Green.
- Powell, A., Axtell.

Sermons, Addresses and Reminiscences and Important Correspondence

- Powell, F., Waco.
- Pratt, C. P., Round Rock.
- Price, Chas., H., Omaha.
- Price, J. A. Rusk.
- Price, L., Montgomery.
- Price, S. M.
- Priel, L., Sutton.
- Primus, S., Waskom.
- Pryor, C. N., Dallas.
- Rabb, F. R., Whitehouse.
- Randall, L. R., Paris.
- Rankin, D. H., Flatonia.
- Rasher, G. W., Crockett.
- Rayford, J. M., Columbus.
- Raynes, S., Hempstead.
- Read, C. M., Pittbridge.
- Recker, J., Caldwell.
- Reed, L., Nacogdoches.
- Reeves, A., Rosebud.
- Reeves, J. L., Dallas.
- Reinhart, J. J., Navasota.
- Rhodes, D., Altair.
- Rhoades, S. C., Bastrop.
- Rhone, Jno., Beaumont.
- Richardson, R., New Berlin.
- Richmond, H. M., Sulphur Springs.
- Riley, H. C., Greenville.
- Riller, J., T., Elgin.
- Rivers, A., Calvert.
- Roach, R. R., Webberville.
- Roberson, S. M., Austin.
- Roberts, A. A., Rosanky.
- Roberts, J., Ladohia.
- Robertson, A. R., San Antonio.
- Robertson, J. W., Wharton.
- Robertson, T. R., Reily Springs.
- Robinson, A., Orange.
- Robinson, C., Rogers Prairie.
- Robinson, D., Valley Mills.
- Robinson, G. G., Gill.

Sermons, Addresses and Reminiscences and Important Correspondence

- Robinson, J. F., Fort Worth.
- Robinson, J. R., Sulphur Springs.
- Rogers, T. W. R., San Antonio.
- Ross, L. L., Tadmore.
- Rowland, A. H., Goliad.
- Rowland, J. H., Goliad.
- Rucker, H., Columbia.
- Rucker, J. W., Pleasanton.
- Rucker, S., San Marcos.
- Russell, D., Denison.
- Russell, S. T., Austin.
- Rutledge, A. R., Pittsburg.
- Sanders, A. J., Crockett.
- Sanders, C., Reagan.
- Sanders, C. S., Calvert.
- Sanders, Jackson, Belmont.
- Sanders, S., Deberry.
- Sapp, D. S., Rockport.
- Scott, D. A., Marshall.
- Scott, J. W., Palestine.
- Scott, L., Littig.
- Scott, L. S., Ellinger.
- Scott, N. S., Taylor.
- Scott, S. C., Troupe.
- Seaton, B. W., Graball.
- Shackles, A. R., Manor.
- Shackles, G. M., Manor.
- Shackles, J. S., Fiskville.
- Shackles, J. T., Manor.
- Sharpe, J. A., Steeles Store.
- Shaw, C. H., Dallas.
- Sheffield, J. H., Seguin.
- Sheldon, Nat., San Antonio.
- Shelton, J., Galveston.
- Shepherd, J., Lewisville.
- Shields, C., Roundtop.
- Shivers, D. H., Bryan.
- Shorter, J., Cookes Point.
- Sidney, John, Caney.
- Simmons, S. S., Wolfe City.

- Simpson, J., Weatherford.
- Sinclair, M. H., Gonzales.
- Skurlock, N. D., Weatherford.
- Sledge, A. L., Chapel Hill.
- Stone, N., Palestine.
- Smith, A. T., Velasco.
- Smith, A. W., D. D., San Antonio.
- Smith, C. H., Houston.
- Smith, D., Denison.
- Smith, G. W., Kingsbury.
- Smith, J. W., Ravenna.
- Smith, L. S., Crockett.
- Smith, S. C., Rockdale.
- Sneed, L. S., Sherman.
- Solomon, G. W., Butler.
- Sparks, C. H., Cameron.
- Spencer, C. C., Big Sandy.
- Spencer, H. G., Weldon.
- Spencer, J., Bertram.
- Standifer, B. F., China Springs.
- Starling, W. H., Lawsonville.
- Staton, G. E., Calvert.
- Stephens, J. S., Tyler.
- Stephens, L., Kyle.
- Sterling, J., Roxton.
- Sterling, W. H., Lawson.
- Steward, R. J.
- Stiles, S., Cuero.
- Stoney, H. E., Hempstead.
- Strong J. W., Corpus Christi.
- Stubble, G., Emory.
- Swancey, J. R., Waxahachie.
- Swanson, Frank, Palestine.
- Swanson, H., Palestine.
- Sweeting, P. T., Wharton.
- Tabb, Burl, Marshall.
- Taylor, A., Dallas.
- Taylor, R. D., San Angelo.
- Taylor, R. F., Corsicana.
- Taylor, R. T., Longview.

Sermons, Addresses and Reminiscences and Important Correspondence

- Taylor, Wm., Gonzales.
- Terrell, M. E., Galveston.
- Thomas, A., Mexia.
- Thomas, E., St. Hedwig.
- Thomas, J. W., Beaumont.
- Thomas, L. D., San Antonio.
- Thompson, A., Waco.
- Thompson, I. T., Giddings.
- Thompson, J. F., Jonesville.
- Thornton, Q., St. Hedwig.
- Tignor, Morgan, Sulphur Springs.
- Tillman, S. A., Sherman.
- Timms, G. W., Brazoria.
- Tisdale, Jas., Wharton.
- Toleston, C. M., Kosse.
- Tolliver, A. R., Temple.
- Tolson, B., Matagorda.
- Tomkins, H., Belton.
- Turner, J. H., Seaton.
- Turner, M., Mossbluff.
- Tyler, J., Rusk.
- Upshaw, P. W., Terrell.
- Vaughn, H., Waco.
- Vincent, J. A., Marshall.
- Wade, B. W., Hempstead.
- Wade, J. W., Greenville.
- Walker, A., Austin.
- Walker, G. W., Hearne.
- Walker, M. J., Longview.
- Walker, S. P., Lyons.
- Walker, W., Marshall.
- Walton, W. A., Anderson.
- Williams, B., Pledger.
- Williams, C., Jones Prairie.
- Ware, H. W., Greenhill.
- Washington, C., Fort Worth.
- Washington, C. H., Serbin.
- Washington, G. B., Huntsville.
- Washington, P. R., Choctaw.
- Waters, . W., Palestine.

- Watson, Elbert, Reinhardt.
- Watts, H., Houston.
- Weaver, E. B., Bosqueville.
- Webb, Max, Mullica.
- Webb, S. F., Flatonia.
- Wells, L. W., Stone City.
- Wesley, P. W., Texarkana.
- Westbrook, F., Bryan.
- Wheeler, A. R., Manor.
- Wheeler, P., Manor.
- Whitaker, D., Nacogdoches.
- White, J. C., Smithville.
- White, M., Loneoak.
- White, R., Dallas.
- Whitehead, F. W., Hungerford.
- Whiteside, J., Rosebud.
- Whitfield, S. W., Boston.
- Whiting, D. W., Huntsville.
- Whiting, M. A., Independence.
- Whitley, Daniel G., Columbus.
- Whitaker, S., Pollok.
- Wiggins, M., Quitman.
- Wilburn, T. W., Wharton.
- Wilkerson, P. J., Brazoria.
- Wilkins F. H., Corsicana.
- Williams, A. J., Purley.
- Williams, Frank, Dallas.
- Williams, H. M., D. D., Sherman.
- Williams, H. W., Chandler.
- Williams, J., Brenham.
- Williams, J. M., Waelder.
- Williams J. P., Brazoria.
- Williams, J. W., Allen.
- Williams, L., Houston.
- Williams, R. Z., Rockdale.
- Williams, S. P., Bremond.
- Williams, T. S., Waco.
- Williams, W. A., Austin.
- Williamson, G. W., Franklin.
- Williamson, W., Fosterville.

Sermons, Addresses and Reminiscences and Important Correspondence

- Willis, K. C., Velasco.
- Willis, S. S., Sandypoint.
- Wilson, Henry, Belmont.
- Wilson, H. R., Marshall.
- Wilson, R. W., Houston.
- Wilson, S., Dallas.
- Wimbish, E. F., Cuero.
- Winn, A. W., Taylor.
- Winn, G. W., Mackiesville.
- Winn, J. H. Manor.
- Winn, R. S., Fayetteville.
- Womack, C., Paris.
- Woods, D., Sandypoint.
- Woods, D. A., Voxpopuli.
- Woodward, F. L., Navasota.
- Wormley, S. W., Bastrop.
- Wormley, W. L., Velasco.
- Wright, E. M., Galveston.
- Wright, I. S., Eagle Lake.
- Wright, R., Kilgore.
- Wyatt, G. W., Hempstead.
- Wynn, G. G., Crockett.
- Yerber, A., Arthur City.
- Young, D., Brazoria.

VIRGINIA.

- Adams, James, Danville.
- Adams, R. G., Danville.
- Adkins, N. A., Emmerton.
- Allen, B. J., Newport News.
- Allen, J. I., Waynesboro.
- Allen, T. M., B. D., Ashland.
- Allison, E. C., Poplarmont.
- Almond, J. W. T., Keysville.
- Alston, L. B., West Norfork.
- Anderson, P. E., Meherrin.
- Anderson, H. H., Portsmouth.
- Anderson, S. A., Cifax.

Sermons, Addresses and Reminiscences and Important Correspondence

- Anthony, M. D., Glasgow.
- Archey, J. W., Menshville.
- Armistead, J. M., D. D., Portsmouth.
- Arvin, J. H., Meherrin.
- Ashburn, W. A., Salem.
- Bagby, N. C., Unionlevel.
- Bailey, H., Alexandria.
- Bailey, L. H., Herndon.
- Bailey, William, Norwood.
- Ball, L. R., Kilmarnock.
- Barco, H. L., Berkley.
- Barnes, Jacob, Norfork.
- Bass, R. J., Richmond.
- Bates, A., Farmville.
- Baxter, C. G., Jennings Ordinary.
- Beasley, E. W., Powellton.
- Berkeley, C. W., Locust Creek.
- Berkeley, R., Sassafras.
- Berkeley, R., Saluda.
- Berry, P. R., Petersburg.
- Binga, A., D. D., Manchester.
- Buford, J. H., Richmond.
- Blair, H., Culpeper.
- Board, A., Richmond.
- Booth, J. W., Ark.
- Booze, C. C., Buchanan.
- Boston, C. S., Newport News.
- Bowles, J. H., North Garden.
- Bowling, R. H., D. D., Norfolk.
- Bowman, T. M., Petersburg.
- Branch, L., Beaverpond.
- Breedlove, J. J., Danville.
- Briggs, Thos., Richmond.
- Brosier, S. S., Suffolk.
- Brown, Abraham, Perrowville.
- Brown, A. J., Pocahontas.
- Brown, Felix, Salem.
- Brown, G. W., Cambria.
- Brown, John M., Abingdon.
- Brown, J. E., Fredericksburg.

- Brown, J. S., Pearch.
- Brown, N. B., Richmond.
- Brown, R. C., Wellville.
- Brown, S., Montreal.
- Brown, Willis, Princess Anne.
- Brown, W. W., Roanoke.
- Burrell, S. C., Richmond.
- Butcher, R. H., New River Depot.
- Butler, J. B. K., Providence, R. I.
- Byrd, G. H. T., Temperanceville.
- Byrd, J. W., Oak Grove.
- Callaway, W. B., Bellevue.
- Campbell, F. C., Portsmouth.
- Casper, W. H., Danville.
- Carr, R. C., Waynesboro.
- Carter, Janius, Danville.
- Carter, J. D., Roanoke.
- Carter, J. S., Hermitage.
- Carter, L. C., Rural Retreat.
- Carter, Samuel, Newcastle.
- Carter, W. J., Pocahontas.
- Cary, H., Buchanan.
- Cary, James, Esmont.
- Casey, T. A., Chamblissburg.
- Cave, D., Charlottesville.
- Cave, N. C., Gordansville.
- Chavis, A., Lawrenceville.
- Cheeseman, E. T., Hampton.
- Chick, T. J. Pulaski City.
- Chiles, H. W., Portsmouth.
- Chisholm, Alfred, D.D., Portsmouth.
- Clarke, John P., Richmond.
- Clark, R. I., Centralia.
- Clarke, W., Mossing Ford.
- Clarkson, R. A., Amherst.
- Clements, H. C., Branchville.
- Cobbs, R. D., Buffalo Forge.
- Coleman, C. S., Scottsburg.
- Coleman, D. A., Chilesburg.
- Coleman, G. C., Manchester.

- Coleman, R., Greenville.
- Coles, James, Franklin C. H.
- Cook, B., Rexburg.
- Cook, W. F., Williamsburg.
- Corbin, J. W., Hampton.
- Corbin, W. H., Alexandria.
- Crosby, David, L., Richmond.
- Crawley, W. H., South Boston.
- Creecy, W., Hatcreek.
- Cross, Israel, South Quay.
- Crudup, E. J., Newport News.
- Curtis, Thos. C., Vinton.
- Cyrus, J. H. A., Port Royal.
- Cyrus, Samuel, Marion.
- Daggert, George, Richmond.
- Daniels, Robert, Fishersville.
- Davis, C. W., Ivor.
- Davis, D. Webster, Richmond.
- Davis, Lewis, New Kent.
- Davis, S., Waidsboro.
- Davis, Wm. R., Hampton.
- Dawson, J. M., Williamsburg.
- Dennis, Elisha, Roanoke.
- Diggs, F. P., Tappahannock.
- Diggs, G. W., Amelia.
- Diggs, W. Philip, Drewryville.
- Dixon, G. L., Fredericksburg.
- Dixon, H., Natural Bridge.
- Dixon, W. H., Newport News.
- Dodson, J. H., Norfolk.
- Douglass, John, Lowmoor.
- Dover, B., West Point.
- Dow, L. R., Desha.
- Duncan, Levi, Pungoteague.
- Dundee, W. D., Cohoke.
- Edwards, T. J., Johnsons Springs.
- Edwards, P. T., Glenns.
- Fauntelroy, John, Richmond.
- Fauntleroy, J. S., Bridges.
- Ferguson, A., Richmond.

- Ferguson, D., Livingston.
- Ferrell, F., Roxbury.
- Ferrell, J. B., Petersburg.
- Fields, D., Millenbeck.
- Fitzgerald, E., Harmony Village.
- Follis, C. G., Roanoke.
- Ford, W. H., Ashland.
- Fowlkes, L. W., Burkeville.
- Fox, B. F., D. D., Salem.
- Fox, R. C., Harrisonburg.
- Fraysier, Lee, Richmond.
- Frazier, C. H., Wytheville.
- Freeman, Sampson, Boykins.
- Friend, J. D., Burtons Creek.
- Fry, W. R., Fishersville.
- Gaines, W. W., Suffolk.
- Gaines, Z., Edgehill.
- Gaines, D. M., Newport News.
- Galvin, A. A., Staunton.
- Garey, W. H., Norfolk.
- Garland, S. A., Lynchburg.
- Gaskin, J., Portsmouth.
- Gayle, A. T., Roanes.
- Gee, Peter, Bagleys Mills.
- Gerst, M. E., Berkley.
- Gibbons, W. E., Surry C. H.
- Givens, E. R., Stoney Creek.
- Goode, G. W., Danville.
- Goodloe, A., Bowling Green.
- Gordon, C. B. W., Petersburg.
- Graham, W. F., D. D., Richmond.
- Grasty, Henry, Danville.
- Gray, A., Rexburg.
- Gray, B., Staunton.
- Green, C. A., Yorktown.
- Gregory, J., Franklin.
- Gregory, R., Mannboro.
- Griffin, J. R., Richmond.
- Griffin, W. H., Whitestone.
- Guest, C., Ringgold.

Sermons, Addresses and Reminiscences and Important Correspondence

- Gurdy, Lewis, Fincastle.
- Hackett, W. J., Covington.
- Haley, M. A., Rockymount.
- Hall, Frank L., Drakes Branch.
- Hall, R. J., Hicks Wharf.
- Hall, S. S., Marion.
- Hall, W. T., Danville.
- Hardy, J. H., Meadowview.
- Hardy, R. B., Charlottesville.
- Harrold, L., Sharps Wharf.
- Harris, Alexander, Newport News.
- Harris, C., Lynchburg.
- Harris, L. J., Cleopus.
- Harris, O. T., Graham.
- Harris, W. H., Norfolk.
- Harris, W. R., Norfolk.
- Harris, W. W., Westpoint.
- Harrison, R. H., Phoebus.
- Hartwell, I. A. D., Glasgow.
- Harvey, J. H., Sheppards.
- Haskins, Elias, Oak.
- Hawkins, N. P., Sherando.
- Henderson, H. J., Catawba.
- Henning, G. E., Lynchburg.
- Henry, R. T., Palls.
- Hill, A., Basic.
- Hill, A., Hampton.
- Hill, Thomas, Norfolk.
- Hobbs, Isham, Wellsville.
- Hobbs, J, Danville.
- Hockaday, S., Brkley.
- Hodge, Philip, Danville.
- Hodges, Willis, Kempville.
- Holloway, O. H., Basic City.
- Holly, James, Thraxton.
- Holmes, L. W., New River Depot.
- Holmes, H. B., Richmond.
- Howard, G. B., Petersburg.
- Howard, W., Fredericksburg.
- Hudson, J. D., Boydton.

- Hughes, P. H., Abington.
- Hughes, Richard, Livingston.
- Hughes, W. T., North Garden.
- Hughes Z., Tanners Creek.
- Hunt, D. W., Hollins.
- Hunt J. W., Whitlock.
- Jackson, E. R., Alexandria.
- Jackson, G., Lexington.
- Jackson, J.J., Brookewood.
- James, Daniel, Richmond.
- James, Winston, Midway Mills.
- Jeffries, L. R., Meadville.
- Jennings, B., Nottoway.
- Johnson, A., Lanexa.
- Johnson, C. C., Forkland.
- Johnson, E. A., Whites.
- Johnson, Felix, Christianburg.
- Johnson, Geo. E., Richmond.
- Johnson, H., Clifton Forge.
- Johnson, H. B., Beulahville.
- Johnson, I. E., Noel.
- Johnson, J., Shiloh.
- Johnson, Jas., Burkeville.
- Johnson, M. E., Salem.
- Johnson, N. C., Boydton.
- Johnson, P., Madison.
- Johnson, R. O., Richmond.
- Johnson, T. H., Mountcastle.
- Johnson, T. T., Hague.
- Johnson, W. D., Wytheville.
- Johnson, W., Lexington.
- Jones, De Witt H., Portsmouth.
- Jones, D. W., Warrenton.
- Jones, H., City Point.
- Jones, J. E., D.D., Richmond.
- Jones, J. J., Prince George C. H.
- Jones, Richard R., Roanoke.
- Jones, Thos., Summit.
- Jones, W. B., Hampton.
- Jordan, N., Farmville.

- Jordan, W. H., Norfolk.
- Kelly, J. W., Tuckerhill.
- Keene, C. L., Danville.
- Kemp, R. C., Richmond.
- Kirby, John W., D. D., Farmville.
- Kizer, James, Bargess.
- Land, M., Norfolk.
- Lane, C. C., Emporia.
- Lee, I., Jr., Cherton.
- Lewis, M., Norfolk.
- Lewis, R., Lyells.
- Lewis, W. A., Mills.
- Lewis, Z. D., D. D., Richmond.
- Lias, Alexander, Waynesboro.
- Lively, L. D., Hampton.
- Lockett, Thos., Grapelawn
- Lovett, John, Poquoson.
- Lucas, C. S., Fredericksburg.
- Madison, H., San Marino
- Marrow, G. W., Sturgeon Point.
- Marshall, L., Warsaw.
- Martin, N. S., Magnolia.
- Mason, F. L., Jarratt.
- Mason, W. R., Boykin.
- McCall, C. W., Petersburg.
- McDaniels, C. H., Farmville.
- McDaniels, J. L., Yellow Branch.
- Meadows, Floyd, Pearisburg.
- Merchant, R. D., Coolwell.
- Metts, L. W. C., Norfolk.
- Miller, R. J., Goshen.
- Minor, G. B., Amherst.
- Minor, J. S., Goodloes.
- Mitchell, H. H., D. D., Norfolk.
- Morgan, J. H., Wildway.
- Morris, L., Yorktown.
- Morris, P. F., D. D. Lynchburg.
- Moseley, Jordan, Redoak.
- Moses, Wm. H., Staunton.
- Moss, Wm., Danville.

Sermons, Addresses and Reminiscences and Important Correspondence

- Nazareth, R. H., Morrison.
- Nelson, C. W., Lively.
- Nettles, T. W., Eastville.
- Newman, C. H. Harmony.
- Nutt, C., Lottsburg.
- Nutt, T. M., Lottsburg.
- Olliver, J. D., Millboro.
- Outlaw, Henry, Norfolk.
- Page, E. W., Roanes.
- Page, Frank, Ark.
- Page, Wm. M., Newport.
- Pannell, M. A., Chatham.
- Pate, Jno. W., Bedford City.
- Paterson, C. D., Blueridge Springs.
- Patterson, F. C., Hollins.
- Patterson, J. W., Shdy Grove.
- Patterson, C. D., Blueridge Springs.
- Payne, Evans, Richmond.
- Pendleton, J. H., Newton.
- Pendleton, J. W., Corbin.
- Penn, G. J., Moores Mill.
- Perry, Elisha, Franklin.
- Phillips, C. H., Beaverdam.
- Pogue, Samuel, Fincastle.
- Porter, N. P., South Quay.
- Porter, R. H., Alexandria.
- Porter, W. H., Emerton.
- Powell, Holland, D. D., Richmond.
- Powell, J. M., Berkley.
- Price, Asa, Berkley.
- Price, Sandy, Bedford Springs.
- Robinson, J. M., Charlottesville.
- Randolph, J. H., Berkley.
- Rather, J. L., Crewe.
- Ray, A., Fredericksburg.
- Reed, D. A., Clifton Forge.
- Reed, W. M., Chuckatuck.
- Reid, G. E., Hampton.
- Richardson, Cyrus, Hampton.
- Richardson, J. B., Waverly Station.

Sermons, Addresses and Reminiscences and Important Correspondence

- Roane, Horace, Beulahville.
- Robinson, Jacob, Ivanhoe.
- Quarles, R. C., Charlottesville.
- Robinson, M., Staunton.
- Robinson, W. M., Fredericksburg.
- Ruffin, Josiah, Petersburg.
- Russ, C., Tuckerhill.
- Russell, Jacob, News Ferry.
- Samuels, Edw., Richmond.
- Satchell, A. J., Accomac.
- Saunders, F. P., Lynchburg.
- Saunders, Samuel Marion.
- Saunders, S. T., Bayview.
- Savage, J., Wardtown.
- Scott, Benj., Friendship.
- Scott, Elcanah, Cambria.
- Scott, L. C., Richmond.
- Scott, R. R., Gala.
- Shadd, P. J., Pulaski City.
- Shorts, T. H., Hampton.
- Simms, A. J., Waynesboro.
- Sims, D. W., Lynchburg.
- Skinner, A. C., Hampton.
- Smith, C. A., Rustburg.
- Smith, F., King William.
- Smith, J. P., Concord Depot.
- Smith, James H., Ark.
- Smith, J. H., Danville.
- Smith, J. K., Hollins.
- Smith, L. R., Richmond.
- Smith, N. A., Gala Water.
- Smith, R., Whaleyville.
- Smith, Silas, Bedford City.
- Smith, S. M., Alexandria.
- Smith, Walter, Salem.
- Spears, D. W., Afton.
- Spiller, R., D. D., Hampton.
- Stephenson, H., Lynchburg.
- Stevens, W. H., Dawn.
- Stewart, A., Madison.

Sermons, Addresses and Reminiscences and Important Correspondence

- Stith, Richard, D., Nottoway.
- Stokes, W. H., Richmond.
- Stovall, J. D., Leda.
- Sumner, J. W., Portsmouth.
- Syms, L. W., Lynchburg.
- Taylor, C. L., Lowmoor.
- Taylor, Ham, Hanover.
- Taylor, W. L., Richmond.
- Thomas, A. S., Richmond.
- Thomas, Elihu, Norfolk.
- Thomas, J. W., Northview.
- Thomas, Wm., Yorktown.
- Thompson, Chas., Evington.
- Thompson, E. C., Bumpass.
- Thompson, W. E., Harmony Village.
- Thompson, W. J., Hewlett.
- Thornton, W., Phoebus.
- Thurston, A., Louisa.
- Todd, S., Sparta.
- Towles, C. R., Urbanna.
- Townes, R. P., Brockville.
- Trent, C. D., Thurman.
- Truatt, A., Alexandria.
- Tucker, Daniel, Hague.
- Tucker, S., Newport News.
- Turner, J. H., Bowling Green.
- Turner, J. H., Gordonsville.
- Tweety, J., Charlottesville.
- Tyrell, Bernard, Lynchburg.
- Vassar, D. N., D. D., Richmond.
- Wales, L. W., Williamsburg.
- Wales, M., Charlottesville.
- Walker, J. R., Heathsville.
- Walker, M., Petersburg.
- Wallace, Percy, Richmond.
- Warring, H. H., Alexandria.
- Washington, C. C., Poromac Mills.
- Washington, G., Norfolk.
- Washington, N.., Brooke.
- Watkins, B. P., Radford.

Sermons, Addresses and Reminiscences and Important Correspondence

- Watson, Luke, Bayview.
- Watson, L. W., Cape Charles.
- Watts, E., Petersburg.
- Watts, S. S., Natural Bridge.
- Waugh, A. K., Glasgow.
- Webb, Wm. R., Bent Mountain.
- Weeden, H. P., Charlottesville.
- Wells, E., Mallow.
- Wells, R., Richmond.
- White, E., Norfolk.
- White, J. W., Farmville.
- White, T. H., Harrisonburg.
- White, W. H., Richmond.
- Whiting, J. B., Williamsburg.
- Whiting, Z. T., Ordinary.
- Wiggins, N. A., Jamaica.
- Williams, B. B., Great Bridge.
- Williams, H. W., Staunton.
- Williams, M. D., Alexandria.
- Wills, Thos., Staunton.
- Willis, W. H., Berkley.
- Wilson, Ellis, Dinwiddie C. H.
- Wills, C. R., Lipcombe.
- Wilson, H. Mayo.
- Wimbush, O. B., Abingdon.
- Winston, D. C., Tappahannock.
- Witt, A., Fisherville.
- Wood, J. N., Greenfield.
- Wood, T. A., Magnolia.
- Woodruff, Z. N., Capron.
- Woodfolk, D. S., Rio.
- Woolridge, Lee, Lexington.
- Wright, Madison, Portsmouth.
- Wright, Thomas, Ino.
- Wright, W. R., Ivanhoe.
- Wyatt, A., Hicks Wharf.
- Wyatt, Baylor, Cabinpoint.
- Wyatt, N. W., Pamplin City.
- Yancey, R. C., Boydton.
- Yates, S., Bedford City.

Sermons, Addresses and Reminiscences and Important Correspondence

- Young, C., Tappahannock.
- Young, H. L., Loretto.
- Young, M. V., Richmond.
- Young, W. H., Newtown.
- Young, W. W., Richmond.

- **WEST VIRGINIA.**

- Adams, J. H., Bluefield.
- Booker, C. H., Nuttallburg.
- Brandon, T. J., Elkhorn.
- Brown, W. R., Huntington.
- Campbell, C. L., Union.
- Christmas, L. T., Charleston.
- Deans, D., Montgomery.
- Farmer, O. V., Thacker.
- Fortner, C. D., Winifrede.
- Fox, R. C., Malden.
- Hall, Moses, St. Albans.
- Hayes, R. D., Talcott.
- Howard, G. B., Charleston.
- Huffine, W. C., Montgomery.
- Hunter, D. C., Sewell.
- Jackson, L.. P., Alderson.
- Jackson, Wm., Sweet Springs.
- Keys, Robert, Charleston.
- Lewis, C., Ronceverte.
- Mason, R., Charleston.
- Mahew, R. M., Charleston.
- McKory, R. H., Elkhorn.
- Orner, D. S., Wheeling.
- Patterson, J. W., Collinsville.
- Payne, C. H., Montgomery.
- Perkins, R. J., Huntington.
- Pollard, A. B., Huntington.
- Rainbow, A., Wheeling.
- Rice, H. B., Charleston.
- Rice, Lewis, Malden.
- Smith, A. J., Montgomery.
- Smith, V. S., Eckman.
- Stratton, David, St. Albans.
- Toney, William, Moundsville.

Sermons, Addresses and Reminiscences and Important Correspondence

- Wade, P. T., Charleston.
- Walker, G. W., St. Albans.
- Washington, S. A., Caperton.
- Williams, H. W., Quinnimont.
- Wimbush, J. H., Keystone.
- Woodley, A. W., Ronceverte.

PICTURE GALLERY.

PEN PICTURES OF DISTINGUISHED MEN.

We present here a new feature in the contents of this book, "The Picture Gallery of Eminent Scholars and Preachers." We regret that our first arrangements were such as to preclude our giving a biographical sketch of each one of the distinguished persons whose faces look out upon the readers of this volume. But they occupy high rank as teachers, preachers and professional men of the race, and are among the ablest men of the day. They are towers of strength in the several communities in which they reside and command the respect of all classes of our citizens. Some are pastors of great churches with memberships ranging from two hundred to three thousand, some are presidents of colleges and high schools, officers of educational boards, editors of newspapers, real estate dealers, politicians, farmers, etc. In addition to their personal worth and influence, most of them are conspicuous representatives of the great National Baptist Convention and have been untiring in their efforts to promote every interest and object of the Convention. This beautiful gallery gives only a forecast of the thousands in reserve who will figure most conspicuously in the solving of the problems which face us at this day. And, indeed, these and others of the race have set about the great work of solving the economic questions of the day, as they effect the race, by setting in motion and operating great enterprises. We give below a brief statement of the position held by each distinguished gentleman whose picture adorns this gallery.

REV. G. L. P. TALIAFERRO, Philadelphia, Pa.

REV. G. L. P. TALIAFERRO, Philadelphia, Pa.

Rev. G. L. P. Taliaferro, D. D., is editor of the "Christian Banner," published at Philadelphia, and the honored pastor of the Holy Trinity Baptist Church. Dr. Taliaferro has for several years been an active leader in the Baptist ranks.

REV. A. N. McEWEN, Mobile, Ala.

REV. A. N. McEWEN, Mobile, Ala.

REV. A. N. McEWEN, Mobile, Ala.

Rev. A. N. McEwen, one of the Vice Presidents of the National Baptist Convention, is one of the great leaders of the Baptists in Alabama. He is a strong advocate of race enterprises and believes in the possibilities of his people; is the pastor of a large church in Mobile, Ala., and editor and manager of the "Southern Watchman."

REV. L. L. CAMPBELL, D. D., Austin, Texas.

Rev. L. L. Campbell, D. D., of Austin, Texas, is among the able and scholarly young men of the race. He is prominent as a leader in the "Lone Star State," and an ardent supporter of the National Baptist Convention. He is editor of the "Texas Baptist Herald," and pastor of a great church.

Sermons, Addresses and Reminiscences and Important Correspondence

REV. A. R. GRIGGS, D. D., Dallas, Texas.

REV. A. R. GRIGGS, D. D., Dallas, Texas.

REV. A. R. GRIGGS, D. D., Dallas, Texas.

Rev. A. R. Griggs, D. D., of Dallas, Texas, is one of the best known men in the denomination, having been for three years President of the Foreign Mission Convention of the United States. He is a leader in his State and devotes most of his time to missionary work. He is noted for his conservatism, and in consequence of which his counsel is often sought on matters of grievance.

REV. CÆSAR JOHNSON, Raleigh, N. C.

REV. CÆSAR JOHNSON, Raleigh, N. C.

REV. CÆSAR JOHNSON, Raleigh, N. C.

Rev. Cæsar Johnson is both a minister and a business man. He is pastor of a flourishing congregation at Raleigh, N. C., and gives time and attention to the collection of rents and the buying and selling of real estate. He has been a prominent figure in our national meetings for several years.

MR. P. KNEELAND, Phillips, Ark.

MR. P. KNEELAND, Phillips, Ark.

Mr. P. Kneeland is a successful farmer and a devoted Christian, as well as an ardent supporter of all the work carried on by the Baptist denomination. He has at his own expense made several visits to the Convention. He says, "I go to see what my boys are doing and to give them some money if they need it."

Sermons, Addresses and Reminiscences and Important Correspondence

REV. H. C. PETTIS, Marianna, Ark.

REV. H. C. PETTIS, Marianna, Ark.

REV. H. C. PETTIS, Marianna, Ark.

Rev. H. C. Pettis of Marianna, Ark., is a prominent leader in the Phillips, Lee and Monroe Baptist Association. He is often called the "Best Preacher in Lee County," and is without doubt a great pulpit orator. His sermons are frequently referred to as "flashes of lightning."

REV. G B. HOWARD, D. D., Petersburg. Va.

REV. G B. HOWARD, D. D., Petersburg. Va.

REV. G B. HOWARD, D. D., Petersburg. Va.

Rev. G. B. Howard, D. D., pastor of Gilfield Baptist Church, Petersburg, Va., is one of the foremost men of the race and denomination. He is an eminent scholar and possesses rare oratorical ability. He is one of the leaders of the National Baptist Convention and never tires of working for the objects of the Boards. For several years he was pastor at Pittsburg, Pa.

REV. J. R. BE N TT

REV. J. R. BE N TT, Hot Springs, Ark.

REV. J. R. BE N TT, Hot Springs, Ark.

Rev. J. R. Bennett, of Hot Springs, Ark., has for many years been prominently connected with the educational work in his state as the Secretary of the Board of Trustees of the Arkansas Baptist College. He is one of the Vice Presidents of the National Baptist Convention and a strong advocate of its principles. He is pastor of a strong church at Hot Springs.

EV. WILLIAM JARRETT, Coffee, Ark.

REV. WILLIAM JARRETT, Coffee, Ark.

REV. WILLIAM JARRETT, Coffee, Ark.

Rev. Wm. Jarrett, of Coffee, Ark., is a man of the race who has made his mark in the accumulation of wealth. He is a successful and practical farmer and owns a splendid and well furnished plantation. He gives liberally to all the worthy causes of the denomination.

HON. G. W. LOWE, Holly Grove, Ark.

HON. G. W. LOWE, Holly Grove, Ark.

HON. G. W. LOWE, Holly Grove, Ark.

Hon. G. W. Lowe, of Holly Grove, Ark., was for several years a member of the Arkansas Legislature and was regarded by all as an able representative. Most of his life, however, has been spent in the schoolroom as a teacher. He is at present serving the Baptists of his district as missionary.

REV. J. P. BARTON, Talladega, Ala.

REV. J. P. BARTON, Talladega, Ala.

Rev. J. P. Barton, of Talladega, Ala., was for several years a prominent leader in the Baptist ranks of his state, having served them as the President of the State Convention. He is widely known and loved by all his brethren.

REV. G. W. LONGWOOD, Monroe, La.

REV. G. W. LONGWOOD, Monroe, La.

REV. G. W. LONGWOOD, Monroe, La.

Rev. G. W. Longwood, of Monroe, La., was a candidate for the mission field of Africa, but owing to his failing health, the Foreign Mission Board decided not to send him out yet.

REV. GEO. W. DUDLEY, Texarkana, Tex.

REV. GEO. W. DUDLEY, Texarkana, Tex.

REV. GEO. W. DUDLEY, Texarkana, Tex.

Rev. Geo. W. Dudley, of Texarkana, Tex., is one of the most noted evangelists of the day, having held successful meetings in most of the cities of America. He is a splendid preacher, a convincing reasoner, and seldom fails of great results in his meetings. He is a prominent member of the National Baptist Convention.

PROF. R. E. BRYANT, Marianna, Ark.

PROF. R. E. BRYANT, Marianna, Ark.

PROF. R. E. BRYANT, Marianna, Ark.

Prof. R. E. Bryant, of Marianna, Ark., has been prominent for many years as a teacher in his county. He is a member of the Board of Trustees of the Arkansas Baptist College and is a hearty supporter of the Convention work. By strict economy and close attention to business he has amassed a comfortable fortune, and is reputed as being the wealthiest colored man in his county. He is only forty-six years old.

REV. J. H. A. CYRUS, Port Royal, Va.

REV. J. H. A. CYRUS, Port Royal, Va.

Rev. J. H. A. Cyrus, of Port Royal, Va., is pastor of two strong country churches and a prominent leader in the "Old Dominion." He has always been an ardent advocate of a national organization by the colored Baptists, and has for three years been the Treasurer of the National Baptist Convention. He is honored and respected by all who know him.

REV. E. H. McDONALD, Syracuse, N. Y.

REV. E. H. McDONALD, Syracuse, N. Y.

REV. E. H. McDONALD, Syracuse, N. Y.

Rev. E. H. McDonald has built and pastored some of the strongest churches in the North. He is said to be one of the greatest church builders in the country. He is always on hand at the national meetings to give his money and influence to the work of the Convention. His present pastorate is Syracuse, N. Y.

REV. C. S. DINKINS, D. D., Selma, Ala.

REV. C. S. DINKINS, D. D., Selma, Ala.

Rev. C. S. Dinkins, D. D., is the able and scholarly president of the Alabama Colored Baptist State University (Selma University), one of the best schools owned by the Negroes in the South. He is prominent in all the affairs of the denomination in his state and the nation.

REV. H. C. COTTON, Belle Alliance, La.

REV. H. C. COTTON, Belle Alliance, La.

REV. H. C. COTTON, Belle Alliance, La.

Rev. H. C. Cotton, of Belle Alliance, La., occupies an exalted place in the hearts of his brethren both at home and abroad. He never loses an opportunity to be at the annual meetings.

REV. C. H. PARRISH, D. D., Louisville, Ky.

REV. C. H. PARRISH, D. D., Louisville, Ky.

REV. C. H. PARRISH, D. D., Louisville, Ky.

Dr. C. H. Parrish, President and Co-founder of the Eckstein Norton University of Cave Springs, Ky., stands in the front ranks of the scholars and preachers of this day. His influence is exerted and felt for good in all our gatherings. He is pastor of Calvary Baptist Church of Louisville, Ky.

HON. J. W. LYONS, Washington, D. C.

HON. J. W. LYONS, Washington, D. C.

HON. J. W. LYONS, Washington, D. C.

Hon. J. W. Lyons, Register of the Treasury at Washington, D. C., stands second to none as a leader on the political field. He is, however, a devout Christian gentleman and has reflected credit upon his race and the administration ever since President McKinley appointed him to office. He contributes liberally to religious causes and is reputed as an advocate of high-class politics.

REV. A. H. MILLER,

REV. A. H. MILLER, Helana, Ark.

Rev. A. H. Miller, of Helena, Ark., whose picture appears in the gallery, was born a slave in St. Francis County, Arkansas, fifty years ago. Immediately after the close of the war he came to Helena and subsequently went to St. Louis, Mo., where he remained for two years and returned to Helena. Having saved some money, he decided to enter Southland College and get an education. Remaining there until his means were exhausted, he returned home and went to work at ordinary day labor. Mr. Miller claims to have had a premonition to the effect that "A man is not free who must go at the sound of the whistles." He at once left off working by the day and started him a dray which he used to success. Soon after he had entered this latter calling, the people of his county elected him as their representative in the Arkansas Legislature. Unlike most of the men who were in politics in those early days, he invested in city real estate, and, in addition to this, engaged in cotton raising for several years, turning his profits into city property. He now owns about sixty-five houses and lots, which are free from debt and, of course, afford him a handsome income. He is perhaps the wealthiest colored man in his county. He is a devout Christian and gives liberally to religious causes. For several years, Mr. Miller was Treasurer of the Arkansas Baptist College Trustees; is at present a member of that Board; is also a member of the Home Mission Board of the National Baptist Convention, and is a school director in his city. He has an interesting family consisting of a wife and three children. The gentleman is an ardent Baptist and was for a while pastor of a large church at Arkadelphia, Ark. His whole time now is devoted to collecting rents and keeping in good condition the more than three score houses, which he owns.

REV. W. F. GRAHAM, D. D., Richmond, Va.

REV. W. F. GRAHAM, D. D., Richmond, Va.

Among the leaders of the race, no one takes a higher rank than Rev. W. F. Graham, D. D., the able and scholarly pastor of the Fifth Street Baptist Church of Richmond, Va. Dr. Graham is also the President of the Richmond Beneficial Insurance Company. He is one of the most active members of the Virginia Baptist State Convention, is associate editor of the Convention Teacher and an ardent supporter of all the work carried on by the National Baptist Convention.

REV. WILLIS ANTHONY HOLMES, Helena, Ark.

REV. WILLIS ANTHONY HOLMES, Helena, Ark.

REV. WILLIS ANTHONY HOLMES, Helena, Ark.

Rev. Willis Anthony Holmes is the editor and proprietor of the "Baptist Reporter," published at Helena, Ark. For eighteen years he has filled the position of Secretary of the Phillips, Lee and Monroe County District Association, and it is due largely to his untiring effort and fidelity to the National Baptist Convention that this Association makes provision each year for a large portion of the means sent up from the churches to go directly to the work of the National Boards. He is a great lover of music, in consequence of which he has been chosen as President of the Vocal and Instrumental Music Association of the State. Mr. Holmes is a man of no ordinary ability, notwithstanding the fact that he never attended school a day in his life. He has learned much by self-effort, and may be called a man of letters. He never fails to be appointed by his Association as its representative at our national meetings.

Sermons, Addresses and Reminiscences and Important Correspondence

REV. I. G. BAILEY, Pine Bluff, Ark.

REV. I. G. BAILEY, Pine Bluff, Ark.

REV. I. G. BAILEY, Pine Bluff, Ark.

One of the meekest and most level-headed men in the Baptist ranks is the Rev. I. G. Bailey, of Pine Bluff, Ark. He is an untiring worker and would rather surrender all of his personal possessions than see his denomination fall behind others.

REV. E. ARLINGTON WILSON, Kansas City, Mo.

REV. E. ARLINGTON WILSON, Kansas City, Mo.

REV. E. ARLINGTON WILSON, Kansas City, Mo.

The West has many great and progressive men, but among the most brilliant of these is the erudite and scholarly young divine, Rev. E. Arlington Wilson, of Kansas City, Kan. He is a useful man and a rising figure in our national work.

REV. E. GREEN, Fordyce, Ark.

REV. E. GREEN, Fordyce, Ark.

REV. E. GREEN, Fordyce, Ark.

Rev. E. Green, who was for many years the moderator of one of the largest associations in South Carolina, but who now lives at Fordyce, Ark., is one of the strong men of the race. He is making an effort to build an orphan's home for his people.

REV. BENJ. W. FARRIS, Boston, Mass.

REV. BENJ. W. FARRIS, Boston, Mass.

REV. BENJ. W. FARRIS, Boston, Mass.

Rev. Benj. W. Farris is a native of Arkansas, but went East to get an education. After graduating, he accepted for a while the pastorate of a church in Kentucky, but later went to Boston where he is now pastor of St. Paul Baptist Church. He has a bright future before him.

REV. J. J. BLACKSHEAR, Indianapolis, Ind.

REV. J. J. BLACKSHEAR, Indianapolis, Ind.

REV. J. J. BLACKSHEAR, Indianapolis, Ind.

Among the men who stand like a stone wall in defense of the denomination and especially the National Baptist Convention is the Rev. J. J. Blackshear, of Indianapolis, Ind.

REV. ROBERT MITCHELL, D. D., Frankfort, Ky.

REV. ROBERT MITCHELL, D. D., Frankfort, Ky.

REV. ROBERT MITCHELL, D. D., Frankfort, Ky.

Rev. Robert Mitchell, D. D., the Auditor of our Home Mission Board, is one of the leading orators of the day. He is well educated and is the honored pastor of a great church at Frankfort, Ky.

REV. WILLIAM BECKHAM, Austin, Tex.

REV. WILLIAM BECKHAM, Austin, Tex.

REV. WILLIAM BECKHAM, Austin, Tex.

Coming up from the ranks to occupy one of the most prominent positions among the Baptists, is the Rev. Wm. Beckham, of Austin, Texas. He is one of the District Secretaries of the National Baptist Publishing Board.

REV. R. H. BOYD, D. D.

REV. R. H. BOYD, D. D.

REV. R. H. BOYD, D. D.

The subject of this sketch, Rev. R. H. Boyd, D. D., was born in Winton County, Miss., about fifty-four years ago, the exact date of his birth not being known--his mother being a slave and unable to keep a record of her children's births. It is known, however, that young Boyd first saw the light of day in the month of March. He was born the slave of Benonia Grey, but was transferred to the estate of the Boyd's when about six years old and was carried by them to the state of Louisiana and subsequently to the state of Texas. During the War Between the States, young Boyd was made to go with the Confederate Army as a waiting boy, and remained with that army until 1864, when he was taken by his young master into Mexico, where they both remained until after the surrender of Lee to Grant. Having been separated from his mother, and having always cherished a fondness for her, his first thought after peace had been declared, was to return to Texas and see if she could be found. On his return he stopped at Fort Bend, where he found a little sister, and, with her, continued to search until 1866, in Grimes County, Texas, he found his mother, with whom he remained and spent the first years of his freedom as a farm hand and in receiving the counsel of her who had so long hoped for such a day of freedom to come upon her children.

In 1868, he was married to a Miss Laura Thomas, who lived only eleven months afterward and passed into the unknown regions beyond. In 1871, he was again married to a Miss Harriet Moore, with whom he has lived happily ever since. The Lord has blessed this latter union with eight children, six of whom are now living and are the source of much comfort and happiness to the father and mother. On the 19th day of December, 1869, he was baptized and united with the Baptist church at Prairie Plains, Texas. Simultaneously with his conversion came his call to the Gospel ministry and was publicly set apart to that work the following year. His first labor as an ordained Baptist minister was that of a district missionary, which position he filled from 1870 to 1874. Dr. Boyd has pastored some of the best churches in the state of Texas, at such points as Palestine and San Antonio. He was Moderator of the Central Association in the year 1879. He also served the State Convention of Texas as the Financial Agent of its educational work.

After the "split" in the State Convention of Texas, in the year 1894, he was chosen by the General Convention as Superintendent of Missions, in which position he served faithfully for nearly two years. He has been a prominent figure in the National Baptist Convention for many years and was one of the first to support the plan for a Negro Baptist publishing house. He was one of the strongest advocates for such an enterprise until a final decision was reached upon that matter in 1893. When the National Baptist Convention, at its session held at St. Louis, had ordered that the Home Mission Board proceed at once to the publication of a series of periodicals, Dr. Boyd was chosen as Corresponding Secretary of the Board, and was subsequently made Secretary and Manager of the Publishing Committee. From that day to the present, he has been officially connected with the Publishing House.

It is needless to say that the wonderful success, which has come to this department of the denominational work, is due largely to the sagacity and business tact of its untiring Secretary and Manager. His ability to manage and operate such a concern becomes magnified when the fact is known that the business which now amounts to about five thousand dollars a month was begun without a dollar, and that, too, with a divided constituency. Since Dr. Boyd has been connected with the Publishing Board of the Convention, he has been the receiver of much abuse of those who have sought the overthrow of this enterprise. But, by his persistent efforts and unsurpassed business genius, he has beaten back all opposition and made the work of his Board to honor himself and to bless the denomination.

C. S. BROWN, D. D., Winston, N. C.

C. S. BROWN, D. D., Winston, N. C.

C. S. BROWN, D. D., Winston, N. C.

C. S. Brown, D. D., the President of the Waters Normal Institute at Winston, N. C., is a prominent leader in his state and is the President of the Lott Carey Convention.

WM. H. PHILLIPS, D. D., Philadelphia, Pa.

WM. H. PHILLIPS, D. D., Philadelphia, Pa.

WM. H. PHILLIPS, D. D., Philadelphia, Pa.

Wm. H. Phillips, D. D., the pastor of the Shiloh Baptist Church, Philadelphia, Pa., stands in the front rank of the progressive men of the race. He was among the first to advocate a Negro Baptist Publishing House.

Sermons, Addresses and Reminiscences and Important Correspondence

REV. J. D. HUMPHREY, Brinkley, Ark.

REV. J. D. HUMPHREY, Brinkley, Ark.

REV. J. D. HUMPHREY, Brinkley, Ark.

Rev. J. D. Humphrey, Brinkley, Ark., is President of the Board of Trustees of the Brinkley Academy, Moderator of the White River Association and pastor of a strong church. He is held in high esteem by his people.

Sermons, Addresses and Reminiscences and Important Correspondence

REV. J. F. THOMAS, Illinois.

REV. J. F. THOMAS, Illinois.

REV. J. F. THOMAS, Illinois.

Pastor J. F. Thomas, of Illinois, has for many years been prominent as a leader and was for a while President of the General Association of the Western States and Territories.

DR. J. A. DENNIS, Seguin, Texas.

DR. J. A. DENNIS, Seguin, Texas.

Dr. J. A. Dennis, Dean of Theology in Guadalupe College, Seguin, Texas, has filled many places of honor among the Baptists. He is an able preacher and a fine scholar.

REV. P. S. L. HUTCHINS, Columbus, Ga.

REV. P. S. L. HUTCHINS, Columbus, Ga.

REV. P. S. L. HUTCHINS, Columbus, Ga.

Rev. P. S. L. Hutchins has been an earnest supporter of the National Baptist Convention for several years, and is a prominent leader in his state, as well as pastor of a large church in his home city, Columbus, Ga.

REV. J. C. BATTLE, Pine Bluff, Ark.

REV. J. C. BATTLE, Pine Bluff, Ark.

REV. J. C. BATTLE, Pine Bluff, Ark.

Rev. J. C. Battle has for many years been the Secretary of the State Baptist Convention of Arkansas, and is one of those leaders who never fail to manifest great interest in the work of our National Baptist Convention. He is well to do and pastor of a great church.

REV. W. G. PARKS, Chattanooga, Tenn.

REV. W. G. PARKS, Chattanooga, Tenn.

REV. W. G. PARKS, Chattanooga, Tenn.

Among the leading men of Tennessee, none occupy a higher place in the affections of the people than the Rev. W. G. Parks, pastor of Shiloh Baptist Church, Chattanooga. Rev. Parks is a prominent member of our Home Mission Board.

DR. C. L. FISHER, Birmingham, Ala.

DR. C. L. FISHER, Birmingham, Ala.

Dr. C. L. Fisher, of Birmingham, Ala., has made his mark as a rising young man. He has proved his adaptability and capability both in the schoolroom and the pulpit. He is a prominent leader in his state.

DR. HARVEY JOHNSON, Baltimore, Md.

DR. HARVEY JOHNSON, Baltimore, Md.

DR. HARVEY JOHNSON, Baltimore, Md.

Dr. Harvey Johnson, of Baltimore, Md., who is often referred to as "The Old War Horse," is doubtless one of the ablest defenders of race enterprise and race possibilities in this country. He is an eminent scholar and a great preacher.

REV. H C HOWELL, Langston City, Okla.

REV. H C HOWELL, Langston City, Okla.

Rev. H. C. Howell, of Langston City, Okla., is a strong man in the growing West. His influence for good is felt and recognized by the people throughout the territory.

Sermons, Addresses and Reminiscences and Important Correspondence

PROF. JAMES H. GARNETT, A. M., D. D., Jefferson City, Mo.

PROF. JAMES H. GARNETT, A. M., D. D., Jefferson City, Mo.

PROF. JAMES H. GARNETT, A. M., D. D., Jefferson City, Mo.

Prof. James H. Garnett, A. M., D. D., easily takes his place among the foremost men of his race. He has filled many high and honorable positions as preacher, teacher and college president. His present work is that of teaching at Jefferson City, Mo.

REV. H. W. BOWEN, D. D., Durant, Miss.

REV. H. W. BOWEN, D. D., Durant, Miss.

REV. H. W. BOWEN, D. D., Durant, Miss.

Rev. H. W. Bowen, D. D., of Durant, Miss., is a leading spirit in the great Mississippi Delta. He is a most active and ardent supporter of the National Baptist Publishing House and a member of the editorial staff.

REV. J. W. McCRARY, Fordyce, Ark.

REV. J. W. McCRARY, Fordyce, Ark.

Rev. J. W. McCrary, who has for many years been Corresponding Secretary of the Arkansas Baptist State Convention, is among the eminent scholars of the race. He is at present principal of the High School at Fordyce.

REV. S. A. MOSELEY, D. D., Pine Bluff, Ark.

REV. S. A. MOSELEY, D. D., Pine Bluff, Ark.

REV. S. A. MOSELEY, D. D., Pine Bluff, Ark.

Rev. S. A. Mosely, D. D., pastor of St. Paul Baptist Church, Pine Bluff, Ark., occupies an exalted place in the hearts of his brethren in the state. He is a prominent member of the National Baptist Convention and is Vice President for Arkansas.

DR. S. E. SMITH, Owensboro, Ky.

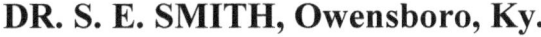

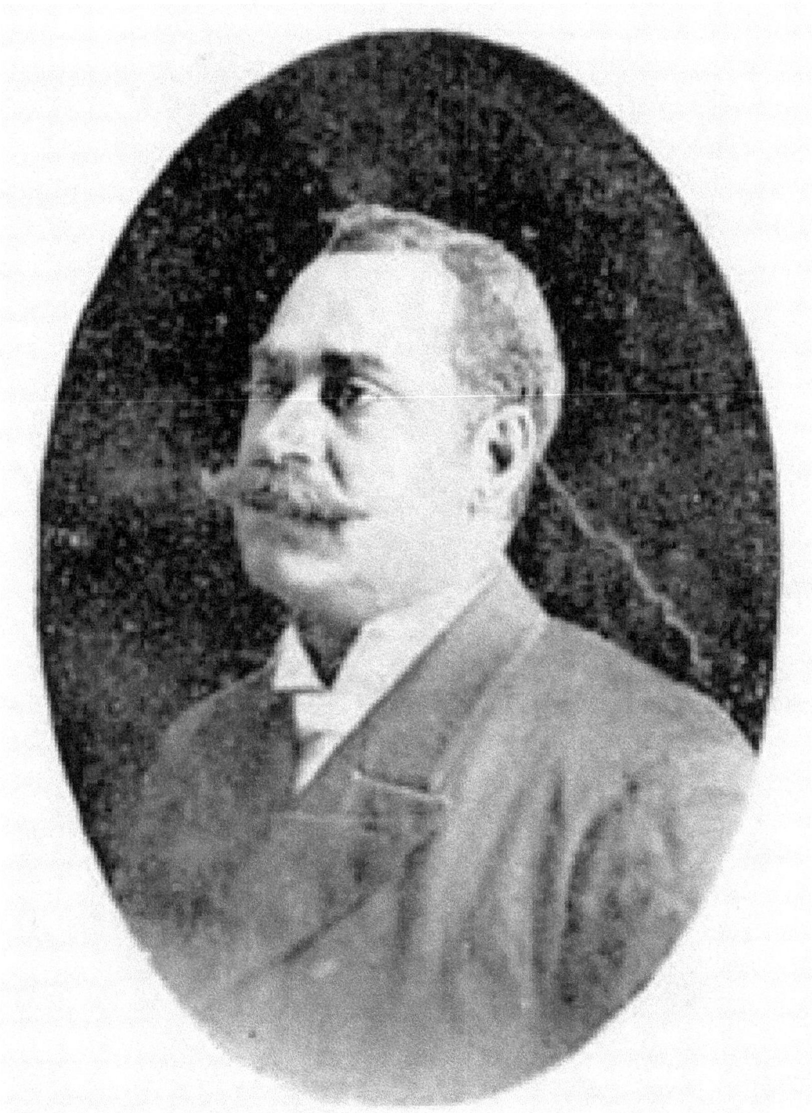

DR. S E. SMITH, Owensboro, Ky.

DR. S. E. SMITH, Owensboro, Ky.

Dr. S. E. Smith, of Owensboro, Ky., is one of our ablest preachers. He is prominent as a political and religious leader in his state. He takes great interest in all that concerns the welfare of the Baptists in this country.

REV. A. A. COSEY, Clarksdale, Miss.

REV. A. A. COSEY, Clarksdale, Miss.

REV. A. A. COSEY, Clarksdale, Miss.

Among the prominent young men in the Mississippi Delta is Rev. A. A. Cosey, editor of the Clarksdale "Journal" and pastor of the Metropolitan Church. Rev. Cosey is an active molder of sentiment and a moving spirit among his people.

REV. W. H. JERNAGAN, Okolona, Miss.

REV. W. H. JERNAGAN, Okolona, Miss.

REV. W. H. JERNAGAN, Okolona, Miss.

Rev. W. H. Jernigan is the President of the State B. Y. P. U. of Mississippi. He is an active and earnest devotee to the interests of the National Baptist Convention and never fails to represent its interests wherever he goes. He is a young man with a promising future.

REV. H. R. McMILLAN, Cottonplant, Ark.

REV. H. R. McMILLAN, Cottonplant, Ark.

REV. H. R. McMILLAN, Cottonplant, Ark.

Rev. H. R. McMillan, of Cottonplant, Ark., is the president of the W. R. C. Academy and pastor of a large Baptist church at Brinkley. He is one of the ablest ministers in his district.

REV. W. H. ANDERSON, D. D., Evansville, Ind.

REV. W. H. ANDERSON, D. D., Evansville, Ind.

REV. W. H. ANDERSON, D. D., Evansville, Ind.

Rev. W. H. Anderson, D. D., of Indiana, is one of the Negro Baptist pioneers and one of the most active supporters of the National Baptist Convention. He is a leader in his state.

REV. C. B. BROWN, Marianna, Ark.

REV. C. B. BROWN, Marianna, Ark.

Rev. C. B. Brown is Moderator of the Phillips, Lee and Monroe District Association of Arkansas, which contributes not less than $100 each year for foreign missions. He has extensive farming interests, and has much of this world's goods.

Sermons, Addresses and Reminiscences and Important Correspondence

REV. W. H. McRIDLEY, A. M., D. D., Cadiz, Ky.

REV. W. H. McRIDLEY, A. M., D. D., Cadiz, Ky.

REV. W. H. McRIDLEY, A. M., D. D., Cadiz, Ky.

Rev. W. H. McRidley, A. M., D. D., of Cadiz, Ky., is a great orator and a splendid preacher. He is at the head of one of our best schools for the education of the youth of our race.

DR. W. H. SUGGS. Little Rock. Ark.

DR. W. H. SUGGS. Little Rock. Ark.

Dr. W. H. Suggs is a prominent physician of Little Rock, Ark., and is a member of the faculty of the Arkansas Baptist College.

PROF. A. W. PEGUES, Ph. D., Raleigh, N. C.

PROF. A. W. PEGUES, Ph. D., Raleigh, N. C.

PROF. A. W. PEGUES, Ph. D., Raleigh, N. C.

Prof. A. W. Pegues, Ph. D., is dean of the Theological Department of Shaw University, Raleigh, N. C. Dr. Pegues is one of our most representative men, and is the author of a book entitled, "Our Ministers and Schools." The book has had wide circulation.

REV. E. B. TOPP, Mississippi.

REV. E. B. TOPP, Mississippi.

Rev. E. B. Topp, D. D., who was at one time missionary to Africa under the Foreign Mission Board of the National Baptist Convention, is one of the leading men of the race in the State of Mississippi.

MR. JNO. S. TROWER, Philadelphia, Pa.

MR. JNO. S. TROWER, Philadelphia, Pa.

MR. JNO. S. TROWER, Philadelphia, Pa.

Mr. Jno. S. Trower, Philadelphia, Pa., is one of the most prominent laymen in the denomination. He is an active Sunday school worker and a great friend and supporter of our National Baptist Publishing Board.

PROF. JOSEPH A. BOOKER, A. M., D. D., Little Rock, Ark.

PROF. JOSEPH A. BOOKER, A. M., D. D., Little Rock, Ark.

Prof. Joseph A. Booker, A. M., D. D., the President of the Arkansas Baptist College, is one of the leading educators of the day. He has been at the head of the educational work of his state for fourteen years.

MRS. M. C. BOOKER, Little Rock, Ark.

MRS. M. C. BOOKER, Little Rock, Ark.

Mrs. M. C. Booker is the accomplished wife of Prof. Jos. A. Booker, A. M., D. D., President of the Arkansas Baptist College. Mrs. Booker is a member of the faculty of the college and is an invaluable assistant to her husband in his great work.

REV. S. L. CANNON, Marianna, Ark.

REV. S. L. CANNON, Marianna, Ark.

REV. S. L. CANNON, Marianna, Ark.

Rev. S. L. Cannon is the President of the Phillips, Lee and Monroe District Sunday School Convention (Ark.), and is an earnest worker in the cause of Christianity.

REV. D. H. HARRIS, Chicago, Ill.

REV. D. H. HARRIS, Chicago, Ill.

Rev. D. H. Harris, of Chicago, Ill., is a minister of deep Christian piety as well as scholarly attainment. He is a conservative race man and an uncompromising Baptist.

REV. J. ANDERSON TAYLOR, D. D., Washington, D. C.

REV. J. ANDERSON TAYLOR, D. D., Washington, D. C.

REV. J. ANDERSON TAYLOR, D. D., Washington, D. C.

Rev. J. Anderson Taylor, D. D., of Washington, D. C., has for many years been one of the most prominent figures at the annual gatherings of the National Baptist Convention. He has, however, been most conspicuous in his efforts to advance the cause of missions in Africa.

Sermons, Addresses and Reminiscences and Important Correspondence

THE MORRIS FAMILY.

THE MORRIS FAMILY.
[The above cut represents the author and his family.]

THE MORRIS FAMILY.

[The above cut represents the author and his family.]

REV. C. T. STAMPS, B. D., Edwards, Miss.

REV. C. T. STAMPS, B. D., Edwards, Miss.

Rev. C. T. Stamps, B. D., of Mississippi, is one of our rising young men. He read a most excellent paper before the last meeting of our National Baptist Convention.

REV. G. W. RAIFORD, Pensacola, Florida.

REV. G. W. RAIFORD, Pensacola, Florida.

Rev. G. W. Raiford, of Florida, is the President of the Baptist State Convention in that State, and a prominent leader in and supporter of the National Baptist enterprises.

REV. J. H. EASON, D. D., Anniston, Ala.

REV. J. H. EASON, D. D., Anniston, Ala.

REV. J. H. EASON, D. D., Anniston, Ala.

Rev. J. H. Eason, D. D., of Alabama, is a young man of most excellent qualities as well as a strong and convincing writer. He is a contributor to the Sunday school periodicals published by the National Baptist Publishing Board.

MRS. W. F. GRAHAM, Richmond, Va.

MRS. W. F. GRAHAM, Richmond, Va.

Mrs. W. F. Graham is the wife of Dr. Graham, of Richmond, Va., who is an acknowledged leader in the Old Dominion. Dr Graham has been a close personal friend of the author for many years.

L. G. JORDAN, D. D.

L. G. JORDAN, D. D.

Dr. Jordan is one of the most progressive and efficient pastors in the denomination. He is a church builder, with rare attainments along this line. As Secretary of the Foreign Mission Board of the National Baptist Convention, he has placed the missionary work on a most substantial foundation, and made the most enviable reputation for this Board which he has served so faithfully.

I. E. ALSUP, Nashville, Tenn.

I. E. ALSUP, Nashville, Tenn.

Deacon Alsup has been for several years one of the most prominent deacons in the Mount Olive Baptist Church of Nashville. He is an earnest church worker, a faithful friend to the pastor and a great admirer of the progress of the denomination. He is engaged in the undertaking business, and is meeting with a marvelous degree of success.

HON. TAYLOR G. EWING, Nashville, Tenn.

HON. TAYLOR G. EWING, Nashville, Tenn.

HON. TAYLOR G. EWING, Nashville, Tenn.

Counsellor Ewing is Attorney for the National Baptist Publishing Board. He has a large, paying pratice as a legal practitioner, and gives general satisfaction. He is engaged also in the operation of a shirt factory, and is meeting with reasonable success in the new business venture.

REV. E. W. D. ISAAC, D. D.

REV. E. W. D. ISAAC, D. D.

REV. E. W. D. ISAAC, D. D.

We present herewith the likeness of one of the most remarkable young men of the times, Rev. E. W. D. Isaac, D. D. Possessing a mind of great native strength, education and research has made him one of the best equipped Negroes in public life. As a writer he wields a trenchant pen, and brings back trophies from every journey that he makes on the literary warpath. His eloquence is marvelous. The fire of his oratory operates as a spell over his hearers, and he has no peer in the art of moving men to action. He is yet a young man, and his future is rich with promise. He is at present the Corresponding Secretary of the National Baptist Young People's Union, and editor of the *National Baptist Union,* the organ of the great Negro Baptist denomination. Prior to his occupancy of his present high position he was pastor of the leading Baptist church of the State of Texas, and editor of the *Western Star,* the organ of the Negro Baptists of that state.

REV. SUTTON E. GRIGGS, B. D.

REV. SUTTON E. GRIGGS, B. D.

REV. SUTTON E. GRIGGS, B. D.

Rev. Sutton E. Griggs is a young man of splendid accomplishments--a ripe scholar, a deep thinker and a magnetic speaker. He is a graduate of Bishop College, Marshall, Tex., also of the Richmond (Va.) Theological Seminary. He is a charming author, and for literary excellence, his productions take high rank among the studious and thoughtful elements in both races. He is now pastor of the First Baptist Church, East Nashville, Tenn.

THE BOYD FAMILY.

THE BOYD FAMILY.
[The above cut represents Rev. R. H. Boyd and Family.]

THE BOYD FAMILY.

www.ingramcontent.com/pod-product-compliance
Lightning Source LLC
Chambersburg PA
CBHW081829170426
43199CB00017B/2679